Hall, J

The permanence of Yeats

DATE DUE

The Permanence of Yeats

edited by JAMES HALL
and MARTIN STEINMANN

THE

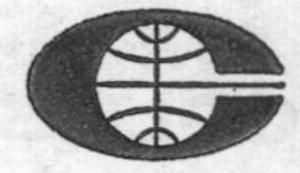

PERMANENCE OF YEATS

COLLIER BOOKS
NEW YORK, N.Y.

This Collier Books edition is published by arrangement with The Macmillan Company.

Collier Books is a division of The Crowell-Collier Publishing Company.

First Collier Books Edition 1961

Printed in the United States of America.

Acknowledgments

The editors are grateful to the following authors and publishers for permission to reprint the essays in this collection:

Jonathan Cape, Ltd., London: pages 53-59 from *Aspects of Literature* by J. Middleton Murry, and pages 115-132 from *The Destructive Element* by Stephen Spender.

Charles Scribner's Sons, New York: pages 26-64 from *Axel's Castle* by Edmund Wilson.

R. P. Blackmur: pages 74-106 from *The Expense of Greatness.*

Cleanth Brooks, Jr., and University of North Carolina Press, Chapel Hill: pages 173-202 from *Modern Poetry and the Tradition.*

John Crowe Ransom and *The Kenyon Review:* "Yeats and His Symbols," from *The Kenyon Review,* I, 3 (summer, 1939), 309-322.

Allen Tate, and Swallow Press and William Morrow and Company, New York: pp. 214-224 from *On the Limits of Poetry.*

David Daiches and University of Chicago Press, Chicago: pp. 128-155 from *Poetry and the Modern World.*

Arthur Mizener and Louisiana State University Press, Baton Rouge: "The Romanticism of W. B. Yeats," from *The Southern Review,* VII, 3 (winter, 1942), 601-623.

Chatto and Windus, London: pp. 27-50 from *New Bearings in English Poetry* by F. R. Leavis.

D. S. Savage, and George Routledge and Sons, London: pp. 67-91 from *The Personal Principle.*

Joseph Warren Beach and Oxford University Press, New York: "Without Benefit of Clergy," from *A History of English Literature* by Craig, Anderson, Bredvold, and Beach.

Austin Warren and University of Chicago Press, Chicago: pp. 66-84 from *Rage for Order.*

Eric Bentley and *The Kenyon Review:* "Yeats as a Playwright," from *The Kenyon Review,* X, 2 (spring, 1948), 196-208.

Kenneth Burke and Louisiana State University Press, Baton Rouge: "On Motivation in Yeats," from *The Southern Review,* VII, 3 (winter, 1942), 547-561.

W. Y. Tindall and Alfred A. Knopf, Inc., New York: pp. 248-263 from *Forces in Modern British Literature* 1885-1946.

Donald Davidson and Louisiana State University Press, Baton Rouge: "Yeats and the Centaur," from *The Southern Review,* VII, 3 (winter, 1942), 510-516.

Elder Olson and *The University of Kansas City Review:* " 'Sailing to Byzantium': Prolegomena to a Poetics of the Lyric," *The University Review,* VIII, 3 (spring, 1942), 209-219.

A. Norman Jeffares and *The Nineteenth Century and After:* "W. B. Yeats and His Methods of Writing Verse," *The Nineteenth Century and After,* CXXXIX, 829 (March, 1946), 123-128.

Delmore Schwartz and Louisiana State University Press, Baton Rouge: "An Unwritten Book," from *The Southern Review,* VII, 3 (winter, 1942), 471-491.

T. S. Eliot and Louisiana State University Press, Baton Rouge: "The Poetry of W. B. Yeats," The First Annual Yeats Lecture, delivered to the Friends of the Irish Academy at the Abbey Theatre, June, 1940; reprinted from *The Southern Review,* VII, 3 (winter, 1942), 442-454.

W. H. Auden and *The Kenyon Review:* "Yeats as an Example," from *The Kenyon Review,* X, 2 (spring, 1948), 187-195.

Morton Dauwen Zabel and *The Nation:* "Yeats: The Book and the Image," from *The Nation,* 151, 15 (October 12, 1940), 160-161; and 156, 10 (March 6, 1943), 348-350.

Walter E. Houghton and University of Chicago Press, Chicago: "Yeats and Crazy Jane: The Hero in Old Age," from *Modern Philology,* XL, 4 (May, 1943), 316-329.

Contents

The Permanence of Yeats

The Seven Sacred Trances

ALMOST EVERYONE IS certain of, and at the same time embarrassed by, Yeats' status as a major poet. If T. S. Eliot, in "A Cooking Egg," has immortalized Madame Blavatsky, it is not too much to say that Yeats has sometimes seemed in danger of losing his immortality through the same medium. For the greatest obstacle to his full acceptance has been the persuasion—stated most brilliantly by R. P. Blackmur—that he is a poet of "magic," and that his poetry partakes of the limitations and especially the rootlessness of magic. An age of formalist criticism has chosen, surprisingly, to deal with Yeats as a problem in cultural values, and thus to make him the only modern poet whose beliefs have been tested enough for us to be reasonably sure that we are distinguishing the poet from the culture hero. To explain this is to explain Yeats' peculiar strength and to suggest why he, even more surely than Eliot or Pound, is certain to remain a major figure in the poetry of the century.

With Eliot (a fair and instructive comparison), this process of separating the poet from the spokesman of an epoch has hardly begun. The theme of the early poems—the spiritual failure of the modern world, the accompanying degradation of the poor and the sterility of the rich—did little to hinder and much to facilitate his acceptance as a poet; but the retreat in recent years from *The Waste Land* to *Four Quartets* has taken place not merely because the latter is newer, but because the mood of the waste land has been quietly evanescing. The waste land of Eliot's successors seems a little self-dramatizing, a trifle showy at the funeral of a Western world that usually has been and predictably will be in a state of crisis. *Four Quartets*, significantly, is receiving the same kind of extraliterary attention that helped the earlier poetry: an Anglo-Catholic criticism which appears to like Eliot first because it likes his doctrine. The *pax Britannica* and the age of taste have shaped Eliot's generation more than we have yet allowed for, and the wearing quality of his myths necessarily remains a major question.

But our respect for Yeats rests on no such ground. Holding—or seeming to hold—the most extraordinary and unfashionable views, he has weathered the kind of nonliterary test that the reputation of a lesser poet could not have survived. Most of the possible ways of getting around, as well as of facing, the question of Yeats' beliefs have been tried, but the intellectual condescension which theosophy, Rosicrucianism, spiritualism, Neo-Platonism, and the system of *A Vision* have aroused in most critics has proved steadily embarrassing to Yeats' defenders and convincing to his detractors. I. A. Richards and Edmund Wilson have written Yeats down as an escapist; Blackmur and Cleanth Brooks see him carrying magic, as opposed to religion, to its ultimate use in poetry (though they differ significantly as to whether this magic involves control of nature); David Daiches and Allen Tate argue that the poetry is more meaningful in other terms than the magical system; and John Crowe Ransom points out that Eliot, too, is reviving an intellectually unacceptable position by investing it with fresh symbols.

Daiches, Ransom, and Tate have the better of this argument. Both Blackmur's objection to the traditionlessness of magic and Brooks' use of *A Vision,* though instructive, imply that a secret discipline is more fundamental in Yeats' work than his concern with the main literary currents of his century. But this emphasis does not explain why, in the later poems, we feel less the remoteness of a special, even a secret, discipline than in the earlier ones—are in fact so struck with their relevance. The real remoteness occurs, then, with Cuchulain. Fortunately, recent evidence—A. Norman Jeffares' printing of earlier versions of some of the best poems, along with data on Yeats' reading—makes it possible now to show more exactly, and more genetically, the role of occultism in the poems and to see Yeats' involvement with the main movements of the time.

When we talk of Yeats and magic, we are speaking of something that exists, of course; but it exists more palpably in the biography, the prose, and many of the lesser poems than it does in the poems which the general consent of the critics here presented has established as Yeats' best. If we are to isolate a major interest in Yeats, we might better emphasize how much more the great poems derive from history and anthropology—used not only in the spirit of Spengler and Toynbee, but in the spirit and mode of Eliot, Mann, and Joyce. In understandable concern with the supernatural, a great deal of the criticism has ignored how much more Yeats belongs to the great anthropological and historical interests of our time than to any magical specific.

The new information about Yeats' reading is suggestive, though of course the poems themselves are the final evidence. Yeats' knowledge of Byzantium came from a history (W. G. Holmes' (*The Age of Justinian and Theodora*), a history of Byzantine art and archaeology (G. M. Dalton's), and a study of Greek and Roman tombstone symbols in Mrs. Strong's *Apotheosis and After-Life*. These lines of investigation are no more Blavatskyish than *Joseph in Egypt* or the Grail, and according them full weight brings the recognition that Yeats has far more in common with Spengler and Toynbee—or with Vico—than with Aleister Crowley.

In "Sailing to Byzantium," history and anthropology predominate clearly over supernaturalism: they provide both the symbolic framework and the bulk of the detail by which the overriding myth is established. The poem, of course, fuses two of Yeats' antitheses—Ireland and Byzantium. The Ireland section, the first stanza, uses neither anthropology nor magic. Yeats' problem in writing it, the earlier versions permit us to see, was to hit upon the symbols that emerge as "salmon-falls," "mackerel-crowded seas," and the like. The second stanza makes a "therefore" statement that Byzantium represents "monuments of [the soul's] own magnificence." After the invocation to the sages, the poem moves to its climactic and only developed use of myth—which turns out to be the medieval legend, extant in numerous versions, of the wrought gold birds singing in gold trees. (Only Yeats among modern poets would have had the directness to set the birds upon an actual "golden bough.") Two lines alone, in the third stanza, involve the supernatural side of the system,

O sages standing in God's holy fire . . .
Come from the holy fire, perne in a gyre,

—and of these Blackmur is undoubtedly correct that "perne in a gyre" is too explicit to survive in force after its novelty has been absorbed. "God's holy fire" does add a level of meaning, but its very isolation indicates how overwhelmingly the poem is expressed in historical-anthropolcgical terms.

How thoroughly Yeats was concentrating upon Byzantium as Byzantium and how little on the specifically magical can be seen in the more extended detail in two earlier versions:

I therefore travel toward Byzantium
Among these sun-brown pleasant mariners
Another dozen days and we shall come
Under the jetty and the marble stair. . . .

and

But now these pleasant dark-skinned mariners
Carry me toward that great Byzantium

Where all is ancient, singing at the oars
That I may look in the great church's dome
On gold-embedded saints and emperors
After the mirroring waters and the foam
Where the dark drowsy fins a moment rise
Of fish that carry the souls to paradise.

Even the "dark drowsy fins"—the dolphins of the later poem—come from the decoration on Roman and Greek tombstones described by Mrs. Strong. And the later condensation of the poem brings no shift in type of symbolism.

"The Second Coming" reveals, however, more than any other single poem, Yeats' own solution to the problem of the esoteric: he *translates* from the private system to symbols in a recognizable tradition. The system provides a starting point, but the extraordinary symbolic framework of the poem depends on Yeats' translating *Magnus Annus* to *Second Coming,* taking symbol out of the realm of the special and cultist and allying the Christian myth, with all its associations, to a myth of even more ancient standing—the Egyptian desert beast. The poem is one of Yeats' greatest achievements precisely because he does not try to impose a specialized definition in place of the one that comes to us instinctively, but translates the special into terms that exist, as he says, in *Spiritus Mundi*—the great storehouse of the race. The main symbols are no more theosophical in Yeats than in Eliot, Mann, or Shelley.

There is magical terminology in the poem, of course—the widening gyre, the centre, *Spiritus Mundi* itself. But among these there is a serious distinction in effect. *Spiritus Mundi* is easily assimilated, a happy metaphor, absorbable as metaphor to our experience and re-enforced by associations, which Brooks and Stephen Spender have noted, with Jung, Freud, etc. The gyre is another matter. There the objection that magic has no tradition applies in considerable force. Even after we have learned all that *A Vision* has to tell us about gyres, we know them as a dictionary definition, a bit from the *Britannica.* We have no associations with this idea or its familiars, the symbol fails to expand, and we have instead allegory. We have been told that the Black Knight is John of Gaunt.

The same translation of the private into the traditional occurs in the Leda sonnet. "A shudder in the loins" introduces a cycle from *A Vision,* but Yeats makes no effort to present it poetically in such terms. The reader sees instead

The broken wall, the burning roof and tower
And Agamemnon dead.

"Byzantium," on the other hand, is Yeats' most difficult poem because he translates only partially. The bulk of the poem derives from concrete detail from *The Age of Justinian and Theodora*, but the walking mummy and the purificatory flame are part of the supernatural concern. But in "Among School Children" Yeats again follows his standard practice and draws on Plato, Aristotle, Pythagoras, icons, and Quattrocento fingers.

The fact is that Yeats was as aware as his critics of the problem of the esoteric, and in the achieved poems the symbols are Christian, Byzantine, Egyptian and Greek. Yeats not only works in the twentieth century mode, but (and it has not been sufficiently accorded him) to a great extent he works with myths that are more directly meaningful than are Eliot's.

But even when we have shown that Yeats habitually translates from his private system to public symbols, we have not automatically scotched the suspicion that his belief in odd manifestations, his private myths, may yet be important as theme. If the cosmology of *A Vision* were, for Yeats, a myth—a systematic, coherent, partly hypothetical, partly verified attempt to account for the workings of the universe, to be believed in as naturalism or Christianity is believed in—we should expect something of the kind to occur. But it is at least an open question whether Yeats accorded the kind of belief to the paraphernalia of *A Vision* which would suit it, as, say, Dante's Thomism was suited, for theme. Even in the early poetry, fairies commonly turn up, not as theme, but as inadequate symbols (Mr. Leavis has even urged for them a certain external validity provided by Yeats' early associations with Sligo peasants, for whom fairies "stood to reason)." But even in so notorious a poem as "The Stolen Child," the theme does not require that we take the poet to believe in fairies; it is, like the theme of the much-anthologized "Innisfree," a romantic standby: the contrast between the world that the senses present, the emotions react to, and the reason interprets, and the world that the poet's fancy select from, and would prefer to the other—the real versus the ideal, in short. (This is not to argue, of course, for the merit of this poem *qua* poem; only that it is the objectification of the theme—the whiff from the shores of Gitchi-Goomi—not the theme itself, which is objectionable.) As for *A Vision*, it is well to note the reservations about the term *belief* that Yeats makes there (Mr. Wilson has called attention to a significant passage) and to remember that the spirits who inspired it came to bring him metaphors for poetry. These reservations are important: they suggest that Yeats believed in his cosmology, not as a child believes in Santa Claus or the Easter Bunny, or as the Sligo peasants believed in fairies, or as Mr. Eliot believes in the XXXIX Articles, but as most Christians believe in the flames of Hell: as symbols for dealing concretely with phenomena that can otherwise be dealt with only abstractly or not at all.

The possibility we are suggesting is that what is fundamental in *A Vision*—the part that Yeats believed literally and used for theme—is what is common to the whole Western Platonic-Aristotelian system. In other words, to the extent that *A Vision* is myth, and is the basis of Yeats' antitheses, it is everyone's myth; to the extent that it is not, it is, as Tate urges, more or less successful metaphor. Certainly, what Daiches, Austin Warren, and (with different intent) D. S. Savage emphasize is true: Yeats needed, and sought, a system more as a poet than as a man. It is certain also that, whatever kind of belief Yeats accorded it, *A Vision* gets into few of the poems as theme. If, as we read the poetry, we try to dissociate it from the prose and the biography, we recognize that his themes have served poets romantic and classical, good and bad: *sic transit gloria mundi*, the conflict of the real and the ideal, the contrast between the physical vitality of youth and the wisdom of age, the permanence of art versus the transience of beauty. Savage and Arthur Mizener are as correct in saying that Yeats' aim never changed—that he was trying for richness, elegance, magnificence at the end as in the beginning—as Daiches and Spender are in saying that, in other ways, he did develop. And the crux of his development was in learning to express this desire for magnificence, this recognition of the Platonic antitheses, in symbols nearer the main interests of the age.

The problem of belief and the allied problem of development have been central in Yeats criticism. But a number of the most valuable essays have been specialized studies—Eric Bentley's and Ronald Peacock's reexaminations of the plays, and W. Y. Tindall's of the relation to French symbolism; Morton Dauwen Zabel's treatment of the autobiographies and the last phase, and Walter E. Houghton's of *Words for Music Perhaps;* Kenneth Burke's and F. O. Matthiessen's discussions of the antitheses; Delmore Schwartz' suggestions for new approaches; L. C. Knights' and Grattan Freyer's reservations on Yeats' aristocratic politics; Elder Olson's detailed reading of "Sailing to

Byzantium"; Horace Gregory's study of the mask of Swift; and Herbert Read's censure of the revisions. The dissents of Leavis, Knights, Savage, and J. Middleton Murry are as significant in their way as the attempts by others to define Yeats' greatness; and if Theodore Spencer's rebuttal to Yvor Winters' championship of T. Sturge Moore against Yeats has lost some interest in the intervening years, the fault can perhaps be assigned to T. Sturge Moore.

The one surprising gap in the criticism is a thorough analysis of Yeats' verse as verse. T. S. Eliot and W. H. Auden have written brilliantly on limited aspects; Elizabeth Drew and John L. Sweeney, Randall Jarrell, and Mizener all touch on the verse in connection with other problems, but a detailed reading is still missing. Auden's suggestion about Yeats' transformation of the occasional poem, however, raises questions about slackness and tension that extend to the whole of modern poetry. His essay concludes that

> Yeats' main legacies to us are two. First, he transformed a certain kind of poem, the occasional poem, from being either an official performance of impersonal virtuosity or a trivial *vers de sociétè* into a serious reflective poem of at once personal and public interest. A poem such as *In Memory of Major Robert Gregory* is something new and important in the history of English poetry. . . .
>
> Secondly, Yeats released regular stanzaic poetry, whether reflective or lyrical, from iambic monotony; the Elizabethans did this originally for dramatic verse, but not for lyric or elegiac. . . .

But Auden does not go on with the analysis.

Yeats has, obviously, a tremendous range of gaits. He can maintain the tension of "Leda and the Swan" or "Byzantium"; he can combine slackness and sudden tension for startling effects, as in "The Second Coming" or "Among School Children"; and he can be very slack indeed. (Not that Yeats has much of what Auden has referred to elsewhere as "the slack attitude" and which his own "Musée des Beaux Arts" best exemplifies.) Yeats' slackness and tension result from ways of putting words together, and not enough attention has been paid to his solution of the problems. Further studies might more profitably take this direction than the miniscule approach to the prose which Tate fears they will take.

This essay is far from an attempt at an exhaustive evaluation of the criticism; it tries to indicate the central problems and to show Yeats as closer to the main current of modern literature than he has sometimes been thought to be. As critics we need to be continually on guard against the assumption that poets are more foolish than we are, or less aware of prevailing values. Yeats in particular deserves to be freed from this suspicion.

J. Middleton Murry

IN THE PREFACE to *The Wild Swans at Coole*, Mr. W. B. Yeats speaks of "the phantasmagoria through which alone I can express my convictions about the world." The challenge could hardly be more direct. At the threshold we are confronted with a legend upon the door-post which gives us the essential plan of all that we shall find in the house if we enter in. There are, it is true, a few things capable of common use, verses written in the seeming-strong vernacular of literary Dublin, as it were a hospitable bench placed outside the door. They are indeed inside the house, but by accident or for temporary shelter. They do not, as the phrase goes, belong to the scheme, for they are direct transcriptions of the common reality, whether found in the sensible world or the emotion of the mind. They are, from Mr. Yeats's angle of vision (as indeed from our own), essentially *verse d'occasion.*

The poet's high and passionate argument must be sought elsewhere, and precisely in his expression of his convictions about the world. And here, on the poet's word and the evidence of our search, we shall find phantasmagoria, ghostly symbols of a truth which cannot be otherwise conveyed, at least by Mr. Yeats. To this, in itself, we make no demur. The poet, if he is a true poet, is driven to approach the highest reality he can apprehend. He cannot transcribe it simply because he does not possess the necessary apparatus of knowledge, and because if he did possess it his passion would flag. It is not often that Spinoza can disengage himself to write as he does at the beginning of the third book of the Ethics, nor could Lucretius often kindle so great a fire in his soul as that which made his material incandescent in *Æneadum genetrix.* Therefore the poet turns to myth as a foundation upon which he can explicate his imagination. He may take his myth from legend or familiar history, or he may create one for himself anew; but the function it fulfils is always the same. It supplies the elements with which he can build the structure of his parable, upon which he can make it elaborate enough to convey the multitudinous reactions of his soul to the world.

But between myths and phantasmagoria there is a great gulf. The structural possibilities of the myth depend upon its intel-

"Mr. Yeats's Swan Song," from *Aspects of Literature*, rev. ed., pp. 53-59.

ligibility. The child knows upon what drama, played in what world, the curtain will rise when he hears the trumpet-note: "Of man's first disobedience. . . ." And, even when the poet turns from legend and history to create his own myth, he must make one whose validity is visible, if he is not to be condemned to the sterility of a coterie. The lawless and fantastic shapes of his own imagination need, even for their own perfect embodiment, the discipline of the common perception. The phantoms of the individual brain, left to their own waywardness, lose all solidity and become like primary forms of life, instead of the penultimate forms they should be. For the poet himself must move securely among his visions; they must be not less certain and steadfast than men are. To anchor them he needs intelligent myth. Nothing less than a supremely great genius can save him if he ventures into the vast without a landmark visible to other eyes than his own. Blake had a supremely great genius and was saved in part. The masculine vigour of his passion gave stability to the figures of his imagination. They are heroes because they are made to speak like heroes. Even in Blake's most recondite work there is always the moment when the clouds are parted and we recognise the austere and awful countenances of gods. The phantasmagoria of the dreamer have been mastered by the sheer creative will of the poet. Like Jacob, he wrestled until the going down of the sun with his angel and would not let him go.

The effort which such momentary victories demand is almost superhuman; yet to possess the power to exert it is the sole condition upon which a poet may plunge into the world of phantasms. Mr. Yeats has too little of the power to be able to vindicate himself completely from the charge of idle dreaming. He knows the problem; perhaps he has also known the struggle. But the very terms in which he suggests it to us subtly convey a sense of impotence:

Hands, do what you're bid;
Bring the balloon of the mind
That bellies and drags in the wind
Into its narrow shed.

The languor and ineffectuality conveyed by the image tell us clearly how the poet has failed in his larger task; its exactness, its precise expression of an ineffectuality made conscious and condoned, bears equal witness to the poet's artistic probity. He remains an artist by determination, even though he returns downcast and defeated from the great quest of poetry. We were inclined at first, seeing those four lines enthroned in majestic isolation on a page, to find in them evidence of an untoward conceit. Subsequently they have seemed to reveal a splendid honesty. Although it has little mysterious and haunting beauty, *The Wild Swans at Coole* is indeed a swan song. It is eloquent of final defeat; the following of a lonely path has ended in the poet's sinking exhausted in a wilderness of grey. Not even the regret is passionate; it is pitiful.

I am worn out with dreams,
A weather-worn, marble triton
Among the streams;
And all day long I look
Upon this lady's beauty
As though I had found in book
A pictured beauty,
Pleased to have filled the eyes
Or the discerning ears,
Delighted to be but wise,
For men improve with the years;
And yet, and yet
Is this my dream, or the truth?
O would that we had met
When I had my burning youth;
But I grow old among dreams,
A weather-worn, marble triton
Among the streams.

It is pitiful because, even now in spite of all his honesty, the poet mistakes the cause of his sorrow. He is worn out not with dreams, but with the vain effort to master them and submit them to his own creative energy. He has not subdued them nor built a new world from them; he has merely followed them like will-o'-the-wisps away from the world he knew. Now, possessing neither world, he sits by the edge of a barren road that vanishes into a no-man's land, where is no future and whence there is no way back to the past.

My country is Kiltartan Cross,
My countrymen Kiltartan's poor;
No likely end could bring them loss
Or leave them happier than before.

It may be that Mr. Yeats has succumbed to the malady of a

nation. We do not know whether such things are possible; we must consider him only in and for himself. From this angle we can regard him only as a poet whose creative vigour has failed him when he had to make the highest demands upon it. His sojourn in the world of the imagination, far from enriching his vision, has made it infinitely tenuous. Of this impoverishment, as of all else that has overtaken him, he is agonisedly aware.

I would find by the edge of that water
The collar-bone of a hare,
Worn thin by the lapping of the water,
And pierce it through with a gimlet, and stare
At the old bitter world where they marry in churches,
And laugh over the untroubled water
At all who marry in churches,
Through the white thin bone of a hare.

Nothing there remains of the old bitter world, which for all its bitterness is a full world also; but nothing remains of the sweet world of imagination. Mr. Yeats has made the tragic mistake of thinking that to contemplate it was sufficient. Had he been a great poet he would have made it his own, by forcing it into the fetters of speech. By re-creating it, he would have made it permanent; he would have built landmarks to guide him always back to where the effort of his last discovery had ended. But now there remains nothing but a handful of the symbols with which he was content:

A Sphinx with woman breast and lion paw,
A Buddha, hand at rest,
Hand lifted up that blest;
And right between these two a girl at play.

These are no more than the dry bones in the valley of Ezekiel, and, alas! there is no prophetic fervour to make them live.

Whether Mr. Yeats, by some grim fatality, mistook his phantasmagoria for the product of the creative imagination, or whether (as we prefer to believe) he made an effort to discipline them to his poetic purpose and failed, we cannot certainly say. Of this, however, we are certain, that somehow, somewhere, there has been disaster. He is empty, now. He has the apparatus of enchantment, but no potency in his soul. He is forced to fall back upon the artistic honesty which has never forsaken him. That it is an insufficient reserve let this passage show:

For those that love the world serve it in action,
Grow rich, popular, and full of influence,
And should they paint or write still it is action:
The struggle of the fly in marmalade.
The rhetorician would deceive his neighbours,
The sentimentalist himself; while art
Is but a vision of reality. . . .

Mr. Yeats is neither rhetorician nor sentimentalist. He is by structure and impulse an artist indeed. But structure and impulse are not enough. Passionate apprehension must be added to them. Because this is lacking in Mr. Yeats those lines, concerned though they are with things he holds most dear, are prose and not poetry.

Edmund Wilson

Born in Dublin in 1865, William Butler Yeats was the son of an Irish Pre-Raphaelite painter, who had given him, at "fifteen or sixteen," Rossetti and Blake to read. Yeats's earliest verse was Pre-Raphaelite and Romantic: his long poem, "The Wanderings of Oisin" (1889), on a subject from Irish mythology, stains a kind of Shelleyan fluidity with a Keatsian richness of color. But, during the nineties, Yeats met Mallarmé in Paris, and though he knew at that time little French, was instructed in the doctrines of Symbolism by his friend Arthur Symons. "I think," he says, "that Symon's translations from Mallarmé may have given elaborate form to my verses of those years, to the latter poems of 'The Wind among the Reeds,' to 'The Shadowy Water.' " And we have seen that he wrote of Symbolism as "the only movement that is saying new things."

If we do not ordinarily think of Yeats as primarily a Symbolist poet, it is because, in taking Symbolism to Ireland, he fed it with new resources and gave it a special accent which lead us to think of his poetry from the point of view of its national qualities rather than from the point of view of its relation to the rest of European literature.

It is easy, however, to see how close Yeats is, even in his later years, to the French poetry of the end of the century, in such a comparatively recent poem as "On a Picture of a Black Centaur":

Your hooves have stamped at the black margin of the wood,
Even where horrible green parrots call and swing.
My works are all stamped down into the sultry mud.
I knew that horse play, knew it for a murderous thing.
What wholesome sun has ripened is wholesome food to eat
And that alone; yet I, being driven half insane
Because of some green wing, gathered old mummy wheat
In the mad abstract dark and ground it grain by grain
And after baked it slowly in an oven; but now
I bring full flavoured wine out of a barrel found
Where seven Ephesian topers slept and never knew
When Alexander's empire past, they slept so sound.
Stretch out your limbs and sleep a long Saturnian sleep;
I have loved you better than my soul for all my words,

And there is none so fit to keep a watch and keep
Unwearied eyes upon those horrible green birds.

Compare this with a characteristic sonnet of Mallarmé's:

Le vierge, la vivace et le bel aujourd'hui
Va-t-il nous déchirer avec un coup d'aile ivre
Ce lac dur oublié que hante sous le givre—
Le transparent glacier des vols qui n'ont pas fui?
Un cygne d'autrefois se souvient que c'est lui
Magnifique mais qui sans espoir se délivre
Pour n'avoir pas chanté la region où vivre
Quand du stérile hiver a resplendi l'ennui.
Tout son col secouera cette blanche agonie
Par l'espace infligée à l'oiseau qui le nie,
Mais non l'horreur du sol où le plumage est pris.
Fantôme qu'à ce lieu son pur éclat assigne,
Il s'immobilise au songe froid de mépris—
Que vêt parmi l'exil inutile le Cygne.

The centaur, the parrots, the wheat and the wine are, like the swan, the lake and the frost, not real things (except that the centaur is something Yeats has seen in a picture), but merely accidental images which, by an association of ideas, have come to stand for the poet's emotion. But where the French poets were obliged to depend almost exclusively upon such symbols, which tended to become more bewildering as they became more heterogeneous, Yeats found in Irish mythology, unfamiliar even to Irish readers, and in itself rather cloudy and vague, a treasury of symbols ready to his hand. He had thus perhaps a special advantage. The Danaan children, the Shadowy Horses and Fergus with his brazen cars—those mysterious and magical beings who play so large a part in Yeats' verse—have little more objective reality than the images of Mallarmé: they are the elements and the moods of Yeats's complex sensibility. But they have a more satisfactory character than such a French Symbolist mythology as Mallarmé's—though Mallarmé does occasionally draw on the Old Testament or the classics for a Salome or a faun—because they constitute a world of which one can to some extent get the hang, where one can at least partly find one's way about.

And, as we follow the progress of Yeats's poetry, this world becomes less dim and iridescent. In "The Wind among the Reeds," which appeared in 1899, we still find "the flaming lute-thronged angelic door" and "the heaven's embroidered cloths—enwrought with golden and silver light" of the earlier Pre-Raphaelite Yeats. But sometime about the beginning of the century, the poet became dissatisfied, he tells us, and set out rigorously to eliminate from his poetry both Romantic rhetoric and Symbolistic mistiness.

The development of Yeats's later style seems to coincide with a disillusionment. The younger Yeats has lived much in fairyland: the heroes of his short stories and poems—Oisin, Red Hanrahan, the Man Who Dreamed of Fairyland—are always deserting the real world for the world of the Sidhe, the fairies. The real world is a sad unsatisfactory place: in one of the very first of Yeats's poems, the fairies warn the child they are stealing away

Come away, O human child!
To the waters and the wild
With a faery, hand in hand,
For the world's more full of weeping than you can understand.

And the mortals who escape to fairyland find eternal love-making and laughter: they dance on twilit lawns to strange music. The Irish fairies of Yeats are not, like the fairies of the ordinary fairy-story, merely smaller human beings like ourselves, possessed of special supernatural powers: they are a different order of beings altogether, existing, as it were, in different dimensions. This strangeness, this real other-worldliness of the fairyland of Yeats's poetry, derives partly, no doubt, it would appear from the fascinating anthology of Irish fairytales which Yeats compiled and edited, from Irish folk-lore itself. The Sidhe were the natural creation of the dreaming and mocking Irish mind amid the illusory uncertain lights and mists of the Irish countryside. But Yeats has made of this Irish fairyland something which puts upon us a stronger spell than the spell even of the folk-tales in his anthology. Yeats's fairyland has become a symbol for the imagination itself. The world of the imagination is shown us in Yeats's early poetry as something infinitely delightful, infinitely seductive, as something to which one becomes addicted, with which one becomes delirious and drunken—and as something which is somehow incompatible with, and fatal to, the good life of that actual world which is so full of weeping and from which it is so sweet to withdraw. There is nothing sinister about the Sidhe in themselves: they are non-moral and relieved of mortal cares; for them, there is not even time; and from our human point of view, their fairy point of view is unseizable. But to the mortal who has lived among the fairies, who has lost the sense of human laws in their world, the consequences may be terrible—

for he has preferred something else to reality—he has escaped the responsibilities of human life and he must fail of its satisfactions. The Man Who Dreamed of Fairyland, in one of the most beautiful of Yeats's early poems, had

. . . stood among a crowd at Drumahair;
His heart hung all upon a silken dress,
And he had known at last some tenderness,
Before Earth made of him her sleepy care;
But when a man poured fish into a pile,
It seemed they raised their little silver heads,
And sang how day a Druid twilight sheds
Upon a dim, green, well-beloved isle,
Where people love beside star-laden seas;
How Time may never mar their faery vows
Under the woven roofs of quicken boughs:
The singing shook him out of his new ease.
He wandered by the sands of Lisadill;

His mind ran all on money cares and fears,
And he had known at last some prudent years
Before they heaped his grave under the hill;
But while he passed before a plashy place,
A lug-worm with its gray and muddy mouth
Sang how somewhere to north or west or south,
There dwelt a gay, exulting, gentle race;
And how beneath those three times blessed skies
A Danaan fruitage makes a shower of moons,
And as it falls awakens leafy tunes:
And at that singing he was no more wise.

And so with all our human needs and passions—the man who dreamed of fairyland is always being distracted from them by intimations of a world outside our world; and even when he is dead, he can find "no comfort in the grave." So in another poem, the joys of the "Happy Townland" where "boughs have their fruit and blossom at all times of the year," where "rivers are running over with red beer and brown beer" and where "queens, their eyes blue like the ice, are dancing in a crowd," are irreconcilable with real life: the enchanted Happy Townland is also "the world's bane."

In the prose stories of Yeats's early period, this fairyland appears under its real aspect as the life of revery and imagination—and of solitude. The narrator of "Rosa Alchemica" exiles himself from the world in a house where tapestries, "full of the blue and bronze of peacocks . . . shut out all history and activity untouched with beauty and peace," and where he is able to find in "antique bronze gods and goddesses . . . all a pagan's delight in various beauty . . . without his terror at sleepless destiny and his labor with many sacrifices." Another solitary, Michael Robartes, lives on the lonely Irish coast in a house which he calls "the Temple of the Alchemical Rose" and where by night the immortal spirits of beautiful long-dead men and women from Egypt and from Greece come to dance in a mosaic-lined room, with a great rose in mosaic on the ceiling. It was characteristic of the *fin de siècle* writers to want to stand apart from the common life and live only in the imagination. I have said that the battle of Symbolism was never properly fought out in English; but there was one writer in England who played a role somewhat similar to that of Mallarmé in France. Walter Pater was, like Mallarmé, a man of much intellectual originality who, living quietly and writing little, had a profound influence on the literature of his time. More nearly than anyone else, he supplied, in his literary criticism, an English equivalent to the Symbolist theory of the French. When Pater says that experience gives us, "not the truth of eternal outlines, ascertained once for all, but a world of fine gradations and subtly linked conditions, shifting intricately as we ourselves change," he is stating a point of view exactly similar to that of the Symbolists. But it was less in the field of aesthetic theory than in that of the appreciation of life that Pater developed this point of view. The famous conclusion to "The Renaissance" fixed the ideal of a whole generation: "To regard all things and principles of things as inconstant modes or fashions has more and more become the fashion of modern thought. . . . The service of philosophy, of speculative culture, towards the human spirit, is to rouse, to startle it to a life of constant and eager observation. Every moment some form grows perfect in hand or face; some tone on the hills or the sea is choicer than the rest; some mood of passion or insight or intellectual excitement is irresistibly real and attractive to us—for that moment only. Not the fruit of experience, but experience itself, is the end. A counted number of pulses only is given to us of a variegated, dramatic life. How may we see in them all that is to be seen in them by the finest senses?" "We looked consciously to Pater for our philosophy," Yeats wrote of himself and his friends; and the tapestried house, the Alchemical Temple, had been invented as ideal abodes where this philosophy might be put into practice—as Yeats's fairyland itself had been but one of the imaginery domains of the *fin de siècle* mind.

But just as Yeats's early poetry presents the fascination of fairyland as something inimical to life in the real world, so these stories of the life of ecstatic revery, unlike the typical writings of the *fin de siècle* aesthetes, are edged with a consciousness of dangers and temptations inescapably involved in such a life. In Yeats, we find the aestheticism of Pater carried through to its consequences. What *is* the consequence of living for beauty, as beauty was then understood, of cultivating the imagination, the enjoyment of aesthetic sensations, as a supreme end in itself? We shall be thrown fatally out of key with reality—we shall incur penalties which are not to be taken lightly. There is a conflict here which cannot be evaded; and Yeats, even in his earliest period, is unceasingly aware of this conflict. But still he prefers to dwell most of the time in fairyland or among the dancers of the Alchemical Temple. He would even transport his human love, his human desire, into the climate of that immortal world, where nothing that is ugly can jar and where nothing that is beautiful fades:

All things uncomely and broken, all things worn out and
old,
The cry of a child by the roadway, the creak of a
lumbering cart,
The heavy steps of the ploughman, splashing the wintry
mould,
Are wronging your image that blossoms a rose in the
deeps of my heart.
The wrong of unshapely things is a wrong too great to be
told;
I hunger to build them anew and sit on a green knoll
apart,
With the earth and the sky and the water, remade, like
a casket of gold
For my dreams of your image that blossoms a rose in the
deeps of my heart.

But now, in the period inaugurated by "The Green Helmet" (published in 1912), the balance is to dip on the other side. In the frustration of early love, apparently, he has paid the price of escaping to fairyland, and the memory of it is bitter: he still champions, he still puts above everything, the nobility and splendor of the imagination; but he must face life's hard conditions. And the consciousness of inexorable limits has brought his art to a sharper focus—the unbinding of "youth's dreamy load" has made him a better poet. No longer content with the ice-eyed queens of fairyland at the same time that he no longer hopes from real life any satisfaction other than the triumph of imagination through art, he applies to poetry all the vigor of his intellect and all the energy of his passion. He would reduce his verse to something definite and hard—at the same time more severe and more passionate. Now the soap-bubble colors vanish; the music of fairyland dies away; we behold only, earthly and clear, the bare outlines of "cold Clare rock and Galway rock and thorn."

In a poem which is at once a description of this style and an admirable example of it, he tells how,

Maybe a twelvemonth since
Suddenly I began
In scorn of this audience
Imagining a man,
And his sun-freckled face,
And gray Connemara cloth,
Climbing up to a place
Where stone is dark under froth,
And the down turn of his wrist
When the flies drop in the stream:
A man who does not exist,
A man who is but a dream;
And cried, "Before I am old
I shall have written him one
Poem maybe as cold
And passionate as the dawn."

Yeats inhabits, in this phase, a world of pure intense emotions expressed in distinct fine images. His words, no matter how prosaic, are always somehow luminous and noble, as if pale pebbles smoothed by the sea were to take on some mysterious value and become more precious than jewels or gold. He is less prodigal now of symbols and names, and his visions have a new austerity:

I call to the eye of the mind
A well long choked up and dry
And boughs long stripped by the wind,
And I call to the mind's eye
Pallor of an ivory face,
Its lofty dissolute air,
A man climbing up to a place
The salt sea wind has swept bare.

When he returns to the heroic world of Irish mythology, he describes it with a new homeliness of detail. And more and more steadily he fixes his attention upon the actual world about him. He has come to desire above everything, as he says in another part of the poem about the fisherman,

To write for my own race
And for the reality.

And again, in another poem:

Through all the lying days of my youth
I swayed my leaves and flowers in the sun;
Now I may wither into the truth.

He finds his subjects now in the events of his own life, no longer transposed into romantic convention, and in the public affairs of Ireland. And he succeeds in dignifying such subjects, as perhaps no other contemporary poet has done, at the same time that he never ceases to deal with them without sentimentality and in the plainest language. He can even challenge comparison with Dante—whom he now describes as "the chief imagination of Christendom"—by his ability to sustain a grand manner through sheer intensity without rhetorical heightening. He assumes, indeed, a kind of Dantesque mask. How he suggests the compactness and point of Dante's two- or three-line allusions in such a passage as,

Traders or soldiers who have left me blood
That has not passed through any huxter's loin,
Pardon, and you that did not weigh the cost,
Old Butlers when you took the horse and stood
Beside the brackish waters of the Boyne
Till your bad master blenched and all was lost . . .

and Dante's epigrammatic bitterness in,

Why should I blame her that she filled my days
With misery, or that she would of late
Have taught to ignorant men most violent ways,
Or hurled the little streets against the great,
Had they but courage equal to desire?

And he has also a Dantesque exaltation—an exaltation no longer the opium dream of fairyland, but such as life has to offer within its limits: the admiration for ancestor or friend, the pride in honor kept or work well done, the wild memory of early love:

And what of her that took
All till my youth was gone
With scarce a pitying look?
How should I praise that one?
When day begins to break
I count my good and bad,
Being wakeful for her sake,
Remembering what she had,
What eagle look still shows,
While up from my heart's root
So great a sweetness flows
I shake from head to foot.

II

With the development of this maturer style, it became impossible any longer to regard Yeats merely as one of the best of the English lyric poets of the nineties. The author of "The Lake of Innisfree," which had so delighted Robert Louis Stevenson, had grown, in an interval of ten years during which nobody outside of Ireland had apparently paid much attention to him, to the unmistakable stature of a master. No other poet writing English in our time has been able to deal with supreme artistic success with such interesting and such varied experience. No other writer has been able to sustain the traditional grand manner of the poet with so little effect of self-consciousness.

And in spite of the immense amount of poetry published and read to-day, the personality truly and naturally poetic seems to be becoming rarer and rarer. It may be true that the kind of dignity and distinction which have been characteristic of the poet in the past are becoming more and more impossible in our modern democratic society and during a period when the ascendancy of scientific ideas has made man conscious of his kinship with the other animals and of his subjection to biological and physical laws rather than of his relation to the gods. It was easy for the lyric poet, from Wyatt's age to Waller's, to express himself both directly and elegantly, because he was a courtier, or, in any case, a member of a comparatively small educated class, whose speech combined the candor and naturalness of conversation among equals with the grace of a courtly society. It was possible for him honestly to take up a residence in an intellectual world where poetic images stood for actualities because the scientific language and technique for dealing with these actualities had not yet come to permeate thought. But the modern poet who would follow this tradition, and who would yet deal with life in any large way, must create for himself a special personality, must maintain a state of mind, which shall shut out or remain indifferent to many aspects of the contemporary world. This necessity accounts partly, I suppose, for Yeats's preoccupation in his prose writings with what he calls the Mask or Anti-Self, a sort of imaginary personality, quite antagonistic to other elements of one's nature, which the poet must impose upon himself. It is hard to imagine a seventeenth-century poet being driven to such a theory—a theory which makes one's poetic self figure as one of the halves of a split personality; and it seems true that Yeats himself has not been able to keep up his poetic role without a certain effort. We find, at any rate, in his criticism and his autobiographical writings a remarkably honest and illuminating account of the difficulties of remaining a poet during the age in which we live.

Yeats seems to be conscious from the first of an antagonism between the actual world of industry, politics and science, on the one hand, and the imaginative poetic life, on the other. He tells us, in his autobiography, that a vital issue seemed to be raised for him, in his boyhood, by the then popular and novel realism of Bastien-Lepage and Carolus Durand as against the mysticism of the Pre-Raphaelite painters. Bastien-Lepage's "clownish peasant staring with vacant eyes at her great boots" represented already to the young Yeats that Naturalistic, scientific vision which contradicted and warred with his own. And he takes up from the beginning, in his criticism, a definite and explicit position in regard to Naturalism: he will stand apart from the democratic, the scientific, modern world—his poetic life shall be independent of it; his art shall owe nothing to its methods. His principles in literature are those of the Symbolists, but he formulates them more clearly and defends them with more vigor than anyone else has yet done in English.

"There is," he asserts in his early essay on the symbolism of Shelley, "for every man some one scene, some one adventure, some one picture, that is the image of his secret life, for wisdom first speaks in images and . . . this one image, if he would but brood over it his whole life long, would lead his soul, disentangled from unmeaning circumstance and the ebb and flow of the world, into that far household, where the undying gods await all whose souls have become simple as flame, whose bodies have become quiet as an agate lamp." All great literature, says Yeats, is created out of symbols: observations and statistics mean nothing; works of art which depend upon them can have no enduring value. "There is something," he says, "of an old wives' tale in fine literature. The makers of it are like an old peasant telling stories of the great famine or the hangings of '98 or from his own memories. He has felt something in the depth of his mind and he wants to make it as visible and powerful to our senses as possible. He will use the most extravagant words or illustrations if they will suit his purpose. Or he will invent a wild parable, and the more his mind is on fire or the more creative it is, the less will he look at the outer world or value it for its own sake. It gives him metaphors and examples, and that is all. He is even a little scornful of it, for it seems to him while the fit is on that the fire has gone out of it and left it but white ashes. I cannot explain it, but I am certain that every high thing was invented in this way, between sleeping and waking, as it were, and that peering and peeping persons are but hawkers of stolen goods. How else could their noses have grown so ravenous or their eyes so sharp?"

And in all his activity as playwright and journalist in connection with the Abbey Theatre, Yeats is leading a reaction against Naturalism. This reaction, which, by way of Germany and under the name of Expressionism, has attracted so much more attention since the War, had not, at the time of the founding of the Abbey Theatre, manifested itself very vigorously on the Continent. Symbolism did not play yet in the theatre the role that it was playing in poetry. Yet its seeds had already sprouted here and there. August Strindberg, returning from Paris to Sweden, wrote between 1899 and 1902 the Symbolistic "To Damascus" and "Dream Play," the prototypes of the German Expressionistic drama; and Maeterlinck, with vague, pale and suave images, quite different from Strindberg's lively, queer and dissonant ones, had created quite a little theatre of Symbolism. Now Yeats, in his own dramatic works, has produced a theatre somewhat similar to Maeterlinck's. The productions of a greater poet, equipped with a richer and more solid mythology, these plays do, however, take place in the same sort of twilit world as Maeterlinck's—a world in which the characters are less often dramatic personalities than disembodied broodings and longings. Yeats's plays have little dramatic importance because Yeats himself has little sense of drama, and we think of them primarily as a department of his poetry, with the same sort of interest and beauty as the rest. But Yeats, the director and propagandist of the Abbey Theatre, does have considerable importance in the history of the modern stage. The Abbey Theatre itself, of recent years, with the Gorky-Chekhovesque plays of Sean O'Casey, has taken a Naturalistic turn which Yeats never contemplated or desired; but his long and uncompromising campaign for a revival of poetic drama contributed much to contemporary efforts to break up the rigid technique and clear the stage of the realistic encumbrances of the Naturalistic drama. Yeats's greatest contribution to the theatre has been, not his own plays, but those of Synge, whom in 1896 he discovered stagnating in Paris and induced to return to Ireland. Synge succeeded, on a small scale, during the few years before he died, in creating for the Abbey Theatre perhaps the most authentic example of poetic drama which the modern stage has seen.

Yeats at this period, the period of the founding and the first battles of the Abbey Theatre, is both active and effective. There has always been more of the public figure and more of the pugnacious Irishman about him than his philosophy invites us to believe. But this philosophy never ceases to insist upon the irreconcilable opposition between the life of self-assertion in the practical world and the life consecrated to the recovery and contemplation of the precious symbol, which, "if he [the poet] would but brood over it his whole life long, would lead his soul, disentangled from unmeaning circumstances and the ebb and flow of the world," into the presence of the gods. Yeats recurs again and again to the necessity of mortifying the will: "Every visionary knows that the mind's eye soon comes to see a capricious and variable world, which the will cannot shape or change, though it can call it up and banish it again"; "We must find some place upon the Tree of Life for the Phoenix nest, for the passion that is exaltation and negation of the will; the style of the dialogue in Synge's plays "blurs definition, clear edges, everything that comes from the will, it turns imagination from all that is of the present, like a gold background in a religious picture, and it strengthens in every emotion whatever comes to it from far off, from brooding memory and dangerous hope," etc.

For the rest, Yeats's prose, in its beginnings, when he is most under the influence of the Pre-Raphaelites and Pater, is a little self-consciously archaic—it has a Renaissance elaborateness and pomposity; and it is a little too close to the language of poetry—the meaning is often clotted by metaphor. But Yeats's prose, like his verse, has, with time, undergone a discipline and emerged with a clearer outline. Yeats is to-day a master of prose as well as a great poet. He was already magnificent in his intermediate period—the period of "Per Amica Silentia Lunae" (1917): "We make out of the quarrel with others rhetoric, but of the quarrel with ourselves, poetry. Unlike the rhetoricians, who get a confident voice from remembering the crowd they have won or may win, we sing amid our uncertainty; and, smitten even in the presence of the most high beauty by the knowledge of our solitude, our rhythm shudders. I think, too, that no fine poet, no matter how disordered his life, has ever, even in his mere life, had pleasure for his end. Johnson and Dowson, friends of my youth, were dissipated men, the one a drunkard, the other a drunkard and mad about women, and yet they had the gravity of men who had found life out and were awakening from the dream; and both, one in life and art and one in art and less in life, had a continual preoccupation with religion. Nor has any poet I have read of or heard of or met with been a sentimentalist. The other self, the anti-self or the antithetical self, as one may choose to name it, comes but to those who are no longer deceived, whose passion is reality. The sentimentalists are practical men who believe in money, in position, in a marriage bell, and whose understanding of happiness is to be so busy whether at work or at play, that all is forgotten but the momentary aim. They find their pleasure in a cup that is filled from Lethe's wharf, and for the awakening, for the vision, for the revelation of reality, tradition offers us a different word—ecstasy."

This is perhaps still a little *too* magnificent, still a little too much like poetry. But in his autobiography, "The Trembling of the Veil" (1922), Yeats has achieved a combination of grandeur with a certain pungency and homeliness which recalls the more lightly and swiftly moving writers of the seventeenth century rather than the more heavily upholstered ones of the earlier Renaissance. The prose of Yeats, in our contemporary literature, is like the product of some dying loomcraft brought to perfection in the days before machinery. The qualities of a good prose style in English to-day are likely to be those of a sound intellectual currency, slipped out by a sharp cutter and stamped by a solvent mint; Rudyard Kipling, Bernard Shaw and T. S. Eliot, however else they may differ, have these characteristics in common. Of Samuel Butler, Shaw's master, Yeats has written that he was "the first Englishman to make the discovery that it is possible to write with great effect without music, without style, either good or bad, to eliminate from the mind all emotional implication and to prefer plain water to every vintage, so much metropolitan lead and solder to any tendril of the vine." The style of the seventeenth century, on the other hand—the style of Walton's "Lives" or Dryden's prefaces—was a much more personal thing; it fitted the author like a suit of clothes and molded itself to the natural contours of his temperament and mind; one is always aware that there is a man inside, whereas with Kipling, Eliot or Shaw, the style seems to aim at the effect of an inflexible impersonal instrument specially designed to perform special functions. Yeats's prose is, however, still a garment worn in the old-fashioned personal manner with a combination of elegance and ease, at the same time that it is unmistakably of our time by virtue of a certain modern terseness and of a characteristically modern trick—we shall encounter it later in Proust—of revealing by unexpected juxtapositions relations of which one had not been aware—"He had been almost poor" writes Yeats of Wilde in the period before his disaster, "and now, his head full of Flaubert, found himself with ten thousand a year"—or of effecting almost startling transitions from the particular to the general and back again. For Yeats has become a critic now not merely of literature, but of human life and society in general: compare the passage on Johnson and Dowson which I have quoted above from "Per Amica Silentia Lunae," with the realistic and subtle analysis, in "The Trembling of the Veil," of the causes for the final breakdown of that "tragic generation."

III

Yeats has shown himself, in his prose writings, a man of both exceptionally wide information and exceptional intellectual curiosity; but, for all the variety of his interests and the versatility of his intelligence, he has, in rejecting the methods of modern science, cut himself off in a curious way from the general enlightened thought of his time. Yet his mind is so comprehensive and so active that he has felt the need of constructing a system: and, finding it impossible to admit the assumptions upon which most modern systems are based, he has had recourse to the only science which his position has allowed him to accept, the obsolete science of Astrology. As a young man, Yeats frequented clairvoyants and students of Astrology and Magic; Madame Blavatsky, the necromantic Theosophist, seems to have made upon him a considerable impression. And in 1901 he was led to formulate, in an essay on Magic, the following set of beliefs, to which he still apparently adheres:

(1) That the borders of our mind are ever shifting, and that many minds can flow into one another, as it were, and create or reveal a

single mind, a single energy.

(2) That the borders of our memories are as shifting, and that our memories are a part of one great memory, the memory of Nature herself.

(3) That this great mind and great memory can be evoked by symbols.

What Yeats was really approaching here was some such systematic study of the symbolism of myths, trances, dreams and other human visions as psychoanalysis and anthropology were attempting from a different direction. And despite the obvious charlatanism or naïveté of most of his instructors and fellow investigators, Yeats's account of his researches is interesting. For it is not merely that Yeats loves the marvellous: he is also intent upon discovering symbols which may stand for the elements of his own nature or which shall seem to possess some universal significance. The results of this research are very curious. When we read Yeats's account of his adventures among the mediums it becomes plain that, in spite of his repudiation of science, he has always managed to leave himself a margin of scientific doubt. Like Huysmans, he betrays an instinct to scrutinize and check up on the supernatural which is disastrous to genuine mysticism. Just as in Huysmans's case, we always feel that the wistful student of Satanism has too much solid Dutch common sense really to deceive himself about his devils, so in Yeats—he himself has confessed it—the romantic amateur of Magic is always accompanied and restrained by the rationalistic modern man. "He and I often quarreled," Yeats writes of himself and A.E., "because I wanted him to examine and question his visions, and write them out as they occurred; and still more because I thought symbolic what he thought real like the men and women that had passed him on the road." Yet Huysmans went so far as to claim—or at least to make one of his characters claim—as genuine examples of demoniacal possession those very hysteria cases of Charcot's which at that moment were leading Charcot's young pupil Freud to his first great discovery of the principle of emotional repression; and Yeats attributes to a sort of supernatural being designated as "Anima Mundi" precisely such universal symbols as are studied by such psychologists as Jung. What is most curious is that Yeats should at last have constructed out of these symbols an elaborate mystical-metaphysical system.

This system was set forth in "A Vision," a work which occupied Yeats for many years and which he published privately in 1926. "A Vision" presented an elaborate theory of the variation of human personality, of the vicissitudes of human history and of the transformations of the soul in this world and the next. This theory was worked out with geometrical diagrams set forth in terms of such unfamiliar conceptions as *daimons, tinctures, cones, gyres, husks* and *passionate bodies.*

Yeats asserts that human personality follows the pattern of a "Great Wheel." That is, the types of personality possible constitute a kind of closed circle—they are regular stages in a circular journey to and fro between complete objectivity at one pole and complete subjectivity at the other; and this journey may be represented by the orbit of the moon, to which it corresponds. Let the moon represent subjectivity and the sun, objectivity: then the dark of the moon, when it is closest to the sun, is the phase of complete objectivity; and the full moon, which is farthest from the sun, is the phase of complete subjectivity. At these two poles of the circle, human life is impossible: there exist only antipodal types of supernatural beings. But along the circumference of the circle, between these two ultra-human poles, there occur twenty-six phases which cover all possible types of human personality.

Yeats's theory of the variation of these types is extremely complicated. He begins by assigning to "incarnate man" four "Faculties": the Will, "by which is understood feeling that has not become desire . . . an energy as yet uninfluenced by thought, action or emotion"; the Mask, which means "the image of what we wish to become, or of that to which we give our reverence"; the Creative Mind, "the intellect . . . all the mind that is consciously constructive"; and the Body of Fate, "the physical and mental environment, the changing human body, the stream of Phenomena as this affects a particular individual, all that is forced upon us from without." The Will is always opposite the Mask: "it looks into a painted picture." The Creative Mind is opposite the Body of Fate: "it looks into a photograph; but both look into something which is the opposite of themselves." We follow the Will around the clock, and by combining it with the other elements according to geometrical laws we calculate the characters of the different phases. Starting at the right of the objective pole, the soul passes first through varieties of almost purely physical life—Yeats takes his examples here from the Bacchuses and shepherds of the poets. It is moving toward subjectivity, however—Walt Whitman, Alexandre Dumas: it is seeking itself, and as it progresses, it becomes more beautiful. The ultra-human subjective phase, which apparently includes Christ, is described as "a phase of complete beauty," where "Thought and Will are indistinguishable, effort and attainment are indistinguishable—nothing is apparent but dreaming Will and the Image that it dreams." This is preceded and followed by phases which include Baudelaire and Beardsley; Keats and Giorgione; Blake and Rabelais; Dante and Shelley; and presumably Yeats himself: men who have withdrawn from the life of the world in order to live in their dream. But once the all-subjective phase is past, the soul

> *. . . would be the world's servant, and as it serves,*
> *Choosing whatever task's most difficult*
> *Among tasks not impossible, it takes*
> *Upon the body and upon the soul*
> *The coarseness of the drudge. Before the full*
> *It sought itself and afterwards the world.*

And it is now leaving beauty behind and headed toward deformity:

> *Reformer, merchant, statesman, learned man,*
> *Dutiful husband, honest wife by turn,*
> *Cradle upon cradle, and all in flight and all*
> *Deformed because there is no deformity*
> *But saves us from a dream.*

The soul has now come full circle: the three final human phases before the phase of complete objectivity are the Hunchback, the Saint and the Fool.

Yeats has worked all this out with great care and with considerable ingenuity. He has described each of the twenty-eight phases and supplied us with typical examples. What we find in this part of the book is Yeats's familiar preoccupation with the conflict between action and philosophy, reality and imagination. (It is amusing and characteristic that, according to his system, the side of humanity closest to the sun—that is, closest the objective nature—should be the side that is bathed in darkness, whereas the side which is furthest from the sun—that is, nearest the subjective nature—should be the side that is bright!) Now this is a subject which has hitherto, in Yeats's prose as well as in his verse, usually inspired him well; the symbols of the Mask, the Sun and Moon, etc., if they have sometimes been a little disconcerting when we encountered them in his critical writings, have created just the right impression of significance in mystery for Symbolistic poetry. And there are, to be sure, certain passages of "A Vision" as brilliant as Yeats at his best. He writes, for example, of the phase of "the Receptive Man," to which he assigns Rembrandt and Synge: "The man wipes his breath from the window pane, and laughs in his delight at all the varied scene." And of the phase of "the Obsessed Man," to which he assigns Giorgione and Keats: "When we compare these images with those of any subsequent phase, each seems studied for its own sake; they float as in serene air, or lie hidden in some valley, and if they move it is to music that returns always to the same note, or in a dance that so returns upon itself that they seem immortal." And, in what is perhaps the most eloquent passage in the book, he returns to a certain type of beautiful uncontemplative woman who has already haunted his poetry: "Here are born those women who are most touching in their beauty." Helen was of this phase; and she comes before the mind's eye elaborating a delicate personal discipline as though she would make her whole life an image of a unified *antithetical* (that is, subjective) energy. While seeming an image of softness, and of quiet, she draws perpetually upon glass with a diamond. Yet she will not number among her sins anything that does not break that personal discipline, no matter what it may seem according to others' discipline; but if she fail in her own discipline she will not deceive herself, and for all the languor of her movements, and her indifference to the acts of others, her mind is never at peace. She will wander much alone as though she consciously meditated her masterpiece that shall be at the full moon, yet unseen by human eye, and when she returns to her house she will look upon her household with timid eyes, as though she knew that all power of self-protection had been taken away, and that of her once *primary Tincture* (that is, objective element) nothing remained but a strange irresponsible innocence. . . . Already perhaps, through weakness of desire, she understands nothing, while alone seeming of service. Is it not because she desires so little and gives so little that men will die and murder in her service?" And there is a strange imaginative power in the conception behind the final sequence of the Hunchback, the Saint and the Fool.

Yet "A Vision," when we try to read it, makes us impatient with Yeats. As a rule, he expounds his revelations as if he took them seriously—that is, as if he believed that *masks* and *husks* and *daimons* and *passionate bodies* were things which actually existed, as if they were as real as those visions of A.E.'s which had been as real to A.E. as the people in the street, but which Yeats had tried to induce him to question; and indeed one would think that to elaborate a mystical system so complicated and so tedious, it would be necessary to believe in it pretty strongly. Yet now and then the skeptical Yeats reasserts himself and we are startled by an unexpected suggestion that, after all, the whole thing may be merely "a background for my thought, a painted scene." If the whole thing, we ask ourselves, has been merely an invented mythology, in which Yeats himself does not believe, what right has he to bore us with it—what right has he to expect us to explore page after page of such stuff as the following description of the habits of the soul after death: "The *Spirit* first floats horizontally within the man's dead body, but then rises until it stands at his head. The *Celestial Body* is also horizontal at first but lies in the opposite position, its feet where the *Spirit's* head is, and then rising, as does the *Spirit*, stands up at last at the feet of the man's body. The *Passionate Body* rises straight up from the genitals and stands in the centre. The *Husk* remains in the body until the time for it to be separated and lost in *Anima Mundi.*"

In "A Packet for Ezra Pound" (1929) a new light is thrown on "A Vision." We learn that Yeats's wife is a medium, and that the theories set forth in this book were communicated through her by supernatural beings. Yeats tells us how, four days after their marriage in 1917, Mrs. Yeats surprised him by attempting automatic writing. "What came in disjointed sentences, in almost illegible writing, was so exciting, sometimes so profound, that I persuaded her to give an hour or two day after day to the unknown writer, and after some half-dozen such hours offered to spend what remained of life explaining and piecing together those scattered sentences. 'No,' was the answer, 'we have come to give you metaphors for poetry.' The unknown writer took his theme at first from my just published 'Per Amica Silentia Lunae.' I had made a distinction between the perfection that is from a man's combat with himself and that which is from a combat with circumstances, and upon this simple distinction he built up an elaborate classification of men according to their more or less complete expression of one type or the other. He supported his classification by a series of geometrical symbols and put these symbols in an order that answered the question in my essay as to whether some prophet could not prick upon the calendar the birth of a Napoleon or a Christ." Yeats describes the manifestations which accompanied these revelations: the perfumes, whistlings, smells of burnt feathers, bursts of music, apparitions of great black birds and of "persons in clothes of the late sixteenth century and of the seventeenth." On one occasion, when an owl was hooting in the garden, the dictating spirit asked for a recess: "Sounds like that," the spirit explained, "give us great pleasure." And there were also mischievous obstructive spirits who attempted to mislead the Yeatses and who were designated as "Frustrators"; "the automatic script would deteriorate, grow sentimental or confused, and when I pointed this out the communicator would say 'from such and such an hour, on such and such a day, all is frustration.' I would spread out the script and he would cross all out back to the answer that began it, but had I not divined frustration he would have said nothing."

We learn also, by the way, a fact which might, for a psychologist, throw a good deal of light on the development of Yeats's personality. It appears that not only has Yeats always succeeded in steering clear of science: he has never till recently read philosophy. "Apart from two or three of the principal Platonic Dialogues I knew no philosophy. Arguments with my father, whose convictions had been formed by John Stuart Mill's attack upon Sir William Hamilton, had destroyed my confidence and driven me from speculation to the direct experience of the Mystics. I had once known Blake as thoroughly as his unfinished confused Prophetic Books permitted, and I had read Swedenborg and Boehme, and my initiation into the 'Hermetic Students' had filled my head with Cabalistic imagery." Now, however, he wants to study philosophy as an aid to understanding the "system." The spirits ask him to wait till they have finished. At the end of three years, when the supernatural revelations have ceased, and "A Vision" is actually in proof, Yeats takes down from Mrs. Yeats, who, it appears, did not share her husband's ignorance, a list of the philosophers she had read. For four years, Yeats applies himself to these, and what he finds makes him uneasy about "A Vision": he feels that he must partly have misinterpreted what the spirits have told him. But the spirits themselves intervene to put an end to this disquieting situation: they make him stop his philosophical studies.

As we read all this, we say to ourselves that Yeats, growing older, has grown more credulous. But we come, at the end, to the following passage: "Some will ask if I believe all that this book contains, and I will not know how to answer. Does the word belief, used as they will use it, belong to our age, can I think of the world as there and I here judging it?" And he intimates that, after all, his system may be only a set of symbols like another—a set of symbols, we recognize, like the Irish myths with which he began.

Into the personal situation suggested by Yeats's account of his revelations, it is inappropriate and unnecessary to go: the psychological situation seems plain. When Yeats, at the crucial period of his life, attempted to leave fairyland behind, when he became aware of the unsatisfying character of the life of iridescent revery, when he completely recreated his style so as to make it solid, homely and exact where it had formerly been shimmering or florid—the need for dwelling with part of his mind—or with his mind for part of the time—in a world of pure imagination, where the necessities of the real world do not hold, had, none the less, not been conjured away by the new artistic and intellectual habits he was cultivating. Where the early Yeats had studied Irish folk-lore, collected and sorted Irish fairy tales, invented fairy tales for himself, the later Yeats worked out from the mediumistic communications of his wife the twenty-eight phases of the human personality and the transformations of the soul after death. Yeats's sense of reality to-day is inferior to that of no man alive—indeed, his greatness is partly due precisely to the vividness of that sense. In his poetry, in his criticism and in his memoirs, it is the world we all live in with which we are confronted—the world we know, with all its frustrations, its defeats, its antagonisms and its errors—the mind that sees is not naïve, as the heart that feels is not insensitive. They meet reality with comprehension and with passion—but they have phases, we are astonished to discover, when they do not seem to meet it at all. Yet the scientific criticism of supernatural phenomena is actually as much a part of the reality of Yeats's world as it is of that of most of the rest of us. And when Yeats writes of his supernatural experiences, this criticism, though it may be kept in the background, is nevertheless always present—his realistic sense is too strong, his intellectual integrity too high, to leave it out of the picture. Though he is much addicted to these fantastic imaginings, though he no doubt needs their support to enable him to sustain his rôle of great poet—yet when he comes to write about his spirits and their messages, he cannot help letting us in on the imposture. He believes, but—he does not believe: the impossibility of believing is the impossibility which he accepts most reluctantly, but still it is there with the other impossibilities of this world which is too full of weeping for a child to understand.

It is interesting to compare "A Vision" with that other compendious treatise on human nature and destiny by that other great writer from Dublin: Bernard Shaw's "Guide to Socialism and Capitalism." Here we can see unmistakably the differences between the kind of literature which was fashionable before the

War and the kind which has been fashionable since. Shaw and Yeats, both coming as young men to London from eighteenth-century Dublin, followed diametrically opposite courses. Shaw shouldered the whole unwieldy load of contemporary sociology, politics, economics, biology, medicine and journalism, while Yeats, convinced that the world of science and politics was somehow fatal to the poet's vision, as resolutely turned away. Shaw accepted the scientific technique and set himself to master the problems of an industrial democratic society, while Yeats rejected the methods of Naturalism and applied himself to the introspective plumbing of the mysteries of the individual mind. While Yeats was editing Blake, Shaw was grappling with Marx; and Yeats was appalled by Shaw's hardness and efficiency. "I hated it," he says of "Arms and the Man"; "it seemed to me inorganic, logical straightness and not the crooked road of life and I stood aghast before its energy." And he tells us that Shaw appeared to him in a dream in the form of a sewing machine, "that clicked and shone, but the incredible thing was that the machine smiled, smiled perpetually."

In his Great Wheel of the twenty-eight phases, Yeats has situated Shaw at a phase considerably removed from his own, and where the individual is headed straight for the deformity of seeking, not the soul, but the world. And their respective literary testaments—the "Vision" and the "Guide"—published almost at the same time, mark the extreme points of their divergence: Shaw bases all human hope and happiness on an equal distribution of income, which he believes will finally make impossible even the pessimism of a Swift or a Voltaire; while Yeats, like Shaw a Protestant for whom the Catholic's mysticism was impossible, has in "A Vision" made the life of humanity contingent on the movements of the stars. "The day is far off," he concludes, "when the two halves of man can divine each its own unity in the other as in a mirror, Sun in Moon, Moon in Sun, and so escape out of the Wheel."

IV

Yet, in the meantime, the poet Yeats has passed into a sort of third phase, in which he is closer to the common world than at any previous period. He is no longer quite so haughty, so imperturbably astride his high horse, as during his middle Dantesque period. With the Dantesque mask, he has lost something of intensity and something of sharpness of outline. In "The Tower" (1928), certain words such as "bitter," "wild," and "fierce," which he was able, a few years ago, to use with such thrilling effect, have no longer quite the same force. He writes more loosely, and seems to write more easily. He has become more plain-spoken, more humorous—his mind seems to run more frankly on his ordinary human satisfactions and chagrins: he is sometimes harsh, sometimes sensual, sometimes careless, sometimes coarse.

Though he now inhabits, like Michael Robartes, a lonely tower on the outermost Irish coast, he has spent six years in the Irish senate, presiding at official receptions in a silk hat, inspecting the plumbing of the government schools and conscientiously sitting through the movies which it is one of his official duties to censor. He is much occupied with politics and society, with general reflections on human life—but with the wisdom of the experience of a lifetime, he is passionate even in age. And he writes poems which charge now with the emotion of a great lyric poet that profound and subtle criticism of life of which I have spoken in connection with his prose.

We may take, as an example of Yeats's later vein, the fine poem in "The Tower" called "Among School Children." The poet, now "a sixty year old smiling public man," has paid an official visit to a girls' school kept by nuns; and as he gazes at the children there, he remembers how the woman he had loved had told him once of some "harsh reproof or trivial event" of her girlhood which had changed "some childish day to tragedy." And for a moment the thought that she may once have looked like one of the children before him has revived the excitement of his old love. He remembers the woman in all her young beauty—and thinks of himself with his present sixty years—"a comfortable kind of old scarecrow." What use is philosophy now?—is not all beauty bound up with the body and doomed to decay with it?—is not even the divine beauty itself which is worshipped there by the nuns inseparable from the images of it they adore?

Labour is blossoming or dancing where
The body is not bruised to pleasure soul,
Nor beauty born out of its own despair,
Nor blear-eyed wisdom out of midnight oil.
O chestnut tree, great rooted blossomer,
Are you the leaf, the blossom or the bole?
O body swayed to music, O brightening glance,
How can we know the dancer from the dance?

Here the actual scene in the convent, the personal emotions it awakens and the general speculations which these emotions suggest, have been interwoven and made to play upon each other at the same time that they are kept separate and distinct. A complex subject has been treated in the most concentrated form, and yet without confusion. Perceptions, fancies, feelings and thoughts have all their place in the poet's record. It is a moment of human life, masterfully seized and made permanent, in all its nobility and lameness, its mystery and actuality, its direct personal contact and abstraction.

R. P. Blackmur

THE LATER POETRY of William Butler Yeats is certainly great enough in its kind, and varied enough within its kind, to warrant a special approach, deliberately not the only approach, and deliberately not a complete approach. A body of great poetry will awaken and exemplify different interests on different occasions, or even on the same occasions, as we may see in the contrasting and often contesting literatures about Dante and Shakespeare: even a relation to the poetry is not common to them all. I propose here to examine Yeats's later poetry with a special regard to his own approach to the making of it; and to explore a little what I conceive to be the dominant mode of his insight, the relations between it and the printed poems, and—a different thing—the relations between it and the readers of his poems.

The major facts I hope to illustrate are these: that Yeats has, if you accept his mode, a consistent extraordinary grasp of the reality of emotion, character, and aspiration; and that his chief resort and weapon for the grasping of the reality is magic; and that if we would make use of that reality for ourselves we must also make some use of the magic that inspirits it. What is important is that the nexus of reality and magic is not by paradox or sleight of hand, but is logical and represents, for Yeats in his poetry, a full use of intelligence. Magic performs for Yeats the same fructifying function that Christianity does for Eliot, or that ironic fatalism did for Thomas Hardy; it makes a connection between the poem and its subject matter and provides an adequate mechanics of meaning and value. If it happens that we discard more of Hardy than we do of Yeats and more of Yeats than we do of Eliot, it is not because Christianity provides better machinery for the movement of poetry than fatalism or magic, but simply because Eliot is a more cautious craftsman. Besides, Eliot's poetry has not even comparatively worn long enough to show what parts are permanent and what merely temporary. The point here is that fatalism, Christianity, and magic are none of them disciplines to which many minds can consciously appeal today, as Hardy, Eliot, and Yeats do, for emotional strength and moral authority. The supernatural

"The Later Poetry of W. B. Yeats," reprinted from *The Southern Review*, II, 2 (autumn, 1936), pp. 339-362; and from *The Expense of Greatness*, by R. P. Blackmur, copyright, 1940, by R. P. Blackmur, Arrow Editions, New York, pp. 74-106.

is simply not part of our mental furniture, and when we meet it in our reading we say: Here is debris to be swept away. But if we sweep it away without first making sure what it is, we are likely to lose the poetry as well as the debris. It is the very purpose of a supernaturally derived discipline, as used in poetry, to set the substance of natural life apart, to give it a form, a meaning, and a value which cannot be evaded. What is excessive and unwarranted in the discipline we indeed ought to dismiss; but that can be determined only when what is integrating and illuminating is known first. The discipline will in the end turn out to have only a secondary importance for the reader; but its effect will remain active when he no longer considers it. That is because for the poet the discipline, far from seeming secondary, had an extraordinary structural, seminal, and substantial importance to the degree that without it he could hardly have written at all.

Poetry does not flow from thin air but requires always either a literal faith, an imaginative faith, or, as in Shakespeare, a mind full of many provisional faiths. The life we all live is not alone enough of a subject for the serious artist; it must be life with a leaning, life with a tendency to shape itself only in certain forms, to afford its most lucid revelations only in certain lights. If our final interest, either as poets or as readers, is in the reality declared when the forms have been removed and the lights taken away, yet we can never come to the reality at all without the first advantage of the form and lights. Without them we should *see* nothing but only glimpse something unstable. We glimpse the fleeting but do not see what it is that fleets.

So it was with Yeats; his early poems are fleeting, some of them beautiful and some that sicken, as you read them, to their own extinction. But as he acquired for himself a discipline, however unacceptable to the bulk of his readers, his poetry obtained an access to reality. So it is with most of our serious poets. It is almost the mark of the poet of genuine merit in our time—the poet who writes serious works with an intellectual aspect which are nonetheless poetry—that he performs his work in the light of an insight, a group of ideas, and a faith, with the discipline that flows from them, which taken together form a view of life most readers cannot share, and which, furthermore, most readers feel as repugnant, or sterile, or simply inconsequential.

All this is to say generally—and we shall say it particularly for Yeats later—that our culture is incomplete with regard to poetry; and the poet has to provide for himself in that quarter where authority and value are derived. It may be that no poet ever found a culture complete for his purpose; it was a welcome and arduous part of his business to make it so. Dante, we may say, completed for poetry the Christian culture of his time, which was itself the completion of centuries. But there was at hand for Dante, and as a rule in the great ages of poetry, a fundamental agreement or convention between the poet and his audience about the validity of the view of life of which the poet deepened the reality and spread the scope. There is no such agreement today. We find poets either using the small conventions of the individual life as if they were great conventions, or attempting to resurrect some great convention of the past, or finally, attempting to discover the great convention that must lie, willy-nilly, hidden in the life about them. This is a labor, whichever form it takes, which leads as often to subterfuge, substitution, confusion, and failure, as to success; and it puts the abnormal burden upon the reader of determining what the beliefs of the poet are and how much to credit them before he can satisfy himself of the reality which those beliefs envisage. The alternative is to put poetry at a discount—which is what has happened.

This the poet cannot do who is aware of the possibilities of his trade: the possibilities of arresting, enacting, and committing to the language through his poems the expressed value of the life otherwise only lived or evaded. The poet so aware knows, in the phrasing of that prose-addict Henry James, both the sacred rage of writing and the muffled majesty of authorship; and knows, as Eliot knows, that once to have been visited by the muses is ever afterwards to be haunted. These are qualities that once apprehended may not be discounted without complete surrender, when the poet is no more than a haunt haunted. Yeats has never put his poetry at a discount. But he has made it easy for his readers to do so—as Eliot has in his way—because the price he has paid for it, the expense he has himself been to in getting it on paper, have been a price most readers simply do not know how to pay and an expense, in time and labor and willingness to understand, beyond any initial notion of adequate reward.

The price is the price of a fundamental and deliberate surrender to magic as the ultimate mode for the apprehension of reality. The expense is the double expense of, on the one hand, implementing magic with a consistent symbolism, and on the other hand, the greatly multiplied expense of restoring, through the *craft* of poetry, both the reality and its symbols to that plane of the quickened senses and the concrete emotions. That is to say, the poet (and, as always, the reader) has to combine, to fuse inextricably into something like an organic unity the constructed or derived symbolism of his special insight with the symbolism animating the language itself. It is, on the poet's plane, the labor of bringing the representative forms of knowledge home to the experience which stirred them: the labor of keeping in mind *what* our knowledge is of: the labor of craft. With the poetry of Yeats this labor is, as I say, doubly hard, because the forms of knowledge, being magical, do not fit naturally with the forms of knowledge that ordinarily preoccupy us. But it is possible, and I hope to show it, that the difficulty is, in a sense, superficial and may be overcome with familiarity, and that the mode of magic itself, once familiar, will even seem rational for the purposes of poetry—although it will not thereby seem inevitable. Judged by its works in the representation of emotional reality—and that is all that can be asked in our context—magic and its burden of symbols may be a major tool of the imagination. A tool has often a double function; it performs feats for which it was designed, and it is heuristic, it discovers and performs new feats which could not have been anticipated without it, which it indeed seems to instigate for itself and in the most unlikely quarters. It is with magic as a tool in its heuristic aspect—as an agent for discovery—that I wish here directly to be concerned.

One of the finest, because one of the most appropriate to our time and place, of all Yeats's poems, is his "The Second Coming."

Turning and turning in the widening gyre
The falcon cannot hear the falconer;
Things fall apart; the centre cannot hold;
Mere anarchy is loosed upon the world,
The blood-dimmed tide is loosed, and everywhere
The ceremony of innocence is drowned;
The best lack all conviction, while the worst
Are full of passionate intensity.

Surely some revelation is at hand;
Surely the Second Coming is at hand.
The Second Coming! Hardly are those words out
When a vast image out of Spiritus Mundi

Troubles my sight: somewhere in sands of the desert
A shape with lion body and the head of a man,
A gaze blank and pitiless as the sun,
Is moving its slow thighs, while all about it
Reel shadows of the indignant desert birds.
The darkness drops again; but now I know
That twenty centuries of stony sleep
Were vexed to nightmare by a rocking cradle,
And what rough beast, its hour come round at last,
Slouches towards Bethlehem to be born?

There is about it, to any slowed reading, the immediate conviction of pertinent emotion; the lines are stirring, separately and in their smaller groups, and there is a sensible life in them that makes them seem to combine in the form of an emotion. We may say at once then, for what it is worth, that in writing his poem Yeats was able to choose words which to an appreciable extent were the right ones to reveal or represent the emotion which was its purpose. The words deliver the meaning which was put into them by the craft with which they were arranged, and that meaning is their own, not to be segregated or given another arrangement without diminution. Ultimately, something of this sort is all that can be said of this or any poem, and when it is said, the poem is known to be good in its own terms or bad because not in its own terms. But the reader seldom reaches an ultimate position about a poem; most poems fail, through craft or conception, to reach an ultimate or absolute position: parts of the craft remain machinery and parts of the conception remain in limbo. Or, as in this poem, close inspection will show something questionable about it. It is true that it can be read as it is, isolated from the rest of Yeats's work and isolated from the intellectual material which it expresses, and a good deal gotten out of it, too, merely by submitting to it. That is because the words are mainly common, both in their emotional and intellectual senses; and if we do not know precisely what the familiar words drag after them into the poem, still we know vaguely what the weight of it feels like; and that seems enough to make a poem at one level of response. Yet if an attempt is made at a more complete response, if we wish to discover the precise emotion which the words mount up to, we come into trouble and uncertainty at once. There is an air of explicitness to each of the separate fragments of the poem. Is it, in this line or that, serious? Has it a reference?—or is it a rhetorical effect, a result only of the persuasive overtones of words?—or is it a combination, a mixture of reference and rhetoric?

Possibly the troubled attention will fasten first upon the italicized phrase in the twelfth line: *Spiritus Mundi;* and the question is whether the general, the readily available senses of the words are adequate to supply the specific sense wanted by the poem. Put another way, can the poet's own arbitrary meaning be made, merely by discovering it, to participate in and enrich what the "normal" meanings of the words in their limiting context provide? The critic can only supply the facts; the poem will in the end provide its own answer. Here there are certain facts that may be extracted from Yeats's prose writings which suggest something of what the words symbolize for him. In one of the notes to the limited edition of *Michael Robartes and the Dancer*, Yeats observes that his mind, like another's, has been from time to time obsessed by images which had no discoverable origin in his waking experience. Speculating as to their origin, he came to deny both the conscious and the unconscious memory as their probable seat, and finally invented a doctrine which traced the images to sources of supernatural character. I quote only that sentence which is relevant to the phrase in question "Those [images] that come in sleep are (1) from the state immediately preceding our birth; (2) from the *Spiritus Mundi*—that is to say, from a general storehouse of images which have ceased to be a property of any personality or spirit." It apparently follows, for Yeats, that images so derived have both an absolute meaning of their own and an operative force in determining meaning and predicting events in this world. In another place (the Introduction to "The Resurrection" in *Wheels and Butterflies*) he describes the image used in this poem, which he had seen many times, "always at my left side just out of the range of sight, a brazen winged beast that I associated with laughing, ecstatic destruction." Ecstacy, it should be added, comes for Yeats just before death, and at death comes the moment of revelation, when the soul is shown its kindred dead and it is possible to see the future.

Here we come directly upon that central part of Yeats's magical beliefs which it is one purpose of this poem emotionally to represent: the belief in what is called variously *Magnus Annus*, The Great Year, The Platonic Year, and sometimes in a slightly different symbolism, The Great Wheel. This belief, with respect to the history of epochs, is associated with the procession of the equinoxes, which bring, roughly every two thousand years, a Great Year of death and rebirth, and this belief, with respect to individuals, seems to be associated with the phases of the moon; although individuals may be influenced by the equinoxes and there may be a lunar interpretation of history. These beliefs have a scaffold of geometrical figures, gyres, cones, circles, etc., by the application of which exact interpretation is secured. Thus it is possible to predict, both in biography and history, and in time, both forwards and backwards the character, climax, collapse, and rebirth in antithetical form of human types and cultures. There is a subordinate but helpful belief that signs, warnings, even direct messages, are always given, from *Spiritus Mundi* or elsewhere, which the poet and the philosopher have only to see and hear. As it happens, the Christian era, being nearly two thousand years old, is due for extinction and replacement, in short for the Second Coming, which this poem heralds. In his note to its first publication (in *Michael Robartes and the Dancer*) Yeats expresses his belief as follows:

> At the present moment the life gyre is sweeping outward, unlike that before the birth of Christ which was narrowing, and has almost reached its greatest expansion. The revelation which approaches will however take its character from the contrary movement of the interior gyre. All our scientific, democratic, fact-accumulating, heterogeneous civilisation belongs to the outward gyre and prepares not the continuance of itself but the revelation as in a lightning flash, though in a flash that will not strike only in one place, and will for a time be constantly repeated, of the civilisation that must slowly take its place.

So much for a major gloss upon the poem. Yeats combined, in the best verse he could manage, the beliefs which obsessed him with the image which he took to be a specific illustration of the beliefs. Minor and buttressing glosses are possible for many of the single words and phrases in the poem, some flowing from private doctrine and some from Yeats's direct sense of the world about him, and some from both at once. For example: The "ceremony of innocence" represents for Yeats one of the qualities that made life valuable under the dying aristocratic social tradition; and the meaning of the phrase in the poem requires no magic for completion but only a reading of other poems. The "falcon and the falconer" in the second line has, besides its obvious symbolism, a doctrinal reference. A falcon is a hawk, and a hawk is symbolic of the active or intellectual mind; the falconer is perhaps the soul itself or its uniting principle. There is also the apposition which Yeats has made several times that "Wisdom is a butterfly/And not a gloomy bird of prey." Whether the special symbolism has actually been incorporated in the poem, and in which form, or whether it is private debris merely, will take a generation of readers to decide. In the meantime it must be taken provisionally for whatever its ambiguity may seem to be worth. Literature is full of falcons, some that fly and some that lack immediacy and sit, archaic, on the poet's wrist; and it is not always illuminating to determine which is which. But when we come on such lines as

The best lack all conviction, while the worst
Are full of passionate intensity,

we stop short, first to realize the aptness of the statement to every plane of life in the world about us, and then to connect them with the remote body of the poem they illuminate. There is a dilemma of which the branches grow from one trunk but which cannot be solved; for these lines have, not two meanings, but two sources for the same meaning. There is the meaning that comes from the summary observation that this is how men are—and especially men of power—in the world we live in; it is knowledge that comes from knowledge of the "fury and mire in human veins"; a meaning the contemplation of which has lately (April, 1934) lead Yeats to offer himself to any government or party that, using force and marching men, will "promise not this or that measure but a discipline, a way of life." And there is in effect the same meaning, at least at the time the poem was written, which comes from a different source and should have, one would think, very different consequences in prospective party loyalties. Here the meaning has its source in the doctrines of the Great Year and the Phases of the Moon; whereby, to cut exegesis short, it is predicted as necessary that, at the time we have reached, the best minds, being subjective, should have lost all faith though desiring it, and the worst minds, being so nearly objective, have no need of faith and may be full of "passionate intensity" without the control of any faith or wisdom. Thus we have on the one side the mirror of observation and on the other side an imperative, magically derived, which come to the conclusion of form in identical words.

The question is, to repeat, whether the fact of this double control and source of meaning at a critical point defeats or strengthens the unity of the poem; and it is a question which forms itself again and again in the later poems, sometimes obviously but more often only by suggestion. If we take another poem on the same theme, written some years earlier, and before his wife's mediumship gave him the detail of his philosophy, we will find the question easier to answer in its suggested than in its conspicuous form. There is an element in the poem called "The Magi" which we can feel the weight of but cannot altogether name, and of which we can only guess at the efficacy.

Now as at all times I can see in the mind's eye,
In their stiff, painted clothes, the pale unsatisfied ones
Appear and disappear in the blue depths of the sky
With all their ancient faces like rain-beaten stones,
And all their helms of silver hovering side by side,
And all their eyes still fixed, hoping to find once more,
Being by Calvary's turbulence unsatisfied,
The uncontrollable mystery on the bestial floor.

I mean the element which, were Yeats a Christian, we could accept as a species of Christian blasphemy or advanced heresy, but which since he is not a Christian we find it hard to accept at all: the element of emotional conviction springing from intellectual matters without rational source or structure. We ought to be able, for the poem's sake, to accept the conviction as an emotional possibility, much as we accept *Lear* or Dostoieffsky's *Idiot* as valid, because projected from represented experience. But Yeats's experience is not represented consistently on any one plane. He constantly indicates a supernatural validity for his images of which the authority cannot be reached. If we come nearer to accepting "The Magi" than "The Second Coming" it is partly because the familiar Christian paradigm is more clearly used, and, in the last two lines what Yeats constructs upon it is given a more immediate emotional form, and partly because, *per contra,* there is less demand made upon arbitrary intellectual belief. There is, too, the matter of scope; if we reduce the scope of "The Second Coming" to that of "The Magi" we shall find it much easier to accept; but we shall have lost much of the poem.

We ought now to have enough material to name the two radical defects of magic as a tool for poetry. One defect, which we have just been illustrating, is that it has no available edifice of reason reared upon it conventionally independent of its inspiration. There is little that the uninspired reader can naturally refer to for authority outside the poem, and if he does make a natural reference he is likely to turn out to be at least partly wrong. The poet is thus in the opposite predicament; he is under the constant necessity of erecting his beliefs into doctrines at the same time that he represents their emotional or dramatic equivalents. He is, in fact, in much the same position that Dante would have been had he had to construct his Christian doctrine while he was composing *The Divine Comedy:* an impossible labor. The Christian supernaturalism, the Christian magic (no less magical than that of Yeats), had the great advantage for Dante, and imaginatively for ourselves, of centuries of reason and criticism and elaboration: It was within reason a consistent whole; and its supernatural element had grown so consistent with experience as to seem supremely *natural*—as indeed it may again. Christianity has an objective form, whatever the mysteries at its heart and its termini, in which all the phenomena of human life may find place and meaning. Magic is none of these things for any large fraction of contemporary society. Magic has a tradition, but it is secret, not public. It has not only central and terminal mysteries but has also peripheral mysteries, which require not only the priest to celebrate but also the adept to manipulate. Magic has never been made "natural." The practical knowledge and power which its beliefs lead to can neither be generally shared nor overtly rationalized. It is in fact held to be dangerous to reveal openly the details of magical experience: they may be revealed, if at all, only in arbitrary symbols and equivocal statements. Thus we find Yeats, in his early and innocuous essay on magic, believing his life to have been imperiled for revealing too much. Again, the spirits or voices through whom magical knowledge is gained are often themselves equivocal and are sometimes deliberately confusing. Yeats was told to remember, "We will deceive you if we can," and on another occasion was forbidden to record anything that was said, only to be scolded later because he had failed to record every word. In short, it is of the essence of magical faith that the supernatural cannot be brought into the natural world except through symbol. The distinction between natural and supernatural is held to be substantial instead of verbal. Hence magic may neither be criticized or institutionalized; nor can it ever reach a full expression of its own intention. This is perhaps the justification of Stephen Spender's remark that there is more magic in Eliot's "The Hollow Men" than in any poem of Yeats; because of Eliot's Christianity, his magic has a rational base as well as a supernatural source: it is the magic of an orthodox, authoritative faith. The dogmas of magic, we may say, are all heresies which cannot be expounded except each on its own authority as a fragmentary insight; and its unity can be only the momentary unity of association. Put another way, magic is in one respect in the state of Byzantine Christianity, when miracles were quotidian and the universal frame of experience, when life itself was held to be supernatural and reason was mainly a kind of willful sophistication.

Neither Yeats nor ourselves dwell in Byzantium. At a certain level, though not at all levels, we conceive life, and even its nonrational features, in rational terms. Certainly there is a rational bias and a rational structure in the poetry we mainly agree to hold great—though the content may be what it will; and it is the irrational bias and the confused structure that we are mainly concerned to disavow, to apologize or allow for. It was just to provide himself with the equivalent of a rational religious insight and a predictable rational structure for the rational imagination that in his book, *A Vision* (published, in 1925, in a limited edition only, and then withdrawn), he attempted to convert his magical experience into a systematic philosophy. "I wished," he writes in the Dedication to that work, "for a system of thought that would leave my imagination free to create as it chose and yet make all that it created, or could create, part of the one history, and that the soul's." That is, Yeats hoped by systematizing it to escape from the burden of confusion and abstraction which his magical experience had imposed upon him. "I can now," he declares in this same Dedication, "if I have the energy, find the simplicity I have sought in vain. I need no longer write poems like 'The Phases of the Moon' nor 'Ego Dominus Tuus,' nor spend barren years, as I have done three or four times, striving with abstractions that substitute themselves for the play that I had planned."

"Having inherited," as he says in one of his poems, "a vigorous mind," he could not help seeing, once he had got it all down, that his system was something to disgorge if he could. Its truth as experience would be all the stronger if its abstractions could be expunged. But it could not be disgorged; its thirty-five years of growth was an intimate part of his own growth, and its abstractions were all of a piece with his most objective experience. And perhaps we, as readers, can see that better from outside than Yeats could from within. I suspect that no amount of will could have rid him of his magical conception of the soul; it was by magic that he knew the soul; and the conception had been too closely associated with his profound sense of his race and personal ancestry. He has never been able to retract his system, only to take up different attitudes towards it. He has alternated between granting his speculations only the validity of poetic myth and planning to announce a new deity. In his vacillation—there is a poem by that title—the rational defect remains, and the reader must deal with it sometimes as an intrusion upon the poetry of indeterminate value and sometimes as itself the subject of dramatic reverie or lyric statement. At least once he tried to force the issue home, and in a section of *A Packet for Ezra Pound* called "Introduction to the Great Wheel" he meets the issue by transforming it, for the moment, into wholly poetic terms. Because it reveals a fundamental honesty and clarity of purpose in the midst of confusion and uncertainty the section is quoted entire.

> Some will ask if I believe all that this book contains, and I will not know how to answer. Does the word belief, as they will use it, belong to our age, can I think of the world as there and I here judging it? I will never think any thoughts but these, or some modification or extension of these; when I write prose or verse they must be somewhere present though it may not be in the words; they must affect my judgment of friends and events; but then there are many symbolisms and none exactly resembles mine. What Leopardi in Ezra Pound's translation calls that 'concord' wherein 'the arcane spirit of the whole mankind turns hardy pilot'—how much better it would be without that word 'hardy' which slackens speed and adds nothing—persuades me that he has best imagined reality who has best imagined justice.

The rational defect, then, remains; the thought is not always in the words; and we must do with it as we can. There is another defect of Yeats's magical system which is especially apparent to the reader but which may not be apparent at all to Yeats. Magic promises precisely matters which it cannot perform—at least in poetry. It promises, as in "The Second Coming," exact prediction of events in the natural world; and it promises again and again, in different poems, exact revelations of the supernatural, and of this we have an example in what has to many seemed a great poem, "All Souls' Night," which had its first publication as an epilogue to *A Vision*. Near the beginning of the poem we have the explicit declaration: "I have a marvelous thing to say" and near the end another: "I have mummy truths to tell." "Mummy truths" is an admirable phrase, suggestive as it is of the truths in which the dead are wrapped, ancient truths as old as Egypt perhaps, whence mummies commonly come, and truths, too, that may be unwound. But there, with the suggestion, the truths stop short; there is, for the reader, no unwinding, no revelation of the dead. What Yeats actually does is to summon into the poem various of his dead friends as "characters"—and this is the greatness, and only this, of the poem: the summary, excited, even exalted presentation of character. Perhaps the rhetoric is the marvel and the evasion the truth. We get an impact as from behind, from the speed and weight of the words, and are left with an ominous or terrified frame of mind, the revelation still to come. The revelation, the magic, was in Yeats's mind; hence the exaltation in his language; but it was not and could not be given in the words of the poem.

It may be that for Yeats there was a similar exaltation and a similar self-deceit in certain other poems, but as the promise of revelation was not made, the reader feels no failure of fulfillment. Such poems as "Easter, 1916," "In Memory of Major Robert Gregory," and "Upon a Dying Lady" may have buried in them a conviction of invocation and revelation; but if so it is no concern of ours: we are concerned only, as the case may be, with the dramatic presentations of the Irish patriots and poets, Yeats's personal friends, and Aubrey Beardsley's dying sister, and with, in addition, for minor pleasure, the technical means—the spare and delicate language, the lucid images, and quickening rhymes—whereby the characters are presented as intensely felt. There is no problem in such poems but the problem of reaching, through a gradual access of intimacy, full appreciation; here the magic and everything else are in the words. It is the same, for bare emotion apart from character, in such poems as "A Deep-Sworn Vow," where the words accumulate by the simplest means an intolerable excitement, where the words are, called as they may be from whatever source, in an ultimate sense their own meaning.

Others because you did not keep
That deep-sworn vow have been friends of mine;
Yet always when I look death in the face,
When I clamber to the heights of sleep,
Or when I grow excited with wine,
Suddenly I meet your face.

Possibly all poetry should be read as this poem is read, and no poetry greatly valued that cannot be so read. Such is one ideal towards which reading tends; but to apply it as a standard of judgment we should first have to assume for the poetic intelligence absolute autonomy and self-perfection for all its works. Actually, autonomy and self-perfection are relative and depend upon a series of agreements or conventions between the poet and his readers, which alter continually, as to what must be represented by the fundamental power of language (itself a relatively stable convention) and what, on the other hand, may be adequately represented by mere reference, sign, symbol, or blue print indication. Poetry is so little autonomous from the technical point of view that the greater part of a given work must be conceived as the manipulation of conventions that the reader will, or will not, take for granted; these being crowned, or animated, emotionally transformed, by what the poet actually represents, original or not, through his mastery of poetic language. Success is provisional, seldom complete, and never permanently complete. The vitality or letter of a convention may perish although the form persists. *Romeo and Juliet* is less successful today than when produced because the conventions of honor, family authority, and blood-feud no longer animate and justify the action; and if the play survives it is partly because certain other conventions of human character do remain vital, but more because Shakespeare is the supreme master of representation through the reality of language alone. Similarly with Dante; with the cumulative disintegration, even for Catholics, of medieval Christianity as the ultimate convention of human life, the success of *The Divine Comedy* comes more and more to depend on the exhibition of character and the virtue of language alone—which may make it a greater, not a lesser poem. On the other hand, it often happens that a poet's ambition is such that, in order to get his work done at all, he must set up new conventions or radically modify old ones which fatally lack that benefit of form which can be conferred only by public recognition. The form which made his poems available was only gradually conferred upon the convention of evil in Baudelaire and, as we may see in translations with contrasting emphases, its limits are still subject to debate; in his case the more so because the life of his language depended more than usual on the viability of the convention.

Let us apply those notions, which ought so far to be commonplace, to the later work of Yeats, relating them especially to the predominant magical convention therein. When Yeats came of poetic age he found himself, as Blake had before him, and even Wordsworth, but to a worse extent, in a society whose conventions extended neither intellectual nor moral authority to poetry; he found himself in a rational but deliberately incomplete, because progressive, society. The *emotion* of thought, for poetry, was gone, along with the emotion of religion and the emotion of race—the three sources and the three aims of the great poetry of the past. Tyndall and Huxley are the villains, Yeats records in his Autobiographies, as Blake recorded Newton; there were other causes, but no matter, these names may serve as symbols. And the dominant aesthetics of the time were as rootless in the realm of poetic import and authority as the dominant conventions. Art for Art's sake was the cry, the Ivory Tower the retreat, and Walter Pater's luminous languor and weak Platonism the exposition. One could say anything but it would mean nothing. The poets and society both, for opposite reasons, expected the poet to produce either exotic and ornamental mysteries or lyrics of mood; the real world and its significance were reserved mainly to the newer sciences, though the novelists and the playwrights might poach if they could. For a time Yeats succumbed, as may be seen in his early work, even while he attempted to escape; and of his poetic generation he was the only one to survive and grow in stature. He came under the influence of the French Symbolists, who gave him the clue and the hint of an external structure but nothing much to put in it. He read, with a dictionary, Villiers de L'Isle-Adam's *Axel's Castle,* and so came to be included in Edmund Wilson's book of that name—although not, as Wilson himself shows, altogether correctly. For he began in the late 'nineties, as it were upon his own account, to quench his thirst for reality by creating authority and significance and reference in the three fields where they were lacking. He worked into his poetry the substance of Irish mythology and Irish politics and gave them a symbolism, and he developed his experiences with Theosophy and Rosicrucianism into a body of conventions adequate, for him, to animate the concrete poetry of the soul that he wished to write. He did not do these things separately; the mythology, the politics, and the magic are conceived, through the personalities that reflected them, with an increasing unity of apprehension. Thus more than any poet of our time he has restored to poetry the actual emotions of race and religion and what we call abstract thought. Whether we follow him in any particular or not, the general poetic energy which he liberated is ours to use if we can. If the edifice that he constructed seems personal, it is because he had largely to build it for himself, and that makes it difficult to understand in detail except in reference to the peculiar unity which comes from their mere association in his life and work. Some of the mythology and much of the politics, being dramatized and turned into emotion, are part of our common possessions. But where the emphasis has been magical, whether successfully or not, the poems have been misunderstood, ignored, and the actual emotion in them which is relevant to us all decried and underestimated, merely because the magical mode of thinking is foreign to our own and when known at all is largely associated with quackery and fraud.

We do not make that mistake—which is the mistake of unwillingness—with Dante or the later Eliot, because, although the substance of their modes of thinking is equally foreign and magical, it has the advantage of a rational superstructure that persists and which we can convert to our own modes if we will. Yeats lacks, as we have said, the historical advantage and with it much else; and the conclusion cannot be avoided that this lack prevents his poetry from reaching the first magnitude. But there are two remedies we may apply, which will make up, not for the defect of magnitude, but for the defect of structure. We can read the magical philosophy in his verse *as if* it were converted into the contemporary psychology with which its doctrines have so much in common. We find little difficulty in seeing Freud's preconscious as a fertile myth and none at all in the general myth of extroverted and introverted personality; and these may be compared with, respectively, Yeats's myth of *Spiritus Mundi* and the Phases of the Moon: the intention and the scope of the meaning are identical. So much for a secular conversion. The other readily available remedy is this: to accept Yeats's magic literally as a machinery of meaning, to search out the prose parallels and reconstruct the symbols he uses on their own terms in order to come on the emotional reality, if it is there, actually in the poems—when the machinery may be dispensed with. This method has the prime advantage over secular conversion of keeping judgment in poetic terms, with the corresponding disadvantage that it requires more time and patience, more "willing suspension of disbelief," and a stiffer intellectual exercise all around. But exegesis is to be preferred to conversion on still another ground, which may seem repellent: that magic, in the sense that we all experience it, is nearer the represented emotions that concern us in poetry than psychology, as a generalized science, can ever be. We are all, without conscience, magicians in the dark.

But even the poems of darkness are read in the light. I cannot, of course, make a sure prognosis; because in applying either remedy the reader is, really, doctoring himself as much as Yeats. Only this much is sure: that the reader will come to see the substantial unity of Yeats's work, that it is the same mind stirring behind the poems on Crazy Jane and the Bishop, on Cuchulain, on Swift, the political poems, the biographical and the doctrinal—a mind that sees the fury and the mire and passion of the dawn as contrary aspects of the real world. It is to be expected that many poems will fail in part and some entirely, and if the chief, magic will not be the only cause of failure. The source of a vision puts limits upon its expression which the poet cannot well help overpassing. "The limitation of his view," Yeats wrote of Blake, "was from the very intensity of his vision; he was a too-literal realist of imagination, as others are of nature"; and the remark applies to himself. But there will be enough left to make the labor of culling worth all its patience and time. Before concluding, I propose to spur the reader, or inadvertently dismay him, by presenting briefly a few examples of the sort of reconstructive labor he will have to do and the sort of imaginative assent he may have to attempt in order to enter or dismiss the body of the poems.

As this is a mere essay in emphasis, let us bear the emphasis in, by repeating, on different poems, the sort of commentary laid out above on "The Second Coming" and "The Magi," using this time "Byzantium" and "Sailing to Byzantium." Byzantium is for Yeats, so to speak, the heaven of the man's mind; there the mind or soul dwells in eternal or miraculous form; there all things are possible because all things are known to the soul. Byzantium has both a historical and an ideal form, and the historical is the exemplar, the dramatic witness, of the ideal. Byzantium represents both a dated epoch and a recurrent state of insight, when nature is magical, that is, at the beck of mind, and magic is natural—a practical rather than a theoretic art. If with these notions in mind we compare the two poems named we see that the first called simply "Byzantium," is like certain cantos in the *Paradiso* the poetry of an intense and condensed declaration of doctrine; not emotion put into doctrine from outside, but doctrine presented as emotion. I quote the second stanza.

Before me floats an image, man or shade,
Shade more than man, more image than a shade;
For Hades' bobbin bound in mummy-cloth

May unwind the winding path;
A mouth that has no moisture and no breath
Breathless mouths may summon;
I hail the superhuman;
I call it death-in-life and life-in-death.

The second poem, "Sailing to Byzantium," rests upon the doctrine but is not a declaration of it. It is, rather, the doctrine in action, the doctrine actualized in a personal emotion resembling that of specific prayer. This is the emotion of the flesh where the other was the emotion of the bones. The distinction should not be too sharply drawn. It is not the bones of doctrine but the emotion of it that we should be aware of in reading the more dramatic poem: and the nearer they come to seeming two reflections of the same thing the better both poems will be. What must be avoided is a return to the poem of doctrine with a wrong estimation of its value gained by confusion of the two poems. Both poems are serious in their own kind, and the reality of each must be finally in its own words whatever clues the one supplies to the other. I quote the third stanza.

O sages standing in God's holy fire
As in the gold mosaic of a wall,
Come from the holy fire, perne in a gyre,
And be the singing-masters of my soul.
Consume my heart away; sick with desire
And fastened to a dying animal
It knows not what it is; and gather me
Into the artifice of eternity.

We must not, for example, accept "perne in a gyre" in this poem merely because it is part of the doctrine upon which the poem rests. Its magical reference may be too explicit for the poem to digest. It may be merely part of the poem's intellectual machinery, something that will *become* a dead commonplace once its peculiarity has worn out. Its meaning, that is, may turn out not to participate in the emotion of the poem: which is an emotion of aspiration. Similarly a note of aspiration would have been injurious to the stanza quoted from "Byzantium" above.

Looking at other poems as examples, the whole problem of exegesis may be put another way; which consists in joining two facts and observing their product. There is the fact that again and again in Yeats's prose, both in that which accompanies the poems and that which is independent of them, poems and fragments of poems are introduced at strategic points, now to finish off or clinch an argument by giving it as proved, and again merely to balance argument with witness from another plane. *A Vision* is punctuated by five poems. And there is the complementary fact that, when one has read the various autobiographies, introductions, and doctrinal notes and essays, one continually finds echoes, phrases, and developments from the prose in the poems. We have, as Wallace Stevens says, the prose that wears the poem's guise at last; and we have, too, the poems turning backwards, reilluminating or justifying the prose from the material of which they sprang. We have, to import the dichotomy which T. S. Eliot made for his own work, the prose writings discovering and buttressing the ideal, and we have the poems which express as much as can be actualized—given as concrete emotion—of what the prose discovered or envisaged. The dichotomy is not so sharp in Yeats as in Eliot. Yeats cannot, such is the unity of his apprehension, divide his interests. There is one mind employing two approaches in the labor of representation. The prose approach lets in much that the poetic approach excludes; it lets in the questionable, the uncertain, the hypothetic, and sometimes the incredible. The poetic approach, using the same material, retains, when it is successful, only what is manifest, the emotion that can be made actual in a form of words that need only to be understood, not argued. If props of argument and vestiges of idealization remain, they must be felt as qualifying, not arguing, the emotion. It should only be remembered and repeated that the poet invariably requires more machinery to secure *his* effects—the machinery of his whole life and thought —than the reader requires to secure what he takes as the *poem's* effects; and that, as readers differ, the poet cannot calculate what is necessary to the poem and what is not. There is always the debris to be cut away.

In such a fine poem as "A Prayer for My Son," for example, Yeats cut away most of the debris himself, and it is perhaps an injury to judgment provisionally to restore it. Yet to this reader at least the poem seems to richen when it is known from what special circumstances the poem was freed. As it stands we can accept the symbols which it conspicuously contains—the strong ghost, the devilish things, and the holy writings—as drawn from the general stock of literary conventions available to express the evil predicament in which children and all innocent beings obviously find themselves. Taken so, it is a poem of natural piety. But for Yeats the conventions were not merely literary but were practical expressions of the actual terms of the predicament, and his poem is a prayer of dread and supernatural piety. The experience which led to the poem is recounted in *A Packet for Ezra Pound*. When his son was still an infant Yeats was told through the mediumship of his wife that the Frustrators or evil spirits would henceforth "attack my health and that of my children, and one afternoon, knowing from the smell of burnt feathers that one of my children would be ill within three hours, I felt before I could recover self-control the mediaeval helpless horror of witchcraft." The child *was* ill. It is from this experience that the poem seems to have sprung, and the poem preserves all that was actual behind the private magical conventions Yeats used for himself. The point is that the reader has a richer poem if he can substitute the manipulative force of Yeats's specific conventions for the general literary conventions. Belief or imaginative assent is no more difficult for either set. It is the emotion that counts.

That is one extreme to which the poems run—the extreme convention of personal thought. Another extreme is that exemplified in "A Prayer for My Daughter," where the animating conventions *are* literary and piety *is* natural, and in the consideration of which it would be misleading to introduce the magical convention as more than a foil. As a foil it is nevertheless present; his magical philosophy, all the struggle and warfare of the intellect, is precisely what Yeats in this poem *puts out of mind,* in order to imagine his daughter living in innocence and beauty, custom and ceremony.

A third extreme is that found in the sonnet "Leda and the Swan," where there is an extraordinary sensual immediacy—the words meet and move like speaking lips—and a profound combination of the generally available or literary symbol and the hidden, magical symbol of the intellectual, philosophical, impersonal order. Certain longer poems and groups of poems, especially the series called "A Woman Young and Old," exhibit the extreme of combination as well or better; but I want the text on the page.

A sudden blow: the great wings beating still
Above the staggering girl, her thighs caressed
By the dark webs, her nape caught in his bill,
He holds her helpless breast upon his breast.

How can those terrified vague fingers push
The feathered glory from her loosening thighs?
And how can body, laid in that white rush,
But feel the strange heart beating where it lies?

A shudder in the loins engenders there
The broken wall, the burning roof and tower
And Agamemnon dead.

Being so caught up,
So mastered by the brute blood of the air,
Did she put on his knowledge with his power
Before the indifferent beak could let her drop?

It should be observed that in recent years new images, some from the life of Swift, and some from the Greek mythology, have been spreading through Yeats's poems; and of Greek images he has used especially those of Oedipus and Leda, of Homer and Sophocles. But they are not used as we think the Greeks used them, nor as mere drama, but deliberately, after the magical tradition, both to represent and hide the myths Yeats has come on in his own mind. Thus "Leda and the Swan" can be read on at least three distinct levels of significance, none of which interferes with the others: the levels of dramatic fiction, of condensed insight into Greek mythology, and a third level of fiction and insight combined, as we said, to represent and hide a magical insight. This third level is our present concern. At this level the poem presents in interfusion among the normal terms of the poem two of Yeats's fundamental magical doctrines in emotional form. The doctrines are put by Yeats in the following form in his essay on magic: "That the borders of our mind are ever shifting, and that many minds can flow into one another, as it were, and create or reveal a single mind, a single energy. . . . That this great mind can be evoked by symbols." Copulation is the obvious nexus for spiritual as well as physical seed. There is also present I think some sense of Yeats's doctrine of Annunciation and the Great Year, the Annunciation, in this case, that produced Greek culture. It is a neat question for the reader, so far as this poem is concerned, whether the poetic emotion springs from the doctrine and seizes the myth for a safe home and hiding, or whether the doctrine is correlative to the emotion of the myth. In neither case does the magic matter as such; it has become poetry, and of extreme excellence in its order. To repeat the interrogatory formula with which we began the commentary on "The Second Coming," is the magical material in these poems incorporated in them by something like organic reference or is its presence merely rhetorical? The reader will answer one way or the other, as, to his rational imagination, to all the imaginative understanding he can bring to bear, it either seems to clutter the emotion and deaden the reality, or seems rather, as I believe, to heighten the emotional reality and thereby extend its reference to what we call the real world. Once the decision is made, the magic no longer exists; we have the poetry.

Other approaches to Yeats's poetry would have produced different emphases, and this approach, which has emphasized little but the magical structure of Yeats's poetic emotions, has made that emphasis with an ulterior purpose: to show that magic may be a feature of a rational imagination. This approach should be combined with others, or should have others combined with it, for perspective and reduction. No feature of a body of poetry can be as important as it seems in discussion. Above all, then, this approach through the magical emphasis should be combined with the approach of plain reading—which is long reading and hard reading—plain reading of the words, that they may sink in and do as much of their own work as they can. One more thing: When we call man a rational animal we mean that reason is his great myth. Reason is plastic and takes to any form provided. The rational imagination in poetry, as elsewhere, can absorb magic as a provisional method of evocative and heuristic thinking, but it cannot be based upon it. In poetry, and largely elsewhere, imagination is based upon the reality of words and the emotion of their joining. Yeats's magic, then, like every other feature of his experience, is rational as it reaches words; otherwise it is his privation, and ours, because it was the rational defect of our society that drove him to it.

Cleanth Brooks, Jr.

WILLIAM BUTLER YEATS has produced in his *Vision* one of the most remarkable books of the last hundred years. It is the most ambitious attempt made by any poet of our time to set up a "myth." The framework is elaborate and complex; the concrete detail constitutes some of the finest prose and poetry of our time. But the very act of boldly setting up a myth will be regarded by most critics as an impertinence, or, at the least, as a fantastic vagary. And the latter view will be reinforced by Yeats's account of how he received the system from the spirits through the mediumship of his wife.

The privately printed edition of *A Vision* appeared so long ago as 1925, but it has been almost completely ignored by the critics even though there has been, since the publication of *The Tower* in 1928, a remarkable resurgence of interest in Yeats's poetry. Indeed, Edmund Wilson has been the only critic thus far to deal with *A Vision* in any detail. His treating it in any detail is all the more admirable in view of his general interpretation of the significance of Yeats's system. For Wilson, as we have already seen, considers the symbolist movement as a retreat from science and reality; and Yeats's system, with its unscientific paraphernalia, its gyres and cones, its strange psychology described in terms of Masks and Bodies of Fate, and most of all its frank acceptance of the supernatural, is enough to try the patience of any scientific modernist. A very real regard for the fineness of Yeats's later poetry has prevented him from carrying too far the view of Yeats as an escapist. But to regard the magical system as merely a piece of romantic furniture is to miss completely the function which it has performed for Yeats.

The central matter is science, truly enough, and Edmund Wilson is right in interpreting the symbolist movement as an antiscientific tendency. But the really important matter to determine is the grounds for Yeats's hostility to science. The refusal to accept the scientific account in matters where the scientific method is valid and relevant is unrealistic, but there is nothing "escapist" about a hostility to science which orders science off the premises as a trespasser when science has tak

"Yeats: The Poet as Myth-Maker," reprinted from *The Southern Review*, IV, 1 (summer, 1938), pp. 116-142; and from *Modern Poetry and the Tradition*, by Cleanth Brooks, Jr., copyright, 1939, by the University of North Carolina Press, Chapel Hill, pp. 173-202.

en up a position where it has no business to be. For example, Victorian poetry will illustrate the illegitimate intrusion of science, and Yeats in his frequent reprehension of the "impurities" in such poetry—far from being a romantic escapist—is taking a thoroughly realistic position. The formulas which Edmund Wilson tends to take up—scientific = hard-headed, realistic; antiscientific = romantic, escapist—are far too simple.

We have argued in earlier chapters that all poetry since the middle of the seventeenth century has been characterized by the impingement of science upon the poet's world. Yeats, after a brief enthusiasm for natural science as a boy, came, he tells us, to hate science "with a monkish hate." "I am," Yeats tells us, "very religious, and deprived by Huxley and Tyndall . . . of the simple-minded religion of my childhood, I had made a new religion, almost an infallible church of poetic tradition, of a fardel of stories and of personages, and of emotions, inseparable from their first expression, passed on from generation to generation by poets and painters with some help from philosophers and theologians." Here is the beginning of Yeats's system.

It is easy, when one considers the system as expressed in *A Vision,* to argue that Yeats's quarrel with science was largely that the system of science allowed no place for the supernatural—visions, trances, and incredible happenings—which began to manifest itself to Yeats at a very early period in his life. Undoubtedly Yeats wished for an account of experience which would make room for such happenings. But if we insist on this aspect of the matter, as most critics have done, we neglect elements which are far more important. Granting that Yeats had never had a single supernatural manifestation, many of his objections to science would have remained. The account given by science is still abstract, unconcerned with values, and affording no interpretations. Yeats wished for an account of experience which would surmount such defects: as he once put it, a philosophy which was at once "logical and boundless." The phrase is an important one. Had Yeats merely been content to indulge himself in fairy tales and random superstitions, he would never, presumably, have bothered with a system of beliefs at all. A philosophy which was merely "boundless" would allow a person to live in a pleasant enough anarchy. The "logical" quality demands a systematization, though in Yeats's case one which would not violate and oversimplify experience.

The whole point is highly important. If Yeats had merely been anxious to indulge his fancy, not caring whether the superstition accepted for the moment had any relation to the world about him—had he been merely an escapist, no system would have been required at all. For the system is an attempt to make a coherent formulation of the natural and the supernatural. The very existence of the system set forth in *A Vision* therefore indicates that Yeats refused to run away from life.

But if he refused to run away from life he also refused to play the game with the counters of science. For the abstract, meaningless, valueless system of science, he proposed to substitute a concrete, meaningful system, substituting symbol for concept. As he states in the introduction to *A Vision,* "I wished for a system of thought that would leave my imagination free to create as it chose and yet make all it created, or could create, part of the one history, and that the soul's." [1]
Or if we prefer Mr. Eliot's terms, Yeats set out to build a system of references which would allow for a unification of sensibility. Yeats wanted to give the authority of the intellect to attitudes and the intensity of emotion to judgments. The counsel of I. A. Richards is to break science and the emotions cleanly apart—to recognize the separate validity and relevance of "statements" (scientific propositions) on the one hand and of "pseudo-statements" (unscientific but emotionally valid statements) on the other.

Yeats, on the contrary, instead of breaking science and poetry completely apart, has preferred to reunite these elements in something of the manner in which they are fused in a religion. His system has for him, consequently, the authority and meaning of a religion, combining intellect and emotion as they were combined before the great analytic and abstracting process of modern science broke them apart. In short, Yeats has created for himself a myth. He says so frankly in the closing paragraphs of *A Vision* (1925 edition): "A book of modern philosophy may prove to our logical capacity that there is a transcendental portion of our being that is timeless and spaceless . . . and yet our imagination remains subjected to nature as before. . . . It was not with ancient philosophy because the ancient philosopher had something to reinforce his thought,—the Gods, the Sacred Dead, Egyptian Theurgy, the Priestess Diotime. . . . I would restore to the philosopher his

[1]This statement occurs in the privately printed edition of *A Vision* which appeared in 1925. The new edition does not differ from the earlier fundamentally in the system that it sets forth, though it has many omissions and revisions of statement, and some extensions.

mythology."

It is because most of us misunderstand and distrust the myth and because we too often trust science even when it has been extended into contexts where it is no longer science that most of us misunderstand the function of Yeats's mythology. A further caution is in order. Yeats has called his system "magical," and the term may mislead us. Yeats even claims for the system a capacity for prediction. In 1917, in his "Anima Hominis," he wrote: "I do not doubt those heaving circles, those winding arcs, whether in one man's life or in that of an age, are mathematical, and that some in the world, or beyond the world, have foreknown the event and pricked upon the calendar the life-span of a Christ, a Buddha, a Napoleon"; and in the earlier edition of *A Vision,* there actually occurs a prophecy of the next two hundred years. But the system does not serve the ends of "vulgar magic." Yeats obviously does not propose to use his system to forecast the movements of the stock market, or to pick the winner of the Grand National. The relation of the system to science and the precise nature of Yeats's belief in it will be discussed later. For the present, the positive qualities of the myth may be best discussed by pointing out its relation to Yeats's poetry.

The system may be conveniently broken up into three parts: a picture of history, an account of human psychology, and an account of the life of the soul after death. The theory of history is the easiest aspect of the system. It bears a close resemblance to Spengler's cyclic theory. (Yeats takes notice of this, but he points out that his system was complete before he had read Spengler.) Civilizations run through cycles of two thousand-odd years, periods of growth, of maturity, and lastly, of decline; but instead of Spengler's metaphor of the seasons, spring-summer-autumn-winter, Yeats uses a symbolism drawn from the twenty-eight phases of the moon. For example, whereas Spengler speaks of the springtime of a culture, Yeats speaks of phases 1 to 8 (the first quarter of the moon). A civilization reaches its zenith at the full moon (phase 15) and then gradually declines, passing through phases 16 to 28 (the dark of the moon) again. Yeats further complicates his scheme by dividing his cycle into two subcycles of twenty-eight phases and of one thousand-odd years each. The phases 15 of these two subcycles which make up the two thousand years of Christian civilization are, for example, Byzantine civilization under Justinian and the Renaissance. Our own period is at phase 23 of the second subcycle; the moon is rapidly rounding toward the dark when the new civilization to dominate the next two thousand years will announce itself—"The Second Coming."

The full moon (phase 15) symbolizes pure subjectivity, the height of what Yeats calls the "antithetical" which predominates from phase 8 (the half moon of the first quarter) to the full moon and on to phase 22 (the half moon of the last quarter). The dark of the moon ("full sun") symbolizes pure objectivity, the height of what Yeats calls the "primary," which dominates from phase 22 to phase 8. The critical phases themselves, 8 and 22, since they represent equal mixtures of primary and antithetical, are periods of great stress and change. So much for the four cardinal phases. Each of the various twenty-eight phases, indeed, is assigned a special character in like manner.

An account of phase 23 will be sufficient illustration—all the more since this phase is the subject of several of Yeats's poems. Yeats regards phase 22 as always a period of abstraction. Synthesis is carried to its furthest lengths and there comes "synthesis for its own sake, organization where there is no masterful director, books where the author has disappeared, painting where some accomplished brush paints with an equal pleasure, or with a bored impartiality, the human form or an old bottle, dirty weather and clean sunshine" (*A Vision*). In the next phase, phase 23, which the present world has already entered upon (Yeats gives the year of transition as 1927) "in practical life one expects the same technical inspiration, the doing of this or that not because one would, or should, but because one can, consequent license, and with those 'out of phase' anarchic violence with no sanction in general principles."[2]

It is a vision of this period which Yeats gives us in what is perhaps the best known of his historical poems, "The Second Coming":

> *Turning and turning in the widening gyre*
> *The falcon cannot hear the falconer;*
> *Things fall apart; the center cannot hold;*
> *Mere anarchy is loosed upon the world . . .*

In "Meditations in Time of Civil War" Yeats gives another vision of the same period, one which employs again the sym-

[2]From the earlier edition. The account of history in the 1938 edition breaks off after the discussion of phase 22.

bol of the hawk but this time joined with the symbol of the darkening moon itself. In Section VII of this poem the poet has a vision of abstract rage, "The rage-driven . . . troop" crying out for vengeance for Jacques Molay, followed by a vision of perfect loveliness—ladies riding magical unicorns. But both visions fade out and

Give place to an indifferent multitude, give place
To brazen hawks. Nor self-delighting reverie,
Nor hate of what's to come, nor pity for what's gone,
Nothing but grip of claw, and the eye's complacency,
The innumerable clanging wings that have put out
the moon.

The moon is used as a symbol of the imagination in its purity, of the completely subjective intellect. It has this general meaning in many of Yeats's poems—for example, in the poem, "Blood and the Moon," where it is played off against blood (which is comparable to the sun, or the dark of the moon) as a symbol of active force—of the objective, or the primary.

An examination of the various meanings of blood in this poem will indicate how flexible and subtle the "meanings" attached to one of Yeats's concrete images can be. The symbol first occurs in the phrase, "A bloody, arrogant power." The tower on which the poet stands has been built by such a force and the symbolic meaning of the term is partially indicated by the characterization of the power as "bloody," shedding blood. But the meaning is extended and altered somewhat in the reference to Swift's heart: "in his blood-sodden breast" which "dragged him down into mankind" Blood here is associated with elemental sympathy, though the reference to Swift's particular quality of sympathy qualifies it properly—a sympathy grounded in one's elemental humanity which cannot be escaped and which—from the standpoint of the pure intellect—may be said to drag one down. The third reference to blood occurs in the phrase, "blood and state," and a third connection emerges—the connection of blood with nobility and tradition.

These references, it is important to notice, do not so much define the meaning of the symbol as indicate the limits within which the meaning (or manifold of meanings) is to be located. That meaning emerges fully only when we reach the last two sections of the poem where the symbols of blood and moon enter into active contrast: action contrasted with contemplation, power with wisdom, the youth of a civilization with its age.

The purity of the unclouded moon
Has flung its arrowy shaft upon the floor.
Seven centuries have passed and it is pure,
The blood of innocence has left no stain.
There, on blood-saturated ground, have stood
Soldier, assassin, executioner,
Whether for daily pittance or in blind fear
Or out of abstract hatred, and shed blood,
But could not cast a single jet thereon.
Odor of blood on the ancestral stair!
And we that have shed none must gather there
And clamour in drunken frenzy for the moon.

Upon the dusty, glittering windows cling,
And seem to cling upon the moonlit skies,
Tortoiseshell butterflies, peacock butterflies,
A couple of night-moths are on the wing.
Is every modern nation like the tower,
Half dead at the top? No matter what I said,
For wisdom is the property of the dead,
A something incompatible with life; and power,
Like everything that has the stain of blood,
A property of the living; but no stain
Can come upon the visage of the moon
When it has looked in glory from a cloud.

The development is very rich, and even though the poet in the last stanza has apparently reduced his meaning to abstract statement, the meaning is fuller than the statement taken as mere statement. We must read the lines in their full context to see how their meaning is made more complex, and, if one likes, more "precise" by the development of the symbols already made.

The tower itself, it is probably unnecessary to add, is the symbol of the poet's own old age and the old age of the civilization to which he belongs—

Is every modern nation like the tower,
Half dead at the top?

The poem itself is a very fine example of the unification of sensibility. As we have said, the poem refuses to be reduced to allegory—allegory which is perhaps the first attempt which man makes to unite the intellect and the emotions when they begin to fall apart—Spenser's *Faerie Queene,* for example. Moreover, the poet has repudiated that other refuge of a divided sensibility, moralization following on a piece of description—Tennyson's *Princess,* for instance. One can imagine how the poem would probably have been written by a Victorian: the old man standing upon the tower surveys from its vantage point the scene about him; then the poet, having disposed of the concrete detail, moralizes abstractly on the scene to the effect that wisdom and power are incompatibles. Instead, Yeats has confidence in his symbols; the concrete and the abstract, thought and feeling, coincide. The poet refuses to define the moralization except in terms of the specific symbols and the specific situation given.

A more special and concentrated example of Yeats's contemplation of the cyclic movement of history is revealed in his "Two Songs from a Play." These poems really represent his account of "the First Coming," the annunciation to Mary of the birth of Christ, the dynamic force which was to motivate the two thousand year cycle of Christian civilization. The first stanza of the second song will further illustrate the close dependence of Yeats's poetry on his system.

In pity for man's darkening thought
He walked that room and issued thence
In Galilean turbulence;
The Babylonian starlight brought
A fabulous, formless darkness in;
Odor of blood when Christ was slain
Made all Platonic tolerance vain
And vain all Doric discipline.

We have already commented on the fact that, according to Yeats's system, new civilizations are born at the dark of the moon—at the first phase. When the moon is dark, the stars alone are to be seen—hence the "Babylonian starlight" may be said to have brought the new force in. But the phrase is used not merely to indicate that the time is that of the first phase of a civilization. Babylon is associated by Yeats with the early study of the stars, and more than this, with a mathematical, historyless measurement of events. The Babylonian starlight, then, is not only eastern starlight but the starlight as associated with the objective and the "primary." (In his system Yeats indicates that he considers the West as dominantly antithetical, the East as dominantly primary; moreover, the two thousand years of Graeco-Roman civilization is dominantly antithetical; the cycle of Christian civilization, dominantly primary.) The phrase "fabulous, formless darkness," one finds (in *A Vision*) to come from a pagan philosopher of the fourth century who described Christianity as "a fabulous, formless darkness" that blotted out "every beautiful thing." The conception of the advent of Christianity on the rational, ordered classic world as a black cloud boiling up out of the ancient East is further developed in the last three lines of the stanza. "Blood," we have already seen, is another one of the primary symbols, and it is the odor of this blood which breaks up the order of classic thought and the classic discipline of action. The implied image, very powerful in its effect, is that of men made frantic and irrational by the smell of blood.

Examination of *A Vision* will also throw light on the first lines of the stanza. Yeats is describing man just before the advent of Christianity:

> Night will fall upon man's wisdom now that man has been taught that he is nothing. He had discovered, or half-discovered, that the world is round and one of many like it, but now he must believe that the sky is but a tent spread above a level floor, and . . . blot out the knowledge or half-knowledge that he has lived many times.
>
> The mind that brought the change [that of Christ], if considered as man only, is a climax of whatever Greek and Roman thought was most a contradiction to its age; but considered as more than man He controlled what Neo-Pythagorean and Stoic could not—irrational force. He could announce the new age, all that had not been thought of or touched or seen, because He could substitute for reason, miracle.
>
> We say of Him because His sacrifice was voluntary that He was love itself, and yet that part of him which made Christendom was not love but pity, and not pity for intellectual despair, though the man in Him, being *antithetical* like His age, knew it in the Garden, but *primary* pity, that for the common lot, man's death, seeing that He raised Lazarus, sickness, seeing that He healed many, sin, seeing that He died.

The celebrated poem, "Leda and the Swan," is of course related to the same general theme, for the annunciation to Leda is felt by the poet to have ushered in the cycle of classic civilization. Leda and her swan are thus felt to be parallel to Mary and her dove. The power with which Yeats handles the old myth resides in part in the fact that his own myth allows him to take the older one in terms of *myth*, reincorporating it into itself. "Leda and the Swan," far from being merely a pretty cameo, a stray *objet d'art* picked up from the ruins of the older civilization, has a vital relation to Yeats in his own civilization of the twentieth century. (One may observe in passing that the section on history in *A Vision* includes the finest rhythmic prose written in English since that of Sir Thomas Browne.)

Remembering Yeats's expressed desire for a system which would make all history an imaginative history, "and that the soul's," one is not surprised to find that Yeats employs the symbolism of the moon also to describe the various types of men. Men are classified on the basis of their mixtures of the subjective and objective. There are not twenty-eight possible types of men, however, but only twenty-six; for phase 1, complete objectivity, and phase 15, complete subjectivity are not mixtures. These phases are therefore supernatural or superhuman and may characterize an age though not an individual person. Several possible misapprehensions may be anticipated here: the phase of an age does not determine the phase of men living in that age. A man of phase 20, for example, like Shakespeare, may live in some other historical phase than 20—Yeats assigns him as a matter of fact to historical phase 16. Moreover, the determination of a man's personality in terms of his own phase is by no means absolute. He is also influenced by his environment. The historical phase thus qualifies the individual phase.

The faculties involved in Yeats's system of psychology are four rather than the Aristotelian three. In Yeats's system Man possesses Will; Mask (image of what he wishes to become or reverence); Creative Mind (all the mind which is consciously constructive); and Body of Fate (physical and mental environment). One need not enter here into the mode for determining the precise relations of the four faculties to each other in a given personality. One relationship among them, however, is of great importance. The four faculties are divided into two sets, and each member of the pair is opposite to the other. A man is classified under the phase to which his Will belongs. The Mask is always opposite to this phase. Thus, if we imagine the twenty-eight phases of the moon drawn in the form of a circle, a man whose Will is of phase 17, will have his Mask directly across the circle at phase 3; in the same way, a man with Will at phase 18, will have his Mask at phase 4. Creative Mind and Body of Fate are paired in opposition in like manner.

The interplay of tensions among the four faculties is very intricate, and this also cannot be treated here. The important thing to notice, one repeats, is this: that the psychology is founded on the conflict of opposites. The basic form of the whole system is the gyre, the one end of which widens concomitantly as the other narrows. Will and Mask are fixed in such a relation in one gyre; Creative Mind and Body of Fate, in another. "All things are from antithesis," Yeats observes, "all things dying each other's life, living each other's death." Will and Mask, desire and the thing desired, among the other elements of Yeats's system, bear such a relationship.

The relationship of Will and Mask especially illuminates Yeats's theory of the artist. Men of the antithetical or subjective phases (8 to 22) must strive in their work to realize the Mask which is the opposite of all that they are in actual life. The poem, "Ego Dominus Tuus," gives an exposition of this view. Keats, for example, a man of phase 14, is described as follows:

His art is happy, but who knows his mind?
I see a schoolboy when I think of him,
With face and nose pressed to a sweet-shop window,
For certainly he sank into his grave
His senses and his heart unsatisfied,
And made—being poor, ailing and ignorant,
Shut out from all the luxury of the world
The coarse-bred son of a livery-stable keeper—
Luxuriant song.

The case of Yeats himself, who apparently considers himself a man of phase 17, will also illustrate. He says of himself in his *Autobiographies* that he is "a gregarious man, going hither and thither looking for conversation, and ready to deny from fear or favor [his] dearest conviction." Frequently he chides himself for his interest in politics. Yet the Mask, the antiself of man of phase 17, hates "parties, crowds, propaganda" and delights in "the solitary life of hunters and of fishers and 'the groves pale passion loves.' " In his own great later poetry it is the "proud and lonely things" which he celebrates, and typically the fisherman:

I choose upstanding men
That climb the streams until
The fountain leap, and at dawn

Drop their cast at the side
Of dripping stone. . . .

So much for antithetical men, men whose Will is at phases dominantly antithetical; but primary men, on the other hand, men of phases 22 to 8, "must cease to desire *Mask* and Image by ceasing from self-expression, and substitute a motive of service for that of self-expression. Instead of the created *Mask* they have an imitative *Mask* . . ." This condition may be illustrated, for example, by Synge (whom Yeats assigns to phase 23), a man who needed to plunge into the objective world to find his true self; or to take another illustration, and one more extremely "primary," there is the saint (phase 27) who must renounce all desire. "His joy is to be nothing, to do nothing, to think nothing; but to permit the total life, expressed in its humanity, to flow in upon him and to express itself through his acts and thoughts."

If Yeats may appear to the reader to have fallen into a mechanical determinism quite as rigid as the scientific determinism which he tried to escape, and one which is fantastic to boot, one should notice that Yeats allows a considerable amount of free will. For each man of every phase, there is a False Mask as well as a True Mask—a course of action which is fatal for him to pursue as well as a course which he should pursue. Shelley, for example (like Yeats, a man of phase 17 and "partisan, propagandist, and gregarious"), too often sought his False Mask and wrote "pamphlets, and [dreamed] of converting the world." More will be said later about the effect of this psychology on Yeats's own development as a poet. For the present purpose it is easiest to pass on at this point to the relation of conscious to subconscious in Yeats's system.

In the first place, one may observe that Yeats accounts for the subconscious in his myth of the Daimon.

The *Four Faculties* are not the abstract categories of philosophy, being the result of the four memories of the *Daimon* or ultimate self of that man. His *Body of Fate,* the series of events forced upon him from without, is shaped out of the *Daimon's* memory of the events of his past incarnations; his *Mask* or object of desire or idea of good, out of its memory of the moments of exaltation in his past lives; his *Will* or normal ego out of its memory of all the events of his present life, whether consciously remembered or not; his *Creative Mind* from its memory of ideas—or universals—displayed by actual men in past lives, or their spirits between lives.

The man's Will is the Daimon's Mask; his Mask, the Daimon's Will; and so likewise with Creative Mind and Body of Fate. The mind of the man and his Daimon are thus related as the narrow and wide ends of a gyre are related. And Yeats had already told us in "Anima Mundi," that the Daimon "suffers with man as some firm-souled man suffers with the woman he but loves the better because she is extravagant and fickle." Moreover, "The Daemon, by using his mediatorial shades, brings man again and again to the place of choice, heightening temptation that the choice may be as final as possible . . . leading his victim to whatever among works not impossible is the most difficult." Man must not refuse the struggle. To do so is to fall under automatism and so be "out of phase." But the most powerful natures may occasionally need rest from the struggle and may fall into an automatism temporarily without becoming out of phase.

Yeats has apparently described such a rest in his own life in his fine but obscure poem, "Demon and Beast."

For certain minutes at the least
That crafty demon and that loud beast
That plague me day and night
Ran out of my sight;
Though I had long perned in the gyre,
Between my hatred and desire,
I saw my freedom won
And all laugh in the sun.

The sun symbolizes, here, the primary life of the men of early phases, instinctive acceptance of and delight in objective nature, in which Yeats as an antithetical man cannot normally participate. The portraits of the dead seem to smile at him and accept him, for their struggle is over, and now that he has ceased to struggle, he is of them. He feels an "aimless joy" seeing a gull and a "portly green-pated" duck on the lake.

Being no more demoniac
A stupid happy creature
Could rouse my whole nature.

But man not only is influenced by his Daimon; he may also be influenced by the dead, and partake in the *Anima Mundi,* the great collective memory of the world. Here one comes upon the third division of Yeats's system, that which deals with the life after death. To deal with Yeats's highly complicated account very summarily, one may say that Yeats holds that the soul after death goes through certain cycles in which it relives its earthly life, is freed from pleasure and pain, is freed from good and evil, and finally reaches a state of beatitude. Unless it has finished the cycle of its human rebirths, it then receives the Cup of Lethe, and, having forgotten all of its former life, is reborn in a human body.

The soul remains in existence, therefore, after the death of the body and under various conditions disembodied souls may communicate with the living—for example, in dreams—though on waking, the dreamer has substituted for the dream, some other image. The reader will remember that in *A Packet for Ezra Pound* Yeats claims, like Kusta Ben Luka in the poem, "The Gift of Harun Al-Rashid," to have received this system of thought itself from the spirits under the mediumship of his wife.

The relation of the artist to the souls of the dead is apparently a highly important one for Yeats, and two of Yeats's finest poems, the "Byzantium" poems, depend heavily upon a knowledge of this relationship.

Byzantium, as Mr. R. P. Blackmur has pointed out, is the heaven of man's mind. But more especially it is a symbol of the heaven of man's imagination, and preeminently of a particular kind of imagination, the nature of which Yeats suggests for us in the following passage from *A Vision.*

I think if I could be given a month of Antiquity and leave to spend it where I chose, I would spend it in Byzantium a little before Justinian opened St. Sophia and closed the Academy of Plato. I think I could find in some little wine-shop some philosophical worker in mosaic who could answer all my questions, the supernatural descending nearer to him than to Plotinus even . . .

I think that in early Byzantium, maybe never before or since in recorded history, religious, aesthetic and practical life were one, and that architect and artificers—though not, it may be, poets, for language had been the instrument of controversy and must have grown abstract—spoke to the multitude and the few alike . . .

[In Byzantium of this period] . . . all about . . . is an incredible splendor like that which we see pass under our closed eyelids as we lie between sleeping and waking, no representation of a living world but the dream of a somnambulist. Even the drilled pupil of the eye, when the drill is in the hand of some Byzantine worker in ivory, undergoes a somnambulistic change, for its deep shadow among the faint lines of the tablet, its mechanical circle, where all else is rhythmical and flowing, give to Saint or Angel a look of some great bird staring at miracle.

So much for the symbol of Byzantium itself. The poem "Sailing to Byzantium," as the less difficult of the two, may properly be considered first.

That is no country for old men. The young
In one another's arms, birds in the trees,
—Those dying generations—at their song,
The salmon-falls, the mackerel-crowded seas,
Fish, flesh, or fowl, commend all summer long
Whatever is begotten, born, and dies.
Caught in that sensual music all neglect
Monuments of unageing intellect.

An aged man is but a paltry thing,
A tattered coat upon a stick, unless
Soul clap its hands and sing, and louder sing
For every tatter in its mortal dress,
Nor is there singing school but studying
Monuments of its own magnificence;
And therefore I have sailed the seas and come
To the holy city of Byzantium.

The poet appeals to the

. . . sages standing in God's holy fire
As in the gold mosaic of a wall,

asking them to

Come from the holy fire, perne in a gyre,
And be the singing masters of my soul.

A quotation from "Anima Mundi" is illuminating at this point: "There are two realities, the terrestrial and the condition of fire. All power is from the terrestrial condition, for there all opposites meet and there only is the extreme of choice possible, full freedom. And there the heterogeneous is, and evil, for evil is the strain one upon another of opposites; but in the condition of fire is all music and all rest . . ." The dead whose souls have gone through all the sequences, and whose sequences have come to an end are in the condition of fire: ". . . the soul puts on the rhythmic or spiritual body or luminous body and contemplates all the events of its memory and every possible impulse in an eternal possession of itself in one single moment."

There is a close connection between the dead living in their passionate memories, and Yeats's theory of *Anima Mundi* or the Great Memory. In an earlier essay he tells us: "Before the mind's eye, whether in sleep or waking, came images that one was to discover presently in some book one had never read, and after looking in vain for explanation in the current theory of forgotten personal memory, I came to believe in a great memory passing on from generation to generation." From this great memory come two influences: first, "that inflowing coming alike to men and to animals is called natural." It is this, for example, that teaches a bird to build her nest or which shapes the child to the womb. But the second inflowing "which is not natural but intellectual . . . is from the fire . . ." It is this inflow which the poet wishes to come to him and to transform him, shaping him to a "bodily form" which is not taken

from any natural thing
But such a form as Grecian goldsmiths make
Of hammered gold and gold enameling . . .

And if we inquire why the symbol of this "unnatural" form is denoted by that of a bird, though a bird of metal, we may find the reason in reading further in "Anima Mundi":

From tradition and perception, one thought of one's own life as symbolized by earth, the place of heterogeneous things [compare "the terrestrial condition" *supra*], the images as mirrored in water and the images themselves one could divine but as air; and beyond it all there was, I felt confident, certain aims and governing loves, the fire that makes all simple. Yet the images themselves were fourfold, and one judged their meaning in part from the predominance of one out of the four elements, or that of the fifth element, the veil hiding another four, a bird born out of the fire.

The poem can be taken on a number of levels: as the transition from sensual art to intellectual art; as the poet's new and brilliant insight into the nature of the Byzantine imagination; as the poet's coming to terms with age and death. The foregoing account of the development of the symbols in the poet's personal experience will not in itself explain the fineness of the poem, or even indicate its aesthetic structure: it will not indicate, for example, the quality of self-irony in his characterization of himself as a "monument of unageing intellect" or as a "tattered coat upon a stick" or the play of wit achieved in such a phrase as "the artifice of eternity." And the account given will, for that matter, do no more than indicate the series of contrasts and paradoxes on which the poem is founded—it will not assess their function in giving the poem its power. But it may indicate in part the source of the authority which dictates the tone of the poem. The real importance of the symbolic system is that it allows the poet a tremendous richness and coherency.

"Sailing to Byzantium," as we have seen, derives its direction from the poet's own sense of loss and decay. The focus of the poem rests in the reader's sense that the poet is in Ireland, *not* Byzantium. The appeal to the sages of Byzantium is made in terms of the man whose soul is "fastened to a dying animal." "Byzantium," on the other hand, a more difficult poem, concerns itself directly with the "condition of fire" and the relation of the living to the living dead. It will furnish therefore perhaps the best illustration of the extent to which Yeats can successfully rely upon his system, for the poem is an undoubted success and yet its relation to the system is detailed and intricate.

BYZANTIUM

The unpurged images of day recede;
The Emperor's drunken soldiery are abed;
Night resonance recedes, night-walkers' song
After great cathedral gong;
A starlit or a moonlit dome disdains
All that man is,
All mere complexities,
The fury and the mire of human veins.

Before me floats an image, man or shade,
Shade more than man, more image than a shade;
For Hades' bobbin bound in mummy-cloth
May unwind the winding path;
A mouth that has no moisture and no breath
Breathless mouths may summon;
I hail the superhuman;
I call it death-in-life and life-in-death.

Miracle, bird or golden handiwork,
More miracle than bird or handiwork,
Planted on the star-lit golden bough,
Can like the cocks of Hades crow,
Or, by the moon embittered, scorn aloud
In glory of changeless metal

Common bird or petal
And all complexities of mire or blood.

At midnight on the Emperor's pavement flit
Flames that no faggot feeds, nor steel has lit,
Nor storm disturbs, flames begotten of flame,
Where blood-begotten spirits come
And all complexities of fury leave,
Dying into a dance,
An agony of trance,
An agony of flame that cannot singe a sleeve.

Astraddle on the dolphin's mire and blood,
Spirit after spirit! The smithies break the flood,
The golden smithies of the Emperor!
Marbles of the dancing floor
Break bitter furies of complexity,
Those images that yet
Fresh images beget,
That dolphin-torn, that gong-tormented sea.

Consider, for example, the lines

A starlit or a moonlit dome disdains
All that man is,
All mere complexities,
The fury and the mire of human veins.

A starlit dome, in contradistinction to a moonlit dome, is one at the dark of the moon (phase 1), and the implication of "moonlit dome" is one lighted by the full moon (phase 15).

Now, as we have already seen at phase 1, complete objectivity, and phase 15, complete subjectivity, human life cannot exist; for all human life represents a mixture of the subjective and the objective, "complexities," "mere complexities" as compared with the superhuman purity of phase 1 or 15. The dependence on the system may also seem excessive. And yet, even in this instance, one may show that the use is not merely arbitrary. The poem describes an appeal to the superhuman, to the deathless images of the imagination; and the starlit or moonlit dome, freed of the "unpurged images of day," and silent with the "Emperor drunken soldiery" abed, may seem a place unhuman and supernatural, and a place in which one might fittingly invoke the superhuman. Yeats's symbols, though they are interwoven into complex organizations, never give way to a merely allegorical construct; the proof that they do not lies in the fact that on their literal level they tend to take the reader in the direction of the system, as in the present case.

The second stanza will be much clarified by a consideration of a number of passages in Yeats's prose. For example, consider with regard to the first lines of the stanza—

Before me floats an image, man or shade,
Shade more than man, more image than a shade;
For Hades' bobbin bound in mummy-cloth
May unwind the winding path . . .

—the following passage from "Hodos Chameliontos" (Yeats is pondering in this passage on the possibility of a great memory of the world): "Is there nationwide multiform reverie, every mind passing through a stream of suggestion, and all streams acting and reacting upon one another no matter how distant the minds, how dumb the lips? A man walked, as it were, casting a shadow, and yet one could never say which was man and which was shadow, or how many the shadows that he cast." The general idea we have already quoted above: "Before the mind's eye whether in sleep or waking, came images that one was to discover presently in some book one had never read. . . ." The image here, "man or shade," is such an image, and a part of the great memory. "Hades' bobbin bound in mummy-cloth" occurs in the earlier poem, "All Souls' Night," where Yeats again summons the dead:

I need some mind that, if the cannon sound
From every quarter of the world, can stay
Wound in mind's pondering
As mummies in the mummy-cloth are wound.

All activity for Yeats, as we have seen, partakes of the whirling motion of the gyre, and the thread wound about the spool is continually used by Yeats as a symbol for experience wound up. Each age unwinds what the previous age has wound, and the life after death unwinds the thread wound on the spool by life. The "winding path" which "Hades' bobbin" may unwind is mentioned in "Anima Mundi." It is the "path of the Serpent" or the "winding movement of nature" as contrasted with the straight path open to the saint or sage. Once more, then, the natural and the human are contrasted with the supernatural and the superhuman. "Death-in-life and life-in-death" are of course the dead themselves, who are for Yeats more alive than the living: "It is even possible that being is only possessed completely by the dead. . . ."

The symbol of the bird in the third stanza, we have already come upon in "Sailing to Byzantium," and also in two passages quoted here from Yeats's prose—that in which he describes Byzantine art and that in which he uses the bird "born out of the fire" to symbolize the fifth element—the supernatural—the veil hiding another four. The allusion to the "cocks of Hades" is to be compared with the reference to the cockerel in the earlier poem, "Solomon and the Witch":

A cockerel
Crew from a blossoming apple bough
Three hundred years before the Fall,
And never crew again till now,
And would not now but that he thought,
Chance being at one with Choice at last,
All that the brigand apple brought
And this foul world were dead at last.

Chance is that which is Fated; Choice, that which is destined or chosen; and they coincide at phases 1 and 15, for at these phases Mask and Body of Fate are superimposed upon each other. "At Phase 15 mind [is] completely absorbed by Being" —at phase 1 "body is completely absorbed in its supernatural environment." The cockerel in the earlier poem "crowed out eternity [and]/Thought to have crowed it in again." The "miracle, bird or golden handiwork" may thus fittingly crow in "the artifice of eternity."

But we shall not understand the third stanza nor the fourth fully unless we understand something of Yeats's theory of spirits. For example the phrase "blood-begotten spirits" is explicable if we consider the following passage from "Anima Mundi": "All souls have a vehicle or body. . . . The vehicle of the human soul is what used to be called the animal spirits," and Yeats quotes from Hippocrates, "The mind of man . . . is not nourished from meats and drink from the belly, but by a clear luminous substance that redounds by separation from the blood." These vehicles can be molded to any shape by an act of the imagination. Moreover, "our animal spirits or vehicles are but as it were a condensation of the vehicle of *Anima Mundi,* and give substance to its images in the faint materialization of our common thought, or more grossly when a ghost is our visitor."

The description of the spirits as flames accords with the fact that they are in the condition of fire, but the additional phrase, "flames begotten of flame," requires reference to Yeats's statement that "The spirits do not get from it [the vehicle] the material from which their forms are made, but their forms take light from it as one candle takes light from another." Indeed, Yeats tells us in the earlier version of *A Vision* that spirits can actually be born of spirits. Being called "Arcons" are born from spirits which are at phases 15 and 1. Those born from spirits at phase 15 are antithetical arcons. The spirit at phase 15, desiring to rid itself of all traces of the primary, accomplishes this by "imposing upon a man or woman's mind an *antithetical* image . . ." This image may be expressed as an action or as a work of art. The expression of it "is a harmonization which frees the Spirit from terror and the man from desire . . ." So much from *A Vision*. In an essay published still earlier, Yeats says that Shelley "must have expected to receive thoughts and images from beyond his own mind, must in so far as that mind transcended its preoccupation with particular time and place, for he believed *inspiration a kind of death* [italics mine]; and he could hardly have helped perceiving that an image that has transcended particular time and place becomes a symbol, passes beyond death, as it were, and becomes a living soul." The passage from *A Vision* quoted above gives merely a schematization of this earlier thought: an explanation of what the dead man gives and what the living man receives, and the reason for the giving. One notices, however, that whereas Yeats gives in the poem a most complex theory of the relation of the Dead to the Great Memory and of their relation to the living, the symbols form more than an exposition of the esoteric: they dramatize the emotional relationships. The spirits must be originally blood-begotten but the blood gives place to flame; the mere complexities give way to purity; the fire "makes all simple." Yet power is of the blood and the flames which "no faggot feeds" are powerless and cannot "singe a sleeve." The balance is maintained.

As for the dance of the spirits, another passage from "Anima Mundi" is relevant:

> Then gradually they [the dead] perceive, although they are still but living in their memories, harmonies, symbols, and patterns, as though all were being refashioned by an artist, and they are moved by emotions, sweet for no imagined good but in themselves, like those of

children dancing in a ring . . . Hitherto shade has communicated with shade in moments of common memory that recur like the figures of a dance in terror or in joy, but now they run together like to like, and their Covens and Fleets have rhythm and pattern.

The fifth stanza is a recapitulation, but a recapitulation with the addition of a new and important image for the Great Memory, an image which Yeats has earlier used for it in his prose: the image of the sea. In "Anima Mundi," after speaking of the Great Memory, Yeats has written:

The thought was again and again before me that this study has created a contact or mingling with minds who had followed a like study in some other age, and that these minds still saw and thought and chose. Our daily thought was certainly but the line of foam at the shallow edge of a vast luminous sea; Henry More's *Anima Mundi*, Wordsworth's "immortal sea which brought us hither. . . ."

Again, in an essay on "The Tragic Theatre," Yeats has used the figure: "Tragic art, passionate art, the drowner of dykes, the confounder of understanding, moves us by setting us to reverie, by alluring us almost to the intensity of trance. . . . We feel our minds expand convulsively or spread out slowly like some moon-brightened image-crowded sea." The phrase, "gong-tormented," emphasizes the connection of the images of *Anima Mundi* with drama:

All men are dancers and their tread
Goes to the barbarous clangour of a gong.
("Nineteen Hundred and Nineteen")

The image of the Great Memory as a sea is introduced by the reference to Arion and the dolphin. The poet can travel in that sea, but only supported on the dolphin's mire and blood. The "golden smithies of the Emperor" are of course those referred to in "Sailing to Byzantium":

Once out of nature I shall never take
My bodily form from any natural thing,
But such a form as Grecian goldsmiths make
Of hammered gold and gold enameling . . .

These artists—the Byzantine "painter, the worker in mosaic, the worker in gold and silver"—are those to whom, because of their craftsmanship, the "supernatural descended nearer . . . than to Plotinus even."

One can allow that much of the poem would be intelligible to a person entirely unacquainted with Yeats's system. But this rather detailed comparison of the poem with the passages from Yeats's prose given above is perhaps justified in showing how rich and intricate the poem becomes when a knowledge of the system is brought to bear on the poem. "Byzantium" is admittedly a somewhat special case, but many of Yeats's other poems—especially those written around 1917—are hardly less dependent on the system.

Most important of all, however, is no notice that from the poet's standpoint the richness and *precision* of such a poem as "Byzantium" is only made possible by the poet's possession of such a system. The system, in these terms, is an instrument for, as well as a symbol of, the poet's reintegration of his personality. It is the instrument through which Yeats has accomplished the unification of his sensibility.

A brief summary of the general function of Yeats's system may be in order here. We have already spoken of the advantages which the poet gains by using concrete symbols rather than abstract concepts and of traditional symbols which make available to him the great symbolism out of the past. The system, to put it concisely, allows Yeats to see the world as a great drama, predictable in its larger aspects (so that the poet is not lost in a welter of confusion), but in a pattern which allows for the complexity of experience and the apparent contradictions of experience (so that the poet is not tempted to over-simplify). The last point is highly important and bears directly on the dramatic aspect of the system, for the system demands, as it were, a continually repeated victory over the contradictory whereby the contradictory is recognized, and through the recognition, resolved into agreement. Yeats's finest poems not only state this thesis but embody such a structure, and his increasing boldness in the use of the contradictory and the discordant in his own poetry springs directly from his preoccupation with antithesis.

It is easy to see, at least from our vantage point of the present, the effect of this emphasis in making possible Yeats's break with Victorianism. The prime defect of Victorian poetry was that it subordinated the imaginative act of assimilating the incongruous to the logical act of matching the congruent. Yeats, in trying to write from his antiself, in trying to be all that he naturally was not—whatever we may think of his Doctrine of the Mask—broke away from Victorian optimism, decorum, and sentimentality, and disciplines his dramatic powers.

One may cite text and verse in corroboration. For example, in a highly illuminating passage in "Anima Hominis," Yeats has written:

> The other self, the anti-self or the antithetical self . . . comes but to those who are no longer deceived, whose passion is reality. The sentimentalists are practical men who believe in money, in position, in a marriage bell, and whose understanding of happiness is to be so busy whether at work or play, that all is forgotten but the momentary aim.

The antiself, then, is incompatible with sentimentality. And in "Hodos Chameliontos" Yeats writes of two such men who sought reality, Dante and Villon, saying of them that "had they lacked their Vision of Evil, had they cherished any species of optimism, they could but have found a false beauty. . . . They and their sort alone earn contemplation, for it is only when the intellect has wrought the whole of life to drama, to crisis, that we live for contemplation, and yet keep our intensity." "Their sort" of poets is that to which Yeats himself must be certainly assigned. And his insistence on the dramatic element is fundamental. In "Anima Hominis" he says:

> If we cannot imagine ourselves as different from what we are, and try to assume that second self, we cannot impose a discipline upon ourselves though we may accept one from others. Active virtue, as distinguished from the passive acceptance of a code, is therefore theatrical, consciously dramatic, the wearing of a mask . . . Wordsworth, great poet though he be, is so often flat and heavy partly because his moral sense, being a discipline he had not created, a mere obedience, has no theatrical element.

So much for the general nature of Yeats's myth and for its relation to his own great poetry; and now, one further reference to the vexing question of Yeats's "belief" in his system. "The saner and greater mythologies," as Richards says, "are not fancies; they are the utterance of the whole soul of man and, as such, inexhaustible to meditation." The statement can be claimed for Yeats's myth. We have already uttered a warning against the use of the misleading term "magic" for Yeats's system. Magical in the sense that it proposes to use unscientific means to accomplish ends better accomplished by scientific means the system is not. Properly speaking it is a world-view or a philosophy—an "utterance of the whole soul of man" having for its object imaginative contemplation.

Yeats, as we have seen, apparently has no objection himself to referring to his system as a myth, but we are to remember that in calling it this, he is not admitting that it is trivial, or merely fanciful, or "untrue." And this is doubtless why Yeats, in answering the question of whether or not he believes in his system, can only reply with a counterquestion as to whether the word "belief," as the questioner will use it, belongs to our age. For the myth is not scientifically true, and yet though a fiction, though a symbolical representation, intermeshes with reality. It is imaginatively true, and if most people will take this to mean that it is after all trivial, this merely shows in what respect our age holds the imagination.

J. C. Ransom

BEFORE I BECOME involved in some local studies in the poetry of Yeats, and some theory which it suggests, I had better record my general tribute to the poet. I concur as instantly as any other critic in the judgment that he had by nature the finest poetic gift in our time, and by technical discipline one of the subtlest and surest instruments in the history of English poetry. This is to see the poet at his best, but the condition is frequent in his later work. He was a great poet—if there are readers who cannot bear to have the ultimate adjective withheld.

He might have failed on the whole, as he did in many poems, if he had not been driven by a powerful sense of vocation. And, particularly, he might have become a sort of Villiers de L'Isle-Adam, or Rimbaud. He was a symbolic poet and might have become a Symbolist one—though there has never quite been one in English poetry, and Blake, who may be thought to have come near to it, was different in an obvious way, while Mr. Eliot is different in another way.

I do not mean disrespect to religion, but quite the contrary, if I schematize the religious impulse in its bold aesthetic phase as being simply the best instance of the poetic impulse. Since I have said that Yeats wrote great poetry, I need not surrender the adjective before remarking that the great style as we have had it in English is the style that works upon the great theme, and this theme is the metaphysical. I had almost called it the supernatural; but that term has become trite and inhibiting to perception. I mean the world which is over or under the natural world, but sustaining and explaining it, not violating it; the world shared by poetry and religion. Yeats was born into a barren or unreligious age, and lived to see it become a naturalistic or irreligious one. That was the background against which he had to exercise his gift of poetry which, like that of Shakespeare and Donne and Milton, was a gift for splendid metaphysical imagery. His importance for us now is that over the facile excitements of swarms of naturalistic poets—the tame villatic fowl we had come to—he has saved our poetic tradition in its dignity.

So far as I know, Mr. Edmund Wilson was the first to offer

"Yeats and His Symbols," reprinted from *The Kenyon Review*, I, 3 (summer, 1939), pp. 309-322, copyright, 1939, by Kenyon College.

significant comments on Yeats, though I think they were inadequate, and Mr. Blackmur later has treated Yeats with the best general sense of his achievement. Criticism of Yeats in the light of the whole of his testament, now that it is finished, would be ideally done if Mr. Wilson and Mr. Blackmur could do it in collaboration. Mr. Wilson would be continually objecting to the vulnerable poems on the ground that intellectual authority did not attach to their metaphysical symbols, and that in using them Yeats was too much like an irresponsible French Symbolist. Mr. Blackmur's service would be to insist that at any rate the symbols were grasped and held to with fierce sincerity; and he would also be able to argue that at many times the symbols were entirely suitable and defensible. Mr. Wilson's part would be negative but important, since in an age of naturalism the poet is properly subjected to the rule of reason. Mr. Blackmur, granting everything that deserved to be granted, would not be deterred from his perception of a magnificence that could not ultimately be diverted, and finally of poems that were objectively and simply magnificent.

Fifteen or eighteen years ago I was saying, and everybody was saying, for it was easy to say: There can be no more poetry on the order of its famous triumphs until we come again upon a time when an elaborate Myth will be accepted universally, so that the poet may work within a religious frame which is conventional, and therefore objective. The saying declared our own difficulties though it echoed Matthew Arnold. Yeats has disproved it. We have no common religion but we have not stopped being religious. There is no one religion but none of the old religions has quite died, for we still respond to its symbols. Yeats did not found a religion though it appears from his prose that he tinkered with a system for private use. In his public poetry he was a tireless religious eclectic and improviser of religious imagery, and this strategy, which was perhaps the only possible strategy, succeeded. There must have been a few ages in which unofficial poetry has kept religion alive if not flourishing during the weakness or the collapse of the establishments. After all, Yeats's accomplishment in this respect is of the same kind as Shakespeare's, though it is far less diffuse and more coherent.

The religious system that was most available was the one he scarcely used. Roman Catholicism, flourishing outwardly at least, was all round him in his Ireland. But, for one thing, it was not congenial with his ethical feelings; and what must have been more forbidding, and is more significant with respect to the difficulties of poets generally, its imagery had gone rather stale. So many generations of poets had explored its handsome framework that now the late poets found themselves anticipated; it was too hard to obtain fresh perceptions within it. I suppose this stage may come for any religion, with its exclusive range of images.

I will try a simple argument without properly citing the supporting evidences; I know I shall be over-simplifying it. While he public religion is crystallizing, and just afterwards, the poets are probably glad to serve it by elaborating the images of ts persons and events. The sacred story is told over and over, and always, as long as real poets are telling it, with fresh invention. This would be a very direct kind of religious poetry; and here we have *Paradise Lost*, which in design is not subtle at all. Milton, always the virtuoso, saw fit to work within the vast but simple range of the ingenuous Du Bartas, not that of the advanced religious lyric poets then current in his England, and to hark back to the first principles of religious poetry; to the direct attack. This means merely, I suppose, that he was intending a heroic poem. But eventually, and all the sooner after a Milton, this sort of thing will have gone as far as the poets can take it, and then they will abandon it.

The next stage in the religion, still speaking of its use for poets, would be the stage of poetic symbols. The poetry here is strategically and structurally more interesting. The poets come down to earth, and they import into their secular or human recitals the powerful symbols which refer to the metaphysical features of the public religion. The symbols keep the natural and the supernatural systems in relation. It is in this stage of more personal religious poetry that we find most of the 17th Century religious poets. But we should recall to ourselves just what sort of poetic device is the symbol, and why it is potent. It is a compendium of imagery, not content with the immediate image evoked by the word, but starting the imagination back upon the realization of the image in its special religious history; and it does not work, it lapses from being a poetic device into being an ordinary tag of identification, if it does not really evoke the image that originated it; it fails all the more if it does not have an image to evoke.

A proper symbol would refer to the authoritative context of public religion. With the French Symbolists began, I suppose, the habit of faking the symbol; the word would look as if it ought to have had a brilliant history within some system of metaphysical images, but one was embarrassed to know just what it could have been. I remember my disgust of years ago with some of Maeterlinck's writing (he must have represented a softer side of the school) where the mere repetition of the word, otherwise a senseless proceeding, invited the reader to import a symbolic meaning into it, when no symbolic meaning came to mind. No amount of repetition will substitute for a history in creating a symbol; and that is just the trouble I find with Miss Gertrude Stein's heavily weighted nonsense prose. We think something must be signified by the little phrases which bear such an emphasis of repetition; but we conclude after a certain time that the thing is an amiable imposture, and nothing special is being signified. The symbol needs its public genealogy.

I do not mean to slander the dead Symbolists whose example accounts for so much that has been brilliant in English poetry since. Tentatively I venture that they felt the force of both of the twin considerations: first, that delicate minds will always relish something better than the stock religious images that serve the obtuse and vulgar, and will have to set up a kind of unformalized religion of their own; second, that in the late days of a religion the stock images are not really images but bare terms of reference. At any rate our impression of Symbolist effects is of symbols uncertain enough to have been taken as either religious or secular, according to the author's convenience. The imagery cannot be objectified. It is arbitrary if it works at all, and by the standards of public discourse it is obscure. The obscurity to which we find ourselves attributing this kind of history is probably the bigger and nobler portion of all that famous obscurity of the moderns. It may be deplorable but it is essential to the pseudo-religious effect, for if unequivocal terms are substituted the depth of this poetry, with the possibility of religious feeling, is drained away.

It must at any rate be said that powerful symbols, like lovely airs, are not immune to wear. With increased familiarity comes the instant "identification" of the thing symbolized, on the part of the economical intellect, and no evocation of imagery. For poetry the religion has lost its standing. (We need not conclude that religion at this stage has finished its highly compounded program.) There has not been for a long time in English a systematic poetry using Christian symbols on a large scale. That was the condition under which Yeats as a poet renounced Christianity.

The best exception I find is the poem, "A Prayer for My Son." If the son is a small child, no religion will answer to the occasion like Christianity, and Yeats's recourse to it is spontaneous. He begins:

Bid a strong ghost stand at the head
That my Michael may sleep sound,
Nor cry, nor turn in the bed
Till his morning meal come round.

By a strong ghost he means one with "sword in fist," for the father's premonition is that actual murder seeks out his son, who is destined to great deeds. Therefore he addresses his prayer to Christ, who has known precisely that situation:

Though You can fashion everything
From nothing every day, and teach
The morning stars to sing,
You have lacked articulate speech
To tell your simplest want, and known,
Wailing upon a woman's knee,
All of that worst ignominy
Of flesh and bone.

And now the account of Yeats will be worse than negative; I have to advert to a creative effort long sustained and all but wasted. He tried with all his might to establish his poetry within the frame of the Ossianic or Irish mythology. It occupied many of his early years, and produced nothing, I believe, that is worthy of his ultimate stature as a poet. But that is a hazard of vocation; at any rate it painfully educates the poet both in technique and in strategy.

The ethical paganism of this religion suited Yeats as a preference over Christian mortification of the flesh; yet it did not have for him the solid structure of an eligible religion. The rehearsal of the legends is of something remote and romantic. Actually Yeats and his friends with all their persuasion did not restore to modern Ireland her Gaelic myth; perhaps because Ireland had been too fully subjugated to the sterner and more intellectual European tradition. Its tense remains the past. It does not yield a present, for symbols do not come out of it to apply to the situations of life. We can see why Yeats, when he has kept these old-Irish poems in his successive editions, has accompanied them with an apology for his youth.

The remainder of the symbolic poetry, so far as the origin of the symbols is concerned, might be lumped together as eclectic. Its religious ancestry goes back to nearly every source with which European tradition is familiar.

It may derive from Greek religion, whether the public one or that of the secret cults; for Yeats was a studious man, and always conceived the way of philosophy to be the way of religion. More commonly it derives from the contemporary occult schools; Rosicrucian, Cabalistic, Hermetic, or all together. The occultists are themselves eclectics, with a hospitality to symbols so promiscuous that they are always forgetting the boundaries of intellectual responsibility. The other modern poet who has Yeats's range of symbols is Mr. Eliot. But there is a great difference in their strategies. Mr. Eliot attaches the occult symbols like captives to his Christian chariot, and it gives a fresh and interesting status to his Christianity. (Changing the figure, it is as if he were the doctor infusing strange blood into a decadent organism, and reviving it for another while. The figure is precisely as reasonable as his poetic strategy). The important achievement for Mr. Eliot lies of course in his really recovering to the Christian symbols some of their original energy as images. Yeats is both more and less orthodox than Mr. Eliot; more orthodox in his intellectual technique, working with one set of symbols at a time; less, in that he does not at all feel bound to take the Christian symbols as his base.

Yeats never—rarely if we look through the whole body of the collected poems, never if we look at that segment of them which seems destined to stand—requires much editorial gloss to explain a symbol because it is the property of an occult sodality or because it is private to himself alone. (In this again he contrasts with Mr. Eliot.) The symbol is objective and easy, or else it is actually developed a little way so that the "impartial spectator" who reads (and who stands in our mind for the test of the poem's objectivity) can go on and obtain a sufficiently clear and exciting image to answer to it. There is an interesting point of biography here which it would be a service in some historian to clear up. Much of the prose of Yeats is far more difficult than any of the verse, being crowded with obscure and unaided symbols. It is as if his scruple in the poetry were his sense of a professional responsibility, while his prose is for his own consumption. Florid Neo-Platonism, theosophy, even a little astrology, for his privacy, but in his poetry only symbols fit for the public currency.

But it is certain that there is a religiousness which is not based on instruction in systematic religion, and that poets will have at least that sort of religiousness if they are not enervated (as by a naturalistic climate), and that Yeats has many poems which come out of this religiousness; these too may be considered under the general head of eclectic. For what it technically called "natural religion" might better be called "poetic religion." Natural religion also consists in having metaphysical images, and carrying them to the natural world. The images are spontaneous and genuine, but they must be valid almost at first sight if they are to carry persuasion. They cannot expect to be entertained as the result of a discipline that has already instructed the public in them as in the images of a dogmatic system; nor can one of them singly imply a whole historical system of images that is intellectually coherent. They are inferior in force to the properly symbolic images; and I mean such pretty improvisations as

But look, the morn, in russet mantle clad,
Walks o'er the dew of yon high eastward hill.

Yeats's unofficial religious images are more significant than this, just as Donne's are, and the reason is the same for both poets: they are educated in the official images, so that they have a superior skill in improvising. I owe this point principally to Mr. Blackmur. He argues to the effect that religious discipline is the making of a fine poet even if he is to throw away every specific image in whose use he has been instructed. It is such a good argument that it deserves to be repeated. It might be extended to cover this principle: that in an age of naturalism the aesthetic hunger obtains many satisfactions, though they may be furtive ones, from images that still echo the old official systems which the revolution has run out of business, and so the age is still living on the remaining works of a capital which it has stopped from further productive employment.

And now I must illustrate the eclectic symbolism from the text.

A famous and startling poem is of course "The Second Coming":

Turning and turning in the widening gyre
The falcon cannot hear the falconer;
Things fall apart; the centre cannot hold;
Mere anarchy is loosed upon the world,
The blood-dimmed tide is loosed, and everywhere
The ceremony of innocence is drowned;

The best lack all conviction, while the worst
Are full of passionate intensity.

Surely some revelation is at hand;
Surely the Second Coming is at hand.
The Second Coming! Hardly are those words out
When a vast image out of Spiritus Mundi
Troubles my sight: somewhere in sands of the desert
A shape with lion body and the head of a man,
A gaze blank and pitiless as the sun,
Is moving its slow thighs, while all about it
Reel shadows of the indignant desert birds.
The darkness drops again; but now I know
That twenty centuries of stony sleep
Were vexed to nightmare by a rocking cradle,
And what rough beast, its hour come round at last,
Slouches towards Bethlehem to be born?

The first part of the poem would consist with any sort of religiosity. It is not a naturalistic passage, to any public experienced in reading poetry; for either the falcon and falconer are symbolic, or else they are a boldly new and cosmic image; and there are the images of the centripetal force of the world turning to centrifugal, of anarchy being loosed upon it (by evil forces or by destiny), and of the blood-dimmed tide which may have an occult meaning or may be a metaphysical image of war. The last two lines sound most naturalistic, and they might be distinguished elsewhere, but here they are the climax and we have to dwell upon them, because it is a metaphysical context which advances to their summary truth; and the more we dwell upon them, the more adequate they become.

The second part sounds Christian in the beginning, but develops an image whose source is not Scripture but Spiritus Mundi, and which concerns something like an Egyptian Sphinx, and the passing of Christ in his favor. The language is worthy of the matter. The matter is valid enough if it is reasonable to say: Twenty centuries have passed, and the ideal they professed has come to perfect ineptitude and impotence; a new millennium will dawn, and we cannot tell what ideal it will obey; very likely, a monstrous ideal of abstract animal power. Even in this substitute form it is not a pure intellectual speculation, but is fringed with metaphysical imagery; and in the poem itself the obvious content is that imagery in distinctness.

Upon an even more famous poem, "Sailing to Byzantium," : have read Mr. Blackmur and Mr. Cleanth Brooks. But I hink the high powered exegesis of the symbols which is ›ossible for the scholar is not really needed for a very deep lay atisfaction in the poem. I omit the first stanza for the sake of space:

An aged man is but a paltry thing,
A tattered coat upon a stick, unless
Soul clap its hand and sing, and louder sing
For every tatter in its mortal dress,
Nor is there singing school but studying
Monuments of its own magnificence;
And therefore I have sailed the seas and come
To the holy city of Byzantium.

O sages standing in God's holy fire
As in the gold mosaic of a wall,
Come from the holy fire, perne in a gyre,
And be the singing-masters of my soul.
Consume my heart away; sick with desire
And fastened to a dying animal
It knows not what it is; and gather me
Into the artifice of eternity.

Once out of nature I shall never take
My bodily form from any natural thing,
But such a form as Grecian goldsmiths make
Of hammered gold and gold enamelling
To keep a drowsy Emperor awake;
Or set upon a golden bough to sing
To lords and ladies of Byzantium
Of what is past, or passing, or to come.

In this poem the old poet, electing the body for his next ıcarnation, chooses to inhabit an artificial Byzantine bird ıat will sing; then he will not have to feel his living body ecay as he does now, and have to pray to be delivered f it. The prayer is addressed to holy sages who dwell I › not know where; it does not seem to matter where, for ıey appear qualified to receive the prayer, and it is a correct and elevated prayer. The poem offers a certain version f Pythagorean philosophy, but that is not too steep for me, ıd the version is a human and charming one.

In these two poems the images are as recondite as Yeats usually permits them to be. If we will put together the fact of his eclecticism, or the catholicity of his symbols, and the fact of his care to see that the symbols are practicable and actually set in motion their intended imagery, we will conclude that he had an excellent understanding of how to use and how not to abuse his symbols; that his religiousness was wholly intelligent. But he has many passages commenting upon his practice. In "Nineteen Hundred and Nineteen" he says, for example:

Some moralist or mythological poet
Compares the solitary soul to a swan:
I am satisfied with that,
Satisfied if a troubled mirror show it,
Before that brief gleam of its life be gone,
An image of its state;
The wings half spread for flight,
The breast thrust out in pride
Whether to play, or to ride
Those winds that clamour of approaching night.

And in "The Tower" he asserts that he like all men has (as we would say) created his gods in his own image; but he does not reprobate himself for doing it; it is the commonest necessity, and as an old man he must now declare it plainly to the proud young men—not the animalists and naturalists—whom he wishes to inherit him:

And I declare my faith:
I mock Plotinus' thought
And cry in Plato's teeth,
Death and life were not
Till man made up the whole,
Made lock, stock and barrel
Out of his bitter soul,
Aye, sun and moon and star, all,
And further add to that
That, being dead, we rise,
Dream and so create
Translunar Paradise.
I have prepared my peace
With learned Italian things
And the proud stones of Greece,

Poet's imaginings
And memories of love,
Memories of the words of women,
All those things whereof
Man makes a superhuman
Mirror-resembling dream.

These terms can be made to do in deriving the epistemology of religion; they are a little bit on the soft and "romantic" side, but philosophy will support them. Concluding this poem, he indicates that as he grows old the "superhuman dream" dispossesses in reality the concerns of the body:

Now shall I make my soul,
Compelling it to study
In a learned school
Till the wreck of body,
Slow decay of blood,
Testy delirium
Or dull decrepitude
Or what worse evils come—
The death of friends, or death
Of every brilliant eye
That made a catch in the breath—
Seem but the clouds of the sky
When the horizon fades;
Or a bird's sleepy cry
Among the deepening shades.

In Yeats there is no element of that seeking for special favors from Heaven, that expectation of being relieved of the incidence of the ordinary physical laws, which makes degenerate religions, or religions in the hands of degenerate priests, positively vicious. The body of his poetry breathes a tragic sense. His gods are true gods rather than easy ones. And to a veteran and accomplished religionist like Yeats a purely secular moment, into which the forms of gods do not enter, is likely to be a context dignified by the sense that gods are immanent within it, and may appear any instant; it is like a prelude to a specifically religious experience. A score of poems could show this. But I will stop with his "Prayer for My Daughter." It might as well be entitled, "Wish for My Daughter," since it is addressed to no particular deities and has no official religious symbolism. The blessings desired are qualified by great modesty and fastidiousness as the father reasons on their serviceability to the woman in her world; and the poem concludes:

And may her bridegroom bring her to a house
Where all's accustomed, ceremonious;
For arrogance and hatred are the wares
Peddled in the thoroughfares.
How but in custom and in ceremony
Are innocence and beauty born?
Ceremony's a name for the rich horn,
And custom for the spreading laurel tree.

The abbreviated quotation as I have it does not suggest what is the fact, that ceremony and custom are climactic for the poem in being identified here with the horn of plenty and the laurel tree, which have had attention earlier. The horn and laurel tree have been treated by a cunning creative imagination, till they virtually, before our eyes, are promoted to something like the status of religious symbols.

Allen Tate

THE PROFUNDITY OF Yeats's vision of the modern world and the width of its perspective have kept me until this occasion from writing anything about poetry of our time which I most admire. The responsibility enjoins the final effort of understanding—an effort that even now I have not been able to make. The lesser poets invite the pride of the critic to its own affirmation; the greater poets—and Yeats is among them—ask us to understand not only their minds but our own; they ask us in fact to have minds of a related caliber to theirs. And criticism must necessarily remain in the presence of the great poets a business for the ant-hill: the smaller minds pooling their efforts. For the power of a Yeats will be given to the study of other poets only incidentally, for shock and technique and for the test of its own reach: this kind of power has its own task to perform.

Ours is the smaller task. The magnitude of Yeats is already visible in the failure of the partial, though frequently valuable, insights that the critics have given us in the past twenty years. There is enough in Yeats for countless studies from many points of view, yet I suspect that we shall languish far this side of the complete version of Yeats until we cease to look into him for qualities that neither Yeats nor any other poet can give us, and to censure him for possessing "attitudes" and "beliefs" which we do not share. Mr. Edmund Wilson's essay on Yeats in the influential study of symbolism *Axel's Castle* asks the poet for a political and economic philosophy; or if this is unfair to Mr. Wilson, perhaps it could be fairly said that Mr. Wilson, when he was writing the essay, was looking for a political and economic philosophy, and inevitably saw in Yeats and the other heirs of symbolism an evasion of the reality that he, Mr. Wilson, was looking for. (If you are looking for pins you do not want needles, though both will prick you.) Mr. Louis MacNeice's book-length study of Yeats says shrewd things about poetry, but on the whole we get the impression that Yeats had bad luck in not belonging to the younger group of English poets, who had a monopoly on "reality." (The word is Mr. MacNeice's.) Those were the

"Yeats's Romanticism: Notes and Suggestions," reprinted from *The Southern Review,* VII, 3 (winter, 1942), pp. 591-600; and from *On the Limits of Poetry,* The Swallow Press and William Morrow and Company, pp. 214-224, copyright, 1948, by Allen Tate.

days when not to be a communist was to be fascist, which is what Mr. MacNeice makes Yeats out to be. (Yeats liked the ancient "nobility," of which for Mr. MacNeice, Wall Street and the City offer examples.)

I cite these two writers on Yeats because in them we get summed up the case for Yeats's romanticism, the view that he was an escapist retiring from problems, forces, and theories relevant to the modern world. While it is true that Yeats, like every poet in English since the end of the eighteenth century, began with a romantic use of language in the early poems, he ended up very differently, and he is no more to be fixed as a romantic than Shakespeare as a Senecan because he wrote passages of Senecan rhetoric. If one of the historic marks of romanticism is the division between sensibility and intellect, Yeats's career may be seen as unromantic (I do not know the opposite term) because he closed the gap. His critics would then be the romantics. I do not think these squabbles are profitable. It is still true that Yeats had a more inclusive mind than any of his critics has had.

II

Two years before Yeats died he wrote to Dorothy Wellesley:

> At this moment all the specialists are about to run together in our new Alexandria, thought is about to be unified as its own free act, and the shadow in Germany and elsewhere is an attempted unity by force. In my life I have never felt so acutely the presence of a spiritual virtue and that is accompanied by intensified desire.

Scattered throughout Yeats's prose there are similar passages, but this one is only from a letter, and it lacks the imaginative reach and synthesis of the great passages towards the end of *A Vision,* where I recall particularly the fine paragraph on early Byzantium and Section III of "Dove or Swan" in which Yeats describes the annunciation to Leda which brought in the classical civilization, as the annunciation to the Virgin brought in the Christian. Of Byzantium he says:

> I think that in early Byzantium, maybe never before or since in recorded history, religious, aesthetic, and practical life were one, that architect and artificers—though not, it may be, poets, for language had been the instrument of controversy and must have gone abstract —spoke to the multitude and the few alike. The painter, the mosaic worker, the worker in gold and silver, the illuminator of sacred books, were almost impersonal, almost perhaps without the con-

sciousness of individual design, absorbed in their subject-matter and that the vision of a whole people.

Mr. Cleanth Brooks has shown that the great sonnet "Leda" is no pretty picture out of mythology, that it gets power from the powerful forces of the imagination behind it. Section III of "Dove or Swan" begins:

> I imagine the annunciation which founded Greece as made to Leda, remembering that they showed in a Spartan temple, strung up to the roof as a holy relic, an unhatched egg of hers; and that from one of her eggs came Love and from the other War. But all things are from antithesis, and when in my ignorance I try to imagine what older civilization that annunciation rejected I can but see bird and woman blotting out some corner of the Babylonian mathematical starlight.

In these three passages I believe that we get the main threads of Yeats's thought expressed in language which refers to the famous "system" but which is nevertheless sufficiently clear to persons who have not mastered the system or who even know nothing of it. Study of the Great Wheel with its gyres and cones might give us extensive references for certain ideas in the passage from the letter. We should learn that we are now in the twenty-third phase of our historical cycle, in which thought is abstract and unity of life must be imposed by force, and that culture is Alexandrian. The picture of a perfect culture that he gives us in Byzantium (which in the poem of that name becomes something more than mere historical insight) where men enjoy full unity of being has too many features in common with familiar Western ideas to be seen as an eccentric piece of utopianism. Byzantium is a new pastoral symbol and will be taken as that by anybody who sees more in the pastoral tradition than ideal shepherds and abstract sheep. The annunciation to Leda offers historical and philosophical difficulties; yet in spite of Yeats's frequently expressed belief that he had found a new historical vision, the conception is not historical in any sense that we understand today. It is a symbol established in analogical terms; that is, our literal grasp of it depends upon prior knowledge of the annunciation to the Virgin. The "Babylonian mathematical starlight" is self-evidently clear without Yeats's scattered glosses on it: it is darkness and abstraction, quantitative relations without imagination; and I doubt that Yeats's definitions make it much clearer that that. If Leda rejected it, we only learn from Yeats's "system" that the coming of Christ brought it back in;

for an entire cultural cycle can be predominantly antithetical or predominantly primary, at the same time that it goes through the twenty-eight phases from primary to antithetical back to primary again.

In the letter to Dorothy Wellesley occurs a sentence which sounds casual, even literally confessional; there is no harm done if we take it at that level; there is merely a loss of insight such as we get in Mr. MacNeice's *The Poetry of W. B. Yeats,* in which Yeats's myth is dismissed as "arid" and "unsound." In the midst of the "attempted unity by force," he writes: "In my own life I have never felt so acutely the presence of a spiritual virtue and that is accompanied by intensified desire." The literal student of *A Vision,* coming upon statements like this, may well wonder what has become of the determinism of the system, which, with an almost perverse ingenuity, seems to fix the individual in a system of coordinates from which he cannot escape. Mr. Cleanth Brooks believes that some measure of free will lies in Yeats's conception of the False Mask, which some unpredictable force in the individual may lead him to choose instead of the True Mask. I believe this is only part of the explanation.

Does not the true explanation here lie in there being *no* explanation in terms of the system? Even if we see Yeats as he saw himself, a man of Phase 17 living in Phase 23 of our civilization, the discrepancy merely introduces a complication which the system can easily take account of. Mr. MacNeice at this point enlightens us almost in spite of himself: "Freedom for Yeats, as for Engels, was a recognition of necessity—but not of economic necessity, which he considered a vulgarism." Yes; and he would have considered psychological necessity, or any inner determinism no less than an outer, economic determinism, a vulgarism also. But in the phrase the "recognition of necessity" we get a clue to Yeats's own relation to his system and to what seems to me the right way to estimate its value. He only wanted what all men want, a world larger than himself to live in; for the modern world as he saw it was, in human terms, too small for the human spirit, though quantitatively large if looked at with the scientist. If we say, then, that he wanted a *dramatic* recognition of necessity, we shall have to look at the system not as arid or unsound or eccentric, which it well may be in itself, but through Yeats's eyes, which are the eyes of his poetry.

If we begin with the poetry we shall quickly see that there is some source of power or illumination which is also in us, waiting to be aroused; and that this is true of even the greater number of the fine poems in which the imagery appears upon later study to lean upon the eccentric system. I would say, then, that even the terms of the system, when they appear in the richer texture of the poems, share a certain large margin of significance with a wider context than they have in the system itself. May we say that Yeats's *A Vision*, however private and almost childishly eclectic it may seem, has somewhat the same relation to a central tradition as the far more rigid structure of the *Divine Comedy* has to the Christian myth? I dare say that Mr. Eliot would not chide Dante for accepting a "lower mythology." Perhaps the central tradition in Dante and Yeats lies in a force that criticism cannot specifically isolate, the force that moved both poets to the dramatic recognition of necessity; yet the visible structure of the necessity itself is perhaps not the source of that power. I do not say that Yeats is comparable in stature to Dante only that both poets strove for a visible structure of action which is indeed necessary to what they said, but which does not explain what they said. I believe that Eliot should undertake to explain why Arnold's Higher Mythology produced poetry less interesting than Yeats's Lower Mythology which becomes in Yeats's verse the vehicle of insights and imaginative syntheses as profound as those which Arnold talked about but never, as a poet, fully achieved. Myths differ in range and intensity, but not I take it as high and low; for they are in the end what poets can make of them.

If Yeats could feel in the midst of the Alexandrian rigidity and disorder the "presence of a spiritual virtue," was he denying the inclusiveness of the system; or could he have seen his senile vigor and insight in terms of the system? Possibly the latter; but it makes little difference.

III

A Vision has been described by more than one critic as a philosophy; I speak of it here as a "system"; but I doubt that it is a system of philosophy. What kind of system is it? Yeats frequently stated his own purpose, but even that is a little obscure: to put myth back into philosophy. This phrase may roughly describe the result, but it could not stand for the process; it attributes to the early philosophers a deliberation of which they would have been incapable. The language of Plotinus, whose *Enneads* Yeats read late in life, is compounded of primitive symbolism, the esoteric fragments of classical myth, and the terms of Greek technical metaphysics; but there is no calculated intention of instilling myth into philosophy.

In what sense is *A Vision* a myth? There are fragments of many myths brought in to give dramatic and sensuous body to the framework, which attains to the limit of visualization that a complex geometrical picture can provide.

A broad view of this picture, with its gyres and cones, to say nothing of the Daimons and the Principle whose relation to the Faculties defies my understanding, gleans at least two remarkable features. I merely note them:

(1) ". . . the subjective cone is called that of the *antithetical tincture* because it is achieved and defended by continual conflict with its opposite; the objective cone is called that of the *primary tincture* because whereas subjectivity—in Empedocles 'Discord' as I think—tends to separate man from man, objectivity brings us back to the mass where we began." From this simple definition—verbally simple, but very obscure—we get the first picture of the intersecting cones; and from this the whole structure is elaborated.

It is clear visually with the aid of the diagrams; but when Yeats complicates it with his Principles and Daimons, and extends the symbol of the gyres to cover historical eras, visualization breaks down. It is an extended metaphor which increasingly tends to dissolve in the particulars which it tries to bring together into unity.

When we come to the magnificent passages on history in "Dove or Swan" all the intricacies of the geometrical metaphor disappear; and the simple figure of historical cycles, which Yeats evidently supposed came out of his gyres, is sufficient to sustain his meaning. Again Yeats's "system" overlaps a body of insight common to us all.

I would suggest, then, for the study of the relation of Yeats's "system" to his vision of man, both historical and individual, this formula: As the system broadens out and merges with the traditional insights of our culture, it tends to disappear in its specific, technical aspects. What disappears is not a philosophy, but only a vast metaphorical structure. In the great elegy, "In Memory of Major Robert Gregory," we get this couplet:

But as the outrageous stars incline
By opposition, square, and trine—

which is the only astrological figure in the poem. Yet it must not be assumed that Yeats on this occasion turned off the system; it must be there. Why does not it overtly appear? It has been absorbed into the concrete substance of the poem; the material to be symbolized replaces the symbol, and contains its own meaning. I would select this poem out of all others of our time as the most completely expressed: it has a perfect articulation and lucidity which cannot be found in any other modern poem in English.

(2) In his early poems Yeats is concerned with the myths of ancient Ireland. We may find unreadable today a poem like the "Wanderings of Oisin" or plays like "Deirdre" or "The Land of Heart's Desire." The later poems are less dependent upon fable and fully developed mythical plots for their structures. And yet Yeats entered his later poetic phase at about the same time he began to be interested in his system, in putting myth back into philosophy. Did this mean that he was taking myth out of his poetry?

Thus the second remarkable feature of the system, as I see it, is that it is not a mythology at all, but rather an extended metaphor, as I have already pointed out, which permits him to establish relations between the tag-ends of myths eclectically gathered from all over the world. For example, there is nothing in the geometrical structure of the system which inherently provides for the annunciation to Leda; it is an arbitrary association of two fields of imagery; but once it is established, it is not hard to pass on through analogy to the Annunciation to the Virgin.

IV

Thus it is difficult for me to follow those critics who accept Yeats's various utterances that he was concerned with a certain relation of philosophy to myth. Any statement about "life" must have philosophical implications, just as any genuine philosophical statement must have, because of the nature of language, mythical implications. Yeats's doctrine of the conflict of opposites says nothing about the fundamental nature of reality; it is rather a dramatic framework through which is made visible the perpetual oscillation of man between extreme introspection and extreme loss of the self in the world of action. The intricacies of Yeats's system provide for many of the permutations of the relation; but it cannot foresee them all; and we are constantly brought back to the individual man, not as a symbolic counter, but as a personality rich and unpredictable. Yeats's preference for the nobleman, the peasant, and the craftsman does not betray, as Mr. MacNeice's somewhat provincial contention holds, the "budding fascist"; it is a "version of pastoral" which permits Yeats to see his characters acting above the ordinary dignity of men, in a concrete relation to life undiluted by calculation and abstraction. I can only repeat here that the "system" is perpetually absorbed into action. If Yeats were only an allegorist, the meaning of his poetry could be ascertained by getting hold of the right key. The poetry would serve to illustrate the "system," as the poetry of the Prophetic Books fleshes out the homemade system of Blake.

V

Mr. Eliot's view, that Yeats got off the central tradition into a "minor mythology," and Mr. Blackmur's view, that he took "magic" (as opposed to religion) as far as any poet could, seem to me to be related versions of the same fallacy. Which is: that there must be a direct and effective correlation between the previously established truth of the poet's ideas and the value of the poetry. (I am oversimplifying Blackmur's view, but not Eliot's.) In this difficulty it is always useful to ask: *Where* are the poet's ideas? Good sense in this matter ought to tell us that while the ideas doubtless exist in some form outside the poetry, as they exist for Yeats in the letters, the essays, and *A Vision,* we must nevertheless test them in the poems themselves, and not "refute" a poem in which the gyres supply certain images by showing that gyres are amateur philosophy.

> *Turning and turning in the widening gyre*
> *The falcon cannot hear the falconer. . . .*

—the opening lines of "The Second Coming." And they make perfect sense apart from our knowledge of the system; the gyre here can be visualized as the circling flight of the bird constantly widening until it has lost contact with the point, the center, to which it ought to be able to return. As a symbol of disunity it is no more esoteric than Eliot's "Gull against the wind," at the end of "Gerontion," which is a casual, not systematic, symbol of disunity. Both Mr. Blackmur and Mr. Brooks—Mr. Brooks more than Mr. Blackmur—show us the systematic implications of the symbols of the poem "Byzantium." The presence of the system at its most formidable cannot be denied to this poem. I should like to see, nevertheless, an analysis of it in which no special knowledge is used; I should like to see it examined with the ordinary critical equipment of the educated critic; I should be surprised if the result were very different from Mr. Brooks's reading of the poem. The symbols are "made good" in the poem; they are drawn into a wider convention (Mr. Blackmur calls it the "heaven of man's mind") than they would imply if taken separately.

I conclude these notes with the remark: the study of Yeats in the coming generation is likely to overdo the scholarly procedure, and the result will be the occultation of a poetry which I believe is nearer the center of our main traditions of sensibility and thought than the poetry of Eliot or of Pound. Yeats's special qualities will instigate special studies of great ingenuity, but the more direct and more difficult problem of the poetry itself will probably be delayed. This is only to say that Yeats's romanticism will be created by his critics.

David Daiches

Eliot's concern with tradition, his attempt to define his relation to the past, his attack on the romantic view of literature as the exploitation of personality, and his deliberate eclecticism in his choice of symbols from past cultures suggest some of the problems of the poet who lives in an age without a stable background. Self-consciousness about symbols and about tradition—and symbols depend upon tradition—is to be found increasingly among European poets from the last decade of the nineteenth century onward. Probably no poet was so aware of his problem and made such a gallant and sustained effort to solve it as W. B. Yeats. Yeats's poetic career, beginning in the 1880's and concluding in the latter part of the 1930's, coincides with the development of that disintegration of belief which had so great an influence both on the technique and on the subject matter of literature. The phases of his poetic activity represent successive attempts to compensate for this disintegration by framing for himself symbolizations of experience in terms of which he could give meaning to his symbols, pattern to his thought, coherence to his interpretation of experience. Though he shared his problem with his generation, he differed from most of his contemporaries in being more conscious and deliberate in his endeavor to solve it. In his earliest period he saw the problem as that of finding a substitute for a no longer tenable religious tradition:

> I am very religious, and deprived by Huxley and Tyndall, whom I detested, of the simple-minded religion of my childhood, I had made a new religion, almost an infallible church of poetic tradition, of a fardel of stories, and of personages, and of emotions, inseparable from their first expression, passed on from generation to generation by poets and painters with some help from philosophers and theologians. I wished for a world, where I could discover this tradition perpetually, and not in pictures and in poems only, but in tiles round the chimney-piece and in hangings that kept out the draft.

In his search for a compensating tradition Yeats went first to romantic literature, and then to mysticism of one kind and another, to folklore, theosophy, spiritualism, Neo-Platonism, and finally elaborated a symbolic system of his own, based on

"W. B. Yeats—I," reprinted from *Poetry and the Modern World,* pp. 128-155, by David Daiches, copyright, 1940, by the University of Chicago, by permission of University of Chicago Press.

a variety of sources, and in terms of this was able to give pattern and coherence to the expression of his thought. It was a search for a system rather than a search for a set of beliefs; he sought a mode of expression rather than a set of dogmas to express. The problem for Yeats was not that of finding what he ought to say: his sensitive and restless mind provided him with a constant supply of subjects and attitudes. His problem was that of giving order and proportion to his insights. He did not even seek a point of view, for his mind, so much more elastic and all-embracing than Eliot's, would never be satisfied, as Eliot's was, with any single formulation of attitude. He sought simply adequacy of poetic communication and for that he needed an ordered system to give meaning to his terms, significance to his symbols, form to his expression, and unity to his individual poems. He did not conceive of this system as demanding the intellectual assent of his readers, though his attempts at prose exposition show that he would have preferred such assent: its function was to be rather that of the frame on which the weaver weaves his patterns, necessary to the weaver though requiring no recognition on the part of those who appreciate the finished product. The analogy is not altogether perfect, for in some cases we do need to know what frame Yeats was using before we can appreciate his finished work. Indeed, there seems to be some confusion in Yeats's conception of the function of his system. Is it a frame for the weaver or a key to be used by the observer in interpreting the pattern aright? In a period of cultural stability such a system would serve both functions, but it would be a system common to writer and reader and it would serve these functions unconsciously. In the modern world, however, the poet who wishes to compensate for the lack of such a tradition has to make up his mind how far the compensation should go. For by attempting too much he may achieve nothing, by trying both to help himself to coherence and to supply a background of belief for his readers he may end by making himself incoherent or by alienating his readers by the privateness of his conceptions. This is a risk which Yeats often runs in his later poetry, and though he often emerges successfully by his power of organization and the brilliance of his phrasing (the first communicating the relation of the symbols to each other, the second evoking sufficient suggestion of their meaning to combine with the suggestion of their relation to each other and produce a significant whole), there are occasions, in some of the poems in "Words for Music Perhaps," for example, where the reader gets only the impression of an esoteric imagination. Did not Yeats possess this double power of organization and of phrasing, his work would be more consistently obscure than in fact it is.

It is a mistake to consider Yeats as a mystical poet. The true mystic is one who seeks to escape from an age of overformulation by repudiating the orthodox categories and seeking identities and correspondences not recognized by more rational speculation. But far from seeking to escape from formulas Yeats is seeking to establish them. He does not wish to escape from orthodox religion but to find a substitute for it. He seeks to impose order, not, as the true mystic does, to break down a too neatly ordered system and get beyond it. He has little in common with a mystical poet like A.E. He turns to mysticism not in search of shattering new insights but in quest of categories, often maintaining a casual skepticism concerning what to the mystics themselves were the essential truths. His discussion of Macgregor Mathers, for example, in *The Trembling of the Veil,* is conducted in an almost ironical spirit; the real point was that "I had soon mastered Mathers' symbolic system," and a new way of ordering experience had been discovered. Like Eliot, Yeats was looking for order. But while Eliot was able to find it in orthodox Christianity, for Yeats, as for so many of his contemporaries, "Victorian science" destroyed the possibility of belief in orthodox Christianity, and he had to turn to less beaten tracks. That Victorian science had also, by implication at least, destroyed the possibility of belief in these other systems did not matter, for Yeats had as a very young man believed in the scientific approach and allowed it to destroy his religious belief which could never after that be re-established, while he came to these other systems after he had repudiated Victorian science (which he soon grew to hate "with a monkish hate") which could thus have no further effect on his attitude. It might be argued that the question of belief was in any case irrelevant, for it was a vague sort of quasi-belief that Yeats came to have in these systems, and why could he not have adopted this same attitude to religion? The answer to this is simply that the religious tradition was too finally blown up for Yeats in his youth for him to be able to turn there for his system. It has often been noted that in an age when religious belief is decaying, belief in all kinds of odd superstitions grows apace: astrology flourishes more vigorously in England today than it did when Christianity was more firmly in the saddle. The truth is that when a religious tradition begins to decay those who are affected by its decay are rarely conscious of any logical process of repudiation which could be applied a fortiori to the superstitions which often take its place; they simply have a vague sense that the tradition has decayed, the position is untenable, relating this feeling, perhaps, to the name of some scientist, as Yeats did to the names of Huxley and Tyndall, which came to take on a symbolic meaning for him.

System, order, ritual—these Yeats sought not for their own sake, not because as a man he would have chosen to subordinate his mind and body to a traditional discipline, but because he needed them as a poet, to help him achieve adequate poetic expression. Again and again in his autobiographical writings we find some such wish expressed:

> I planned a mystical Order which should buy or hire the castle, and keep it as a place where its members could retire for a while for contemplation, and where we might establish mysteries like those of Eleusis and Samothrace; and for ten years to come my most impassioned thought was a vain attempt to find philosophy and to create ritual for that Order. I had an unshakable conviction, arising how or whence I cannot tell, that invisible gates would open as they did for Blake, as they opened for Swedenborg, as they opened for Boehme, and that this philosophy would find its manuals of devotion in all imaginative literature, and set before Irishmen for special manual an Irish literature which, though made by many minds, would seem the work of a single mind, and turn our places of beauty or legendary association into holy symbols. I did not think this philosophy would be altogether pagan, for it was plain that its symbols must be selected from all those things that had moved men most during many, mainly Christian, centuries.

Here Yeats is expressing his desire for an eclectic symbolic system which would at once be a source of literary symbolism and derive from the symbolism of imaginative Irish literature. The reference to Ireland in this connection is interesting; for we cannot hope to understand Yeats if we do not realize that his search for a symbolic system was bound up in a very complex manner with his desire to utilize traditional Irish material —literary, historical, mythical, and popular. In some way Ireland had to be involved in his system; Irish symbols had to be employed to give the proper emotional quality to his work. Yeats was attempting to solve two problems—the general problem of symbols in literature in an age lacking a common tradition and the particular problem presented by the confusions of the Irish situation. We have only to go through Yeats's autobiographical writings to see at once that the chaotic nature of the Irish scene—politically, culturally, socially—imposed a task on him from the beginning, the task of imposing order on this chaos. It was, of course, a subjective order primarily, a pattern in his own mind which would enable him to utilize Irish material in his poetry. He was no politician and did not feel called upon to solve the practical problems of his time. But he was impelled to find a way of putting Ireland into some mental order, so that cultural symbols of dependable significance would be at the disposal of the artist. This double task —one posed by the cultural problem of his time, the other resulting from his relation to Ireland—was faced boldly by Yeats, and his development as a poet is the record of how he attempted to carry it out.

When Yeats first began writing poetry, he accepted as a matter of course the thinned-out romantic tradition which demanded that poetry should be concerned with a "beautiful" world of dream, employing a language chosen for its vague emotional suggestiveness and conventional poetic associations. He had at this period no clear ideas concerning his relation to his Irish background; the influences on him were English rather than Irish, and in his treatment of Irish themes he displayed the normal English romantic attitude toward things Celtic. But even in this earliest period his thin poetizing seems to have meant more to Yeats than the conventional practice of a craft; the images of beauty and strangeness which he collected out of Spenser and Shelley and other less distinguished influences were intended in some vague way to represent an imaginative world of values which would compensate him both for his lost religion and for the confused and prosaic nature of everyday existence. He was already seeking his "infallible church of poetic tradition." But he had as yet no thought of a system; his church was to be built on the romantic word, compensating for the grayness of contemporary reality:

The woods of Arcady are dead,
And over is their antique joy;
Of old the world on dreaming fed;
Grey Truth is now her painted toy;
Yet still she turns her restless head:
But O, sick children of the world,
Of all the many changing things
In dreary dancing past us whirled,
To the cracked tune that Chronos sings,
Words alone are certain good.

There are poems on Indian subjects, too, among this early group, India being chosen for its remoteness and its romantic suggestions in accordance with a tradition established by generations of English poets. At this time—he was not yet twenty—Yeats held the belief that "only beautiful things should be painted, and that only ancient things and the stuff of dreams were beautiful." His poetry was frankly escapist, like most early verse of nineteenth-century poets, and its purpose was not to interpret life but to compensate for it. Spenser, Shelley, Rossetti, and Blake shaped his adolescence, and he struck Byronic poses to his reflection in shop windows.

It was Ireland that rescued him from this imitative romanticism. In the folklore that he picked up while staying with his grandparents in Sligo he found a subject matter as effective for his purposes as India or Arcadia and much less hackneyed, while in the peasant speech of the Irish country people he found a diction and a rhythm which, while poetic, was fresh and vigorous. We have only to compare "The Stolen Child" or "To an Isle in the Water" with "The Indian to His Love" or "Anashuya and Vijaya" to see what the introduction of the Irish folk element meant for Yeats's poetry. There is a new precision of imagery and a greater vitality in diction in the former poems, whose theme and setting are Irish, introducing the imagination of the Irish peasants and the places—Rosses, Sleuth Wood, Sligo—that he knew. The substitution for vague romantic landscapes of specific Irish scenes associated with local folklore of a kind that combined wild imagination with homely realism—stories of fairies, ghosts, goblins, local spirits—was the first important step in the development of Yeats's individuality as a poet.

This change worked slowly in Yeats's poetry, and its full effect was not immediately noticeable. It would be quite wrong to think of Yeats as suddenly turning to realistic poetry while still in his teens. The general nature of his poetry remained the same, but the imagery became more precise, the setting more clearly seen and so more clearly presented, the themes less pretentious. *The Wandering of Usheen* (later spelled by Yeats *The Wanderings of Oisin*), written in his early twenties, still shows very clearly his early influences—Spenser and Shelley and the Pre-Raphaelites—and in its general trappings and looseness of structure displays Yeats's most youthful characteristics. Yet this elaborate narrative poem, based on an Irish mythological theme, contains passages of sharp and disciplined writing that stand out from the prevailing luxuriance as heralds of the later Yeats.

But it was not simply Irish folklore and peasant speech that influenced Yeats's poetry at this time. A more important impetus came from his Irish background. Yeats has explained it himself:

> I think it was a Young Ireland Society that set my mind running on "popular poetry." We used to discuss everything that was known to us about Ireland, and especially Irish literature and Irish history. We had no Gaelic, but paid great honour to the Irish poets who wrote in English, and quoted them in our speeches. . . . I knew in my heart that most of them wrote badly, and yet such romance clung about them, such a desire for Irish poetry was in all our minds, that I kept on saying, not only to others but to myself, that most of them wrote well, or all but well. I had read Shelley and Spenser and had tried to mix their styles together in a pastoral play which I have not come to dislike much [*The Island of Statues*], and yet I do not think Shelley or Spenser ever moved me as did these poets. I thought one day—I can remember the very day when I thought it—"If somebody could make a style which would not be an English style and yet would be musical and full of colour, many others would catch fire from him, and we would have a really great school of ballad poetry in Ireland. If these poets, who have never ceased to fill the newspapers and the ballad-books with their verses, had a good tradition they would write beautifully and move everybody as they move me." Then a little later on I thought, "If they had something else to write about besides political opinions, if more of them would write about the beliefs of the people like Allingham, or about old legends like Ferguson, they would find it easier to get a style." Then, with a deliberateness that still surprises me, for in my heart of hearts I have never been quite certain that one should be more than an artist, I set to work to find a style and things to write about that the ballad writers might be the better.

Yeats is beginning to be conscious of his search for a tradition and at the same time to use Ireland to help him in his search.

By this time the "Irish revival" had got under way, and Yeats did not have to depend entirely on his own eye and ear in utilizing Irish motives in his poetry. Already in 1878 Standish O'Grady had published his *History of Ireland, Heroic Period,* a florid and high-spirited work which, whatever its faults as a piece of scholarship, was a tremendous importance in making available to the public the old Gaelic heroic legends. Wrote Yeats:

> In his unfinished *History of Ireland* [O'Grady] had made the old Irish heroes, Fion, and Oisin, and Cuchullan, alive again, taking them, for I think he knew no Gaelic, from the dry pages of O'Curry and his school, and condensing and arranging, as he thought Homer

would have arranged and condensed. Lady Gregory has told the same tales . . . but O'Grady was the first, and we had read him in our teens.

While O'Grady's history thus made available material from the heroic age of Irish history, the popular legends and folk literature of Ireland were collected and edited soon after, providing even richer subject matter for the poets. George Sigerson's *Poets and Poetry of Munster* began this task as early as 1860, and it was followed by the same author's *Bards of the Gael and Gall* in 1897, which contained about a hundred and fifty traditional Irish poems translated in a meter which endeavored to capture the movement of the Gaelic originals. Douglas Hyde's *Love Songs of Connacht* (1893) was even more influential; the Gaelic poems were translated by Hyde into "that dialect which gets from Gaelic its syntax and keeps its still partly Tudor vocabulary," and Yeats profited greatly.

> Nothing in that language of his was abstract, nothing worn-out; he need not, as must the writer of some language exhausted by modern civilization, reject word after word, cadence after cadence; he had escaped our perpetual, painful, purification. . . . When I first read it, I was fresh from my struggle with Victorian rhetoric. I began to test my poetical inventions by translating them into like speech.

Yeats has several times testified to the importance for him of Hyde's *Love Songs of Connacht* and "that English idiom of the Irish-thinking people of the West."

But in London Yeats's poetic milieu was the Rhymers' Club, "which for some years was to meet every night in an upper room with a sanded floor in an ancient eating-house in the Strand called The Cheshire Cheese." Here he met with Lionel Johnson, Ernest Dowson, Richard Le Gallienne, T. W. Rolleston, John Todhunter, John Davidson, and others. Of these "companions of The Cheshire Cheese" only Rolleston and Todhunter had any association with the Irish movement, and the latter's was brief. Though there was little agreement on poetic ideals among the group, the prevailing aim was that of a rather tired sensationalism, and Yeats was not very sure whether to dissociate himself from it or not. The influence of the French Symbolists reinforced that of the Pre-Raphaelites, and gradually "the reds and yellows that Shelley gathered in Italy" faded out of his poetry to give place to less violent colors. His Irish material, too, encouraged him in his tendency, but on the whole the lessons he was learning from Ireland and those he was learning from the "decadent" poets in London hardly fitted together, and, as is clear from his autobiographical writings, Yeats remained in a rather confused state of mind throughout the late 1880's and early 1890's.

Among Irish sources he continued his search of new myths and a living speech that could be used in poetry, and he did so less as a patriot than as a poet. He had as yet no literary plans for Ireland or for himself in Ireland; he was waiting for something, though he was not quite clear what it was. He was in fact waiting for some kind of opportunity to integrate the disparate elements of a poetic creed that he had picked up in Ireland and in London. It became increasingly clear to him that only in Ireland, only by defining his relation to Ireland and putting the symbols of Ireland in order in his mind, could he achieve the kind of poetic system he was groping after. In 1890 he wrote, significantly: "We are preparing, likely enough, for a new Irish literary movement—like that of '48—that will show itself in the first lull in politics." As long as the Irish revival remained primarily a political movement Yeats at this stage could derive little from it as a movement, and give little to it; but with a "lull in politics" he might be able to make Ireland serve his purpose.

The death of Parnell, following rapidly on the virtual collapse of his movement, provided that lull for which Yeats was waiting. There came to him "the sudden certainty that Ireland was to be like soft wax for years to come," and he bestirred himself to insure that he should be the one to mold that wax to a shape that would serve both literature and himself. He founded the Irish Literary Society in London and the National Literary Society in Dublin and began to conceive of himself as taking part in a movement. He came into intimate contact with the most important leaders of Irish thought of the day, whose portraits he draws in "Ireland after Parnell" (*The Trembling of the Veil,* Book II). But his practical schemes did not come to anything; he argued and quarreled and became increasingly aware of his isolation. And this was not because he was essentially an impractical person who was bound to bungle things of this sort—some years later while working for the Abbey Theatre with Lady Gregory he achieved a great deal—but because he was out in search of a mythology, a tradition, a system to help him in writing poetry, while his colleagues were interested in more objective aims. Until he had patterned his thought to his own satisfaction he could be of little use to even literary movements; his procedure was to plunge into them, engage in a short spell of great activity during which he had a great many ideas and talked a great deal, and then retire with his booty, as it were. What he was seeking is perhaps indicated by the fact that during this same activity he was also frequenting "a house in Ely Place, where a number of young men lived together, and, for want of a better name, were called Theosophists." Here lived artists, Neo-Platonists, hypnotists, vegetarians, mystics of several varieties, a motley group of unorthodox thinkers (A.E. was the "saint and genius" of the community) whose discussions Yeats attended. It was at this time that he had the conviction that the invisible gates would open for him as they opened for Blake and imaginative literature would become the storehouse of the symbols of the new philosophy.

The Neo-Platonic ideas which he picked up at Ely Place and from Spenser and Shelley were used by Yeats at this time to give meaning and pattern to the Irish heroic themes which were coming more and more into his poetry. *The Rose* (1893) is a collection of poems whose general theme is the symbolization of Platonic "ideas" by means of figures from Irish mythology and early history. The Platonism of Shelley and Spenser is clearly seen in his conception of the Rose as a symbol of the idea of beauty, though in a note to these poems written in 1925 Yeats comments: "I notice upon reading these poems for the first time for several years that the quality symbolized as The Rose differs from the Intellectual Beauty of Shelley and of Spenser in that I have imagined it as suffering with man and not as something pursued and seen from afar." The relation of the Rose to the Irish figures is indicated in the opening poem of the group:

Red Rose, proud Rose, sad Rose of all my days!
Come near me, while I sing the ancient ways:
Cuchulain battling with the bitter tide;
The Druid, grey, wood-nurtured, quiet-eyed,
Who cast round Fergus dreams, and ruin untold;
And thine own sadness, whereof stars, grown old
In dancing silver-sandalled on the sea,
Sing in their high and lonely melody.
Come near, that no more blinded by man's fate,
I find under the boughs of love and hate,
In all poor foolish things that live a day,
Eternal beauty wandering on her way.

And the concluding lines are significant:

Come near; I would, before my time to go,
Sing of old Eire and the ancient ways:
Red Rose, proud Rose, sad Rose of all my days.

Ireland, especially the Ireland of heroic legend, is welcomed as his new subject, to be interpreted through his Neo-Platonic system. The influence of O'Grady's *History* is to be seen here again and again, but it is an influence absorbed and utilized for Yeats's own purpose. With the increased confidence afforded him by the mental pattern that underlies these poems Yeats was able to achieve a new power of phrase and effectiveness of structure. "The Rose of the World," perhaps the most perfect of his early poems, shows a careful discipline in language and control over form that are to be the outstanding features of Yeats's later poetry. The luxuriance and the romantic beating about the bush of his very first poems, when he sought his system in words merely ("Words alone are certain good"), have given place to an artistic restraint which carries much greater power:

Who dreamed that beauty passes like a dream?
For these red lips, with all their mournful pride,
Mournful that no new wonder may betide,
Troy passed away in one high funeral gleam,
And Usna's children died.

The use of classical and Irish names as illustration and climax to the Neo-Platonic theme, the handling of the line-lengths, the skilful placing of the emphatic words, and the simple yet effective tripartite structure of the complete poem show that this temporary synthesis of Yeats's ideas (he was to move on to many others) helped him to mature as a poet.

It was not only Irish heroic motives which Yeats managed to treat in this symbolic manner in the poems of *The Rose;* folk themes are also employed in the same manner. "The Man Who Dreamed of Faeryland," one of the most interesting and most successful of the poems using folk themes, treats popular beliefs and superstitions in a highly symbolic way, so that the story of a man involuntarily in touch with supernatural forces emerges from a catalogue of wonders:

He stood among a crowd at Drumahair;
His heart hung all upon a silken dress,
And he had known at last some tenderness,

Before earth took him to her stony care;
But when a man poured fish into a pile,
It seemed they raised their little silver heads,
And sang what gold morning or evening sheds
Upon a woven world-begotten isle
Where people love beside the ravelled seas;
That Time can never mar a lover's vows
Under that woven changeless roof of boughs:
The singing shook him out of his new ease.

The contrasts wind through the subsequent stanzas, becoming at once more complicated and more clear, until the climax, where the man's restless and unwanted desire for supernatural truth reaches its culmination: he is dead and would have slept in peace

Did not the worms that spired about his bones
Proclaim with that unwearied, reedy cry
That God has laid His fingers on the sky,
That from those fingers glittering summer runs
Upon the dancer by the dreamless wave.
Why should those lovers that no lovers miss
Dream, until God burn Nature with a kiss?
The man has found no comfort in the grave.

We see here what is to become Yeats's characteristic ability to create a myth whose meaning lies in its form, its pattern, rather than in its precise connotation. The connotations of such a myth as that expressed in "The Man Who Dreamed of Faeryland" are numerous, perhaps infinite, and this is true of a great deal of Yeats's later poetry and plays. He was concerned with truth as pattern rather than with truth as a "state of affairs."

This feature of his poetry can once again be related to that conscious desire to create a system, to build a body of tradition in terms of which his symbols would have significance, which we have noted as one of the central facts about Yeats's development as a poet. We note in these early poems a general tendency to construct a pattern in terms of a simple pair of contrasts. Human activity as opposed to fairy activity, the natural as opposed to the artificial, the familiar as opposed to the remote and strange, the domestic as opposed to the heroic, the contemporary as opposed to the ancient, the transient as opposed to the permanent—these contrasts provide nearly all the themes in *Crossways* and *The Rose*. Yeats's awareness of a dichotomy in human experience was central in his thought; his earlier attitudes are concerned largely with expressing this dichotomy, while in his later work we see him endeavoring to resolve it. But always it is the pattern that matters. The terms in which this division is expressed vary from poem to poem, but the fact of the division is constant. And so in his later work—*The Tower* and *The Winding Stair*—where he constructs elaborate symbols and strange myths in order to achieve a resolution of this contrast, it is the resolution rather than the terms of the resolution that matters. If we understand this important aspect of Yeats's thought, we shall find his later poetry less obscure and his mythology less irritating.

About the same time that he was writing the poems contained in *The Rose* group, Yeats was collecting and recording in simple prose the folk material from which he drew his symbols in the poems. These records are contained in the group of prose sketches which he called *The Celtic Twilight;* they include descriptions of his favorite spots—of Drumcliff and Rosses, for example—accounts of local superstitions, and all sorts of folk tales and folk beliefs. To some extent this collection represents the raw material out of which the poems were constructed. Yet they are not simply that; Yeats intended to achieve in this simple recording the same task that he sought to achieve in his poetry. He tells us in his Introduction:

> I have desired, like every artist, to create a little world out of the beautiful, pleasant, and significant things of this marred and clumsy world, and to show in a vision something of the face of Ireland to any of my own people who would look where I bid them. I have therefore written down accurately and candidly much that I have heard and seen, and, except by way of commentary, nothing that I have merely imagined.

Here again is the desire for order, for pattern, with Irish material used as a means of achieving it.

Though Yeats's participation in Irish affairs at this time, his foundation of the literary societies, and his utilization of Irish material arose from his desire to satisfy his personal need as a poet, he nevertheless believed that in thus making use of Irish material he was contributing as much to Ireland as the politicians and the fighters. The concluding poem of *The Rose*, "To Ireland in the Coming Times," makes this point quite clearly:

> *Know, that I would accounted be*
> *True brother of a company*

That sang, to sweeten Ireland's wrong,
Ballad and story, rann and song;
Nor be I any less of them
Because the red-rose-bordered hem
Of her, whose history began
Before God made the angelic clan,
Trails all about the written page.

And he goes on to claim kinship with the more political of the Irish writers:

Nor may I less be counted one
With Davis, Mangan, Ferguson,
Because, to him who ponders well,
My rhymes more than their rhyming tell
Of things discovered in the deep,
Where only body's laid asleep.

We have here his expression of the relation between his philosophic and his patriotic interests.

In *The Wind among the Reeds* (1899) the influence of the French Symbolists—of Mallarme, of Verlaine, of Villiers de L'Isle Adam, and also of Maeterlinck—is more clearly seen than anywhere else in Yeats's work, but it is still Irish figures and Irish themes that supply the bulk of his symbols. He had been reading the mystical writers, too, Bohme and Swedenborg, and studying Blake for the edition of Blake's prophetic books which he undertook along with Edwin Ellis. His prose works *The Secret Rose* and *The Tables of the Law* present the result of the various mystical speculations in which he had been engaged in the 1890's, while some of the essays in *Ideas of Good and Evil* express the view of poetry which he came to hold as a result. His symbolic system became more elaborate and tied up more definitely with specific figures in Irish mythology and Irish heroic history. Yet the precise significance of these symbolic figures—Hanrahan, Michael Robartes, Aedh, and others—is not always clear; they are used to give pattern and general implication rather than precise denotation to the poems, as is indicated by the fact that Yeats dropped these names from his later revisions of the poems, substituting simply the pronoun "he." Thus the title "Michael Robartes Remembers Forgotten Beauty" becomes in the revision "He Remembers Forgotten Beauty" and similarly "Aedh Mourns for the Loss of Love" is altered to "The Lover Mourns for the

Loss of Love." This change is an important clue to the function of Yeats's symbolic systems, indicating that they were intended to help himself more than the reader, so that once he hed completed the poem the framework could later be removed without loss. Once again we see Yeats's search for order and system, to be imposed on a world without tradition.

Yet the views on symbolism which Yeats had by this time come to hold showed certain confusions, in particular the confusion between mysticism and magic which is one of the qualities that distinguish him from the true mystic. His discussion of magic in *Ideas of Good and Evil* (1901) illustrates his state of mind on these matters:

> I find in my diary of magical events for 1899 that I awoke at 3 A.M. out of a nightmare, and imagined one symbol to prevent its recurrence, and imagined another, a simple geometrical form, which calls up dreams of luxuriant vegetable life, that I might have pleasant dreams. . . . I find another record, though made some time after the event, of having imagined over the head of a person, who was a little of a seer, a combined symbol of elemental air and elemental water. This person, who did not know what symbol I was using, saw a pigeon flying with a lobster in his bill. I find that on December 13, 1898, I used a certain star-shaped symbol with a seeress. . . . She saw a rough stone house, and in the middle of the house the skull of a horse. . . . I know that my examples will awaken in all who have not seen the like, or who are not on other grounds inclined towards my arguments, a most natural incredulity. It was long before I myself would admit an inherent power in symbols. . . . I cannot now think symbols less than the greatest of all powers whether they are used consciously by the masters of magic, or half unconsciously by their successors, the poet, the musician and the artist. . . . The symbols are of all kinds, for everything in heaven or earth has its association, momentous or trivial, in the great memory, and one never knows what forgotten events may have plunged it; like the toadstool and the ragweed, into the great passions.

And he concludes the essay with this appeal:

> Who can keep always to the little pathway between speech and silence, where one meets none but discreet revelations? And surely, at whatever risk, we must cry out that imagination is always seeking to remake the world according to the impulses and the patterns in that great Mind, and that great Memory?

He puts the matter concisely at the beginning of the same essay:

> . . . I believe in three doctrines, which have, as I think, been handed down from early times, and been the foundations of nearly all magical practices. These doctrines are—

(1) That the borders of our minds are ever shifting, and that many minds can flow into one another, as it were, and create or reveal a single mind, a single energy.

(2) That the borders of our memories are as shifting, and that our memories are a part of one great memory, the memory of Nature herself.

(3) That this great mind and great memory can be evoked by symbols.

Yeats clarifies his view further in his essays on "Symbolism in Painting" and "The Symbolism of Poetry" (the first written in 1898, the second in 1900). In the former essay he quotes with approval a German Symbolist who insisted that "Symbolism said things which could not be said so perfectly in any other way, and needed but a right instinct for its understanding; while Allegory said things which could be said as well, or better, in another way, and needed a right knowledge for its understanding." This distinction between symbolism and allegory clarifies some aspects of Yeats's art: it explains his casualness in providing (or not providing) his readers with keys to the esoteric systems on which so much of his symbolic poetry and drama is based. If the symbols fell into the right order and had the right relation to each other, the reader with "a right instinct" would grasp their significance. Precise knowledge was unnecessary.

The importance of arrangement is stressed by Yeats himself more than once, for example in discussing these misquoted lines of Burns—

The white moon is setting beyond the white wave,
And Time is setting with me, O!

These lines Yeats calls "perfectly symbolical" and explains: "Take from them the whiteness of the moon and of the wave, whose relation to the setting of Time is too subtle for the intellect, and you take from them their beauty. But, when all are together, moon and wave and whiteness and setting Time and the last melancholy cry, they evoke an emotion which cannot be evoked by any other arrangement of colours and sounds and forms." According to Yeats, the indefinable yet precise emotions possessed by "all sounds, all colours, all forms" arise either from their "pre-ordained energies" or from "long association." He is not careful to distinguish these sources in practice, and indeed the two are often confused. The emotional value of the names of the old Irish heroes, for example, arises from the nature of the stories in which they figure, from the part they have played in history, mythology, and in previous literature, and no theory of "pre-ordained energies" is necessary to explain it. Yet Yeats seemed at one time to believe that each of these names possessed such a preordained energy, which could be depended on to communicate itself to the reader. However, his theory never quite controlled his practice, and his use of place names and the names of Irish figures in *The Wind among the Reeds* suggests no consistent reliance on these energies.

The poetry of *The Wind among the Reeds* contains some of the most effective of the tenuous symbolic poetry that Yeats wrote. He left behind now for good the lush romantic descriptions of his earliest period, while at the same time the tapestry quality of so many of the poems of *The Rose* has given place to a more fluid kind of verse. This change is not unrelated to the development in Yeats's attitude—his elaboration of a symbolic system and of a theory of symbolism—as he explains himself:

> If people were to accept the theory that poetry moves us because of its symbolism, what change should one look for in the manner of our poetry? A return to the way of our fathers, a casting out of descriptions of nature for the sake of nature, of the moral law for the sake of the moral law, a casting out of all anecdotes and of that brooding over scientific opinion that so often extinguished the central flame in Tennyson, and of that vehemence that would make us do or not do certain things. . . . With this change of substance, this return to imagination, this understanding that the laws of art, which are the hidden laws of the world, can alone bind the imagination, would come a change of style, and we would cast out of serious poetry those energetic rhythms, as of a man running . . . and we would seek out those wavering, meditative, organic rhythms, which are the embodiment of the imagination, that neither desires nor hates, because it has done with time, and only wishes to gaze upon some reality, some beauty.

It might be argued that in all his critical and expository work Yeats was moved by a desire for over-rationalization, that he was seeking to find a rational explanation of ways of writing which he had already come to practice intuitively. There is some truth in this; we find in Yeats constantly the order-seeking intellect glossing and expounding and rationalizing texts which might have more meaning if left to speak for themselves. But this does not mean that we should be justified in ignoring his prose work when discussing his poetry, for his prose does show more explicitly than his poetry the lines along which his mind was moving at the time and thus provides valuable help in an endeavor to explain and interpret his changing attitudes and the relation of these changes to his poetic practice. The eccentricity—and on occasions the plain silliness—of Yeats's thought is sometimes taken as an example of an innate confusion of mind, but the very opposite is the truth. It was his nostalgia for order and system in a world whose orthodox systems had ceased to be able to provide them that led Yeats into these esoteric paths. Of course, there were other reasons too: the fact that he began to develop as a poet in the 1880's and 1890's left a permanent legacy to his poetry that one is tempted to dismiss too lightly in view of the extreme individuality of Yeats's later achievement. But the fact remains that Yeats became an esoteric symbolist for the same reason that Eliot became an Anglican and W. H. Auden a Socialist: each was seeking a solution to the problem presented by a disintegrating tradition.

We find in the poems of *The Wind among the Reeds* the same deep sense of contrast which we have already noted in Yeats's earlier poetry. The Christian is opposed to the pagan, the normal to the supernatural, the passing to the changeless. The opening poem, "The Hosting of the Sidhe," describes the gathering of the fairy folk with a tremendous sense of their difference from humanity and a careful exploitation of proper names:

> *The host is riding from Knocknarea*
> *And over the grave of Clooth-na-Bare;*
> *Caoilte tossing his burning hair,*
> *And Niamh calling* Away, come away:
> Empty your heart of its mortal dream.

In "The Everlasting Voices" we have the contrast between life in time and life outside time, round which the poem is constructed: a similar contrast between the fairy and the human (related to the contrast between the pagan heroic and the Christian) is the basis of "The Unappeasable Host"; while the contrast between the world of human morality and the changeless values of "the mystical brotherhood/Of sun and moon and hollow and wood" is the theme of "Into the Twilight." These are random examples, but they illustrate a feature of Yeats's poetic structure which is one of the most central facts about his art. He continually uses his symbols to express a sense of difference, not of identity, and he does this in innumerable forms, until finally, in his later verse, he finds in the symbol of the winding stair the key to a new attitude and a new kind of expression. This is a point to be stressed, for our interpretation of Yeats's later poetry depends on it.

But the folk strain was still running through Yeats's poetry, curbing his esoteric impulses and producing every now and again a simple, realistic poem which foreshadows what some critics have called his "realistic period," which comes in the middle of his poetic career. "The Song of the Old Mother," for example, is a short, simple, realistic poem describing the hard domestic life of an Irish peasant woman. Theories of symbolism seem to have been forgotten, and all Yeats is doing is etching a picture he remembers having seen. It was fortunate for Yeats that he kept his photographic eye; it was one of the anchors that kept him tied to earth even in his wildest and most fantastic speculations. The recurring ballads and simple descriptive poems in his work show that he never surrendered himself to any single theory of what poetry ought to be.

With *The Wind among the Reeds* what one might call Yeats's first period comes to a close. It is of course silly and unrealistic to draw hard and fast lines between the different phases of a poet's development; all one can say is that from his earliest work to this collection Yeats is working in some modification of the "romantic"tradition of the late nineteenth century, with the influence of Shelley, Blake, and the Pre-Raphaelites clearly noticeable in his poetry. He was not yet clearly distinguishable from any of the other poets of the period who were concerned with beauty, antiquity, and the exploitation of a meditative romantic imagination. With *In the Seven Woods* (1904) we see clearly the transition not only to a new style—that had been seen already—but also to a new poetic ideal. In *The Green Helmet and Other Poems* (1910) that transition is completed and the first great metamorphosis of Yeats is achieved. What that change was and what is meant is worth some inquiry.[1]

[1]Mr. Daiches takes up the nature and meaning of this change in "Yeats, Chapter II," which is extremely relevant and should properly be included here (our inforced practice of including only one chapter from each critic slights also excellent chapters by Mr. Brooks, Mr. Blackmur, and Mr. Ransom).

Arthur Mizener

Never had I more
Excited, passionate, fantastical
Imagination, nor an ear and eye
That more expected the impossible. . . .
—The Tower

THERE SEEMS TO be pretty general agreement among critics that the later poetry of Yeats is superior to the kind he was writing at the turn of the century. But the tendency has been to analyze the difference between the two either in terms of the change in Yeats's style, of the development of what Mr. MacNeice thinks "we might call the neo-classic beauty" of the later poetry, or in terms of the part played in this change by Yeats's commitment to magic and the system set forth in *A Vision*. It seems to me possible that the points aimed at by these analyses can be made clearer if we are willing to recognize that Yeats was, to the end of his career, a poet of the romantic '90's and that the greatness of the later poetry is a kind of greatness inherent in the '90's attitude.

No one, I suppose, will wish to argue that the style of the later poems is not different from the style of the earlier ones, but it is a curious fact that Yeats remained all his life devoted to the idea of Style in the 1890's sense, scoring, as he must have supposed, some of his most telling points off George Moore, for instance, with anecdotes which demonstrated Moore's inability to write like Pater. And late in *Dramatis Personae* he is still talking, with all the lack of historical perspective which characterized the 90's on this point, of "style, as it has been understood from the translators of the Bible to Walter Pater" as distinguished from "a journalistic effectiveness." (*Autobiography*, p. 373.) Yeats's own conception of his later style was that he had cunningly used "occasional prosaic words" because "if we dramatise some possible singer or speaker we remember that he is moved by one thing at a time, certain words must be dull and numb." (*Autobiography*, p. 371.) The achievement of the end suggested by these quotations was, I think, very near the heart of Yeats's astonishing success in the later poems.

"The Romanticism of W. B. Yeats," from *The Southern Review*, VII, 3 (winter, 1942), pp. 601-623.

But that success did not consist in making "something memorable and even sensuous out of ordinary words, austere rhythms and statements bleakly direct" (*The Poetry of W. B. Yeats*, p. 100), or at least this is a distorted account of both the means and their result.

If we are to talk of style in the abstract, as both Yeats and Mr. MacNeice are inclined to, it would be better to say that Yeats, retaining to the end an 1890's conception of style, learned to use for the purpose of style a much larger vocabulary and a number of colloquial—though never either loose or simple—rhythms; that above all he learned to give an impression of the "active man" speaking, to dramatize the speaker of the poem, by a cunning mixture of the "dull and numb" words and the colloquial rhythms with the romantic diction and rhythms of his earlier poetry. But he never sought to write verse that was "journalistically effective," and the result of supposing so is the notion that in Yeats's later poetry there is "an almost Wordsworthian simplicity"—a somewhat curious gloss on "neo-classic beauty." This is a description patently inappropriate to Yeats's great symbolic poems, for these poems are as exotic in their splendor as anything well could be. And it is a description equally if perhaps less obviously inappropriate to the great poems of meditation. I think Yeats would not forgive us for so describing these achievements of what he believed the "calm . . . of ordered passion." Wordsworth was certainly capable of that combination of great dignity and passion which Yeats is aiming at in these poems, but not when he was being "simple." The difference between a poem by the early Yeats and the late Yeats is not the difference between a rhetorical poem and a poem of Wordsworthian simplicity. It is the difference between a poem where rhythm and vocabulary are obvious and conventional, because the poet has deliberately eliminated from it the dramatic and the concrete, and a poem where neither is obvious or conventional—in either the bad or the good sense—because the poet is bent on including both.

What happened to make Yeats's later poetry different from his early poetry was that he came to feel the early poetry unsatisfactory, not because its theme was unsatisfactory, but because its manner of realizing its theme was. He wanted not only to present his theme but to present it in terms of the "real" world; he wanted his poems to be true not only to the dreams where his responsibility began but also to the facts; he wanted, when he wrote, to hold not only justice but reality in a single thought. This is a development rather than a conversion, a technical change rather than a substantial one. And it is the development of something present in Yeats from the start, for he was a very young man on that occasion when he walked down the street eying himself in the shop windows and wondering why his tie did not blow out in the wind as Byron's did in the picture.

The obvious moral of this incident is that Yeats was not satisfied simply to dream the pictures in which his desires were realized; he wanted to realize them in fact. It is, if less obviously, also its moral that the picture he dreamed was always a romantic one and that it never occurred to Yeats to modify it at any point in order that it might conform with the demonstrable habits of the wind. Yeats could not change the habits of the wind, nor could he ever quite bring himself to leave the miraculous intervention to which he was committed in other hands than his own. What he could do was his best always to stand on corners where the wind was most likely to blow to his satisfaction; and he tried hard to believe that the ensuing flutter of tie-ends was the result of the wind's ordinary habits, not the result of his careful selection of corners. As a consequence his poetry and, I suspect, his life were, when the wind came up to snuff, intensely dramatic, if they were also sometimes merely theatrical.

Yeats was, as he knew, a man with a "faint perception of things in their weight and mass" as such, who nevertheless had a desire for the world of these things, the world where men were "almost always partisans, propagandists and gregarious." He therefore sought, as he says in *A Vision* (pp. 142-43) men of his phase must, "simplification by intensity." For he knew himself also one of those who define themselves "mainly through an image of the mind" (p. 127), and he was too much of a romantic ever to believe the task of defining the world of weight and mass could be anything like of equal importance with the definition of self:

I turn away and shut the door, and on the stair
Wonder how many times I could have proved my worth
In something that all others understand or share;
But O! ambitious heart, had such a proof drawn forth
A company of friends, a conscience set at ease,
It had but made us pine the more. The abstract joy,
The half-read wisdom of daemonic images,
Suffice the ageing man as once the growing boy.

Speaking in the *Autobiography* of the early career here referred to Yeats said that he "overrated the quality of anything that could be connected with my general beliefs about the world" (p. 138); and, he might have added, was willing to use almost any ingenuity of interpretation in order to connect what he found moving with these general beliefs. He was, as Rothenstein remarked (*Scattering Branches,* p. 38), "too easily impressed by work which showed a superficial appearance of romance of mysticism." He never wholly conquered this habit; it sufficed the aging man as once the growing boy. It is a result of this fact that Yeats's later poetry never has a consistently representational surface, never represents the shows of things. What it does have is a marvelous concreteness and immediacy which is the result of Yeats's presenting with the maximum specification of sensuous detail a startling variety of objects which were attached, by some more or less obscure implication which Yeats found in them, to his general beliefs; it is here, and here only, that they find their unity and value for Yeats.

The later Yeats, then, desired what he called "reality," that is simplicity, order and concreteness; and in this sense it is true, as Mr. Reed Whittemore has said, that Yeats was a romantic who did not want to be one; not, however, because he wanted to be something different, but because he wanted to be something more. He wanted reality, but only on his own terms, and the main requirement of these terms was that particular version of the romantic objective on which the '90's concentrated: intensity of feeling. In desiring reality only on his own terms, Yeats was of course desiring something he could not get, since this pragmatical, preposterous pig of a world, its farrow that so solid seem, have a certain stubborn independence of the mind's theme, in spite of God-appointed Berkeley, whom Yeats seems to have thought God appointed to prove He does not exist rather than that He does. Imagination, by which he meant emotion, he thought "is always justified by time, thought hardly ever. It can only bring us back to emotion." (*Autobiography,* p. 403.) This devotion to imagination in the sense of emotion, to what the heart says, was for Yeats, as for all romantics, the defining characteristic of the artist. "Since Phase 12," he wrote in *A Vision* (p. 135), "the *Creative Mind* has been so interfused by the *antithetical tincture* that it has more and more confined its contemplation of actual things to those that resemble images of the mind desired by the *Will.* The being has . . .

been more and more the artist."

The 1890's, in their reductio ad absurdum way, were prepared to sacrifice "reality" altogether ("as for living . . .") to the aesthetic expression of the passionate self, for "to maintain this ecstasy is success in life." But Yeats, knowing the lives of Johnson and Wilde, knew that one could not live wholly in the imagination. It was plain from the experience of the '90's that to refine ecstasy to perfection, to a purely aesthetic and contemplative thing, was self-defeating. It was self-defeating because life will have its revenge; it was self-defeating because, since passion and energy were physical things, to have them only in contemplation, or in the ritual of manners and the ancestral houses out of which the "bitter and violent" living had passed, was not to have them.

O what if gardens where the peacock strays
With delicate feet upon old terraces,
Or else all Juno from an urn displays
Before the indifferent garden deities;
O what if levelled lawns and gravelled ways
Where slippered Contemplation finds his ease
And Childhood a delight for every sense,
But take our greatness with our violence?

It was, then, in life, with its bitterness and violence, its fury and mire, and not in the contemplative peace of the imagination, that ecstasy could be realized. In one sense it was an intolerable insult that this should be so, an insult to the doll-gods, the Magi in their stiff painted clothes, the lifeless but beautiful gods of the poet's imagination. For it was in the Great Memory, that conglomeration of all that men with high imaginations like Yeats's had dreamed, that ecstasy was perfectly conceived, and to such, mere human love was "A noisy and filthy thing." Always Yeats found it "a poor and crazy thing that we who have imagined so many noble persons cannot bring our flesh to heel." (*Autobiography*, p. 37.) On the other hand, it was precisely in what was temporal and evanescent, in the unaesthetic mess of physical life, that ecstasy had its realized being.

It was thus that Yeats came to think of life as at once a horror and a glory:

Why must those holy, haughty feet descend
From emblematic niches and what hand

Ran that delicate raddle through their white?
My heart is broken, yet must understand.
What do they seek for? Why must they descend?
For desecration and the lover's night.

It was thus that he came to dream of a paradise where ecstacy could disdain ("distain," as Yeats first wrote it, free itself from the stain of and so be free to scorn)

All that man is,
All mere complexities,
The fury and the mire of human veins. . . .

Here ecstasy would achieve perfection and permanence of simplicity and intensity, though at the terrible cost of not being able really to burn at all:

Where blood-begotten spirits come
And all complexities of fury leave,
Dying into a dance,
An agony of trance,
An agony of flame that cannot singe a sleeve.

In such a paradise one could burn with this hard gem-like flame, could maintain this ecstasy, eternally; here "religious, aesthetic and practical life were one" and "the strain one upon another of opposites," the conflict of desires for the subjective and objective lives, was resolved. Yet Yeats so loved the flame that can singe a sleeve, that all his poems which describe this paradise are prayers that he may be relieved of that love:

O sages standing in God's holy fire . . .
Consume my heart away; sick with desire
And fastened to a dying animal
It knows not what it is. . . .

For all his conviction that

He who can read the signs nor sink unmanned . . .
Has but one comfort left: all triumph would
But break upon his ghostly solitude;

for all this conviction, he could not forget the ecstasy of the heart:

But is there any comfort to be found?
Man is in love and loves what vanishes,
What more is there to say?

Sometimes, for a moment, Yeats was able to visualize a romanticized version of some actual life which approached what he wanted. This privately mythologized version of actuality he could give his heart to because it seemed actually to realize his heart's desire, a life of that "calm which is . . . an ordered passion." "Yet is not ecstasy," he wrote, speaking of the proper end of tragedy, "some fulfillment of the soul in itself, some slow or sudden expansion of it like an overflowing well? Is not this what is meant by beauty?" (*Autobiography,* p. 402.) And precisely this same metaphor he applied, conditionally, to the life of the Irish gentry:

Surely among a rich man's flowering lawns,
Amid the rustle of his planted hills,
Life overflows without ambitious pains,
And rains down life until the basin spills,
And mounts more dizzy high the more it rains
As though to choose whatever shape it wills
And never stoop to a mechanical
Or servile shape, at others' beck and call.

But the mood of romantic irony follows quickly upon this always.

So long as Yeats had remained in the strict sense a poet of the '90's he had been able to rely on that vague, traditional order which the conventional romantic metaphors and symbols had acquired through constant use, and this was adequate for his purposes. But when he began to draw for symbols and metaphors not merely on the supply of conventional ones but also on the world of his personal and felt experience, he lost even that minimum support. It is clear enough when the moon, rather vaguely, symbolizes emotion, dreams, imagination; we are all at home with such a symbol because it is held down by the many previous contexts which constitute its traditional meaning. But when Yeats tells us by the use of this symbol the familiar story of how the romantic imagination scorns the limitations and complexities of ordinary life, we are likely to be in difficulties. For instead of using the traditional impedimenta of the moon, he entirely re-equips her with such startling armor as the domes of St.

Sophia and, by adducing starlight, adds, to his own satisfaction at least, that the lowest state of being, the state of "complete Plasticity," shares with the high state of pure imagination, the state of "complete Beauty," this scorn.

> *A starlit or a moonlit dome disdains*
> *All that man is,*
> *All mere complexities,*
> *The fury and the mire of human veins.*

Yeats realized this difficulty quite clearly himself. "It is not," he said, "so much that I choose too many elements, as that the possible unities themselves seem without number." (*Autobiography*, p. 319.) It was his hope that *A Vision* would remedy this situation.

So far as it goes to provide enough logical content to give his poems that amount of "thought" required by the romantic poem, *A Vision* is perfectly satisfactory. But this is a much smaller achievement than Yeats aimed at. Always Yeats's primary concern with an account of the world, an experience or a story, was that it should satisfy what he called the imagination, his feelings. But always also a part of him desired to believe that what did so satisfy him was not only satisfactory to the imagination, but true in fact, that it belonged not only to the soul but to history. So he sought to produce in *A Vision* "a system of thought that would leave my imagination free to create as it chose and yet make all it created, or could create, part of one history, and that the soul's." Without doing violence in any way to what his heart felt to be right and just, he was going to produce an account of the phenomenal world which would be systematic and inclusive. By this means he would make it possible for himself "to hold reality and justice in a single thought," for "he has best imagined reality who has best imagined justice." This is a large order; it requires that observation, analysis and feeling shall be unified, not with due respect for all, but by an absolute subordination of observation and analysis to feeling. This is the same Yeats who had such trouble with his tie, still quite unrepentant, "Still," as Matthew Arnold wrote of the romantics,

> *bent to make some port he knows not where,*
> *Still standing for some false, impossible shore.*

For Yeats, though he refused to restrain its freedom to bulge in whatever direction it would, still hoped that his "hands" might have the power to

> *Bring the balloon of the mind*
> *That bellies and drags in the wind*
> *Into its narrow shed.*

A Vision inevitably disappoints this hope, and I think Yeats knew it did.

> Finally I asked: "What then is your solution for these ills?" Dropping his hand, which was never still, the brown hand with the symbolic ring, upon his knee, in a gesture which to me revealed his moods of despair, he replied: "O my dear, I have no solution, none," [*Letters to Dorothy Wellesley*, p. 196]

At a sufficient remove of generalization it was of course possible to state the pattern of Yeats's feelings, for those feelings responded most positively to whatever seemed to represent life lived for ecstasy, and most negatively to what seemed to represent life lived merely for practical ends, the life of submission not to the "sense of glory" but to the facts. This was the pattern Yeats felt in his own life and it was the pattern his imagination sought to impose on all life. Men and history would satisfy his sense of justice only if it could be made true that they were in reality instances of this conflict between the desire to live the subjective life or—as Yeats (who did not love the "dull and numb words") liked to call it—the *antithetical* life, and the desire to live the objective or *primary* life.

But Yeats does not appear to have been able—and certainly did not choose—to develop, by a process of strict definition and consistent logical elaboration, this initial insight into a complete and self-contained system of thought. "I had never put the conflict in logical form, never thought with Hegel that the two ends of the see-saw are one another's negation, nor that the spring vegetables were refuted when over." (*A Vision*, pp. 72-73.) Yeats has his right, of course, to disagree with Hegel, though it is a little ironic to remember that Hegel, in principle if not always in practice, agreed with Yeats that a contrary was not a contradictory and that negation is a refutation of a thing only in so far as that thing claims a false absoluteness. But surely this is a curious confession for one who is producing a "system of thought." Whether reality is logical or not (and it is hard not to feel that Yeats denied it was only because he did not realize the full possibilities of logic), a system of thought must be, if it is to be a system at all. Nor was Yeats, with a lifetime's cultivation of the habit of treating the observable world selectively and of getting hold of such objects as he grasped by the most convenient handle, able to make a systematic examination of men and history in terms of this insight.

What *A Vision* does is to set up this insight as a general framework and to improvise around it the consequences which Yeats "felt" must follow, that is, which he connected to it by the rather vague use of one or another of the possible ways of looking at things, of the "possible unities . . . without number" which he was so unhappily—from the point of view of system—aware of. He strove to give these improvisations the authority which they could not gain from logic by claiming they were revelation, though he was shrewd enough—or *antithetical* enough—to make it part of his theory that revelation was really the "playing back" to us, as it were, of our communal dreams, "that the communicators are the personalities of a dream shared by my wife, by myself, occasionally by others." (*A Vision*, pp. 22-23—Yeats qualifies this belief somewhat to the advantage of the supernatural.) Which is after all only to elevate to the status of dogma a familiar enough romantic fancy which must, I suppose, go back to the influence on nineteenth-century thought of the anthropological theory that the gods are merely the projections of man's hopes and fears.

Such a "system" does not give us much help toward finding for Yeats's poems what Mr. Winters would call "a paraphrasable content" of any great precision, and in so far as Yeats longed to write poems like Dante's ("We can [those hard symbolic bones under the skin] substitute for a treatise on logic the Divine Comedy."), he failed. For behind the *Divine Comedy* is a logical, self-contained system of thought which accounts completely for the observable world. Dante, by disciplining his feelings until they felt the world to be arranged exactly as it was by this system, could describe the world he saw as it was, and feel the justice of its being so; he could describe the world his age knew literally and yet find that world allegorically and analogically explicable at every point. But what is under the skin of Yeats's poems is at best gristle. They realize with immense eloquence and concreteness Yeats's rather specialized kind of justice, the 1890's vision of a ritually ordered life of ecstatic joy, and its contrary. But they achieve their concreteness by an eclectic and sometimes anarchic interpretation of "reality," which it is impossible to systematize. In so far, then, as Yeats was trying to produce a *Summa* in *A Vision,* he failed. From this point of view it is a ha'penny worth of bread for the mind to live by to an intolerable deal of sack of the very best quality.

For if it was the unachievable secondary need of Yeats's temperament to produce a completely logical poetry like Dante's, it is not necessary to our admiration for him that we should claim he did so. *A Vision* gives us a general notion of what Yeats's major symbols mean, which is probably as precise an intellectual content as they had for Yeats himself. And this is a great help, for it is hardly to be expected that one man, however visionary, will produce a revelation universally recognizable and wholly without its private eccentricities. And Yeats was in fact a mystic only in so far as any lifelong romantic is. Wordsworth, Keats and Tennyson, none of whom appears to have been a congenital mystic, had similar visions, though they did not insist on the absolute authority of these visions, did not

> . . . *mock Plotinus' thought*
> *And cry in Plato's teeth,*
> *Death and life were not*
> *Till man made up the whole,*
> *Made lock, stock and barrel*
> *Out of his bitter soul. . . .*

For these early romantics had not yet had completely destroyed in them their ability to believe that something beside their own imaginations had made the universe, nor were they so hard pressed by the complete unwillingness of the scientific thought of their day to lend itself to their purposes. It may even, indeed, be that they were somewhat better advised than Yeats of the difficulties of solipsism, out of which Yeats was constantly struggling, only to slip back again at the thought that he might be depriving the mind of some of its freedom to change its theme. Beyond this, *A Vision* gives sometimes very moving and always, in their '90's way, rhetorically very distinguished displays of that clustering of emotive images around a tenuous "paraphrasable content" which is characteristic of Yeats's poetry.

I am acutely conscious that this view of Yeats's poetry,

and especially of *A Vision* which is the crux of the disagreement, puts me at odds with a number of critics whose general position seems to me true. Mr. Cleanth Brooks, for example, who has written brilliantly about Yeats, has remarked that "the section on history in *A Vision* includes the finest rhythmic prose written in English since that of Sir Thomas Browne." It is certainly very beautiful prose, for Yeats was, by the time he came to write *A Vision*, a master of his particular kind of rhetoric:

> We say of Him because His sacrifice was voluntary that He was love itself, and yet that part of Him which made Christendom was not love but pity, and not pity for intellectual despair, though the man in Him, being *antithetical* like His age, knew it in the Garden, but *primary* pity, that for the common lot, man's death, seeing that He raised Lazarus, sickness, seeing that He healed many, sin, seeing that He died. [p. 275]

The coupling of this prose with Browne's is an instance of Mr. Brooks's general argument that at a certain point "symbolist poetry coalesces with metaphysical." This is a point, not in the development of the two kinds, but in our understanding of them; we see that both kinds have "imaginative unity" and that the difference in their methods is merely "a distinction of strategy." But Mr. Brooks is as aware as any of us that differences in strategy produce differences in the kind and value of the imaginative unity and this coupling of Browne and Yeats must be intended to suggest not only a similarity of value in their achievements but also a similarity of intention and method in the two writers. This suggestion is reinforced by Mr. Brooks's comparison of Yeats to Donne and his discovery of "the syllogistic framework which characterizes so much of metaphysical poetry" in Yeats's poems. It seems to me a misleading suggestion.

Browne's prose is the product of a multiple commitment on his part to several worlds, the world of science, the world of Christianity, the world of pagan mythology, the world of history. Its wit is a metaphysical wit, an attempt to juggle these worlds, to keep them all afloat in the air of his discourse at once, not because Browne is trying to explain them all in terms of one world to which he is finally committed but for the very reason, as Mr. Willey says, of his "not being *finally committed* to any one world":

> But in this latter Scene of time we cannot expect such Mummies unto our memories, when ambition may fear the Prophecy of *Elias,* and *Charles* the fifth hope to live within two *Methuselas* of *Hector.*

There is not, as Mr. Willey also says, any effort at quaintness or Beauty behind this; it is simply the result of Browne's complex honesty. But in the Yeats passage there is a striving for Beauty. It was written by a man to whom it never occurred that the translators of the Bible and the rest of the seventeenth century did not have the same self-conscious conception of style as Pater. Yeats, by the skillful rhetorical manipulation of the profoundly resonant Christian material, has given his passage an emotional tension which it has no right to; for Yeats was no Christian. He is using the emotional appeal of this material, with great skill, as Pater used similar material in *Marius,* aesthetically. The Yeats passage is, in other words, an example of a procedure very like what Mr. Winters calls "pseudo-reference by transference of values." For Yeats was committed to one world, a very tenuous world, which was given an air of substantiality by the accretion to it of selected items from many other worlds, items which were then presented as movingly as Christ here is. The logic of Yeats's own position can, then, justify this very moving description of Christ only in the most tenuous way, and the description is therefore what I suppose Mr. Brooks would call "sentimental," a word which carries an unhappy burden of pejorative implications. But it is hard to find a word for Yeats's procedure which does not, for our day, carry such a burden, since we are today almost pathologically sensitive about our romanticism, as up-to-date critics must, in Wordsworth's day, have been about their neo-classicism.

Mr. Brooks's whole treatment of Yeats seems to me to be devised to free him from the horrid charge of being a romantic. It was a charge Yeats himself was prepared to endure:

We were the last romantics—chose for theme
Traditional sanctity and loveliness. . . .

It is, it seems to me, because he cannot endure this charge that Mr. Brooks argues of Yeats's verse, as he has suggested is the case with Yeats's prose, that its symbols are not vague, but rather rich and complex. But his attempt to demonstrate their complexity consists mainly in adducing a series of similarly symbolic passages from Yeats's prose which parallel but do not elucidate the poetry.

I would, if I can, meet Mr. Brooks upon this honestly. No one is more anxious than I am to assert the emotive richness and complexity of Yeats's poetry. It seems to me precisely in this quarter that his greatness lies, that here he leaves Tennyson and Swinburne, to say nothing of Rossetti and Dowson, nowhere. But this is not the kind of richness and complexity I take Mr. Brooks to be claiming for Yeats, for he is not quite prepared to admit that Yeats's poetry achieves its richness of what Mr. Tate has called "intension" by a very considerable sacrifice of "extension," of coherence of thought. Mr. Brooks outlines the "syllogistic framework" of "Sailing to Byzantium" as follows:

His country is a land of natural beauty, beauty of the body. But his own body is old. The soul must, therefore, sing the louder to compensate for the old and dying flesh. . . . But there is no singing school for the soul except in studying the works of the soul. "And therefore" he has sailed to Byzantium, for the artists of Byzantium do not follow the forms of nature but intellectual forms, ideal patterns. He appeals to them to

Consume my heart away; sick wtih desire
And fastened to a dying animal

and by severing him from the dying world of a body, to gather him into what is at least "the artifice of eternity."

This seems to me unexceptionable as a general paraphrase, save for the ease with which Mr. Brooks gets himself past the point in the poem where, by a species of overlap dissolve, Yeats's appeal to the invoked artisans of Byzantium, those "philosophic workers in mosaic," becomes an appeal to "sages standing in God's holy fire" who are surely something different from Byzantine artisans, however true Yeats's claim that to these the supernatural descended nearer than to Plotinus. This is a characteristic trick of Yeats; it seems to me to show a rare disregard for the substantial reality of Byzantium, even granting that Yeats's conception of historical Byzantium is true in every respect.

But the full acceptance of Mr. Brooks's outline of the poem's "syllogistic framework" leaves us still with many doubts. In what sense of singing is it that the singing of the soul will compensate—I do not say compensate adequately, but compensate in any sense—for the failure of the flesh? It does not seem to me that the terms here are coordinate. Nor do we know, either from the poem or from external sources, precisely what Yeats means by soul, as we would in the case of a metaphysical poet; it is not a term that is defined in *A Vision,* though in general it is clear enough that *soul, heart,* and *imagination* are for Yeats roughly synonymous. And is there anything but an 1890's prejudice to make it necessary that the forms of eternity, "the works of the soul," should be artifacts? Would not one logically expect them to be songs, since Yeats seems to have committed himself to the notion that singing is the compensatory activity of the soul? I do not raise these questions as objections to Yeats's poem, but as objections to Mr. Brooks's claim that it has the same kind of syllogistic framework to be found in certain metaphysical poems.

I feel reasonably sure, in any event, that Mr. Brooks would not claim that this syllogistic framework, this "extensive" dimension of the poem, extends into every detail of it as is the case with a metaphysical poem. Yeats was very clever in his handling of detail and it is a cleverness which I admire and find satisfactory, but it is not a kind of cleverness which satisfies the claims Mr. Brooks, if I understand him, is making for it. For instance, Yeats begins by referring in the first stanza to himself, with an ironic glance at the fact that his own love of "that sensual music" notoriously endured unimpaired into his old age, as a "Monument of unageing intellect." In the next stanza, having announced the necessity for the soul to clap its hands and sing more and more loudly, he adds

Nor is there singing school but studying
Monuments of its own magnificence.

He wants "singing *school*" because he thinks of the symbolic Byzantium as a place where one studies earnestly to learn the hard lesson of the delight of a completely non-sensual life. But he also must have *monument,* because he is determined to transcend the previous stanza's irony at the expense of the non-sensual life of the soul, and he wants therefore to parallel the contrasting references to this life as sharply as possible. The result is, however, to put a considerable strain on the syntax at this point, since the purpose of monuments in singing schools is not at once evident. Yeats does not mean that there are no singing schools but only schools of sculpture, for that would make nonsense of his claim that old men must study singing; *monuments* must here, then, be taken "as great previous masterpieces of song." Nevertheless, one must somehow think of these masterpieces as monuments in the next stanza, and indeed, as music frozen into a Byzantine mosaic from which Yeats for a moment asks us to fancy the figures stepping to serve as his singing masters, as he believed the spirits might truly step from God's holy fire into the world of time and serve as the masters who would teach him how to live the life of the soul. This is a version of the romantic fancy that the characters of great writers have a kind of independent existence and may be appealed to, though it seems perhaps more puzzling because the Byzantine mosaic is less familiar than Shakespeare's plays. (Compare Mrs. Jameson's *The Girlhood of Shakespeare's Heroines* and de la Mare's *Characters from Shakespeare*, for example.)

If these figures from the mosaic are successful, they will in effect gather Yeats into the artifice of which they are a part, into the mosaic, the monument. The advantage of the echo of *monument* in *artifice* is its suggestion of permanence ("Not marble nor the gilded monuments. . . ."). But Yeats cannot afford the word *monument* here, because he is about to shift back to the soul's singing in the next stanza, where he says he will take the artificial form of a bird "Of hammered gold and gold enamelling" ("Miracle bird or golden handiwork"). This will be "monumental" in its permanence, it will be an eternal artifice, but it will scarcely be a monument. This artificial bird will then sing, which is to say the poet will have learned to enjoy the eternal life of pure imagination. The bird here, according to Yeats's note, is the result of his having "read somewhere that in the Emperor's palace at Byzantium was a tree made of gold and silver, and artificial birds that sang." This may be the source of the whole idea of representing the eternal life of the soul as a life of song, though I suspect the idea really derives from Yeats's feeling that his poet's imagination, out of which he wrote his songs, was his immortal soul. Yeats is, in any event, adding the '90's admiration for artifice to the traditional romantic symbol of the bird as the "blithe spirit." And it is the singing of this artificial skylark that determines Yeats's description of the physical life as "sensual *music*" and, with the not inconsiderable help of "birds in the trees," leads him to describe "The young/In one another's arms" as "at their song." This is a considerable triumph, for Yeats was always anxious to equate the ecstasy of the soul, of the lover and of the poet. This is a sufficiently romantic idea, as Theseus was happy to observe with such amusement:

The lunatic, the lover, and the poet
Are of imagination all compact,

an account of the matter to which Yeats, if allowed to take the word *lunatic* quite literally, would have been able to assent with perfect seriousness. Indeed, in Yeats's hands, the idea is usually given an almost pure '90's cast. "The Muses," he wrote in *A Vision* (p. 24), "resemble women who creep out at night and give themselves to unknown sailors and return to talk of Chinese porcelain." And the figure is such pure Beardsley Period that one half suspects it of coming from some parody like *The Green Carnation* or Mr. Eliot's "Portrait of a Lady."

But wherever the idea of representing the life of the soul as a life of song comes from, it is certainly these artificial birds which cause the birds in the trees to turn up in the first stanza. Having turned up there, they seem to have reminded Yeats of the "fish, flesh or fowl" of the popular saying, and he appropriated this triad as a convenient temporary shorthand description of the sensual life and as a consequence produced the magnificent though not altogether relevant line about fish (it is salmon, not salmon-falls, which are relevant here). In all this Yeats's near-sightedness and his lack of interest in external nature, which as Dorothy Wellesley observed, "was almost an obsession," must have helped him; it was what gave that fine, clear but remote quality to the whole description of sensual life. And the "fish, flesh or fowl" bred other triads: "Whatever is begotten, born, and dies," "Of what is past, or passing, or to come."

This kind of construction, which is not, I take it, the kind Mr. Brooks calls metaphysical, is the kind Yeats used in all his great poetry, whether of the more concentratedly symbolic kind which "Sailing to Byzantium" represents or of the meditative kind. It is obviously impossible for me to try to demonstrate this contention at length, but the last stanza of "Among School Children" may serve as an example of the method at work in a meditative poem.

Labour is blossoming or dancing where
The body is not bruised to pleasure soul,
Nor beauty born out of its own despair,
Nor blear-eyed wisdom out of midnight oil.
O chestnut tree, great rooted blossomer,
Are you the leaf, the blossom or the bole?
O body swayed to music, O brightening glance,
How can we know the dancer from the dance?

Just before this stanza Yeats invokes the "Presences/That passion, piety or affection knows," those Presences which are born of his own passionate recollection of Maud Gonne, the pious faith of the nuns, and a mother's affectionate reverie. But these Presences, though they symbolize all heavenly glory, also break our hearts, they are "self-born mockers of man's enterprise."

In the stanza in question Yeats sets up two metaphors to describe what that "labour," which is both an enterprise and a birth, would be like were it wholly satisfactory. The first of these is the chestnut tree, an example of beauty and dignity and (I suppose) "the wisdom of nature"; the second is dancing, a highly artificial formalization of the human and physical life. In both these cases the soul's end is achieved without injuring the body, as the Maud Gonne and the Yeats of stanza IV had; without the despair the child of stanza V knows; without the blearing of eyes from midnight oil that Plato, Aristotle, Plotinus and Yeats come to in stanza VI. And this is the case with nature at its best and with perfect art because in both, as is not the case with humanity, the conception and the instrument are one, the end and the means are inseparable, and it is impossible to say whether the chestnut tree is "the leaf, the blossom or the bole," as it is impossible to "know the dancer from the dance."

But as always with poetry which uses Yeats's method, it is impossible to say precisely what some of the lovely, concrete, sensuous details of the stanza mean in terms of this "syllogistic framework." The reader will observe these for himself, and I notice only one or two. It is necessary to remember the Yeats of stanza IV, with his "pretty plumage," to understand how the child of stanza V is an example of "beauty born out of its own despair." This is forcing things pretty hard, though it may be thought enough to make the "shape," as Yeats calls it, on the mother's lap what it is not otherwise likely to appear, a notable example of beauty. It is the blossoming of the chestnut tree which Yeats thinks of as its achievement of the dreamed-of end, but blossoming can hardly be thought of as an ideal pattern which the Mask holds before the chestnut tree's mind as an end, as the dance is held before the dancer's. Nor, if the dancer is the perfect instrument, indistinguishable in its perfection from its ideal object, the dance, ought we to hear about both the leaf and the bole—unless we are also to hear about the arms and legs of the dancer. What we do hear of, and it is quite perfect of its kind, is rather the "body swayed to music" and the "brightening glance"; the first of these corresponds to the bole and the second to what must, I think, be thought of as the sun-drenched leaves of the tree. This is very effective in its way, but the bole is not related to the blossoming as the body is to the dance, and this is equally true of the leaf and the glance, which are, in addition, not strictly relevant to the poem's "syllogistic framework." These do not exhaust the instances in this stanza where details are chosen primarily for their emotive force and then fitted to the argument by a series of inconsistent but cunning devices, but they may serve to indicate how typical of Yeats's method this stanza is.

That Yeats limited himself to this at once narrow and highly eclectic, though very powerful version of reality, in order that reality might be meaningful to him, is the result, I think, of his belonging to the tradition of nineteenth-century romanticism. Romantic poetry in general has not required such a limitation. A romantic poet like Shakespeare, for example, could accept completely the life which submits to practical necessity, however intensely conscious he was of its conflict with the life of the imagination which insists always on the insignificance of practical necessity. Yeats's opinion of Shakespeare, whom he found it hard to approve of, is revealing:

> Shakespeare's people make all things serve their passion, and that passion is for the moment the whole energy of their being—birds, beasts, men, women, landscape, society, are but symbols, and metaphors, nothing is studied in itself, the mind is a dark well, no surface, depth only. [*Autobiography*, p. 248.]

This is to recognize only that aspect of Shakespeare's mind which Yeats could agree with, though he partly conceals this fact by his bland assumption that some of Shakespeare's people are the same thing as Shakespeare. But Hamlet and Lear are no more representative of Shakespeare than Bolingbroke and Touchstone; nor are all of them together Shakespeare. But it is true that Shakespeare the playwright also mythologizes the objects in his plays. It is not true, however, that in doing so he ignores the way they were believed in his day in fact to act, that he fails to study them "in themselves." Shakespeare's plays have surface as well as depth because he not only submitted the shows of things to the desires of the mind but also submitted the desires of the mind to the shows of things. Yeats, however, hated character, the practical virtues, and loved personality, the insistence, in the teeth of the evidence, that things are as the mind desires them. He was, in his approach to experience, "like some man, who serves a woman all his life without asking whether she be good or bad, wise or foolish." (*Autobiography*, p. 185.)

Precisely as Pater—both More and Mr. Eliot have demonstrated this—is nearer to Arnold than to Sir Thomas Browne, and nearer than Arnold would have been happy to believe possible, so Yeats is nearer to Browning than to Shakespeare, and assuredly nearer than Browning would have enjoyed having him. Beneath the Christian terminology of Browning's poetry lies a conception of things which is the ancestor of Yeats's. Browning too thought the supernatural was made up of man's dreams and aspirations eternally preserved:

All we have willed or hoped or dreamed of good shall exist;
Not its semblance, but itself; no beauty, nor good, nor power
Whose voice has gone forth, but each survives for the melodist
When eternity affirms the conception of an hour.

But Browning had, like Yeats, a hard time believing that "not its semblance, but itself" could exist in a supersensual heaven, and was half inclined to think that those in heaven sometimes envied those on earth:

By passion and thought upborne,
One smiles to one's self—"They fare
Scarce better, they need not scorn
Our sea, who live in the air!"

So Browning's heaven, too, yearns down toward the gong-tormented sea of temporal life, for all its limitations. For Browning, like Yeats, tended to think of the good as passionate and violent ("The Statue and the Bust") and, at its most perfect, as a work of art, the passionate moment become artifice: "We substitute, in a fashion,/For heaven—poetry." As Abt Vogler builds his marvelous, momentary, improvised structure of music, therefore,

. . . the emulous heaven yearned down, made effort to reach the earth,
As the earth had done her best, in my passion, to scale the sky.

And for a moment Abt Vogler finds himself in Byzantium:

For earth had attained to heaven, there was no more near nor far.
Nay more; for there wanted not who walked in the glare and glow, Presences plain in the place . . .

. . . the wonderful Dead who have passed through the
body and gone,
But were back once more to breathe in an old world
worth their new:
What never had been, was now; what was, as it shall
be anon;
And what is,—shall I say, matched both? for I was
made perfect too.

The later poetry of Yeats is far finer than the poetry he wrote for the '90's, and it is finer because in it he sought to shape life to his heart's desire not merely in fancy but in fact. But it remains the poetry of a man committed to the heart's desire, a romantic poetry. As such it is at once colloquial and orotund, straightforward and full of astounding, "irrelevant" implications. As such it is full of enthusiastic and crotchety extremes which are forever on the verge of destroying its coherence or statement or its unity of style. It knows neither decorum of idea ("For love has pitched its mansion in/The place of excrement") nor decorum of vocabulary ("perne in a gyre"). This is not the logical, decorous, "neo-classical" poetry so many of Yeats's critics appear to be trying to make it out, and it is not because it rests on that conviction which Hulme the neo-classicist was at such pains to deny: that the divine is life at its intensest. Mr. Winters's low opinion of it is a perfectly logical judgment from his point of view, and I do not see how we are to dissent from his account of Yeats's procedure, however much we may disagree with his evaluation of its results. The poetry of *The Tower* is not harder and drier and more logical than the poetry of *The Rose;* it is only more concrete, more skillful in rhetoric, and more crowded with what Yeats found solid in life. For he might have been speaking of himself when he wrote of the Irish story-teller:

His art, too, is often at its greatest when it is most extravagant, for he only feels himself among solid things, among things with fixed laws and satisfying purposes, when he has reshaped the world according to his heart's desire. He understands as well as Blake that the ruins of time build mansions in eternity [*Cuchlain in Muirthemne,* p. xiii].

F. R. Leavis

An account of Mr. Yeats's beginnings is an account of the poetical situation in the 'eighties and 'nineties. "I had learned to think," he tells us in *Essays,* "in the midst of the last phase of Pre-Raphaelitism." And he describes his hostility to the later fashions in painting that his father favoured: "I had seen the change coming bit by bit and its defence elaborated by young men fresh from the Paris art schools. 'We must paint what is in front of us,' or 'A man must be of his own time,' they would say, and if I spoke of Blake or Rossetti they would point out his bad drawing and tell me to admire Carolus Duran and Bastien-Lepage." But Mr. Yeats knew differently: "In my heart I thought that only beautiful things should be painted, and that only ancient things and the stuff of dreams were beautiful."

He had made *Prometheus Unbound* his "sacred book," and had begun to write poetry in imitation of Shelley and Spenser, whose styles he had "tried to mix together" in a pastoral play. His father introduced him to *The Earthly Paradise* and he came to know William Morris personally, and found him a congenial spirit. When he became one of the Rhymers' Club along with Johnson, Dowson and the rest he readily adopted the current accent and idiom: "Johnson's phrase that life is ritual expressed something that was in all our thoughts." They had their high-priest—"If Rossetti was a subconscious influence, and perhaps the most powerful of all, we looked consciously to Pater for our philosophy"—and no one exceeded Mr. Yeats in devotion. His early prose is sometimes comic in its earnestness of discipleship, in its unctuously cadenced concern for "the transmutation of art into life":

> . . . tapestry, full of the blue and bronze of peacocks, fell over the doors, and shut out all history and activity untouched with beauty and peace; and now when I looked at my Crevelli and pondered on the rose in the hand of the Virgin, wherein the form was so delicate and precise that it seemed more like a thought than a flower, or my Francesca, so full of ghostly astonishment, I knew a Christian's ecstasy without his slavery to rule and custom. . . . I had gathered about me all gods because I believed in none, and experienced every pleasure because I gave myself to none, but held myself apart, individual, indissoluble, a mirror of polished steel.

From *New Bearings in English Poetry,* pp. 27-50. Chatto and Windus, London, 1932.

Yet if, dutifully, he "noted also many poets and prose-writers of every age, but only those who were a little weary of life, as indeed the greatest have been everywhere," there is a recurrent theme, a recurrnt tone, as, for instance, in his reference to "simpler days before men's minds, subtilised and complicated by the romantic movement in art and literature, began to tremble on the verge of some unimagined revelation," that betrays later influences than Pater's. Pater modulates into the pronounced esotericism indicated by the title, *Rosa Alchemica;* an esotericism that was among the things brought back by Arthur Symons from Paris. The title Yeats gives to his autobiography over these years, *The Trembling of the Veil,* comes from Mallarme, "while," he tells us, "Villiers de L'Isle Adam had shaped whatever in my *Rosa Alchemica* Pater had not shaped." It is difficult for us to-day to regard *The Symbolist Movement in Art and Literature* as a work of great importance, but it was such to Yeats and his contemporaries, and this fact, together with the Continental developments that the book offers to reflect, may serve to remind us that the Victorian poetic tradition was not merely a poetic tradition, but a response to the general characteristics of the age.

"I am very religious," says Mr. Yeats in his *Autobiographies,* and "deprived by Huxley and Tyndall, whom I detested, of the simple-minded religion of my childhood, I had made a new religion, almost an infallible church of poetic tradition, of a fardel of stories, and of personages, and of emotions, inseparable from their first expression, passed on from generation to generation by poets and painters with some help from philosophers and theologians. I wished for a world where I could discover this tradition perpetually . . . I had even created a dogma: 'Because those imaginary people are created out of the deepest instinct of man, to be his measure and his norm, whatever I can imagine those mouths speaking may be the nearest I can go to truth.'" He hated Victorian science, he tells us, with a "monkish hate," and with it he associated the Victorian world. Of *A Doll's House* he says characteristically: "I hated the play; what was it but Carolus Duran, Bastien-Lepage, Huxley and Tyndall all over again; I resented being invited to admire dialogue so close to modern educated speech that music and style were impossible." Modern thought and the modern world, being inimical to the hopes of the heart and the delight of the senses and the imagination, are repudiated in the name of poetry—and of life.

This last clause, or the emphasis due to it, distinguishes him from the other Victorian romantics, distinguishes him too from his fellow esoterics. He may quote as epigraph to *The Secret Rose* Villiers de L'Isle Adam's "As for living, our servants will do that for us"; but there is about his contemplated withdrawal a naively romantic, whole-hearted practical energy that reminds us more of Shelley than of Rossetti or Pater. "I planned a mystical Order," he tells us in *Autobiographies*, "which should buy or hire the castle, and keep it as a place where its members could retire for a while from the world, and where we might establish mysteries like those of Eleusis and Samothrace; and for ten years to come my most impassioned thought was a vain attempt to find philosophy and create ritual for that Order. I had an unshakable conviction, arising how or whence I cannot tell, that invisible gates would open as they opened for Blake, as they opened for Swedenborg, as they opened for Boehme, and that this philosophy would find its manuals of devotion in all imaginative literature, and set before Irishmen for special manual an Irish literature which, though made by many minds, would seem the work of a single mind, and turn our places of beauty or legendary association into holy symbols." It is not for nothing that the *Prometheus Unbound* had been his sacred book. And the latter part of this passage has another significance: Mr. Yeats was an Irishman.

But I anticipate: it is at his poetry that we should be looking by now; it is only as they arise directly out of his poetry that the considerations I have touched on in the last paragraph matter. His early verse bears out what he tells us of his beginnings. William Morris could say with truth, "You write my sort of poetry." This (but for the last two lines, which suggest Tom Moore) Morris himself might have written:

Autumn is over the long leaves that love us,
And over the mice in the barley sheaves;
Yellow the leaves of the rowan above us,
And yellow the wet wild-strawberry leaves.

The hour of the waning of love has beset us,
And weary and worn are our sad souls now;
Let us part, ere the season of passion forget us,
With a kiss and a tear on thy drooping brow.

And Tennyson is behind this (though it could hardly be mistaken for Tennyson):

"Your eyes that once were never weary of mine
Are bowed in sorrow under pendulous lids,
Because our love is waning."
And then she:
Although our love is waning, let us stand
By the lone border of the lake once more,
Together in that hour of gentleness
When the poor tired child, Passion, falls asleep:
How far away the stars seem, and how far
Is our first kiss, and ah, how old my heart!"

And this, with its characteristic burden, modulates into Keats and out again:

The woods of Arcady are dead,
And over is their antique joy;
Of old the world on dreaming fed;
Grey Truth is now her painted toy;
Yet still she turns her restless head:
But O, sick children of the world,
Of all the many changing things
In dreary dancing past us whirled,
To the cracked tune that Chronos sings,
Words alone are certain good.
Where are now the warring kings,
Word be-mockers?—By the Rood
Where are now the warring kings?
An idle word is now their glory,
By the stammering schoolboy said,
Reading some entangled story:
The wandering earth herself may be
Only a sudden flaming word,
In clanging space a moment heard,
Troubling the endless reverie.

The long poem which gave its name to the collection of 1889 (his first) might be described as Mr. Yeats's *Alastor* and *Endymion*. Its importance is what is indicated by this note: ". . . from the moment when I began the *Wanderings of Usheen* . . . my subject matter became Irish." Mr. Yeats starts in the English tradition, but he is from the outset an Irish poet. The impulse behind the poem is the familiar one. A poet's day-dream could not easily be more cloudy and tenuous than the wistful Elysium of his Irish theme, with its "dim, pale waters" and its realms

Where Aengus dreams from sun to sun
A Druid dream of the end of days;

and yet there is a paradoxical energy about the poem that distinguishes it from any of Morris's day-dreams: its pallor and weariness are not the exquisite aesthetic etiolation familiar to the

Poets with whom I learned my trade,
Companions of the Cheshire Cheese . . .

For Mr. Yeats's Irishness is more than a matter of using Irish themes and an Irish atmosphere. It means that his dream-world is something more than private, personal and literary; that it has, as it were, an external validation. It gives him the kind of advantage that he has in mind here:

I filled my mind with the popular beliefs of Ireland. . . . I sought some symbolic language reaching far into the past and associated with familiar names and conspicuous hills that I might not be alone amid the obscure impressions of the senses, . . . or mourned the richness or reality lost to Shelley's *Prometheus Unbound* because he had not discovered in England or in Ireland his Caucasus.

The advantage is put even more significantly here:

I did not believe with my intellect that you could be carried away body and soul, but I believed with my emotions and the belief of the country people made that easy.

In the world created with this kind of sanction he could preserve the "higher reality" that his imagination and emotions craved, and without which life seemed worthless. His second collection of poems, *The Rose* (1893), frankly brings the cult of "Eternal beauty wandering on her way," with its Red Rose of "an unimagined revelation," into the world of Irish lore. But there is still a certain esoteric languor about this phase:

Beauty grown sad with its eternity
Made you of us, and of the dim grey sea;

and we are again reminded that we are in the 'nineties. ("With a rhythm that still echoed Morris I played to the Red Rose.") Here, too, belongs the unfortunate *Innisfree;* unfortunate, because it is Mr. Yeats's most anthologized poem and recalls to us his own note: "I tried after the publication of *The Wanderings of Oisin* to write of nothing but emotion, and in the simplest language, and now I have had to go through it all, cutting out or altering passages that are sentimental from lack of thought."

But with *The Wind Among the Reeds* (1899) the dream-reality takes on a new life, and the poet inhabits it surely. And although the imagery of the Celtic Twilight is heavily worked —"pale," "dim," "shadowy," "desolate," "cloud-pale," "dream-heavy,"—there is no languor or preciosity here. Indeed, "passion-dimmed" and "pale fire" are equally important in the vocabulary. For a new force has entered Mr. Yeats's poetry—love. It is mainly despairing love, and the poetry is extremely poignant. But for us the essential thing to note is how Mr. Yeats turns both exaltation and despair to the heightening of his dream-world, his substitute for the drab quotidian actuality of Huxley, Ibsen and Bastien-Lepage.

When my arms wrap you round I press
My heart upon the loveliness
That long has faded from the world.

It is a perfectly sincere application of the platonic habit, but a very odd one:

For that pale breast and lingering hand
Come from a more dream-heavy land,
A more dream-heavy hour than this;
And when you sigh from kiss to kiss
I hear white Beauty sighing, too,
For hours when all must fade like dew,
But flame on flame, and deep on deep,
Throne over throne where in half sleep,
Their swords upon their iron knees,
Brood her high lonely mysteries.

—Transcendental Beauty, the mystical reality, belongs to a more dream-heavy hour even than that of the poetry, which is thus the dream of a dream. The syntax of the passage, curiously elusive as it is, suggests the equivocal status of Yeats's "reality." It is more than a literary fiction; love and the Irish background ("I believed with my emotions and the belief of the country people made that easy") enabled him to make it so. The resulting poetry has a fresh unliterary spontaneity comparable to that of Shelley's, but a spontaneity that has behind it a Victorian literary sophistication instead of Wordsworth and the French Revolution, and so is the more remarkable an achievement. Yet everywhere there is a recognition, implicit in the shifting, cloudy unseizableness of the imagery, that this "reality" must be illusory, and that even if it could be reached it would leave human longing unslaked. And this recognition is subtly turned into a strength: it validates, as it were, the idealizing fanaticism of the poetry and counterpoises the obsession with the transcendental, just as the exaltations and despairs of love are counterpoised by the sense that

> *. . . time and the world are ever in flight;*
> *And love is less kind than the grey twilight,*
> *And hope is less dear than the dew of the morn.*

The poetry of *The Wind Among the Reeds*, then, is a very remarkable achievement: it is, though a poetry of withdrawal, both more subtle and more vital than any pure product of Victorian romanticism. We might, as bearing on the strength it was to Mr. Yeats to be Irish, note further that with the Irish element in the poetry was associated a public and practical aim. Early and long service in the cause of a national renaissance, and, above all, of a national theatre might be expected to turn even a poet of the Victorian dream-world into something else; and Mr. Yeats devoted to the Irish cause rare qualities of character and intelligence. Yet his resolute attempt upon the drama serves mainly to bring out the prepotence of the tradition he started in. His plays repudiate the actual world as essentially as his incantatory lyrics and his esoteric prose repudiate it. "As for living, our servants will do that for us"—the epigraph might cover all three. A drama thus devoted to a "higher reality" of this kind could hardly exhibit the dramatic virtues.

How insidious was the atmosphere that poets of his time breathed comes out in his critical writings. "Tragic art," he will tell us in a discussion of poetic drama, "passionate art, the drowner of dykes moves us by setting us to reverie, by alluring us almost to the intensity of trance." And so obviously acute is the critical intelligence at work that we try to find much virtue in that "intensity." Yet "reverie" and "trance" are dangerous words, and in the critic who announces that "All art is dream" we fear the worst. "Drama," he will tell us again, "is a means of expression . . . and the dramatist is a free to choose where he has a mind to, as the poet of *Endymion,* or as the painter of Mary Magdalene at the door of Simon the Pharisee. So far from the discussion of our interests and the immediate circumstances of our life being the most moving to the imagination, it is what is old and far-off that stirs us the most deeply." Reading this, we may applaud the challenge to Shaw and Ibsen, but we more than suspect the kind of dream he has in mind. Indeed, we know, for the bent is inveterate. "Every writer," he says, "even every small writer, who has belonged to the great tradition, has had his dream of an impossibly noble life, and the greater he is, the more does it seem to plunge him into some beautiful or bitter reverie." This comes from an essay on Synge, and of Synge's rhythm he says: "It is essential, for it perfectly fits the drifting emotion, the dreaminess, the vague yet measureless desire, for which he would create a dramatic form. It blurs definition, clear edges, everything that comes from the will, it turns imagination from all that is of the present, like a gold background in a religious picture, and it strengthens in every emotion whatever comes to it from far off, from brooding memory and dangerous hope."

Mr. Yeats the dramatist, that is, remains the poet who had "learned to think in the midst of the last phase of Pre-Raphaelitism." He differs from the Victorian romantics in the intensity with which he seeks his "higher reality." This difference we have attributed to his being Irish; but it will not do to let this explanation detract from his rare distinction of mind and spirit. "I had an invincible conviction . . . that the gates would open as they opened for Blake . . ."—this is not the anaemic reverie of Victorian romanticism: to nurse a luxury of defeat was not in Mr. Yeats's character; he was too strong and alive. He fought, paradoxical as it may seem, for victory, and it was not through any lack of intelligence or contempt for it that he found such a Quixotry possible. "The dream-world of Morris," he writes, "was as much the antithesis of daily life as with other men of genius, but he was never conscious of the antithesis and so knew nothing of intellectual suffering." Mr. Yeats knew much of intellectual suffering, for the antithesis was terribly present to him: he had a magnificent mind, and less than the ordinary man's capacity for self-deception. "It is so many years before one can believe enough in what one feels even to know what the feeling is," he notes, exemplifying that rare critical self-awareness of which the signs abound in his *Autobiographies* and *Essays*. "I ceased to read modern books that were not books of imagination," he reports; but he read these last, one might almost say, in a scientific spirit. Indeed, his dealings with spiritualism, magic, theosophy, dream and trance were essentially an attempt to create an alternative science. The science of Huxley and Tyndall he had rejected in the name of imagination and emotion, but he had an intelligence that would not be denied. He exhibits for us the inner struggle of the nineteenth-century mind in an heroic form—heroic, and, because of the inevitable frustration and waste, tragic. "From the moment when these speculations grow vivid," he tells us, "I had created for myself an intellectual solitude."

We may relate to this lonely struggle a remarkable change that manifests itself in Mr. Yeats's poetry when we compare *The Wind Among the Reeds* (1889) with *The Green Helmet* (1912). It is hard to believe that the characteristic verse of the later volume comes from the same hand as that of the earlier. The new verse has no incantation, no dreamy, hypnotic rhythm; it belongs to the actual, waking world, and is in the idiom and movement of modern speech. It is spare, hard and sinewy and in tone sardonic, expressing the bitterness and disillusion of a man who has struggled and been frustrated:

> *The fascination of what's difficult*
> *Has dried the sap out of my veins, and rent*
> *Spontaneous joy and natural content*
> *Out of my heart.*

It is true that the struggles he specifies here belong to the practical world, to "this blind, bitter land":

> *My curse on plays*
> *That have to be set up in fifty ways,*
> *On the day's war with every knave and dolt,*
> *Theatre business, management of men.*

But this is not the whole tale; and if it is time that has brought this maturity, there are reasons why this maturity should be so sour.

> *Though leaves are many, the root is one;*
> *Through all the lying days of my youth*
> *I swayed my leaves and flowers in the sun;*
> *Now I may wither into the truth*

runs a quatrain headed *The Coming of Wisdom with Time*. Actuality has conquered:

The holy centaurs of the hill are vanished;
I have nothing but the embittered sun;
Banished heroic mother moon and vanished,
And now that I have come to fifty years
I must endure the timid sun.

It is like an awakening out of drugs, a disintoxication; the daylight seems thin and cruel. He recognizes the real world, but it is too late; his strength has been wasted, and habit forbids readjustment.

But I grow old among dreams,
A weather-worn, marble triton
Among the streams.

The poem this last comes from has for title *Men Improve with the Years,* which suggests well enough Mr. Yeats's peculiar bitterness, a bitterness mingled with scorn for humanity.[1]

Nevertheless, the poetry of this later phase is a remarkable positive achievement: Mr. Yeats was strong enough to force a triumph out of defeat. He speaks of a beauty

. . . won
From bitterest hours,

and it is this he serves instead of the cloudy glamour of the *Celtic Twilight;* a

. . . beauty like a tightened bow, a kind
That is not natural in an age like this.

The verse, in its rhythm and diction, recognizes the actual world, but holds against it an ideal of aristocratic fineness. It is idiomatic, and has the run of free speech, being at the same time proud, bare and subtle. To pass from the earlier verse to this is something like passing from Campion to Donne. The parallel, indeed, is not so random as it might seem. At any rate, Donne's name in connection with a poet capable of passionate intellectual interests, who from such a start achieved

[1] Cf. *We had fed the heart on fantasies,*
The heart's grown brutal from the fare,
More substance in our enmities
Than in our love;
The Tower, p. 27.

such a manner, leads us to reflect that if the poetic tradition of the nineteenth century had been less completely unlike the Metaphysical tradition Mr. Yeats might have spent less of his power outside poetry. The speculation is perhaps idle, but it calls attention to the way in which his verse developed into something that has the equivalent of certain seventeenth-century qualities. His use of the idiom and rhythm of speech is not all:

Plato thought nature but a spume that plays
Upon a ghostly paradigm of things;
Solider Aristotle played the taws
Upon the bottom of a king of kings;
World-famous golden-thighed Pythagoras
Fingered upon a fiddle stick or strings
What a star sang and careless Muses heard:
Old clothes upon old sticks to scare a bird.

—This (and the context more than bears out the promise of flexibility and variety of tone) is surely rather like seventeenth-century "wit" more like it than anything we expect to find in modern verse outside the work of certain post-war poets—poets who exhibit no completed escape from the Victorian poetical. The volume it comes from, indeed appeared after the war. But *The Tower* (1928) merely develops the manner of *The Green Helmet* (1912), *Responsibilities* (1914), and *The Wild Swans at Coole* (1919).

In *The Tower* Mr. Yeats achieves a kind of ripeness in disillusion. The scorn so pervasive before is gone: his tragic horror at the plight of Ireland (as, for instance, in *Meditations in Time of Civil War*) is something different and more generous. There is indeed bitterness, but it is not the sterile kind. His raging against

Decrepit age that has been tied to me
As to a dog's tail

goes with a sense of ardent vitality:

. . . *Never had I more*
Excited, passionate, fantastical
Imagination, nor an ear and eye
That more expected the impossible;

and the excitement is as apparent as the bitterness in this poetry of the last phase. Each gives value to the other. He is capable of excitement, for instance, about the "abstract things" that he describes as a *pis aller*. He turns with a pang from the varied "sensual music" of the world, but he is drawn positively towards the "monuments of unaging intellect":

> *An aged man is but a paltry thing,*
> *A tattered coat upon a stick, unless*
> *Soul clap its hands and sing, and louder sing*
> *For every tatter in its mortal dress.*

This (though there is always an ironical overtone) is the voice of one who knows intellectual passion. He does not deceive himself about what he has lost, but the regret itself becomes in the poetry something positive. His implications, in short, are very complex; he has achieved a difficult and delicate sincerity, and extraordinary subtle poise.

What, then, it might be asked after this account of Mr. Yeats's achievement, is there to complain of? Does it really show that the tradition in the nineteenth century might with advantage have been other than it was? If he had to struggle with uncongenial circumstances, has not every great artist had to do so; and did he not, by admission, make triumphs of them? Mr. Yeats himself gives the answer in the bitter sense of waste he expresses characteristically, in the latest work as elsewhere. His poetry is little more than a marginal comment on the main activities of his life. No one can read his *Autobiographies* and his *Essays* without being struck by the magnificent qualities of intelligence and character he exhibits. His insight shows itself in his analysis of his own case, an analysis that suggests at the same time the complete achievement he was fated to miss: "In literature," he wrote in 1906,[2] "partly from the lack of that spoken word which knits us to the normal man, we have lost in personality, in our delight in the whole man—blood, imagination, intellect, running together—but have found a new delight in essences, in states of mind, in pure imagination, in all that comes to us most easily in elaborate music." And we find him remarking in *Autobiographies* "how small a fragment of our own nature can be brought to perfect expression, nor that even but with great toil, in a much divided civilisation." Again, by quoting his own verse, he ex-

[2]Cf. "Donne could be as metaphysical as he pleased . . . because he could be as physical as he pleased."—*Autobiographies*.

plicitly relates the general reflection to his own case: "Nor did I understand as yet how little that Unity [of Being], however wisely sought, is possible without a Unity of Culture in class or people that is no longer possible at all.

> *The fascination of what's difficult*
> *Has dried the sap out of my veins, and rent*
> *Spontaneous joy and natural content*
> *Out of my heart."*

At this point it might be commented that Mr. Yeats turns out an unfortunate witness to have called. What he testifies against is not the poetic tradition, but the general state of civilization and culture; a state which, he contends, makes waste inevitable for the sensitive. But he implies nothing against holding that if the poetic tradition had been different, as it might very well have been, he might have brought more of himself to expression. Writing of the early Synge he says significantly: ". . . the only language that interested him was that conventional language of modern poetry which has begun to make us all weary. I was very weary of it, for I had finished *The Secret Rose,* and felt how it had separated my imagination from life, sending my Red Hanrahan, who should have trodden the same roads with myself, into some undiscoverable country." It is true that he successfully dropped this "conventional language of modern poetry"; but early habits of mind and sensibility are not so easily dropped. The incidental confession he makes in a later poem—

> *I have no speech but symbol, the pagan speech I made*
> *Amid the dreams of youth—*

has such significance. For "symbol" in his technical sense—symbol drawn from his cult of magic and the Hermetic sciences—is commonly felt to be an unsatisfactory element in his later verse, and to come from an unfortunate habit of mind. And his magic and occultism, of course, are the persistent and intense expression of the bent that expressed itself first of all in the "conventional language of modern poetry"

> — . . . *The abstract joy,*
> *The half read wisdom of daemonic images,*
> *Suffice the aging man as once the growing boy.*

Disillusion and waste were indeed inevitable; but not in the form in which Mr Yeats suffered them. They might have been more significant. For Victorian romanticism was not the only possible answer to those modern conditions that Mr. Yeats deplores. If it were, poetry would cease to matter, Adult minds could no longer take it seriously. Losing all touch with the finer consciousness of the age it would be, not only irresponsible, but anaemic, as, indeed, Victorian poetry so commonly is. Mr. Yeats's career, then, magnificent as the triumph was that he compelled out of defeat, is a warning. It illustrates the special disability of the poet in the last century, and impressively bears out my argument about the poetic tradition. And it cannot be repeated. No Englishman in any case could have profited by the sources of strength open to Mr. Yeats as an Irishman, and no such source is open to any one now. No serious poet could propose to begin again where Mr. Yeats began.

Stephen Spender

W. B. YEATS is an isolated figure in modern writing, whose achievements at first seem only to be explained by his extreme individuality.

His individuality is emphasized by the romantic line of his development, which is reminiscent of Goethe. He began as the writer of romantic, twilight poetry. Late in life, he is now writing his best poetry, most of which is inspired by contemporary political events, and by the lives of his friends. His awareness, his passionate rhythms, breaking away completely from the limp early work, remind one of the opening stanzas of Goethe's *West-Oestlicher-Divan,* written also in a time of European revolution, following on a terrible series of wars.

Nord und West und Sud zersplittern,
Throne bersten, Reiche zittern,
Flüchte du, im reinen Osten
Patriarchenluft zu kosten!
Unter Lieben, Trinken, Singen
Soll dich Chisers Quell verjüngen

compares with:—

At midnight on the Emperor's pavement flit
Flames that no faggot feeds, nor steel has lit,
Nor storm disturbs, flames begotten of flame,
Where blood-begotten spirits come
And all complexities of fury leave,
Dying into a dance,
An agony of trance,
An agony of flame that cannot singe a sleeve.

The command to flight, except into the pride of his own individualism, is not there in Yeats; at the end of his life he goes further than Goethe in renouncing his romanticism.

Like Goethe, the stream of Yeats's romantic poetry was interrupted by his public life. The effect of politics on his writing was revolutionary.

This development, which at first seems unique, was the re-

"Yeats as a Realist," from *The Criterion,* XIV, 1 (October, 1934), pp. 17-26; and *The Destructive Element,* Jonathan Cape, Ltd., London, 1935, pp. 115-132.

sult of three main influences: the influence on him of certain changes in social life that took place during his life and that of his friends; the influence of his interest in magic; the influence on him of symbolist theories of poetry.

Although at one time he sought very consciously to root his poetry in the popular ballad poetry of Ireland, the literary influences which are to be found in his earliest, as in his most recent verse, are contemporary writing and writers. He does not go back, with the completeness of Eliot in *The Waste Land,* to the late Elizabethans, and achieve by his diction a striking historic comparison of the earlier period's greatness and decay with our own. His early poetry is, in spite of its ballad style (in fact, because of it), unashamedly of the 'eighties, just as his present writing is perhaps almost a little too dazzlingly "modern." As a young man, his friends were such men as Dowson, Arthur Symons, Lionel Johnson and all the Rhymers. He was obviously, in his middle period, excited by the French symbolists: to-day it is not difficult to appreciate that he is an admirer of Ezra Pound and that he has read T. S. Eliot.

But his earlier work also shows that to a poet of his stature a contemporary influence, even when combined with a very great talent, is not enough. Beautiful as some of these poems are, they are enervating and contain a weariness of which Yeats seems, in his old age, quite incapable. One cannot imagine him saying to-day: "I will arise and go now, and go to Innisfree"—which calls up the image of a young man reclining on a yellow satin sofa. There would be a roar of thunder, a flash, and he would be off.

In *Adam's Curse* this sense of the inadequacy of his earlier inspiration seems to reach a climax. The poem is a dialogue between the poet and a woman, whose art of love is supposed to be as great as the poet's art of poetry. The poet first boasts of the trouble he takes over his versifying:

"A line will take us hours maybe;
Yet if it does not seem a moment's thought,
Our stitching and unstitching has been nought."

Then he complains of being thought an idler:

". . . by the noisy set
Of bankers, schoolmasters, and clergymen
The martyrs call the world."

Of whose air of reality, he seems oddly envious.

The woman then replies, " 'That we must labour to be beautiful,' " and the poet, of course, concludes that she is referring to the difficult art of love.

The two speakers then sit silent and watching the day die and "A moon, worn as if it had been a shell." Then the poem ends with the curious reflection:

I had thought for no one's but your ears:
That you were beautiful, and that I strove
To love you in the old high way of love;
That it had all seemed happy, and yet we'd grown
As weary-hearted as that hollow moon.

This poem seems to mark the end of a phase, because the poet's inability to love in the old high way, and his feeling that the symbol of the moon was hollow, reveals a conscious dissatisfaction with his art.

In the series of poems published in 1910 and called *The Green Helmet and Other Poems,* he seems tempted to abandon poetry altogether. In one of the poems he explains:

All things can tempt me from this craft of verse:
One time it was a woman's face, or worse—
The seeming needs of my fool-driven land.

The weakness of the second line—only rescued by the dash and comma—indicates the writer's somewhat distracted mood. The inspiration of Yeats's best poetry is mostly occasional, but here the poems seem to have an altogether occasional nature, in the sense that they form the background to various activities which engaged Yeats at the time, and also to his preoccupation with Irish politics. There are poems on such subjects as *A Friend's Illness, At Galway Races, Upon a House Shaken by the Land Agitation.* There is one poem called *The Fascination of What's Difficult,* in which he complains of the passing of inspiration.

Nevertheless, these poems contain a germ impregnated by the external world which grew up into the later poems. They seem to be a drying up, but, really, they are the beginning of something quite different and new.

The kind of poetry which is considerable as art and which is not based on a consciously sought-out tradition, is likely to be rooted deeply not so much in the writing of contemporaries, which forms its superficial soil, and which is merely an influence, as in the actual life of the time. Yeats's book of *Autobiographies*—which form so strange a mixture of discretion and self-revelation—show how deep was his thirst for the life around him.

The world of the *Autobiographies* is very different from that of *The Celtic Twilight*. The scene is, for the most part, London. The actors—and they were actors—are Lionel Johnson, Wilde, Morris, George Russell and all the literary and Irish-political figures of that time. These people are not in the least idealized, very few of them are fairies, and then only in a worldly sense; they are seen in a hard, clear, but undramatic light, and the sordid aspect of their lives—their drink, dope and debts—is not concealed.

Yeats's attitude to what he calls the "Tragic Generation," the generation of *The Yellow Book* and the Rhymers' Club, was that of one who felt that their destiny was his own, and who yet felt dissatisfied with them and critical. The central point of his criticism was what involved him most deeply in his own work: the relation of their emotional, unbalanced lives to their accomplished, trance-like poetry. "Another day," he writes, when attempting to explain to himself the series of domestic tragedies that overcame so many of them, "I think that perhaps our form of lyric, our insistence upon emotion which has no relation to any public interest, gathered together overwrought, unstable men; and remember, the moment after, that the first to go out of his mind had no lyrical gift, and that we valued him mainly because he seemed a witty man of the world; and that a little later a man who seemed, alike as man and writer, dull and formless, went out of his mind, first burning poems which I cannot believe would have proved him, as the one man who saw them claims, a man of genius."

So that he was not only in contact with the literary movements of his time, he was also deeply involved with the people who made it. He took his tradition, not so much from books (as he had at first imagined he should do), as from the lives of those people who created his cultural environment, and whose lives presented a picture of civilization to him in its most vivid form. Their lives, deeply rooted in the lives of their ancestors, saturate his later poetry; especially the poetry of *The Tower*. I only wish sometimes that he had allowed his interest to extend still further, outside the immediate circle of his friends, into the social life that surrounded him.

I believe that what distinguished Yeats from those other

writers is not so much—as Dr. Leavis has said—his power of self-criticism, as his realism. He is far too rhetorical a writer to be self-critical. It is clear from the style of his prose that he must constantly be presenting himself to himself in a dramatic manner; and his conversation gives the same impression. He is capable, because he has the highest intelligence and because his rhetoric is not the rhetoric of the politician, of passionate seriousness, of penitence, and of an almost excessive sense of responsibility. No lines ring truer in his verse than:

> *Things said or done long years ago,*
> *Or things I did not do or say*
> *But thought that I might say or do,*
> *Weigh me down, and not a day*
> *But something is recalled,*
> *My conscience or my vanity appalled.*

This verse shows how realism is not inconsistent with a certain romanticism, especially when it is self-dramatizing, and indeed one might say that it was Yeats's sense of reality which made him exploit his gift as a romantic poet; but he is certainly not a master of self-criticism, as Eliot is.

Yeats was strengthened in his attitude to the life around him by certain of his intellectual experiences. The chief of these were the three influences of the Irish Literary Renaissance, Magic and Symbolism, and his interest in contemporary politics, which seem in the last years to have broadened into a prophetic concern (which resembles that of Stefan George, during and after the war) with the destiny of Europe.

At first sight the Irish Renaissance, so venomously featured by George Moore in his *Hail and Farewell,* seems inextricably tangled with the Magic and Symbolism. But actually it played a conflicting role in his work, directing it towards the Irish legends and the Celtic Twilight, whereas the Magic and Symbolism became essentially part of his approach to the world around him. One also has to distinguish between the Symbolism which had to do with the Magic and the Symbolism which was part of the symbolist movement in poetry. This close connexion between the mystery of magical symbols and the literary movement of H. D., Ezra Pound and their followers, is typical of Yeats. However mysterious and shadowy it is, his poetry has always the stamp of success, and his magic invocations always have a slightly public air.

The beginnings of the Irish Renaissance were directed towards creating a folk poetry which would be strictly Irish. "When Lionel Johnson and Katherine Tynan (as she was then), and I myself began to reform Irish poetry," he writes (in a business-like way) in *Poetry and Tradition,* "we thought to keep unbroken the thread running up to Grattan which John O'Leary had put into our hands, though it might be our business to explore new paths of the labyrinth. We sought to make a more subtle rhythm, a more organic form than that of the older Irish poets who wrote in English, but always to remember certain ardent ideas and high attitudes of mind which were the nation itself, to our belief, so far as a nation can be summarized in the intellect." In the essay on *The Celtic Element in Literature,* in *Ideas of Good and Evil,* the subject-matter which is suitably Celtic is indicated. This essay is a short account of the Celtic Sagas, and we are told how the Bards "took the blossoms of the oak, and the blossoms of the broom, and the blossoms of the meadow-sweet, and produced from them a maiden the fairest and most graceful men ever saw; and they baptized her and called her the Flower Aspect." It is in this world of dream that *The Wanderings of Oisin* and the early ballad poetry moves.

But even the Irish Renaissance dragged Yeats away from its own mysteries, and forced many practical problems upon his attention, and surrounded him with an active social life. The Abbey Theatre was founded, and in it he must have met many people who were distressingly unlike the fairies of his dreams.

Magic was closely linked with his Irish childhood. He was so accustomed to think and speak of ghosts and fairies, that it is unlikely he could have completely escaped from their influence. *The Celtic Twilight* is, as Forrest Reid remarks, "thick with ghosts. . . . Drumcliff and Rosses are the places where they are to be found thickest." The "good people" abound, and they carry off the souls of peasants.

As a young man in London, he scientifically developed his magical experiences by attending seances, visiting haunted houses, and calling on Madame Blavatsky. Mrs. Katherine Tynan Hinkson (as she became) describes an alarming seance in which the spirits became very annoyed and where "Willie Yeats was banging his head on the table as though he had a fit, muttering to himself. I had a cold repulsion to the whole business."

His own descriptions of what happened at seances leave me with the same sort of bewilderment as do the dully sensational messages rapped out on turning tables. I am impressed by the appearance of a man in black and a hump-backed woman who are apparently engaged in making flesh by mechanical means, but I search vainly in myself for any scale of values which can make such appearances seem to have significance.

His own interest in these phenomena seems, at least partly, to have been a scientific curiosity, for they have little relation to the part that the theory of magic plays in his poetry. A system of magic forms his approach to certain problems, corresponding to the psychological approach of such writers as Joyce or Lawrence. In this essay on *Magic,* he writes:

> I believe . . .
> (1) That the borders of our minds are ever shifting, and that many minds can flow into one another, as it were, and create or reveal a single mind, a single energy.
> (2) That the borders of our memories are as shifting, and that our memories are a part of one great memory, the memory of Nature herself.
> (3) That this great mind and great memory can be evoked by symbols.
> I often think I would put this belief in magic from me if I could, for I have come to see or to imagine, in men and women, in houses, in handicrafts, in nearly all sights and sounds, a certain evil, a certain ugliness, that comes from the slow perishing through the centuries of a quality of mind that made this belief and its evidences common over the world.

I do not think that D. H. Lawrence would have quarrelled with these sentiments, although he may not have admired Yeats's work. Also, the whole passage is suited to appear in any psychological textbook.

Later, he expands this belief into another observation, which explains the subject of much contemporary psychological literature:

> All men, certainly all imaginative men, must be for ever casting forth enchantments, glamours, illusions; and all men, especially tranquil men who have no powerful egoistic life, must be continually passing under their power. Our most elaborate thoughts, elaborate purposes, precise emotions, are often, as I think, not really ours, but have on a sudden come up, as it were, out of hell or down out of heaven.

This may be linked with his theory of symbolism, which is even more orthodoxly psychological:

> I cannot now think symbols less than the greatest of all powers whether they are used consciously by the masters of magic or half

consciously by their successors, the poet, the musician and the artist. At first I tried to distinguish between symbols and symbols, between what I called inherent symbols and arbitrary symbols, but the distinction has come to mean little or nothing. Whether their power has arisen out of themselves, or whether it has an arbitrary origin, matters little, for they act, as I believe, because the great memory associates them with certain events and moods and persons. Whatever the passions of man have gathered about, becomes a symbol in the great memory, and in the hands of him that has the secret, it is a worker of wonders, a caller up of angels or of devils.

His theory of symbolism led him firstly to search for a mysterious symbol which would contain everything outside the writer's self:

By the help of an image
I call to my own opposite, summon all
That I have handled least, least looked upon.

By an inverse process, symbolism also leads to a universal signficance being attached to certain images in his poetry, which in other romantic poetry would only remain details of observation or of invocation. It thus enables him to exploit to the utmost his very limited power of observing nature. George Moore has described how Yeats would walk about the country without ever looking at anything. The visual experiences of his whole life which have found their way into his poetry could probably be counted on the fingers of both hands. The Tower, the moorhen, the wild swans at Coole, a few trees (without leaves, for the most part), the winding stair, the fisherman, a hare, certain of his friends, have all the same significance in Yeats, as cats and negresses have in Baudelaire's poetry.

In the early symbolist poems, in *The Wind among the Reeds,* the symbolism, the magic and the twilight are all interwoven, and the symbols therefore lose power because they are not sufficiently isolated.

I hear the Shadowy Horses, their long manes a-shake,
Their hoofs heavy with tumult, their eyes glimmering white;
The North unfolds above them clinging, creeping night,
The East her hidden joy before the morning break,
The West weeps in pale dew and sighs passing away,
The South is pouring down roses of crimson fire.

Here the reader may fail to realize that far more than a mere mood of trance is being conjured up: the symbols all really stand for something.

Or when Yeats writes:

Do you not hear me calling, white deer with no horns?
I have been changed to a hound with one red ear;

the reader, unless he is well up in magical practices, may fail to realize that he has really been turned into a hound with one red ear.

Symbols derived from witches and the moon, unless they are used in some very particular sense, as in Baudelaire—in the sense that they are *evil*—naturally lose the full force of an isolated crystal experience into which the poet is gazing.

It therefore happens that the method is most successful when it is applied to objects which are, in the magical sense, least symbolic. The friends of his youth whom he names, the particular tower which he owns, the particular fisherman who he met,

Although I can see him still,
The freckled man who goes
To a grey place on a hill
In grey Connemara clothes
At dawn to cast his flies,
It's long since I began
To call up to the eyes
This wise and simple man

about whom he wrote the

Poem maybe as cold
And passionate as the dawn.

Yeats is a poet who, finding himself in a desperate situation, has buttressed and shored up his work—as though it were, perhaps, his ancestral Tower—on every side. The reader is at every stage perplexed. First, he imagines that all is to be mystery and twilight and that he dare hardly listen, he must be so silent, for fear lest he disturb the fairies. To his disappointment he hears the fairy song grow fainter and fainter, until it disappears over the crest of the twilit hill. But Yeats has not disappeared. On the contrary, the reader now discovers that the fairies were only a part of a theory that by writing about them one could create a popular Irish ballad poetry. The fairies then merge into a theory of magic: but the magic, although much talked of, and although the poet never fails to produce a hush-hush solemn atmosphere, seems always to be something of a hoax. It has an element in it of spiritualist seances attended by a journalist, in order that he broadcast his impressions of them.

In the first place, Yeats's attitude to magical events seems always to be that of a doctor instead of a witch doctor, and, in the second place, his poetry is only magical in the sense that he can produce a certain atmosphere. Yeats has written plenty of romantic poetry, plenty of obscure poetry, some nonsense, and much mystification, but nothing which one could say was magical. Nothing, for instance, which has the magical quality of Eliot's poem, *The Hollow Men.* No lines to compare with:

Eyes I dare not meet in dreams
In death's dream kingdom
These do not appear:
There, the eyes are
Sunlight on a broken column
There, is a tree swinging
And voices are
In the wind's singing
More distant and more solemn
Than a fading star.

Not even the magic, plus theories of symbolism and pure poetry, have enabled him to reproduce the effect of the line which he so admires in Nashe: "Brightness falls from the air." Lastly, to complete his ambiguity, the result of the search for one symbol was the discovery that almost anything might become that symbol.

What one admires in Yeats's poetry is, in fact, not its mystery, its magic or even its atmosphere: but its passion, its humanity, its occasional marvellous lucidity, its technical mastery, its integrity, its strength, its reality and its opportunism.

Why, then, is this romantic facade at all necessary? Or, since it exists, why does it not falsify the whole effect? The answer is that Yeats's poetry is devoid of any unifying moral subject, and it develops in a perpetual search for one. Although he has much wisdom, he offers no philosophy of life, but, as a substitute, a magical system, which, where it does not seem rhetorical, is psycho-analytic, but not socially constructive. Reverent as he is, he does not convey any religion; instead, we are offered, in such poems as *Prayer for My Daughter,* an aristocratic faith. It is illuminating to consider what exactly Yeats does pray for his daughter, because presumably these are the qualities which he considers most important to a human being. (1) He wants her to be beautiful, but not too beautiful. (2) Courteous.

(3) *O may she live like some green laurel*
Rooted in one dear perpetual place.

(4) *An intellectual hatred is the worst,*
So let her think opinions are accursed.
(*Cf.* Henry James.)

(5) *And may her bridegroom bring her to a house*
Where all's accustomed, ceremonious;
For arrogance and hatred are the wares
Peddled in the thoroughfares.
How but in custom and in ceremony
Are innocence and beauty born?
Ceremony's a name for the rich horn,
And custom for the spreading laurel tree.

I have quoted the last verse in full because it shows how Yeats's rhetoric illustrates his thought, rather than develops it. This poem does a good deal to explain why Yeats should have taken refuge from the modern world at first in magic, and why in his later poems, although there is a great show of intellectualism, he rests really always on certain qualities, rather than ideas, such as breeding and courtesy. For the thought is hopelessly inadequate to his situation. And the reader who goes to Yeats hoping to find in his work thought which is as profound as his contemporary awareness, goes away as a hungry sheep unfed.

His awareness is shown best of all in that extraordinary poem *The Second Coming:*

Things fall apart; the centre cannot hold;
Mere anarchy is loosed upon the world,
The blood-dimmed tide is loosed, and everywhere
The ceremony of innocence is drowned;
The best lack all conviction, while the worst
Are full of passionate intensity.

The courageous acceptance of this poem makes the set of virtues which Yeats wishes his daughter seem more than ever unsuitable, and even impossible. Indeed, his insistence on aristocratic qualities of mind even limits his humanity, which is his greatest virtue. If one turns from *Prayer for My Daughter* to Wilfred Owen's poem, *Strange Meeting*, one sees that Owen was already a poet of far deeper human understanding. These lines seem almost like an answer to Yeats's *fortissimo* lyrics:

"Strange friend," I said, "here is no cause to mourn."
"None," said the other, "save the undone years,
The hopelessness. Whatever hope is yours,
Was my life also; I went hunting wild
After the wildest beauty in the world,
Which lies not calm in eyes, or braided hair,
But mocks the steady running of the hour,
And if it grieves, grieves richlier than here.
For by my glee might many men have laughed,
And of my weeping something had been left
Which must die now. I mean the truth untold,
The pity of war, the pity war distilled.
Now men will go content with what we spoiled.
Or, discontent, boil bloody, and be spilled.
They will be swift with swiftness of the tigress,
None will break ranks, though nations trek from progress.
Courage was mine, and I had mystery,
Wisdom was mine, and I had mastery;
To miss the march of this retreating world
Into vain citadels that are not walled.
Then, when much blood had clogged their chariot-wheels
I would go up and wash them from sweet wells,
Even with truths that lie too deep for taint.
I would have poured my spirit without stint
But not through wounds; not on the cess of war.
Foreheads of men have bled where no wounds were.
I am the enemy you killed, my friend."

Yeats has found, as yet, no subject of moral significance in the social life of his time. Instead of a subject, he offers us magnificent and lively *rapportage* about his friends. The only exception is in the poem called *The Second Coming*. He has put up a great many props, the largest prop of all being his own noble egotism. And he has created an atmosphere of legend. In such poems as the second section of *The Tower*, and *All Souls' Night*, Yeats's friends—the real characters from the *Autobiographies* and the fantastic characters from the early stories, and all the imagery of the earlier poetry—become inextricably mixed into a world of legend which, although it has no moral and no religion, provides authentically a personal vision of life.

D. S. Savage

> *The intellect of man is forced to choose*
> *Perfection of the life, or of the work,*
> *And if it take the second must refuse*
> *A heavenly mansion, raging in the dark. . . .*

NO QUESTION IS of greater moment for the understanding of modern poetry than that of the relationship of art to life. The various schools and movements of the last hundred years have all been conditioned in one way or another by the disparity existing between the poet's private world and the public world in which he is situated as a social being and which, with the expansion of mechanical civilization, has increasingly separated itself from the private and personal values. In this way all later movements may be seen as offshoots of the Romantic Revival, which was the initial movement of the creative mind in its attempt deliberately to dissociate itself from the realm of collective values and to centre itself upon the personal life of the individual. After the romantics the movement known in France as Symbolism took the personalistic revolution a stage further, purifying poetry of the social and moralistic elements within romanticism, and in doing this it helped to clarify the essential nature of poetry. But Symbolism in turn led to the weakened, inverted romanticism of aestheticism. And it is from the point of view of aestheticism that we must consider the career of W. B. Yeats.

The symbolists attempted to purge poetry of all that was foreign to it, to concentrate upon essentials, and this meant the exclusion from art of those elements which in life had receded into the realm of the general, the commonplace. Thus the symbolists tended to repudiate outer actuality, which they identified with bourgeois civilization, and, retiring into themselves, to concentrate upon their own experience, which became more and more private and personal. The symbolists, if by that word we mean principally the poets Baudelaire, Verlaine and Mallarme, were not led by their ideas to a repudiation of life, i.e. of experience. But in their search for an ideal Beauty lying behind the world of appearances their grip on actual life was weakened, and this made it easier for

"The Aestheticism of W. B. Yeats," from *The Kenyon Review,* VII, 1 (winter, 1945), 118-134, copyright, 1944, by Kenyon College; and from *The Personal Principle,* George Routledge and Sons, London, 1944, pp. 67-91.

successors to turn away from actuality altogether and to preoccupy themselves with dreams. All art is rooted in experience. The flaw in symbolism, which helped to make possible its utilization by the exponents of aestheticism, was its imperfect realization of this truth and its too intense endeavour to break outside the limits of life, its over-specialization and the reactionary tendency which made it concentrate too exclusively upon the exotic, the bizarre. Symbolism and aestheticism must not, however, be confused. The first is a doctrine of art, springing from artistic practice; the second derives from theory and tends to become an attitude to life—a very different thing. Yet it is not hard to see how this doctrine of art lent itself to the less austere and integral gospel of aestheticism which, as a way of apprehending life rather than a way of writing poetry, involved a turning away from actuality and a concentration upon certain elements in life which were considered to be superior to the rest.

As is well enough known, Yeats began his career in a literary environment heavily saturated with the aestheticism of Pater, of Wilde, and of the lesser figures of the eighteen-nineties, the dominant influences upon his mind being those of Pater and Villiers de L'Isle Adam, *Axel* being one of his "sacred books." Of the three main threads which ran together through his life and thought, each deriving from a common source: that is, aestheticism, nationalism, and occultism, it is the first which may most profitably be taken as the key to his development. Yeats absorbed certain of the doctrines of Symbolism (as preached by Mallarme) through the medium of Arthur Symons, who called him "the chief representative of that movement in our country." Nevertheless, Symbolism meant something quite different to the English followers than to their French masters. Baudelaire, Verlaine and Mallarmé were not aesthetes; they were poets, seekers after reality, visionaries, and the practice of their art was rooted in, although it was an attempt to transcend, experience. It had a religious quality about it, and was in a sense the culmination of a mystical way of life, of apprehension. The aesthetes, however, who took over and adapted for their own uses the doctrines of Symbolism, lacked this intense seriousness. They were dilettantes, and interested less in the ardours of artistic creation than in the use to which artistic precepts could be put in the alleviation of living. The elements in life which aestheticism took to be superior to the others were its poetic elements, and therefore when they took to creative work their art was a reflection of a reflection. Dream and decoration were characteristics of their work because dream and decoration were what they sought for in life. Where the practice of poetry for Mallarme implied a mystical vision of life, for Yeats it meant a turning away from life and the making of poetry out of moods and dreams, while his "mysticism," so far from being inherent in his artistic practice, was imported from outside in the form of the alien paraphernalia of theosophy, magic and the rest.

Art can never be divorced entirely from life, from experience, although it can concentrate on certain limited aspects of life and disregard others. The serious artist cannot afford not to take life seriously. For, although art is the creation of a superior world—superior to that of commonplace existence—it must take its elements from life. It is not so much the creation of an ideal world remote from life as the record of the perception of an organic and meaningful order within the disparate universe of day-to-day experience. The life of the poet is thus in the nature of a religious discipline, in which the whole personality engages, to find forms within which experience can be held in organic wholeness, where it becomes illuminated with meaning. Life and art thus become united and yet separate, each dwelling within the other. Art grows from life, and in return illuminates it. Yet they remain distinct, and for their continued existence the boundaries between each must be clearly preserved.

The aesthetes obliterated this distinction. They wanted life to be art—in other words, they wanted a life purged of all its coarse, vulgar, trivial elements. Accordingly they turned away in life from all its inartistic elements. Where the poet's primary impulse may be said to be a "religious" one, the attempt to grapple with experience and to find order and significance in it, and his artistic impulse only secondary, a continuation of the same impulse—the desire to embody and transmit his vision—the aesthetes made a religion out of art. They inverted the order of the creative mind and replaced the dynamic "religious" principle at the centre by the static "artistic" principle and relegated the "religious" principle to the periphery, where it became immobilized and nullified.

It was such a doctrine of aestheticism, to which the symbolists were already pointing the way, that Yeats came to accept. His difference from his fellow-aesthetes of the 'nineties is shown by his combination of aestheticism with apparently alien factors—with Irish nationalism and occult supernaturalism. Where the aestheticism of many of the minor poets of that time, with its colourful bohemian diabolism, shows a reaction from bourgeois social and moral standards, Yeats's attitude appears remarkably pure of such taints. Yeats did not become an aesthete only through circumstances, his aestheticism derived straight from a central detachment. And he remained an aesthete throughout his life.

Poets are commonly of two kinds, or of intermixtures of those kinds. There are those creative spirits whose work is a process of self-revelation and self-realization, who proceed from an inner impulse working through their personal experience, through which experience is formulated and compelled into organic patterns. Their work is a personal, dynamic activity deriving from personal necessity, their impulse is essentially spiritual. And there are those men of talent whose work, deriving from a much weaker inner impulse, is much more impersonal, miscellaneous, exterior in character. These latter writers are they who, less vehemently original, are able to share to a much greater extent than the former the values of the society in which they are brought up. In a culturally homogeneous society they will be quite at home, and busy writing the long narratives or pastorals or didactic poems which their society demands. Their main preoccupation will be with the mechanics of their craft, their subject-matter will be readily available, dictated to them by the conventions of their age. And their religious life will be adequately cared for by the current orthodoxy. Yet what happens to writers of this kind in a culturally *disrupted* society—those, in particular, who, through the nature of their gift and mental inclination, remain writers of verse? Deprived on the one hand of that cultural give-and-take between poet and public which sustains the classical poet, and on the other hand lacking that fiery inner dynamism which distinguishes the original poet, the creative mind, will they not easily drift towards the acceptance of such doctrines as the aestheticism of the *fin-de-siecle*, the doctrines of art for art's sake? This, it seems to me, was the position of Yeats. Essentially a non-dynamic mind, he was saved from dissipation or vulgarization of his gifts by the narrowness of his interests and the strictness of his devotion to his craft. Inwardly he lacked the visionary intensity of the creative spirit, and his art developed peripherally, unaccompanied by any very interesting inward, personal development.

Yeats's view of art as a religious surrogate is expressed in an essay, "William Blake and the Imagination," written in 1897, in which he says of Blake that

> . . . He announced the religion of art, of which no man dreamed in the world he knew. . . . In his time educated people believed that they amused themselves with books of imagination, but that they "made their souls" by listening to sermons and by doing or by not doing certain things. When they had to explain why serious people like themselves honoured the great poets greatly, they were hard put to it for lack of good reasons. In our time we are agreed that we "make our souls" out of some one of the great poets of ancient times, or out of Shelley or Wordsworth, or Goethe or Balzac, or Flaubert, or Count Tolstoy, in the books he wrote before he became a prophet and fell into a lesser order, or out of Mr. Whistler's pictures, while we amuse ourselves, or, at best, make a poorer sort of soul, by listening to sermons or by doing or by not doing certain things.

This is hardly an adequate representation of Blake, who, whatever he might have been, was certainly not cut to the shape of a 'nineties aesthete. Yet the passage is enlightening for its revelation of Yeats's completely impervious aestheticism, to which he seems to have felt a special impulse to attach the writings of mystics like Bohme, Blake and Swedenborg, using them as elements in a purely aesthetic scheme of his own.[1]

Lacking inner dynamism, the religious impulse to grasp hold of life and make it surrender its meaning, and lacking, by the exigencies of his situation, the classical artist's interest in a variety of outward expressions of life and his participation in an orthodox form of religious worship, Yeats, looking inwards, could see only a static universe of moods and dreams, and this he translated into his work. The repugnance to the world of actuality which aestheticism typifies severely limits the material and scope of art, and in the early Yeats this is restricted to a small range of dream-imagery used to convey a predominant, static emotion of world-weariness and ineffectual and objectless longing. "Dream" is itself a recurrent key-word. There is no need to give examples of this sort of writing, although "The Song of the Happy Shepherd" might be given as a good expression of Yeats's central theme:

[1]There is a revealing account in the *Autobiographies* of how Yeats, wandering in a remote part of Ireland and discovering an old castle in a romantic spot, falls to thinking what an excellent retreat this would make for some esoteric religious order, and then begins to attempt the formulation of the rule and mysteries of some such order which could suitably make use of the castle. The inversion is characteristic.

The woods of Arcady are dead,
And over is their antique joy;
Of old the world on dreaming fed;
Grey Truth is now her painted toy;
Yet still she turns her restless head:
But O, sick children of the world,
Of all the many changing things
In dreary dancing past us whirled,
To the cracked tune that Chronos sings,
Words alone are certain good. . . .

Here we note—a significant inversion—that the world *feeds* on dreams, but merely *toys* with Truth.

Practice apart, Yeats's idea of the nature and function of poetry is formulated in certain essays written in the eighteen-nineties, from which it is apparent that he regards it as having no commerce with the world of experience, its task being to conjure up certain enchanted states of mind in which the mind is made aware of some bodiless, timeless reality. As he writes in "The Symbolism of Poetry":

> The purpose of rhythm, it has always seemed to me, is to prolong the moment of contemplation, the moment when we are both asleep and awake, which is the one moment of creation, by hushing us with an alluring monotony, while it holds us waking by variety, to keep us in that state of perhaps real trance, in which the mind liberated from the pressure of the will is unfolded in symbols.

And he continues:

> If people were to accept the theory that poetry moves us because of its symbolism, what change should one look for in the manner of our poetry? A return to the way of our fathers, a casting out of descriptions of nature for the sake of nature, of the moral law for the sake of the moral law, a casting out of all anecdotes and of that brooding over scientific opinion that so often extinguished the central flame in Tennyson, and of that vehemence that would make us do or not do certain things; or, in other words, we should come to understand that the beryl stone was enchanted by our fathers that it might unfold the pictures in its heart, and not to mirror our own excited faces, or the boughs waving outside the window. With this change of substance, this return to imagination, this understanding that the laws of art, which are the hidden laws of the world, can alone bind the imagination, would come a change of style, and we would cast out of serious poetry those energetic rhythms, as of a man running, which are the invention of the will with its eyes always on something to be done or undone; and we would seek out those wavering, meditative, organic rhythms, which are the embodiment of the imagination, that neither

desires nor hates, because it has done with time, and only wishes to gaze upon some reality, some beauty. . . .

An aestheticism of this kind has a similar effect upon both art and life. As an essentially static attitude to life, an attitude which "has done with time," it fails to see meaning or purpose in everyday living, and therefore turns from this to preoccupy itself with that which lies outside the borders of normal human life. Thus Yeats's interest in dreams, in magic, in spiritualism, in astrology, in theosophy, in anything of a religiose or mystical flavour which did not, like true religion, invade and claim the right to transform the actual texture of existence. The texture of existence for Yeats remained, for this reason, commonplace.

In art, the same applies. To avoid a monotonous reiteration of the same mood and imagery, this attitude necessitates a continual search for subject-matter, and this it likewise tends to seek in that which is exotic and remote. Together with his early vein of dreamy sorrow and romantic longing to have "done with time," Yeats learned to exploit Irish legend, as later he was to exploit his own personal legend and Irish nationalist politics. But always his first interest in these things was as material for poetry.

The static nature of Yeats's life-attitude is revealed in his doctrine of the Mask, the need for the poet to cultivate a style, both in art and in life. He wrote in 1909 that "Style, personality—deliberately adopted and therefore a mask—is the only escape from the hot-faced bargainers and the money-changers." And: "There is a relation between discipline and the theatrical sense. If we cannot imagine ourselves as different from what we are and assume that second self, we cannot impose a discipline upon ourselves, though we may accept one from others. Active virtue as distinguished from the passive acceptance of a current code is therefore theatrical, consciously dramatic, the wearing of a mask. It is the condition of arduous, full life." And again, late in life, he writes in his diary: ". . . my character is so little myself that all my life it has thwarted me. It has affected my poems, my true self, no more than the character of a dancer affects the movements of a dance." Throughout his work the negative and static quality of Yeats's personality is revealed. The famous undulating prose style derives directly from it. In his *Essays* we find, not an active, dynamic intellect driving towards some object, not a style which, subordinated to the power of thought, becomes tense, supple and directioned, a vehicle for meaning; but a meandering intermixture of speculation and reminiscence in which the style turns upon itself, becomes ornamental and florid. Everything is shadowy and vague, the ideas are powerless and do not grip, rhetoric and incantation flood the meaning. A similar vagueness and paucity is discovered in the *Autobiographies*. Where we might expect a delineation of the organic growth of an original personality, shaping itself through its manifold contacts with life, we are given a series of blurred impressions, an aesthetic drifting in which scene follows scene but statically and without development. Throughout the *Autobiographies*, Yeats, despite the information he gives about himself, remains a flat and shadowy figure.

II

Yeats, as we have seen, made a "religion" of art, which means in effect that he neutralized religion. Religious activity is the dynamism of the soul in its efforts to comprehend ultimate or absolute truth, meaning and purpose, and to bring actual life into a relationship with them. This did not concern Yeats. The effort to bring actual life into the radius of the ultimate implies the possibility of correspondence between the supernatural and the natural worlds, through which the life of man is given meaning and purpose. It is therefore interesting to find, in Yeats, the predication of a supernatural realm, the world of Faery, of the "Ever Living," which, however, exists in an *antithetical* relationship to the world of humanity. This means that for him human life is lived in a closed circle, a purposeless efflorescence denied the significance which can be given it only by an integral relationship with the absolute, while the supernatural world is such another closed circle. This is a perfect theological justification for aestheticism! There are certain inevitable consequences of such a view of the independence of the natural and supernatural spheres. Not only will the supernatural sphere be seen as the realm of the *inhuman,* but the natural will be despiritualized. In Yeats's poems and plays, mortals who have felt the attraction of the land of Faery wander about in a hopeless daze, fall into trances, or feel themselves to be under some accursed enchantment which turns life to ashes in their mouth.

Yeats's development from the poet of a monotonous dreamy twilight to the poet of the harsh and acrid light of day is to some extent involved with his changing attitude towards the supernatural. But basically his view remained the same, the alteration being one of emphasis. As a young man he dreamed and wrote about the inhuman world of Faery, and this naturally limited the scope of his art. In middle life he approached nearer humanity, but because of his view of the separation of the two worlds he wrote poetry of disenchantment, was not able to take human life seriously, and in his old age fell back on the de-spiritualized natural world and celebrated the brutal, sensual life of the blood. There is something inhuman, or soulless, about Yeats all the way through.

His concern with fairies was apparent from the start. A juvenile poem began:

A man has the hope of heaven
But soulless a fairy dies . . .

and an early poem, "The Stolen Child," has for refrain:

Come away, O human child!
To the waters and the wild
With a faery, hand in hand,
For the world's more full of weeping than you can understand.

In the early play, *The Land of Heart's Desire,* the theme is of a young woman who is wrapt away to the deathless but inhuman world of the fairies. And in the *Wandering of Oisin* (1889) this legendary Irish hero who has lived three hundred years with Niamh his bride in the land of the immortals returns only by a mishap to find his years fall suddenly on him and himself condemned to drag out the rest of his existence in a Christianized Ireland which has no place for the ancient heroes. *The Shadowy Waters,* the final version of which appeared in 1910, has a similar theme in that it represents the voyage of the life-rejecting poet and lover Forgael over the "waste seas" in search of an ideal happiness in that " 'country at the end of the world/Where no child's born but to outlive the moon.' " While he was writing in this vein, Yeats's language was decorative and languorous. But it was not an inexhaustible vein, and a poet of Yeats's artistic conscientiousness could not be content with endless repetition of himself. After *The Shadowy Waters* his verse began to show a more personal bitterness than that contained in the musical melancholy of the early poems. The rather fluent world-weariness gives place to a more acrid dissatisfaction with life. The poem "Adam's Curse" reveals a movement towards realism and away from a lofty, other-world romanticism, and this trend is continued in *Responsibilities* (1914). The bitterness of disillusionment and waste of life runs through the prefatory verses to the latter collection, in which the poet, addressing his ancestors, requests:

Pardon that for a barren passion's sake,
Although I have come close on forty-nine
I have no child, I have nothing but a book,
Nothing but that to prove your blood and mine.

It is notable that in these volumes begins utterance occasioned by public events. And here too is the poem in which the poet speaks of the lying days of his youth when he swayed his leaves and flowers in the sun and now prays that he may "wither into the truth." In these poems generally the language is barer, more sinewy, the metaphors more exact:

. . . There's something ails our colt
That must, as if it had not holy blood,
Nor on Olympus leaped from cloud to cloud,
Shiver under the lash, strain, sweat and jolt
As though it dragged road metal. My curse on plays
That have to be set up in fifty ways,
On the day's war with every knave and dolt,
Theatre business, management of men . . .

and from this time on, it is to be observed, occurs the more frequent and ironical use of broken rhythm and false rhyme.

The cause of this change of mood, subject-matter and style lay in Yeats's dissatisfaction with a poetry of dreams which reflected his dissatisfaction with dreams themselves. Yeats was growing older, the woman about whom he had woven his romantic fantasies appeared with time in a different perspective, he could now admit his to be "a barren passion." "Theatre business, management of men" had brought his idealistic visions of a national cultural renascence to the hard test of practical realization, and in writing for the stage he had had to adapt his style to the understanding of the theatre audience. And with all this he had come to be convinced of the wrongness of his own poetic method of the exclusion of what seemed non-essential from his search for Beauty. But that his attitude to life had indeed changed, or more truly that the perspective of his vision of the relationship of the ideal to the actual world had shifted, is made apparent in the fabular poem entitled "The Two Kings," in which the old theme of the human and the supernatural lover is taken up for the last time, but is given a new and significant twist. In this poem Edaine, the wife of King Eochaid, is tricked to a meeting-place where she is confronted by a supernatural being who claims her love on the grounds of pre-natal priority. In spite of all the spirit's arguments of the transitoriness of mortal love and the superiority of life among the immortals, Edaine rejects him and returns to her husband, to whom she recounts her adventure. Here, though the variance in emphasis which differentiates it from previous allegories is apparent, it should be noted that the alteration is merely one of emphasis: the situation remains basically the same. Edaine rejects the supernatural and chooses the human, but there is no suggestion that human life is anything more than merely mortal, that there is any mitigation of the absolute cleavage between natural and supernatural. The inference clearly is that Yeats has turned away from an impossible ideal for the sake of a reality known to be and accepted as unspiritual, and which is still, therefore, something less than human.

In "The Hour Before Dawn" the altered emphasis is brought out even more unmistakably. The beggar, "a cursing rogue with a merry face" who stumbles on a deep hollow where he finds a drinker with a tub of enchanted beer which will keep him asleep till the day of judgment when all phenomena will pass away, represents the acceptance of life; the drinker, whom he curses and pummels and flees from with prayers and curses on his lips, is an obvious symbol of rejection. The reversal here in Yeats's implied attitude to "dreams" is complete. But here again human life, whose values the poem implicitly decides for, is represented by a beggar, sensual humanity at its commonest level. To the same period belongs the poem "Beggar to Beggar Cried" which, foreshadowing Yeats's later "frenzied" manner, is also a fairly frank piece of self-revelation.

The volume in which Yeats approaches most nearly to the condition of humanity, in which there is some indication of an awareness of the pathos, irony and suffering within human existence, *The Wild Swans at Coole,* is also that which marks Yeats's weakest level of creation. There is little dramatizing here, and less adventitious supernaturalism. The book conveys, as a whole, an impression of a cold, ashy sadness, the sadness of the unachieved and the unrealized; but this sadness is not fully faced and poetically overcome, and it lingers miasmally around the verge of the poems, where its effect is desolate and depressing. The total effect is only to show how far from a deep and rich human sympathy Yeats really is. His lack of grasp is reflected in a technical laxity, and some of the poems, "The People," "The Dawn," "The Sad Shepherd," "Presences," "Broken Dreams" and others, are garrulous and prosy, while such didactic pieces as "The Phases of the Moon" and "Ego Dominus Tuus" suffer from a flatness where all is on the surface, mere dissertation. The movement towards a deeper sympathy with and a greater honesty of approach to human life is partial only, and is not a success, nor is it surprising to find in such a poem as "The Collar-Bone of a Hare," to me a strangely unpleasing and distasteful poem, what amounts to a confession of inhumanity. The slightly "touched" irresponsibility of this, the half-idiotic cackle at the "old bitter world where they marry in churches," is not pretty, particularly in the reminiscential, old-mannish context of the book.

Yeats was not happy with humanity: he refused to suffer. Nor did any miracle occur to alter his approach and cause him to accept human life in a far deeper sense than he had ever done hitherto. Instead, after the hesitations of *The Wild Swans at Coole,* he made a sudden and decisive movement towards entrenching himself in his old supernatural-natural dualism. "Ego Dominus Tuus" and "The Phases of the Moon," besides the prose essay *Per Amica Silentia Lunae,* had shown his gropings towards some kind of private esoteric system, and now in the years after the Great War, in the early days of his marriage, there came the ideas and inspirations which were to result in the work eventually published under the title, *A Vision.*

Yeats himself described the system expounded in this book as a construction which enabled him to purge his poetry of explanation and abstraction and to find a simplicity he had previously sought in vain. The system itself is entirely peculiar to Yeats, it is doubtful whether it would be of use to any other person. The theses upon which it is built are all put forward as *a priori* arguments; the entire construction is arbitrary and seems to have no nexus in real existence. The material upon which it is based purports to have been supplied by "spirits," and it is entirely in keeping that when Yeats, as he says, offered to spend the rest of his life explaining and piecing together the material they gave him, they should have replied, "No, we have come to give you metaphors for poetry." It seems clear that the purpose of this peculiar and ingenious system in relation to Yeats was purely functional. Yeats's static aestheticism precluded him from the living pursuit of truth within experience. Truth was of no interest to him, he wanted either material for poetry or material for that which would provide the pre-conditions for poetry, in this case an idiosyncratic, self-sufficient system which, cutting arbitrarily across all living currents of thought, would enshrine his own feelings about life and justify his concentration upon his deep and narrow vein of poetry. "Some will ask," he wrote in *A Vision,* "whether I believe in the actual existence of my circuits of sun and moon. . . . To such a question I can but answer that if sometimes, overwhelmed by miracle as all men must be when in the midst of it, I have taken such periods literally, my reason has soon recovered; and now that the system stands out clearly in my imagination I regard them as stylistic arrangements of experience comparable to the cubes in the drawing of Wyndham Lewis and to the ovoids in the sculpture of Brancusi. They have helped me to hold in a single thought reality and justice."

The system here expounded confirms Yeats's fast division between natural and supernatural, with the difference that here the "supernatural" as spiritual reality is virtually eliminated, existing only as a blind power driving the wheel of birth and rebirth in which man and the cosmos are involved. The system is rigidly deterministic. Man, according to it, is an inert substance caught up in a cyclic mechanism of successive incarnations in which he passes from pure subjectivity to pure objectivity, the tension between which poles of being determines fate, life and character. Human life exists for no purpose beyond its own mere being, nor is there seemingly any escape from the wheel. The static, deterministic nature of the cosmic process precludes progress of any kind, even individual striving. Thus, by implication, moral effort is redundant, both as operating within the personal life and as directed towards the maintenance of the equilibrium of society. The individual is freed from all responsibility, since everything is regulated automatically by the cosmic mechanism, and there is no possibility of really changing or improving things. While war, famine, destruction of civilizations, are all inevitable and pre-ordained, this is cancelled out by the inevitability of renewal and reconstruction, so that catastrophes are not to be taken very seriously and may, indeed, be accepted with rejoicing as providing a little interest and excitement in the tedium of a prearranged existence. There is obviously no place for the humane emotions, love, pity and the rest. All the individual can do is to accept the life thus thrust upon him and, since there is really no alternative, exult in it. Vitality becomes a value in its own right.

It will be seen how such a system fitted in with Yeats's predilections, and how it helped to make possible the attitude to life of hard, scornful acceptance out of which the poems in *The Tower* and *The Winding Stair* drew their origin. Freed from all uncertainties he could go on to that celebration of blind, passionate, aimless life out of which some of his most magnificent verse arose:

I am content to live it all again
And yet again, if it be life to pitch
Into the frog-spawn of a blind man's ditch,
A blind man battering blind men;
Or into that most fecund ditch of all,
The folly that man does
Or must suffer, if he woos
A proud woman not kindred of his soul.

I am content to follow its source
Every event in action or in thought;
Measure the lot; forgive myself the lot!
When such as I cast out remorse
So great a sweetness flows into the breast
We must laugh and we must sing,
We are blest by everything,
Everything we look upon is blest.

III

Yeats's poetry has received a greater degree of recognition than that of any modern British poet. Therefore no harm will be done if for a moment we refuse to be hypnotized by his reputation and probe more critically into the nature of his achievement than current valuations might seem to encourage. And that there are unsatisfactory features about his poetry seems to me apparent.

The sense of dissatisfaction with the poetry of Yeats—to speak from my own experience—is faint at the first but increases after familiarity, when the mind has recovered from its first bedazzlement and begins to grope after a permanent relationship, to find a place for it in its life. And Yeats's poetry, it seems to me, is one which, though it compels our admiration, contains an element (or the absence of such) which prevents us from finding a place for it close to our heart. It is too remote, both too characteristic and too impersonal; it is, again, for want of a better word, too inhuman. We can live with a speaking or a singing voice, but not with a bellow or shriek pitched violently or ecstatically beyond the range of the human ear. This inhumanness is not a feature of the later verse only. It runs throughout Yeats's work. I have never been able to think of Yeats's work in the abstract or to read a number of poems concretely without receiving the impression of a sort of ghostly shining phosphorescence, and this impression puzzled me for a long time until I began to see its origin and meaning. It is this peculiar quality which imparts an atmosphere of unreality to his work. This unrealness is very noticeable in the early poetry:

You need but lift a pearl-pale hand,
And bind up your long hair and sigh;
And all men's hearts must burn and beat;
And candle-like foam on the dim sand,
And stars climbing the dew-dropping sky,
Live but to light your passing feet.

This is very delightful; but nothing could be falser, more exaggerated, more out of touch with life. We are able to accept the poem only if we accept the poet's premises and permit ourselves to enter into his dream. Now although as Yeats developed he left behind this dim world of dreams and began to incorporate more of concrete imagery into his verse, and although a dreamy vagueness of mood gave place to the sharpness of disenchantment and bitterness or a kind of ironical joy, nevertheless he retained his ineradicable tendency to exaggerated statement the effect of which was necessarily to place his poetry at a remove from human life and sympathy. Even in his middle period his love-poetry is born out of a dramatic attitude rather than out of an honest relationship to experience. This exaggeration and over-heightening, this indulgence in dramatics, is exemplified by the repeated use of hyperbolic phrases and of resounding words whose effect is to inflate the meaning. Some of Yeats's favourite words of his later period, "passionate," "rage," "turbulent," "frenzy," "murderous," "agony," "miraculous," "bitter," "blind," "wild," he overworked no less than, during his early period, he overworked words like "dim," "dreams," "pale," "desolate," "sorrow" and the rest. Yeats carries off his use of these words, and the overdramatic attitude implied in that use, in his later verse no less successfully than in his earlier work; but they do not ring any truer to the perceptive ear. As with the early poems, one must grant the poet his own ground, which means here entering the remote world of reminiscence and reverie which he has built up around his lonely ego, before one is able to accept his work. Yeats's art persuades us to do so. But his is a world which we cannot endure, or interest ourselves in, for long. Yeats's pattern of experience is provincial not only thematically but spiritually, and while we can force it into temporary relationship with our own we cannot truly make it ours.

This hyperbolism of Yeats which on familiarity becomes wearisome and hollow, and which sometimes leads him into tremendous, nonsensical asseverations, finds a counterpart in his lack of contemporaneity, itself a grave fault in any poet when, as nearly always, it signifies a poverty of observation which in turn reflects an incapability before the fullness of experience. On Yeats's part it is certain that it does reflect an inability to overcome and bring into the scope of his art more than a strictly limited range of experience, namely, that which lends itself to a stylized "dramatic" treatment. It is not necessary to suppose that no modern poem can be regarded as valid unless it contains repeated references to pylons, gas-works or grain-elevators to realize the truth that we live in a world which is full of these and similar things, that these therefore constitute much of the background of our experience, and that in mastering experience and translating it into the terms of poetry we are bound to use the images with which experience presents us. Yeats ignores the contemporary scene, which means that he ignores much of his own experience, and when he attempts at times to incorporate a contemporary reference into his verse requiring the exploitation of modern imagery the result is not fortunate. Modern war, for instance, is hardly presented adequately to the imagination in his otherwise admirable poem "Lapis Lazuli," when he writes:

For everybody knows or else should know
That if nothing drastic is done
Aeroplane and Zeppelin will come out,

Pitch like King Billy bomb-balls in
Until the town lie beaten flat.

Yeats is much happier in the same poem when he is describing an antique work of art:

Two Chinamen, behind them a third,
Are carved in lapis lazuli,
Over them flies a long-legged bird,
A symbol of longevity;
The third, doubtless a serving man,
Carries a musical instrument.

Every discoloration of the stone,
Every accidental crack or dent,
Seems a water-course or an avalanche,
Or lofty slope where it still snows
Though doubtless plum or cherry-branch
Sweetens the little half-way house
Those Chinamen climb towards, and I
Delight to imagine them seated there. . . .

And might it not also be possible to view Yeats's attachment to an idiosyncratic use of mechanical verse-metres in the light of his insensibility to those rhythmical currents in the life of our time which have been influential in determining the subtler verse-forms of more sensitively contemporary poets? Yeats's complete absence of discrimination in his response to contemporary work—*vide* the unfortunate *Oxford Book of Modern Verse*—seems to bear this out.

The substance of the poems in *The Tower* and *The Winding Stair,* superficially so impressively full, dwindles on acquaintance and investigation to a very small residue. Yeats's exploitation of his personality and of his personal history is consciously dramatic. The resounding dramatic *effect* achieved, there is very little to hold on to. The poem sequence which gives its title to *The Tower* opens effectively enough, and the second section promises to unfold the poem well, with:

I pace upon the battlements and stare
On the foundations of a house, or where
Tree, like a sooty finger, starts from the earth;
And send imagination forth
Under the day's declining beam, and call
Images and memories

From ruin or from ancient trees,
For I would ask a question of them all.

But thereafter, instead of a fulfilment of the expectancy aroused in these opening lines, we have—a descent to anecdote:

Beyond that ridge lived Mrs. French, and once
When every silver candlestick or sconce
Lit up the dark mahogany and the wine,
A serving man that could divine
That most respected lady's every wish,
Ran and with the garden shears
Clipped an insolent farmer's ears
And brought them in a little covered dish.

And the poem continues in such a reminiscential, rambling, inconsequent manner, only held together by the poet's rhythmical and rhetorical skill.

The poems in these two volumes, indeed, bear out the implications of attitude made in such a poem as "The Hour Before Dawn." Here sensual human life is celebrated: but a life which when detached from all intercourse with spiritual meaning, is regarded as an aimless and meaningless proliferation. Yeats's creed consists in the not very interesting or subtle exaltation of brute vitality:

Whatever stands in field or flood,
Bird, beast, fish or man,
Mare or stallion, cock or hen,
Stands in God's unchanging eye
In all the vigour of its blood;
In that faith I live or die.

In choosing "perfection of the work" in false opposition to "perfection of the life," Yeats, through his artistic devotedness, was able to develop his poetry without developing at the same time a wider and deeper insight into life, and his early otherworldliness, springing from a defect of deep and warm humanity, being too rarefied and phantasmal, found its level in the blood, lust and mud of the last poems. For Yeats there is no human mean between the supernatural and the bestial, the inhuman purity of the moon and the animal ragings of the blood. The culmination of this tendency is to be seen in Yeats's last works, *A Full Moon in March* and the *Last Poems and*

Plays. In the play which gives its title to the former volume, the virginal Queen, "whose emblem is the moon," promises to give herself to whatever man can move her by his song. A swineherd, dressed in "foul rags" and with hair "more foul and ragged than" his rags, and with "scratched foul flesh," comes to sing before her:

"I tended swine, when I first heard your name.
I rolled among the dung of swine and laughed.
What do I know of beauty?"

And when the Queen asks what she gains if, proclaiming his song the best, she leaves her throne for his sake, he answers:

"A song—the night of love,
An ignorant forest and the dung of swine,"

adding to himself:

"She shall bring forth her farrow in the dung."

Insulted, the Queen has the swineherd beheaded. The severed head being brought to her, she takes it in her hands and dances, pressing her lips to the lips of the head. In the *Last Poems and Plays* we have the glorification of violence and war, the celebration of sexuality, the same inner emptiness revealed either in an expression of a sense of personal futility or in the insistence upon a hysterical and nihilistic exultation. In certain of the poems, "Why Should Not Old Men Be Mad?," "Are You Content?," "What Then?," Yeats questions himself, but then drowns any conceivable reply with a randy ballad or a ballad of violence, a political lampoon or a marching song. "Come swish around my pretty punk" and " What shall I do for pretty girls/Now my old bawd is dead" alternate with "The Ghost of Roger Casement/Is beating on the door" and "The Roaring Tinker if you like,/But Mannion is my name,/And I beat up the common sort/And think it is no shame." In "The Circus Animals' Desertion" the poet speaks of his search for a theme, enumerates half regretfully, half ironically, his earlier use of legendary subjects, and concludes:

Now that my ladder's gone,
I must lie down where all the ladders start,
In the foul rag-and-bone shop of the heart . . .

while in "The Spur" he confesses:

You think it horrible that lust and rage
Should dance attention on my old age;
They were not such a plague when I was young;
What else have I to spur me into song?

Certain of these last poems have a barbaric beauty and splendour, although it is a splendour of desolation and emptiness, and an inhuman beauty. But what are we to think of a poet who, with all his occasional impressiveness, is in one moment capable of such a descent into banality as the following:

Irish poets, learn your trade
Sing whatever is well made,
Scorn the sort now growing up
All out of shape from toe to top,
Their unremembering hearts and heads
Base-born products of base beds.
Sing the peasantry, and then
Hard-riding country gentlemen,
The holiness of monks, and after
Porter-drinkers' randy laughter;
Sing the lords and ladies gay
That were beaten into the clay
Through seven heroic centuries;
Cast your mind on other days
That we in coming days may be
Still the indomitable Irishry.

The indomitable Irishry! It is one of the enigmas of Yeats as a poet that he should be capable of mixing real tragic grandeur with such fatal vulgarity and commonplaceness. Whatever may be the conventional verdict on his work, it is certain that at its centre is a hollowness which time is bound increasingly to reveal.

IV

Other things apart, Yeats is a demonstration of the superficiality of the "romantic-classical" antithesis as commonly applied to poetry. On the surface there has never been a more "romantic" poet than Yeats, with his self-dramatization, his dandyism, his exaggerated emotionalism (springing from an inner coldness: one thinks of his impossible love and his marriage in middle age) and the rest. Yet, probing beneath the surface, we find a contradictory conservation and reliance upon outward conditions. The qualities and conditions of a stable, heirarchical social order in which poetry and the poet would have their recognized official places. As Mr. MacNeice says in his study of Yeats: "His desire for a creed and for poetry whose imagery, as well as ideas, is based on that creed, is in tune with his desire for schools of poetry. In spite of his Romantic genealogy he had a Roman liking for the poet in a formal niche; poets were to be members of a priesthood, handing down their mysteries to their successors, and conferring with one another when they wished to develop or modify their ritual." This is nothing if not retrogressive. The fact that he regarded the poet's function as ideally a public (i.e. impersonal) one is shown in several of his remarks about his own poetry during his later life, and by his reversion to the "bard" in his ballad-writing on Irish political themes.

We cannot understand Yeats until we realize that his inner attitude was quite static; his philosophy, his politics, his life and his work were all shaped by this fact. Custom and ceremony are the conditions he exalts when he writes, in "A Prayer for My Daughter," of the perquisites of the good life. His "romantic" peculiarities were developed only as a substitute for that acceptable external framework of convention and custom which, given him by a different society, a different age, would have proved him indubitably a "classical" artist. Yeats flaunts his "personality," but in reality is an extremely impersonal artist; his personality is a "mask," a dramatic convenience for the writing of verse; true personality is not idiosyncratic but anonymous, and does not flaunt itself. Yeats did not place any high value upon the personal qualities and upon human personality itself. He evaded Christianity, which exalts and enshrines the values of human personality (and which brings the supernatural down into the natural), and it is not therefore surprising to find that he took great pride in his ancestry, his family, the nation of his birth. The fact that he toyed with fascism in his later years and took a keen interest in eugenics (racial purity) is but another revelation of his anti-personalism. In default of a principle of personal dynamism within himself, and of such a stable classical order and accepted orthodoxy, Yeats assembled a homemade, gimcrack order and "religious" system out of the exotic fragments he found here and there beyond the borders of commonplace life; thus his apparent romanticism. An artificer or bard, without a context, without standards he could accept from outside and without an inner spiritual pressure directed upon life, he turned inwards to centre his attention upon art, he became an aesthete, and there resulted the development which is revealed in his work: a development in a vacuum.

Joseph Warren Beach

When it is said that Yeats was, by common critical judgment, the finest of British poets in his time, one has a reminder of the high level of poetic technique prevailing among them, the variety of incidental charm represented, as well as of the general remoteness of poetry from the common concerns of intellectual man, its want of rooting in the solid cultural soil of the period. And considering the long stretch of years over which his activity extended and his susceptibility to changing fashions in poetry, one has a measure of the radical alteration in poetic taste and theory. Under the influence of his artist father and his Dublin friends (George Russell, Edward Dowden, Katherine Tynan, etc.) Yeats's training consisted in a heavy inoculation with the cultural dilettantism of Pre-Raphaelite romanticism.[1] In London in the late eighties and nineties he was an intimate of men like Lionel Johnson and Arthur Symons. The shaping influences on his poetry for many years were Pater, Villiers de l'Isle-Adam, Mallarmé, Morris, Blake, and Shelley (in his more visionary and "symbolist" aspects). Of *The Wanderings of Oisin and Other Poems* (1888), Morris said, "You write my kind of poetry." As early as 1886 he had come out strongly in favor of "Celtic Ireland." In 1893 his volume of stories, *The Celtic Twilight,* offered a blueprint of that shadowy realm of faerie glamour, and invited the new racial consciousness of his time thither for inspection and support.

During this period Yeats was a devoted student of theosophy and magic, and member of a society of Christian Cabalists. He was highly eclectic in his occultism, which embraced the lore of fairies, banshees, *revenants,* astrology, automatic writing, second-sight, and prophetic dreams. Much of his later poetry was built around an elaborate transcendental system for determining the twenty-eight phases of personality by reference to a "great wheel"—obviously derived, on the nat-

[1] This is used in a broad non-technical sense. Richard Ellmann, in *Yeats: The Man and the Masks,* emphasizes the fact that, in many points, Yeats took up positions opposed to his father's in the effort to establish his personal independence. Thus his religious mysticism was in part a reaction against his father's rationalism, and as a student of painting he preferred the Pre-Raphaelites to the "anti-romantic French impressionists" who were his father's models.

This article from *A History of English Literature* by Craig, Anderson, Bredvold and Beach, New York, in press. Printed by permission of Oxford University Press, Inc.

ural plane, from esoteric treatises in print, but revealed to him directly, on the supernatural plane, by the voice of disembodied spirits. In short, Yeats, lacking the discipline of either theology or science, and resolutely determined to resist "the mechanical simplification of life of Darwin and the English thinkers" (Hone), yielded himself up through life to the seductions of superstition of every imaginable form. Some critics consider Yeats is to be prized as a poet because he had the wit to invent a mythos which would serve the needs of his mind. One had rather thought that myths were cultural phenomena with a broader basis than one man's deliberate invention and drew their force from the serious participation of the tribe.

Of course, Yeats employed myths, early and late, as symbolic bearers of his emotions. In the earlier time, his Rosicrucian and faerie lore equally served his nostalgic aspiration after states of being more satisfactory than those provided by experience. The Sidhe and the old heroes were calling to the wearied idealist to come, come away "into the twilight," to "the townland that is the world's bane," adjuring him to "brood on hopes and fears no more." He would that he and his beloved were "white birds on the foam of the sea." With wandering Aengus he will follow the magic girl "through hollow lands and hilly lands," and through the looking glass of time, and pluck her "the silver apples of the moon,/The golden apples of the sun." Or else it is the secret rose of the world, symbol of supernal beauty, which is one with truth, and the denial in the world of ideals of all that in reality is "uncomely and broken, all things worn out and old," and which reigns inviolate "beyond the stir and tumult of defeated dreams."

In his later phase, Yeats's nostalgia (or seeking of the spirit) takes another direction, or employs a different terminology. If he still longs to escape from the world of realists, chafferers and snarling politicians, it is no longer into an "other world" of "dreams" that he wishes to be gathered, but into the "artifice of eternity,"—that is, broadly, into the world of pure ideas. It is there, with "sages standing in God's holy fire," that the soul of the old man would "clap its hand and sing, and louder sing/For every tatter in its mortal dress." Thus Yeats wins at last, by way of meditation on the phases of the moon, to the intellectual world of the Platonists. There is, in Yeats's system, nothing of the Socratic method, though a good deal of Pythagorean abracadabra; and he carries none of the metaphysical baggage of Spenser and Shelley in their

Platonism. But the mind was a good one, though untrained, and it worked powerfully, though on eccentric lines. What is most engaging in him here is the frank recognition, as poet, that the pure idea is so abstract that it robs one of the poetry, at the same time that it raises one above the indignities, of mortal experience. This dilemma is poignantly set forth in "A Dialogue of the Self and Soul" and wittily summarized in "Vacillation" in the following interchange:

> The Soul. *Seek out reality, leave things that seem.*
> The Heart. *What, be a singer born and lack a theme?*
> The Soul. *Isaiah's coal, what more can a man desire?*
> The Heart. *Struck dumb in the simplicity of fire!*
> The Soul. *Look on that fire, salvation walks within.*
> The Heart. *What theme had Homer but original sin?*

It is this dialectic of idea and fact that gives their strength to the later poems,—this counterpoint of ideal reality and surface character, with the vibrant tensions constantly operating in the field of their polarity. It informs Yeats's poems on his friends and relatives, on the paradoxes of his own personality, and the esthetic and political controversies of the day; it points his scorn for middle-class ways and thought, and perpetually accompanies the hermetic process of hammering out for himself a character (or "persona") suited equally to the dignity of the spirit and the hardness and pride of the gentleman and man of the world. It gives substance and pattern to his poems as works of the imagination; it guarantees that the beauty of effect shall be "earned" (to use Brooks' and Warren's pregnant phrase) in the spirit's contention with circumstance.

The earlier poems are remarkable for their dreamy sweetness and their traditional song-like ballad rhythm, whether they are in ordinary iambics, like "The Song of Wandering Aengus," or in the more haunting, curiously modulated cadence of "The Lake Isle of Innisfree." Very little of common life is admitted; the vocabulary is rather strictly limited to what would suit the general tonality of late-Victorian romanticism, and further limited in the effort to give the effect of Irish folk literature. In his later poetry Yeats cultivates subtler, more varied and more dramatically balanced cadences; his vocabulary is greatly enlarged with terms both vernacular and learned. The metaphors are fresher and taken from a vastly wider range of reference, and the imaginative structure is both more firmly wrought and more spontaneous and natural in effect. The "metaphysical" has come back, with its artful dissonances and its composition of contrasting tonalities. And the final effect is an enrichment of the early "glamour" with the help of the familiar and the difficult. In all this Yeats has been a leader in that school of writing which includes such names as Eliot, Auden, Ransom, Stevens, Ronald Bottrall and Dylan Thomas.

His later style begins to show strongly in the 1910 and 1914 volumes in such poems as "No Second Troy," "The Fascination of What's Difficult," and "The Cold Heaven." In 1919 he has completely found his voice as a poet in whom feeling is penetrated with thought and the imagination is rooted in experience and enriched by reference to a considerable range of assimilated knowledge. The defining of himself, with the pursuit of his ideal double or anti-self, occupies him in many of his most intriguing poems in this and later volumes—"Ego Dominus Tuus," "The Phases of the Moon," "The Tower," "A Dialogue of the Self and Soul." "Sailing to Byzantium" is justly the most famous as it is the most direct and lyrical of these poetic statements.

Another subject that ocupies his feeling meditations is the political dissensions and distresses of contemporary Ireland and the problem of reconciling political activity with the finer demands of the spirit. It would be tiresome to enumerate the subjects and attitudes reflected in such distinctive and moving poems as "The Wild Swans at Coole," "Among School Children," "All Souls' Night." One may deprecate the strain of social complacency in many poems in which he develops his ideal of the aristocratic personality. He makes a little too much of the artistic integrity that precluded popular appeal with "the noisy set/Of bankers, school-masters, and clergymen/The martyrs call the world." In the misunderstanding between poet and bourgeois, the bourgeois has the advantage of security and the poet must make the most of his command of the verbal trumpet. But after all, it *is* spiritual and not material distinction that Yeats celebrates; and if he cannot find this in the chapman and the Whig, he finds it readily in the beggar, the fisherman, the drunkard and the saint. And he celebrates it without vulgarity, or with as little of this as is compatible with self-conscious pride.

The wisdom that Yeats assiduously cultivated through all the strain of public and private life was not the practical wisdom of the forum nor the philosophical wisdom of the academy. It was the wisdom of the spirit and the imagination. One has strongly the impression of a man who with great seriousness and pertinacity shaped himself a character and submitted himself to a discipline. It was his weakness and misfortune that this discipline had, as it were, no common terms with the systematic knowledge and reason of his time. He does not, like Dante or Goethe or Donne, not even, like Pope or Shelley or Hardy, have the intellect of his time under him for support. He was, indeed, the most gifted representative in English of an age of poets who were in reaction against their age because they did not understand it, and, for lack of an adequate humanism, mistook science and reason for their enemies, and found little to stiffen their imaginative constructions but pick-me-up mythologies. It is hardly right to use the past tense in this connection, since contemporary poets are largely in the same position, and it is hard to sight among his successors any one equally endowed who has managed to make his peace with the intellectual culture of our time and find the poetic terms in which to give it voice.

It would be very hard to put a name on the faculty in him by virtue of which his life and work have a seriousness beyond the mythologies that intrigued his fancy and provided him with a symbolism, but which—his biographers agree—he was inclined to take with a grain of salt. To call this faculty intuition would be to beg all the metaphysical questions involved. It is safer to call it moral tact and let it go at that. It was this, along with sheer imaginative power, and with the good taste that was his one best cultural inheritance, that combined in the end to produce poetry of a singular distinction of tone—elevated without pomposity, refined without mawkishness, and intense without violence. Mr. Ellmann has indicated some of the psychological factors that gave direction to his personal force. But leaving aside such questions of etiology, we may say that the motive power of the whole machine was an unusual urgency of the spirit driving toward the satisfactions of the spirit. It is this that gives to his work its peculiar inner glow as of inspiration and classes it among our poetical monuments, if not precisely among "monuments of unaging intellect."

Austin Warren

YEATS NEEDED RELIGION less as a man than as a poet, and his need was epistemological and metaphysical: he needed to believe that poetry is a form of knowledge and power, not of amusement. One might say of the early Yeats that he thought of poetry as incantation and meant the word as more than metaphor; of the later Yeats, one would have to say that his metaphors were meant as more than illustrative analogies. Of symbolism, the juncture between religion and poetry, he could never have admitted its "mereness": symbols are vehicles as well as intimations. If mathematical and chemical formulas are recipes for the control of matter, images and liturgy have power over minds; they reach farther and deeper than do abstractions. Men become what they contemplate.

The last decades of the ninteenth century did not lack the sense, now become more ominous, of being at the "end of our time." Men were asking, practically—not as ritual prelude to catechetical instruction—whether life was worth living. They were doubting the gain of improved instrumentalities. Unable to hold their old faith, they were unable to relinquish it and were tormented by their indecision. "Seigneur, prenez pitie du chretien qui doute, de l'incredule qui voudrait croire." Des Esseintes's melodramatic cry, muted, can be heard in the suave, sad pages of *Marius*. Frederick Myers writes, in 1900, of "the deep disquiet of our time. . . . On the one hand, health, intelligence, morality,—all such boons as the steady progress of planetary evolution can win for man,—are being achieved in increasing measure. On the other hand, this very sanity, this very prosperity, do but bring out stronger relief the underlying *Weltschmerz,* the decline of any real belief in the dignity, the meaning, the endlessness of life."

Young Yeats read Darwin and Huxley and accepted them as "established authority." But upon consideration he saw that their beliefs contravened his imagination; and he could not accept as doctrines their assumptions and methods. While others lauded "progress," he turned to that kind of traditionary primitivism which supposes central insights into human nature to occur more easily at the beginning of a culture than

"William Butler Yeats: The Religion of a Poet," reprinted from *The Southern Review,* VII, 3 (winter, 1942), pp. 624-638; and from *Rage for Order,* by Austin Warren, pp. 68-84, copyright, 1948, by the University of Chicago, by permission of University of Chicago Press.

at the end of civilization. Like A.E. he was not a university man; he had indeed a prejudice against meed readers in libraries; and—by reaction as well as chance, doubtless—he sought out first the unprofessional books professing to teach wisdom of life. In search of a philosophy "at once logical and boundless" he read Baron Reichenbach on Odic Force, Boehme, Swedenborg. An "authoritative religion," he decided, could be assembled from the affirmations of the poets—especially Spenser, Blake, and Shelley.

His emancipated father took no stock in religion; and it was this parental unbelief which forced the son to examine the arguments and the evidences with care. "I weighed this matter perpetually with great anxiety, for I did not think I could live without religion." Much later, writing of his occult studies, he protests that he has not taken them up "wilfully nor through love of strangeness nor love of excitement . . . but because unaccountable things had happened even in my childhood and because of an ungovernable craving."

The grandparents were Anglicans of the Evangelical persuasion; and they took the child to church, where he found pleasure in the hymns, the sermon, and the poetry of Ecclesiastes and the Apocalypse—predicatable tastes. In later life he occasionally visited Anglican churches; but, as an Irish boy in a London school, under a clerical headmaster "as temperate in his religious life as in all else," he had been repelled by the ease with which English religion passed into respectability. Nor could the moderations and negations of the altarless Church of Ireland be expected to attract the devotion of a young man in search of symbolism and audacity. And "Protestant Ireland seemed to think of nothing but getting on in the world."

Despite his close friendships with Dowson and Lionel Johnson and his subsequent association with Baron von Hugel, Yeats never seriously considered becoming a Catholic. Though impressed by the neo-Catholic movement among the young French intellectuals (Claudel, Péguy, Psichari), he was also puzzled: such concern for the church as he had known in the nineties was the concern of Barbey d'Aurevilly and Huysmans—Catholics with a taste for magic, sadism, or Satanism. To be sure, Celtic Ireland is also Catholic. But in *Ireland's Literary Renaissance* (1916), Ernest Boyd, who can cite only Katherine Tynan as a Catholic writer, remarks the Irish impossibility of *grands convertis* like Huysmans or Verlaine. The "Protestantism of the Irish Catholic is such as to deprive the

Church of precisely those elements which are favourable to literary and intellectual development, and have rallied so many artists to her support." If the Church of Ireland is very Protestant, so, and in another sense, is the Catholic church in Ireland. And so, to find a faith really suited to the Irish genius, the "Dublin mystics" (as Boyd calls Eglinton and A.E.) adopted the ancient Irish pantheon, the *Tuatha De Danann,* and the *sidhe.* With his friends, Yeats turned from St. Patrick (whether Catholic or Anglican) to Oisin and Niamh and Aengus. He began to chart the Sacred Mountains of Ireland on his map, to wander about raths and fairy hills, to question old peasants; he longed to be carried away by fairies; he found beneath the Catholic stratum more primitive deposits of faith. A countrywoman told him that she disbelieved in ghosts and hell—the latter, an invention of priests for their own profit; "but there are fairies," she hastened to supplement, "and little leprechauns, and waterhorses and fallen angels": Whatever else she doubts, one never doubts the fairies, for—as another peasant said to the same inquirer, "They stand to reason."

Thus encouraged, Yeats rejected Christian authority. There must, he maintains, be a "tradition of belief older than that of any European Church, and founded upon the experience of the world before the modern bias." He writes to a French friend: "I have not found my tradition in the Catholic Church, which was not the church of my childhood, but where the tradition is, as I believe, more universal and more ancient." And to this position he persuaded Lady Gregory. "I have longed to turn Catholic that I might be nearer to the people," she testified; "but you have taught me that paganism brings me nearer still."

Of course Yeats pointed out to Lady Gregory that neither she nor her peasants were pure pagans; and in earlier days he did not oppose such a properly contaminated Christianity as a peasant might practice or an esoteric Christian speculatively construct. Both *The Celtic Twilight* (1893) and *The Secret Rose* (1896) use thematically the interplays—the rivalries and interpenetrations—of the Christian and the pagan. In "The Crucifixion of the Outcast," the White Friars put to death a pagan gleeman because his mythic sons, so different from those of their own pious poets, arouse "forgotten longing in their hearts." But when, in another story, Puritan troopers break down the door of the abbey and shoot the White Friars at the altar, and the abbot, crucifix high over his head, condemns the profaners to dwell among the ungovernable shadows, it is the Gaelic deities who lead them to destruction. One and the same "happy theologian" has visions of Christ and of the people of fairy.

Yeats himself early became a pagan. Reading *Walden*, he was inspired to conquer bodily desire and become a hermit: living "as Thoreau lived, seeking wisdom"; it was this desire for the ascetic's solitude which he commemorated in the early popular lyric, "The Lake Isle of Innisfree." Recurrent for him, throughout his life, is the image of Milton's hermetic scholar.

Or let my lamp at midnight hour
Be seen in some high lonely tower
Where I may oft outwatch the Bear
With Thrice-Great Hermes, or unsphere
The spirit of Plato. . . .

But such desire for solitude and lonely contemplation is less characteristic of his confessedly gregarious spirit than a series of entries into esoteric cults, communion of adepts.

In 1885, when he was twenty, he met with A. P. Sinnett's *Esoteric Buddhism*, a chief scripture of the Theosophical movement; he interested his friend, Charles Johnson, who founded the Hermetic Society, soon renamed the Dublin Lodge of the Theosophical Society. In London, shortly after, Yeats nightly frequented the establishment of Theosophy's discoverer and founder, Mme. Helena Blavatsky. The Society for Psychical Research had just finished its scrutiny of the Theosophical revelations; it had pronounced them fraudulent, and the movement had dwindled. But Yeats felt an instinctive admiration, not subsequently renounced, for this "sort of old Irish peasant woman with an air of humour and audacious power," this "great passionate nature, a sort of female Dr. Johnson, impressive . . . to every man or woman who had themselves any richness." One night a week she answered questions on her system, was calm and philosophic; on other evenings she was busy, shrewd, racily humorous—played patience, reckoning her score on the green baize table while cranks "from half Europe and from all America" talked into her imperturbable ears.

Esoteric Buddhism, Yeats's introduction to Theosophy, purports to publish the secret teaching of spiritual adepts living in the remotest Himalayas. As a movement, Theosophy offers itself as an interpretation of the inner meaning of world religion, Christian as well as Buddhist; it attaches much historical importance to Alexandrian Neo-Platonism, both pagan and Christian, as its ancestor; it has developed historically, from the spiritualist movement; it is sympathetic in its attitude toward astrology, alchemy, and such. Like pure Buddhism, Theosophy has no God and consequently no atonement and no prayer. It teaches Hindu and Buddhist doctrine of karma: that our rewards or punishments in future incarnations proceed, as by natural law, from our characters in the last. Like Buddhism, it exhorts to the destruction of desire and anticipates the eventual release from the wheel of existence and entrance into nirvana.

At the British Museum, Yeats encountered S. L. MacGregor Mathers, Bergson's brother-in-law. Mathers, who had assisted Mme Blavatsky in her *Secret Doctrine* and translated *The Kabbalah Unveiled,* founded, at London, the Irish-Urania Temple of the Hermetic Students of the Golden Dawn, an order which professed to derive its rituals from old Rosicrucian manuscripts. Yeats was initiated into the order in its first year, 1887; and Mathers had a long, deep, and acknowledged influence over him. In "All Souls' Night" of 1920, Yeats remembers his adept:

I call up MacGregor from the grave,
. . . .
He had much industry at setting out,
Much boisterous courage, before loneliness
Had driven him crazed;
For meditations upon unknown thought
Make human intercourse grow less and less.

It was presumably Mathers who introduced Yeats to the "Christian Cabbala"—a name loosely given to writings of the sixteenth and seventeenth centuries, notably those of Pico della Mirandola, Reuchlin, Cornelius Agrippa, Henry More, and The Kabbala Denudata of Rosenroth.[1] Yeats frequently cites Agrippa's *De occulta philosophia,* a work which has much to say of magic and magical images and astrology and the World Soul. According to Agrippa, all terrestrial things owe their power to their celestial patterns; and by a proper knowledge of their correspondences we may use the earthly images to in-

[1]Cf. J. L. Blau, *The Christian Interpretation of the Cabala in the Renaissance* (New York, 1944). For Mathers' Order and its contexts, cf. A. E. Waite, *Brotherhood of the Rosy Cross* (London, 1924); and Alvin B. Kuhn, *Theosophy . . .* (New York, 1930).

duce the occult powers. Each sign of the zodiac, each face of each sign, each planet, has its image; and these images imprinted in seals and rings, made at proper times and of proper materials, can effect these powers; so, too, can images not celestial which are made at the astrologically proper times: thus, to procure love one devises figures embracing one another; to bring about disaster, one breaks an image.

Under Mathers' instruction, Yeats learned how to paint cabalistic symbols on cards and how to use them for evoking states of reverie in himself and sometimes trance states in others. Yeats tells some extraordinary stories of these experiments; but at the end of "Hodos chameliontos," he passes a judgment of rejection, not denying power to the symbols chosen but perceiving that irresponsible play with them brings danger. The images that really matter to men of genius and culture are the images which are not chosen but given; and the unity of a culture comes from a given image—the figure of Apollo or of Christ.

In Paris at the end of the century, Yeats scrutinized the chief occultists. With the followers of the eighteenth-century mystic, Saint-Martin, he tested the vision-producing potency of hashish. He met a young Arabic scholar possessing a ring of alchemical gold. He visited the "mysterious house" of Marquis Stanislas de Guaita, founder (in 1889) of the Ordre Kabbalistique de la Rose-Croix and author of *La Clef de la magie noire* and *Le Serpent de la Genèse;* admired the Marquis as "the one eloquent learned scholar who has written of magic in our generation." He met also the great Sar Peladan, founder (in 1890) of yet another, a professedly Catholic, order of the Rosy Cross. Péladan, described by Max Nordau in his once famous *Degeneration,* claimed to be the descendant of the old Magi, the inheritor of the arcane wisdom of Zoroaster, Pythagoras, and Orpheus; and his order purported to revive and unite with the Rosicrucians the Knights Templars and the order of the Holy Grail. The Rosicrucians, professing to reconcile Christianity with Cabalism, provided Yeats with his obsessive symbol of the rose—especially the "Rose upon the Rood of Time" (1893); and in his essay of 1895, "The Body of the Father Christian Rosencrux," he symbolizes an old myth of the order, according to which, two hundred and fifty years after the founder's death, his disciples found in a sealed temple his imperishable body.

In "Hodos chameliontos," Yeats confesses that he had himself ambitions of becoming founder of a "mystical order" which should buy or hire a castle in Lough Kay, a castle affording at one end "a stone platform where meditative persons might pace to and fro." This castle on the rock would provide a place "where its members could retire for a while for contemplation, and establish mysteries like those of Eleusis and Samothrace." For ten years (1888-98?) he sought "to find philosophy and create ritual for the Order." Perhaps, as for Boehme, Swedenborg, and Blake, so again the gates of revelation would open; and he was prepared that the new scripture should, like that of the great mystics whom he had read, use Christian symbols as well as pagan. "Is it true that our air is disturbed, as Mallarmé said, by 'the trembling of the veil of the temple, or that our whole age is seeking to bring forth a sacred book?' Some of us thought that book near towards the end of last century, but the tide sank again."

Acquaintance with Theosophists, Cabalists, and Rosicrucians lay behind Yeats's endeavor to write a novel, the hero of which should "see all the modern visionary sects pass before his bewildered eyes, as Flaubert's St. Anthony saw the Christian sects." This abandoned manuscript of 1896, which must have owed much to Pater as well as to Flaubert, may well be represented by the three tales, "Rosa Alchemica," "The Magi," and "The Tables of the Law," published in 1897 and introducing the figures of Michael Robartes and Owen Aherne, the adepts who reappear in "The Phases of the Moon" and elsewhere. Told in the elaborate, thick harmonies of the *Imaginary Portraits,* these stories summon up adepts in risk of losing their sanity as they have already lost their taste for huma intercourse, even for intercourse with other students—me like Pater's Van Storck, like Huysmans's Des Esseintes, lik Villier's Axel. The narrator is a reformed adept, now a Catho lic, who, though conscious of the malign in esoteric cults, ha but half suppressed his desire for the dangerous, for that "in definite world" which invites the soul to waver, wander, an perish. While professing renunciation, the vain soul still hover over her former state, proud to have sinned. The other tale offer the same image of the divided soul. In the second, Owe Aherne has grown wise to his own damnation. It has bee revealed to him that only through sin and separation from Go can he come to God; but he cannot sin, he cannot pray. " have seen the Whole," he says, "and how can I come again belief that a part is the whole?" In the third tale, concerne with the return of the Magi and the beginning of a new cycl a Second Coming, the teller speaks of dreading the illusio which accompany any age of revelation; and he concludes: "I no longer live an elaborate and haughty life, but seek to lose myself among the prayers and the sorrows of the multitude. I pray best in poor chapels, where the frieze coats brush past me as I kneel, and when I pray against demons. . . ." Despite their perioded style, these pieces have their power and horror —a horror drawn not from blasphemy or diabolism but from the fear of madness.

All the cults to which Yeats attached himself vary a single pattern—that of an arcane wisdom traditionally clothed in myth but now, to some group of initiates, "unveiled"; all of them—even Theosophy, the most elaborate of the systems—are inclusive of magic, alchemy, astrology, and spiritualism. These concerns of Yeats are all defined and defended by Mme Blavatsky, who devoted the first volume of her *Isis Unveiled* to magic, past and present; who asserted that "astrology is to exact astronomy what psychology is to exact physiology"; and who pointed out that, under the emblems of sulphur, mercury, and salt, alchemy may concern itself with human and cosmic mysteries.

Yeats played with alchemy and its symbolisms. He imagined himself as writing a little work, in the style of Sir Thomas Browne, which should interpret the alchemic quest as the "transmutation of life into art." He learned to cast horoscopes; in the Preface to his early novel, *John Sherman,* he writes: "I am something of an astrologer, and can see" in these pages a young man "born when the Water-Carrier Aquarius was on the horizon, at pains to overcome Saturn in Saturn's hour, just as I can see in much that follows his struggle with the still all-too-unconquered Moon, and at last, as I think, the summons of the prouder Sun." Technical terms of the "science" are not infrequent in *A Vision;* more significant, however, is the general analogy between the "Twenty-eight Incarnations" and the structure of a popular manual like Evangeline Adams' *Astrology* (1927). Both offer sequences of characterological types, illustrated from the biography of genius; both offer shrewd, suggestive analyses of types and individuals. But, unlike Miss Adams, Yeats is not offering a literal equation of celestial influences and terrestrial products; he professes that the fitting of the lunar series into the solar year is purely arbitrary and that the whole series is a "parable." In a fashion for which astrologers offer no authority, he orders his types so that they constitute a gradual progression from the most objective to the most subjective and back again; and he combines a psychology with a history by making the same diagram serve at once for a vertical view of two thousand years (the Great Wheel, comprising twenty-eight successive incarnations) and a horizontal view of all types contemporarily occurrent.

His degree of faith in the predictive power of horoscopes is difficult to estimate; but it is not difficult to conjecture the imaginative and philosophical value which the "science" held for him: it lay in the honorific connection astrology establishes between man and nature and in its imprecise determinism of the individual and the state.

One must be at least equally cautious in estimating Yeats's attitude towards spiritualism, apparently the latest to develop of his occult interests. He was critical of alleged communications with the dead and the interpretation of the "messages." He did not forget the warnings of Swedenborg (whose *Heaven and Hell* he read in his youth) that the spirits who can reach men through mediums are either earthbound or devils counterfeiting the virtuous dead. In his discourse prefatory to "The Words upon the Window-Pane," he argues that every manifestation of a spirit is "first of all a secondary personality or dramatisation created by, in, or through the medium." He even suggests, though he but half accepts his suggestion, the theory that the communicators of *A Vision* were not spirits of the dead but the "personalities of a dream" shared by his wife and him; the test of truth for him lies certainly not in the mode of its delivery but in its coherence and illumination. For the credulous "millions who have substituted the seance-room for the church" he had only pity and contempt.

Whatever the precise nature of his interest in spiritualism, it had little to do with curiosity concerning man's post-mortem existence and much to do with possible unseen worlds surrounding man now. In his *Human Personality* (1903), a book admired by William James and A.E. and surely known to Yeats, Myers discovers the cure for man's "spiritual solitude" in the law of telepathy, defined as the transference of ideas and images from living brain to living brain and as communion between incarnate and discarnate spirits. From the painful sense of the self's isolation, Yeats turned to the doctrine that beneath our conscious selves there is a communal psyche, an *Anima mundi*. The sharing of the same dream by two living persons and the invasion of the living man's dream by the dead man's memories are beliefs interconnected in Yeats's faith: they are parts of the same release from the uniqueness of the self.

How far Yeats believed in these mysterious worlds and powers is a question to which his critics have long addressed themselves. The answer has often been skeptical. Before the publication of *A Vision,* Yeats was customarily, in contrast to A.E., viewed as one who toyed with mysticism, used it for literary effect. And certainly *The Celtic Twilight* (1893) is full of hints that Yeats is being romantic and misty and that the real Yeats is the shrewd observer who says of "A Visionary" (clearly A.E.) that there is in him "the vast and vague extravagance that lies at the bottom of the Celtic heart." But there are intimations of another attitude, hints of a Pyrrhonism which finds dreams as credible as facts, of a fideism which is not disturbed by the current and changing "truths" of science. "Everything exists, everything is true" is one fashion of putting this; another is to ask, rhetorically, "When all is said and done, how do we not know but that our own unreason may be better than another's truth?"

Autobiographically considering his earlier self, Yeats suggests the Pascalian antithesis between the reasons of the head and the reasons of the heart: "My critical mind—was it friend or enemy?—mocked, and yet I was delighted." And of his youthful talks with peasants: "I did not believe with my intellect that you could be carried away body and soul, but I believed with my emotions, and the belief of the country people made that easy." But when he conversed with educated people he grew timid: "I was always ready to deny or turn into a joke what was for all that my secret fanaticism. When I had read Darwin and Huxley and believed as they did, I wanted, because an established authority was upon my side, to argue with everybody." Even in *A Vision* Yeats leaves room for the reader to think that he is being offered prose commentary on the symbolism of the poems.

Yet, if the earlier Yeats is whimsical or otherwise evasive on the subject of the occult, the later Yeats has cut himself off from such ambiguity. With whatever hesitations, cautions, and reserves, he ranges himself on the side of the supernaturalists. Responsibility of belief markedly increases from *The Celtic Twilight* to *A Vision.* In the Preface to the 1902 edition of the former, he announced, "I shall publish in a little while a big book about the commonwealth of faery, and shall try to make it systematic and learned enough to buy pardon for this handful of dreams." This announcement, which his critics took as further whimsy, indicates rather that Yeats was unsatisfied to leave his convictions in the twilight of poetic prose, that intellectual integrity required him to produce some philosophical defense of his convictions. The essays called "Magic" (1901) and "Per amica silentia lunae" (1917) represent preliminary efforts at such defense; but it is *A Vision* which, incorporating and developing the earlier ideas of the *Anima mundi,* of the self and its antithetic mask, especially fulfills the intention of 1902. "Learned" and "systematic" are relative terms, of course; but they can stand as descriptive of the intention toward which Yeats moved.

Until comparatively late, he had restricted his reading to the "poets and the mystics," avoided the philosophers, even the philosophers of mysticism—as though the purity of his intuitive belief might be violated by acquaintance with rival positions and criteria. But now, after making the initial notes for *A Vision,* he reads Plotinus, medieval philosophy, Berkeley, Hegel, Wundt, McTaggart, willing not only to see his own "philosophy" in terms of its historical parallels and oppositions but to make it as coherent as possible; and he reads biography and especially history with the intent of grounding his myth in the world of secular fact. This movement from the Rosicrucians to Plotinus and Berkeley is strikingly paralleled by the increasing comprehensiveness of Yeats's mythic Ireland. Whereas in the *Twilight* and the *Rose* he almost limits himself to the lore of peasants and the "pride of the adept," to a pre-Christian, or, failing that, a pre-Reformation, Ireland, the later Yeats is able to find heroes in the persons of the Anglo-Irish Augustans—Swift, Burke, Goldsmith, and Berkeley—and to find Irish philosophy in their writings.

And haughtier-headed Burke that proved the State a
tree,
That this unconquerable labyrinth of the birds, century
after century,
Cast but dead leaves to mathematical equality;

And God-appointed Berkeley that proved all things a
dream,
That this pragmatical, preposterous pig of a world, its
farrow that so solid seem,
Must vanish on the instant if the mind but change its
theme.

Yeats's early traffic with ghosts, sorcerers, and fairies was probably, instigated by a desire to loosen the bonds of logic

In his essay on "Demonology" Emerson speaks of the great interest which dreams, animal magnetism, and omens have for "some minds. They run into this twilight and say, 'There's more here than is dreamed of in your philosophy.' " Young Yeats was surely one of these "minds"; he desired to say: Life is not all rule, order, reason, system, common sense; nature and the human mind have their "night-side" of the subconscious, of dusk and half-lights. Religion he saw as the search for the irrational, the irruptive, the unpredicatable. But, without exaggerating the antithesis, one may represent the later Yeats as finding its own logic and order in the supernatural.

In all these respects, Yeats may be judged to have matured. In his early traffic with Rosicrucians and Cabalists, he is disarmingly easy to satirize as the adolescent enamored of ritual wardrobes, passwords, and the "pride of the adept"; the self-awareness of the later Yeats is, in the earlier, sometimes theatrical, posed. Yet the maturity is anticipated in certain persistencies—belief in the imagination, balance of sensibility and sense, moral courage. Like his contemporary, Irving Babbitt, Yeats could stand removed from the current intellectual orthodoxy without losing either his sharp sense of dissent or his own faith. He was not afraid to seem adolescent until he could achieve maturity on something like his own terms and win, by steadfast adherence, some respect for his outmoded causes. After 1900 we hear little more of arcane societies; Yeats turns from planning an occult ecclesiasticism to the organization of an Irish Theatre. The occult pursuits consolidate into a general defense of a more variously comprehensive universe that a positivist science will admit.

A central property of Yeats's religion which remains unchanged from youth to age is its lack of a consequent ethics. His old companion in theosophy, A.E., was fond of quoting the injunction, "For every step that you take in the pursuit of the hidden knowledge, take three steps in the perfecting of your own character." But Yeats, so far as one can see, never postulated an ascetical discipline preliminary to a religious experience. He had his moral code, and he had his ritual; but, as in primitive religions, the two were unrelated. Catholic Christianity is mystical, sacramental, ethical, and seeks, at whatever tension, to realize this character. With liberal Protestantism, the numinous disappears as *Aberglaube*, and religion becomes morality. In Yeats, religion returns to its pre-Christian and indeed pre-monotheistic character, becoming the search for knowledge of the unseen and for gnostic power.

Temperamentally, Yeats seems to have been an optimistic monist. If his magic seems generally "white," if he had no appetite for diabolism or blasphemy he was correspondingly free from any sense of sin or need of redemption. In the broad sense, he remained, in *A Vision*, theosophic, by implication entertaining the belief in karma, reincarnation, and the eventual delivery from rebirth into the peace of nirvana; but it does not appear that his "heart" ever accepted the Orient's pessimistic view of existence or the ethical release of the Four Noble Truths. Such a statement, however, needs modification; if the earlier Yeats identifies vision with reverie and virtue with abstention from Philistine ambitions, the later Yeats, with his doctrine of the will and its achievements of its True Mask, holds a more strenuous conception. And the later Yeats finds in the grasp of a "Vision of Evil" a chief differentiation between great poets like Villon, Dante (and himself), and such, for his last judgment, superficial poets as Emerson, Whitman, and A.E. Though his is a vision not of man's sin but of necessary pain, an unflinching view of world history which moves characteristically not by smooth progressions but by revolutions, reversals, and brutalities, it is an advance in Yeats's apprehension that he insists upon this realism.

Eric Bentley

It cannot be said that Yeats has much of a reputation as a playwright. Literary critics speak of his plays at best as something that helped him to write poems. Theatre people outside Dublin have never heard of him. Even in Dublin his plays were never the favorites, and by now most of them have disappeared from the Abbey Theatre's repertoire.

If we are undaunted by all this and decide to look into Yeats's plays for ourselves, we are apt to approach them by way of two very depressing literary movements—the "Irish Renaissance" and the Poetic Drama of the late-Victorian and post-Victorian era. The Irish Renaissance is depressing because it didn't exist, the Poetic Drama movement because it did. Read Edward Martyn and A.E., read the verse plays of Bridges and Masefield and Sturge Moore and Gordon Bottomley, and you will quickly lose interest in the Irish Renaissance, the revival of poetic drama, and perhaps even in life itself.

A generation ago, Granville-Barker tells us, everyone you met at a literary lunch had a blank-verse play in his pocket. These plays seem to have been very bad. They were dead; and they were buried by T. S. Eliot when in several essays and plays he showed an alternative path to poetry in the theatre. That Yeats's plays were among the buried is most often taken for granted—as for instance by Bonamy Dobree in an essay he contributed some years ago to the *Southern Review*.

Mr. Dobree clinches the point by quoting passages from the plays of Yeats, Eliot, and several post-Eliot playwrights. The quotations are entirely fair. Open Yeats's plays anywhere, and Eliot's too, and the contrasts will be much what Mr. Dobree says they are. In all his plays at any rate, Yeats uses the literary language of the 19th Century tradition, the feeblest language in all modern literature. Eliot uses a language that is at once more up to date and more popular, the language of living men. Yeats uses blank verse, the dramatic possibilities of which seem to have been exhausted three hundred years ago. Eliot replaces the dead thump of modern blank verse with a swift colloquial irregularity of accent that matches his naturalness of phrase.

There is no passage in Yeats's dialogue that has the histri-

"Yeats as a Playwright," reprinted from *The Kenyon Review*, X, 2 (spring, 1948), pp. 196-208, copyright, 1948, by Kenyon College.

onic force and brilliance of the best passages in Eliot. It is likely that the dramatic poets of today, if there are any, will follow in the tradition of the younger man. There is one fact they should not overlook, however: Eliot has never yet created a drama. He has written down his ideas about drama, and he has put together many admirably dramatic passages. But no number of dramatic passages adds up to a drama. Before we have that, we require a dramatic conception and a dramatic whole in which the conception is realized. Eliot's plays suffer from the lack of these. Finally, even the dialogue—the one thing that is really dramatic in Eliot—suffers, for no ingredient in a work of art can develop and flourish in isolation from the others. There are places in *The Family Reunion* where the dialogue wears much thinner than in the best prose drama, which Eliot disparages.

Yeats, admittedly, is less prepossessing than Eliot. One cannot quote from his plays any passage of indubitable greatness or many of indubitable brilliance. There are no passages as superbly dramatic as some of Yeats's own non-theatrical work such as "'A sudden blow. The great wings beating still/ Above the staggering girl. . . ." Yet I am going to claim that Yeats is a considerable playwright, the only considerable verse playwright in English for several hundred years. Beside the solid achievement of his forty years in the theatre, Eliot's dramatic work seems merely suggestive and fragmentary. For Yeats composed dramas, as Eliot did not. In the first place, he was able to start from a genuinely dramatic conception and carry it through. In the second, he had at his command the essential, even if secondary and non-verbal arts of the theatre.

The first point has been well made already by Mr. Ronald Peacock in the best essay yet written on Yeats's plays. Mr. Peacock is not contrasting Yeats with Eliot. He is defending him from the trite charge of being a pure lyrist. In every play of Yeats you can point to a central dramatic situation—and that for the simple reason that pretty much everything else has been cut away. Yeats is not only a dramatist but a classic dramatist. As Mr. Peacock puts it, each play consists of a single knot, a rather loose one, which is untied in a single movement. Beginning with *Four Plays for Dancers* Yeats's one-act plays have the beauty of structure of a Jamesian *nouvelle*. Like James, Yeats makes much of the special often oblique point of view from which a story is seen with an extraordinarily high degree of selectivity in the seeing

We should praise him the more for achieving in drama itself that dramatic idea which James could realize only in a non-dramatic medium. The case of Yeats shows that the dramatic talent of the 20th Century need not be deflected, as it mostly has been, into fiction and non-dramatic poetry.

Sweeney Agonistes is a triumph, and a dramatic one, because it shows how much drama there can be in words alone. This is the only sort of theatricality any of Eliot's plays have. That is why producers and actors are usually at a loss what to do with them. Whatever they decide on has to be their own idea, so little is suggested, as to spectacle, movement, and bodily expression, in the script. What George Jean Nathan wrongly said of Pirandello's plays might truthfully be said of Eliot's: they seem to have been written by a blind man, or, more precisely, by a man who is blind in the theatre. For all his remarks against closet drama, Eliot has remained to a large extent a "literary dramatist" in the vulgar sense. Yeats has not. Even his most untheatrical early plays, such as *Land of Heart's Desire,* were revised in the light of his steadily improving stagecraft.

Nothing much could be done with *Land of Heart's Desire,* however, beyond lopping off excess decoration. A playwright's stagecraft is needed at the very inception of his work, not merely when the time comes for revision. With the turn of the century, and the establishment of the Abbey Theatre, we find Yeats thinking out his plays in theatrical terms. In terms of stage design, for example. It is not only that he wants the setting to be subordinated to the actor (it must be the background of a portrait, he said), it is that he never writes for the stage without knowing what he wants in visual terms. The "literary dramatist" sees the characters in his mind's eye moving about in their natural setting. The genuine playwright sees them in the highly unnatural setting of the stage. Under the influence of Gordon Craig, Yeats was able to discard realism and to see the stage picture in its elements: as pure color, line, and three-dimensional form, all dominated by the then new electric light.

> I wrote it [Yeats writes of *The Player Queen*] my head full of fantastic architecture invented by myself upon a miniature stage, which corresponds to that of the Abbey in the proportion of one inch to a foot, with a miniature set of Gordon Craig screens and a candle; and if it is gayer than my wont it is that I tried to find words and events that would seem well placed under a beam of light reflected from the ivory-coloured surface of the screens.

Such notes as these prove that Yeats visualized his subjects under stage conditions from the start. He saw them, that is, not as natural and raw material but as realized dramatic art.

No other playwright, unless it is Garcia Lorca, has told us so clearly in stage directions how much of his drama should be communicated by a particular color or shape. Even more remarkable, if we recall how unmusical Yeats was, is his use of music. He seems to have understood music very well from the peculiar standpoint of the playwright. He watched his musicians jealously. He knew how easily they can destroy poetry and drama in the very process of creating song and opera. He knew that you can seldom follow a singer's words. He not only refused to let music predominate; he did not want it to have an interest independent of the drama. From early years he was fascinated by the possibility of using musical tone and rhythm solely to re-inforce words. He knew that, whatever charming form of entertainment might be possible when words cease to be central, it would not be drama.

Of course Yeats carries the use of music further in his dance plays than he ever had in working out his sung poems with Florence Farr and Sarah Allgood. But even in the dance plays his discretion should amaze a generation brought up on radio drama, sound movies, and college productions of Shakespeare. Years before Doris Humphrey and Martha Graham, Yeats combined dance and spoken words. But while Martha Graham's work in this line is dance with words, Yeats's is words with dance. You might suppose that, since Yeats regarded lofty emotion—ecstasy in fact—as the aim of drama, he might have withdrawn almost entirely and left everything to his musicians and dancers; for music and dance are closer, surely, than literature to pure emotion. Actually, Yeats lowered his status to that of a librettist only once (in *Fighting the Waves*). Sometimes, it is true, he achieves his climaxes by music and dance alone (in *A Full Moon in March* and *The Death of Cuchulain*, for instance). Even here, though, the musical-choreographic climax has a literary context which defines its meaning.

With the dancer, there comes into the theatre an element not provided by stage design and music: acting. For from the dramatist's standpoint—which Yeats knew how to preserve—dance is an extension of acting. Nowhere is the dramatic superiority of Yeats to Eliot clearer than here. For the latter, the actor scarcely exists. Eliot is really writing radio plays for elocutionists—the outstanding performer of

Becket was, in fact, the outstanding elocutionist of the B.B.C. With Yeats, acting begins at home. He was himself histrionic. Compare his face with Eliot's, or his voice, or his necktie. To Yeats, as to Bernard Shaw, the histrionic pose, the theatrical mask, was very important.

> There is a relation [Yeats writes] between discipline and the theatrical sense. If we cannot imagine ourselves as different from what we are and assume that second self, we cannot impose a discipline upon ourselves, though we may accept one from others. Active virtue as distinguished from the passive acceptance of a current code is therefore theatrical, consciously dramatic, the wearing of a mask.

Thus while Eliot got into the theatre by mistake (he was more at home in church) and never stayed long, Yeats, like Shaw, needed a theatre, *had* to have one. This is the primordial histrionic longing, the adult equivalent of the child's love of dressing up. The true playwright has an actor's nature; and if he turns out not to be a great stage actor, he will probably act all the better in private life. Yeats and Shaw are Irish. How close the histrionism of Irish life could be to actual stage performance is indicated by the fact that the role of Yeats's Cathleen ni Houlihan was first played by a woman who had little training except that she was playing the role *outside* the theatre, Maud Gonne.

Yeats had much to learn about acting, of course, even after he wrote his first plays. He had to see what first-rate actors could put into plays for *his* benefit before he could know what he should put into plays for theirs. Until he writes for actors—that is, with acting in mind—no one is a really professional playwright. Conversely, what our amateur or "literary" playwrights lack is a sense of how actors work and what they can do. Eliot is a highly unprofessional playwright. Shaw is, in this respect, the most professional playwright of our time. Every speech, every period, every phrase in his big roles has grown out of his knowledge of first-rate performance; that is why any first-rate performer finds certain Shaw roles fitting him like a glove.

With the help of the actors of the Abbey Theatre, Yeats made himself fully professional. His verse is often far from great, but—so W. G. Fay tells us—the actors always found it eminently nimble on the tongue. Of how many poetic playwrights can *that* be said?

II

If this account of mine were the whole truth you would expect to find Yeats becoming one of the great figures of the modern stage—an Ibsen or a Chekhov. We can begin our investigation of why he was *not* such a figure, and of what sort of a figure he really was, with this very art of acting, which, I have said, Yeats learnt to understand.

While Bernard Shaw could base his kind of drama on the sort of performance in which the post-Ibsen actor excelled, a performance marked by a clear grasp of psychology and idea, by urbanity and pace, by colloquial tone and realistic facial expression, in a word, by prose excellence, Yeats's whole theory and practice were devised in revulsion from the whole Ibsenite-Shavian movement. He proposed two alternatives. The first was to cut below it. Beneath the surface of middle-class civilization there still lurked, in Ireland, at least, a peasant culture possessing a living speech and not yet wholly robbed of simple human responses. Not feeling competent to tap this vein himself, Yeats pushed Lady Gregory and J. M. Synge into doing so. For him, the second alternative: to rise above "the play about modern educated people," a drama confined to "the life of the drawing room," in a drama of symbol and myth. He asked for a theatre that was everything the naturalistic theatre was not—something "remote, spiritual and ideal," he wrote as a young man. "Distinguished, indirect, symbolic," was his later characterization. Throughout his career he believed in "a drama of energy, of extravagance, of phantasy, of musical and noble speech." It was to be a theatre to liberate the mind, a theatre in which one would feel no unease when the final curtain falls, a theatre in which all would be caught in "one lofty emotion," an "emotion of multitude."

Yeats was asking for something neither the Abbey Theatre nor any existing theatre could provide. Even if there had been a public, there were no actors for it. The acting profession is not divided into radically different schools of practice. A particular style dominates the whole profession for a good many years; then under the impetus of a new major force in the theatre—usually a playwright—a new style breaks through and in turn becomes the only one. Now Yeats began to write for the theatre at a time when such a new style—that of naturalism—was in the first flush of energy. If he could not make use of it—many anti-naturalistic playwrights did—he could not easily make use of the modern theatre. After all, much as

W. G. Fay acted in Yeats, his favorite modern playwright was J. M. Barrie!

Being a poet, Yeats was not frightened by the prospect of isolation. He simply declared: "I want, not a theatre, but the theatre's antiself." And: "I want . . . an unpopular theatre." Since by this time—the time of the first World War—he had been thoroughly schooled in theatre practice, isolation would do him no harm, if he could stand it; the older Ibsen was almost as isolated. Indeed isolation meant to Yeats the freedom to work with the dramatic techniques he had acquired unhampered by the thousand bothersome circumstances of every actual theatre. Cut loose from the box office, as well as from Stanislavskyan actors, he could range as widely as he chose. Even as far afield as Japan.

It was Ezra Pound who introduced Yeats to the Noh plays, Japan's "unpopular" drama. They gave him a sort of dramatic equivalent for his new verse style: something terse, refined, solid, cryptic, beautiful. They also showed Yeats how to simplify his staging by radical conventions and how to combine music and dance with words without letting the words get swamped. Apart from such general principles, and the formal framework, Yeats's dance plays are as distinct from their Japanese prototypes as from Western drama. The Noh play can become anything you want to make it. Brecht's Noh plays—*Der Jasager* and *Der Neinsager*—are utterly different in spirit from Yeats's.

The Noh form was, so to say, an excuse for departing from even the most deeply entrenched Western pattern. As Mr. Peacock has pointed out, Yeats's most radical act was his rejection of the form common to Ibsen, Shakespeare, and Sophocles—the drama which was a moral analysis of character within a framework of more or less logical appearances. It is the absence of this form that the modern reader finds bewildering when we first encounter Yeats's plays. Is the play really there? asks the reader. What on earth am I supposed to do with these roles? asks the actor. And those of us who are more impressed ask: What does Yeats put in the place of the regular plot-and-character pattern? One's first inclination, especially if one has read his essays, is to say that he is following in the wake of Maeterlinck, and that what he is attempting is mood and atmosphere. One recalls that Yeats found in tragedy itself only emotion, and hence would not allow that Shakespeare is a tragedian. Mr. Peacock goes deeper than this when he writes:

The coherent action-sequence that illustrates essentially the *moral* nature of life gives place to a complex pattern communicating a spiritual insight.

If we see this, we see that Yeats's rejection of character was no mere whimsy. It is not the psychology of Cuchulain that concerns him but the spiritual world to which Cuchulain can lead us.

It would be a stirring adventure [he once wrote] for a poet and an artist, working together, to create once more heroic or grotesque types, that, keeping always an appropriate distance from life, would seem images of those profound emotions that exist only in solitude and in silence.

This passage helps us to see the connection between Yeats's theatre and the theory of the arts enunciated in his two essays on Symbolism. The poetic image, for Yeats, is a symbol of inner experience, which is otherwise incommunicable. So with the histrionic image, the image of Deirdre or Countess Cathleen or Cuchulain.

The same passage illuminates Yeats's stage technique and shows how it grows from the need for expression and not from a hankering after experiment. "Keeping always an appropriate distance from life," he says. A crucial matter for any playwright is the degree of aesthetic distance he needs to establish. The big modern theatre begins by separating audience from actor by the proscenium arch and then proceeds to try to cancel the distance thus established with fourth-wall illusionism. Yeats's procedure is clean contrary. He insists on a very small auditorium—"a friend's drawing-room"—with no stage at all, let alone a proscenium arch. This gives him intimacy, which is needed if one is to hear his delicate pianissimo. Aesthetic distance, in the absence of physical distance, has to be established by stylization of decor, costume, gesture, movement, speech, and finally, the human face. Note how exactly technique expresses intention. Every item in this stylization helps Yeats to ignore psychology (or character) and to limit himself to symbols of "the soul life," the inner "deeps." An intention that might seem too subjective and insubstantial for the stage is thus given objective form and substance.

As he states it, I do not think Yeats's theory of the drama is satisfactory. It is the "pure poetry" theory of the 'nineties transferred to the theatre. It would suggest that Yeats was a second Maeterlinck, one who invites us to consider him profound on the grounds that he conveys a purely emotional intimation of spirituality. Maeterlinck's emotions are delicate, to be sure, but what is profound about them? Today, I think, we demand also meaning; and, in fact, if not in intention, Yeats provides it. He is opposed to literature that teaches only, I believe, when the teaching differs from his own. In some of his best work, he is at least as didactic as Ibsen. To check this assertion, and to verify my general description of Yeats's dramaturgy, let us look at one of the finest examples of his histrionic art, *A Full Moon in March*.

In this play Yeats tells the story of a queen. She is to marry the suitor who, in her own opinion, best sings her passion. A swineherd comes and is much too confident for her taste. She has him beheaded. But his severed head sings, and lures her till she makes love to it.

Yeats's version of the tale is a drama, not a dramatic poem. It is based on a pattern familiar to all students of dramaturgy (I will mention Musset's *Fantasio* and Garcia Lorca's *Don Perlimplin*): the victory of a "good" man, who seems to be fighting a losing battle, over a "bad" woman. The man dies for the woman, and the woman's life is brought to some sort of climax or fulfillment.

To some extent, Lorca and Yeats put this pattern to the same uses. Both start with folk material and create an atmosphere of fairy tale. Both make masterly use of the non-verbal arts of the theatre, visual and auditory. But where Lorca seeks richness, Yeats, whose early plays had staggered under a load of decoration, seeks that stabbing violence of emotion which the drama above all other arts can produce.

The play is a close structure in four short movements. The first is an introduction in the form of a stanzaic poem establishing the theme of love, which, we learn, is alternately "crown of gold" and "dung of swine." Next comes the main body of the dialogue, which is a blank-verse duet of Queen and Swineherd, who are identified with "crown of gold" and "dung of swine" respectively. We find that the Swineherd is not interested in winning a kingdom for himself but in introducing the Queen to love, the forest, and the dung of swine. Then we see the violent part of the folk-tale refashioned into a symbol of the sexual act and procreation. A gesture—the Queen "drops her veil"—indicates the Swineherd's victory.

The third movement consists of the Queen's dance with the Swineherd's severed head. It is in the dance that the play reaches its climax in the kind of tragic ecstasy that is well enough in accord with Yeats's theories. If the ecstasy were all, however, the play could stop here. The fact is that Yeats extracts a theme from his subject, and that the theme is given very explicit statement in the two sung poems that constitute the fourth and last movement. The Swineherd has risen, we learn, out of his dung and has become a "twinkle in the sky." The Queen, we infer, is like a statue of a saint descending from its niche into the dung. Though saints carry in pitchers "all time's completed treasure" they lack one essential thing: "their desecration and the lover's night." The penultimate poem—"The moon shone brightly . . . A full moon in March" —sends us back to an earlier point in the play in which the Queen confessed herself "cruel as the *winter* of virginity." Before the end of the action, the winter snow has melted beneath the moon of the spring equinox. Speaking of the story of the severed head in his preface, Yeats says: "It is part of the old ritual of the year: the mother goddess and the slain god."

Thus *A Full Moon in March* illustrates just about all the points I have tried to make about Yeats and the theatre: that he starts from a dramatic situation and resolves it in a single incident; that he employs the non-verbal arts while subordinating them to the words; that he asks for absolutely un-Stanislavskyan actors who dance, and speak behind masks; that his situation is not used to define individual character or as the starting point of a plot but as a gateway to the "deeps" of the "soul life"; and, finally, that we are not left holding a mere Maeterlinckian mood, but are given a theme, namely, that, if we are to live, our wintry and saintly virginity must descend into the dung of passion.

I am afraid that I have made it sound as if Yeats's theme were simply tacked on at the end. And, to be sure, it is not merely embodied. It is given very explicit statement as in the didacticists whom Yeats hated. Nevertheless, it is organically incorporated in the play—not by the logic of event but by rhythm, by form. One recalls Kenneth Burke's description of the tragic rhythm: from purpose to passion to perception. Is not that exactly the rhythm and shape of *A Full Moon in March?* From the Swineherd's boldly affirmed purpose, to the Queen's climactic passion, to the perception on our part of what it all signifies. A familiar rhythm indeed, though the play seems in most other ways an unfamiliar sort of play. Might one not call it a dramatic meditation? For, though Yeats disliked the naturalistic drama of thought, he himself called for a theatre that was "masculine and intellectual," a place of "intellectual excitement," "that unearthly excitement that has wisdom for fruit." *A Full Moon in March* is a general meditation upon life. But I call it a *dramatic* meditation because the generalities, the thoughts, are thoroughly assimilated into the rich and varied art of the theatre. The art of the theatre includes much, of course, that is not literature, just as the art of literature includes much that is not theatre. Where literature and theatre overlap, you have drama. The plays of Yeats are an instructive case in point.

Kenneth Burke

I SHALL HERE consider some basic correlations of theme, or motif, in Yeats, noting how the Many are collapsed into the One and the One is ramified into the Many.

"We have come to give you metaphors for poetry," said the spirits which, Yeats tells us, dictated through automatic writing on the part of his wife and himself, and through the mediumship of his wife asleep, the intricate account of cosmic motivation described in *A Vision*.

And critics, whose job it is to look a gift horse in the mouth, will probably again and again puzzle over this ambiguous document, a document so ambiguous, in fact, that the author even endows it with a double genesis. For besides telling us that it was communicated to him by the spirits, he offers a playful, and occasionally even mildly ribald, narrative to explain its discovery. This narrative, in an earlier version, had originally been used in order to avoid reference to the roles played by himself and his wife in the "communications." Yet even after he had dropped this pretense, he retained the story, in an amended form. Presumably, he retained it because its frankly fictive character was also felt to be a proper way of signalizing the quality of the "revelation." A vision that was sent to help a poet with his metaphors might well deserve a metaphorical introduction.

As for the kind of "truth" which the "vision" itself really did possess: Yeats says that it is to be taken as "symbolical," that he took it literally only when "overwhelmed by miracle, as all men must be when in the midst of it." And recalling a remark in an early essay on magic to the effect that visions are "symbolical shadows of the impulses" that have formed the dominant moods and events of a man's life, "messages as it were out of the ancestral being of the questioner," we might couple it with a remark in his present preface to the effect that he regards the details of the system "as stylistic arrangements comparable to the cubes in the drawing of Wyndham Lewis and to the ovoids in the sculpture of Brancusi." Then we might resolve this particular ambiguity thus: we might say that the scheme describes the *form* in which his imagination is cast, but that he gives this form the kind

"On Motivation in Yeats," from *The Southern Review*, VII, 3 (winter, 1942), pp. 547-561.

of names that go with *content*. And though he knows that the content names are not quite correct, at the same time he could not call them simply untrue, since they do represent real forms. For instance: Imagine a mode of thought using, let us say, some general notion of *reciprocality;* next, imagine dividing this notion into that of two complementary forms; and next, imagine calling one of them "masculine" and the other "feminine" in some contexts, "solar" and "lunar" in other contexts, "primary" and "antithetical" in other contexts, "democratic" and "aristocratic" in other contexts, etc. Could one quite exactly say that his terms were or were not "true"? They would be "true" in the sense that they did correctly represent the form of reciprocality, and in the sense that in the poet's experience this form did acquire body by precisely such specific designations. Yet they would be "untrue" in the sense that no specific designation could properly designate the form *in its sheer formality*. (This is, perhaps, but another way of saying what Cleanth Brooks has said in his discussion of Yeats's truth as "imaginatively" true.)

The communications, we recall, are said to have taken as their point of departure a distinction Yeats had made "between the perfection that is from a man's combat with himself and that which is from a combat with circumstance." And upon "this simple distinction" there was built up "an elaborate classification of men according to their more or less complete expression of one type or the other." In reading the account as fully elaborated in *A Vision,* I have regretted that this distinction became obscured. For here are certainly two very different concepts of motivation. But this theme tends to retreat behind an interest in augury, as we are given geometrical designs that should enable us to "prick upon the calendar the birth of a Napoleon or a Christ." There are references to a distinction between fate, which is imposed from without, and destiny, which moves us from within; there is the analogy of the *Commedia dell'Arte* to indicate a range of improvisation permitted to men within the limits of the roles they must enact; there are references to a moment when Choice and Chance are one; and certainly the fundamental distinction between the "solar" and the "lunar," which is quite close to that between "extrovert" and "introvert," can be related to the two kinds of motive which are named as the point of departure. Yet the great preoccupation with the machinery of augury usurps so much of the attention that one cannot, even with an effort, conceive of the book in general as one that points up the distinction between these two kinds of combat.

Indeed, I think that the machinery by which the augury is to be accomplished is itself of a nature to obliterate the distinction. For if the whole involves a basic distinction between "solar" and "lunar" motivations, and a Great Wheel is designed on the basis of that distinction, yet this Great Wheel itself is divided into twenty-eight phases of the *moon*. Thus, though we have sun and moon as antithetical, the fact that both are treated in terms of the moon would, to my mind, mean that the lunar is the true psychological ancestor of this pair; and the sun would be under the sign of the moon, or perhaps but a reflection of the moon. Imagine, for instance, someone saying: "You can take a direction either East or West," and then putting you on a fast train moving West; let us suppose that you, in the front car, walked Eastward to the rear of the train; on this train, then, you could go either Eastward or Westward, but if the train was going Westward, over and above all you too would be going Westward. This example should illustrate why I would interpret a sun-moon distinction as lunar when it is developed by the featuring of lunar terms. Indeed, when we recall the major role played by the moon in Yeats's early poetry, and his "Lines Written in Dejection" on his fiftieth birthday ("I have nothing but the embittered sun;/Banished heroic mother moon and vanished"), we must concede that the spirits who chose Yeats as the writer to whom they would communicate their teachings about the Twenty-Eight Phases of the Moon selected one who was well prepared by temperament to receive a moon-lit message.

I might suggest another way of indicating that in *A Vision* the distinction between solar and lunar is itself "lunar." For we are told that the lunar is "antithetical" and the solar is "primary." We are also told that "the whirlpool is an *antithetical* symbol, the descending water a *primary*." And finally, we are told that the symbol of the whirlpool, rather than the symbol of descending water, would be used for designing the motivations of the world we live in. For the "natural" world, we are told, is "lunar." Solar light (symbolically speaking) is the light of the incarnate world, where the light "is thought not nature."

We are told that we may think of the Great Wheel "as an expression of alternations of passion" (which would be another expression for two kinds of motivation). We can "think of the power of the woman beginning at symbolical East . . . and of the power of the man . . . beginning at symbolical West." Or we may "think of the Wheel as an expression of the birth of symbolical children bound together by a single fate." And "all the symbolism of this book applies to begetting and birth, for all things are a single form which has divided and multiplied in time and space." Since the two kinds of motivation (solar-masculine and lunar-feminine) prevail at different parts of the day, different parts of the month, different parts of the year, and different parts of the Great Year, it is obvious that we have many opportunities for improvisation on the part of one who would assign the quality of motivation for an act. For instance, would the solar part of the day in the lunar part of the month be solar or lunar?

I point this out, not to be so brash as to search for fallacies in the exposition of the spirits, but to excuse myself for not offering a very lucid summarization of the Great Wheel. In trying thus to indicate that the design itself is intricately elaborated with motives and cross-motives, I am seeking to offer a justification for attempting here not to summarize the design, but rather to bring out the essence of its motivation. Were I to do otherwise, attempting simply to review the details of the Wheel as Yeats has given them, I should but be doing sketchily what the book itself does thoroughly—and when I got through our study of the underlying themes would have been advanced not a jot.

"Ultimate reality," we are told, "is a phaseless sphere" that but "becomes phasal in our thoughts." Here all things are present as an eternal instant. Thus, each symbol used "has evoked for me some form of human destiny, and that form, once evoked, has appeared everywhere, as if there were but one destiny, as my own form might appear in a room full of mirrors." What, similarly, would be the "ultimate reality" of this discussion of "ultimate reality"? The quality that would be present everywhere? Stephen Spender, in a moment of impatience with the Yeatsian symbol, has written: "The result of the search for one symbol was the discovery that almost anything might become that symbol." We are here trying to suggest that, in *A Vision,* the key word for that One would be "lunar."

And then, as we expanded it back into a Many, we could select the various equations indicated in the book without concern for the intricacies of the Wheel, its "phaseless" informing unity so "divided and multiplied" into phases that, as applied to a given individual in a given historical circumstance, one would find motives of choice and motives of necessity variously assisting one another and at odds, in a great welter of contrasts, conflicts, reinforcements, modifications, disguises, or processes of death and birth that move the soul from the stage of illusion or delusion to the stage of understanding (part of this taking place during carnate existence, part during incarnate interims, as the soul develops through the twenty-eight phases of the Wheel).

Cutting across this "equationally," then, we find as key traits for this central motive: antithetical or natural (in contrast with primary or reasonable); "towards Nature" rather than "towards God"; second and third quarters of the moon, the two surrounding full moon (in contrast with the first and fourth, surrounding the dark moon); inner world of desire and imagination (in contrast with the stress upon that which is external to mind, "actual facts"); carnate, in contrast with incarnate; "subjectivity, unity of being, beauty" (at the full moon), in contrast with "objectivity, passivity, plasticity" (at the dark of the moon, the "solar" phase).

The design also features four "Faculties": Will, Mask, Creative Mind, and Body of Fate. Will and Mask are related as desire and the object of desire. Creative Mind and Body of Fate are related as thought and the objects of thought, "knower and known." Of these, Will and Mask (the subjective, individualistic members of the four) are lunar. However, these four "Faculties" are set against four corresponding "Principles," which are their "innate ground"—and from the standpoint of this pairing, all the Faculties are lunar, and all the Principles solar. The Principles, we are told, are the Faculties "transferred from a concave to a convex mirror." They "reveal reality but create nothing," whereas "in the *Faculties* the sole activity and the sole unity is natural or lunar." But the set of Faculties is so superimposed upon the corresponding set of Principles that "lunar south is solar east" (a formula that Yeats several times repeats). It is important to remember when considering the Byzantium poems. For "lunar south" is at full moon, golden Byzantium is East, Yeats in his essay on Magic has told us that "solar symbols often call up visions of gold and precious stones," and in *A Vision* he tells us that, if he could have been "given a month of Antiquity" and leave to spend it where he chose, he would have spent it "in early Byzantium"; and finally, he says that the full moon "amid east-ward-moving thought . . . brought

Byzantine glory."

I mention all this to back up my claim that even "solar" golden Byzantium may properly be treated as a derivative of the lunar ("all things dying each other's life, living each other's death"). For we have been told that the mark of the lunar is beauty, unity of being—and in *A Vision* Yeats says of Byzantium: "I think that in early Byzantium, maybe never before or since in recorded history, religious, aesthetic and practical life were one."

Were I to go beyond the readily available evidence of the page, utilizing traditional psychoanalytic lore (on the grounds that, as Yeats might say, his symbolism is derived from the Great Memory that is the common pool of all mankind, a condition we could also state less mystically by saying that the generally uniform neural structure of men provides the stimulus for a generally uniform pattern of experience and its symbolic reflections)—were I thus to speculate beyond the readily available facts on the page, I should suggest that the lunar white of Yeats's imagery is related to the seminal, and the solar gold related to the excremental. (These being, we might say, at the bottom of the ladder, with lunar white and solar gold bearing their sublime correspondences at the top.) This would account for the bitter mode of expression in his later realism, with its stress upon decay (notably, in "The Circus Animals' Desertion," his complaint that all "those masterful images" had begun in "a mound of refuse"; and "Now that my ladder's gone,/I must lie down where all the ladders start,/In the foul rag-and-bone shop of the heart"). Particularly in his early poems, I think it would be easy to reveal the seminal ambiguity lurking behind the imagery of white. In "Sailing to Byzantium," he accepts the "decay" of age in an ecstatic glow which gives us but the higher registers of the golden "ladder." But in later years, as the new love of women was denied him, he had many years in which his first exhilaration, in accepting age and death thus glorified, had full opportunity to abate. The sun, no longer vivified by reflection from the moon, could not thus continue to glow. And so the extremely poignant realism results. And whereas he could say of his early verse, "the quality symbolized as The Rose differs from the Intellectual Beauty of Shelley and of Spenser in that I have imagined it as suffering with man and not as something pursued and seen from afar," in his realism we find again a suffering-with, but this time it is he himself causing himself to suffer in the very act of excoriation.

However, though Yeats's doctrine of the Great Memory would justify me in thus treating his symbolism in accordance with psychoanalytic interpretation in general (and if we recall his poems of white birds, we may not leave unnoticed his remark in *A Vision* to the effect that "My imagination was for a time haunted by figures that, muttering 'The great systems,' held out to me the sun-dried skeletons of birds"), I shall hurry back to treatment of motive on the upper rungs of the "ladder" (an interesting simplification, by the way, of the "gyring" climb that Yeats made so much of in his imagery of the Tower). So, let us note another version of contrasting motives:

> What if Christ and Oedipus or, to shift the names, Saint Catherine of Genoa and Michael Angelo, are the two scales of a balance, the two butt-ends of a seesaw? What if every two thousand and odd years something happens in the world to make one sacred, the other secular; one wise, the other foolish; one fair, the other foul; one divine, the other devilish?

Accordingly, he had written to Pound, "I send you the introduction of a book which will, when finished, proclaim a new divinity." That is, it would "proclaim a new motive," since men's gods are their terms for the motives common to their group. The book could hardly be said to have succeeded in doing this, though we can, when we read it, understand why the hunchback, the saint, and the fool figure as a prophetic trio in his verse, for they would be the three most suited to stand at the point of such a grave transition.

One of the most striking contributions which the Vision of the motivational Wheel seems to have made to Yeats's metaphors is to be seen in that mighty sonnet on "Leda and the Swan," printed at the head of Book V. His basic sexual parallel between the motivational source of Greek culture and that of the Christian culture centers in his concept of the two annunciations: the one made to Mary, into whom the new life of the Holy Ghost penetrated through the ear; the other made to Leda, when Zeus descended to her in the guise of a swan (a union out of which were born Helen, Castor and Pollux—"love" and "war").

To my mind, the most effective moment in the Leda sonnet comes at the turn from octave to sestet. In the octave Yeats has built up the imagery of the event in its sheer physicality. The sestet will give us its "moral" equivalent, the ideational translation of the events in the octave. The physical concreteness of the octave is symbolic; the sestet will tell us what it is symbolic of. Or rather, that would be the most "businesslike" way of treating the subject. But the special effectiveness at this point arises from the fact that the "translation" is not a mere statement as to what the events in the octave "mean." Instead, it is itself a new act:

A shudder in the loins engenders there
The broken wall, the burning roof and tower
And Agamemnon dead.

That is: since offspring are to come of this annunciation, implicit in its present there is a future. But since the offspring is the offspring of a god (and gods are terms for the motivating center of a culture)[1] this future that is implicit in the present must comprise not merely the *persons* that are to come of it, but also the entire play, with all its scenes, in which these persons are to enact their roles. In the annunciation, the fertilizing of the egg is implicit; in the fertilized egg, Helen is implicit; and in Helen is implicit all the incidents leading up to and away from the sack of Troy, about which the whole of Greek-Roman antiquity is disposed.

It is in their contribution to this intensity of implication, I think, that the spirits did carry out their purpose, to give the poet new metaphors. For one of the most important thoughts underlying the concept of the motivational Wheel is the notion that not only is a man's character inherited from prior incarnations, but also the environment that is in conformity with this character is inherited. The agent, to enact the role that belongs to him as an agent, must also have the scene to which such an act belongs. It is a dramatist's concept, the sort of concern we read much of in Henry James's prefaces, where he is offering us an analysis of the novelist's motives in terms of the dramatist's exigencies. And it thus contributes vitally to the dramatic result.

I can think of no more felicitous fusion of personal and impersonal factors (in an egg that contains not merely a biological outcome, but also biographical and historical ones, with the sense of these personal elements also intensified by their very contrast with the non-human form of Zeus as prime motive).

[1] When Yeats writes, of another swan, "That stormy white/But seems a concentration of the sky," is he not here covertly responding to the connotations that Leda's particular swan has for him? Indeed, we might trace a movement through his works thus: in his early poems, there are the white birds, which are "seminal" aspects of himself; these become deified in taking the form of Zeus, as a swan; and in this form they again descend to earth.

Of course, sensitivity in the use of such a form for harmonious effects also implies sensitivity to its potentialities in the conveying of a harshness. Thus with his poem "Three Things" (to a refrain that we could have mentioned with relevance when in our psychoanalytic speculations: "A bone wave-whitened and dried in the sun") he gets a jarring effect by alternately, through three stanzas, building up this bone into a *person,* with the qualities of loveliness, and then reducing it again to the barren object named in the refrain.

However, though the spirits fulfilled their promise in bringing Yeats good metaphors, even to the last (enabling him, ironically, to retain such stylistic youthfulness until the very end as would equip him to speak with eloquence of the old age that afflicted him), he does not seem to have kept his own promise to bring us a "new divinity." For precisely in his later work, where one would most expect to find some reliance upon the supernatural for solace, we find him proclaiming as his motive:

You think it horrible that lust and rage
Should dance attention upon my old age;
They were not such a plague when I was young;
What else have I to spur me into song?

The vision was after all, it seems, "towards Nature" rather than "towards God." And the spirits were then right in holding that it should be explained in lunar terms (the lunar being towards Nature). And the promise of Byzantium was not in the supernatural future, but in the nature of poems back a couple of decades in the past. Among the stark complaints that the metaphors enabled him to make poignant in confronting the bleakness, there is one called "The Apparitions," having the somewhat enigmatical refrain:

Fifteen apparitions have I seen;
The worst a coat upon a coat-hanger.

Some correlations can, I think, help to fill out for us the significance of this symbol. Thus, when discussing the "Principles" that underlie the "Faculties," Yeats writes:

My instructors have described the *Marriage* [a stage in the rebirth of the soul] as follows: "The *Celestial Body* is the Divine Cloak lent to all, it falls away at the consummation and Christ is revealed," words which seem to echo Bardesan's "Hymn to the Soul," where a

King's son asleep in Egypt (physical life) is sent a cloak which is also an image of his body. He sets out to his father's kingdom wrapped in the cloak.

And he adds in a footnote:

A living man sees the *Celestial Body* through the *Mask*. I awoke one night when a young man to find my body rigid and to hear a voice that came from my lips and yet did not seem my voice saying, "We make an image of him who sleeps that is not him who sleeps and we call it Emmanuel."

However, this is about a "cloak," and the reader may object that "cloak" can be in a quite different compartment of associations from "coat." But there is a poem "A Coat" in the volume *Responsibilities*, beginning cheerfully enough:

I made my song a coat
Covered with embroideries
Out of old mythologies
From heel to throat.

The poem then turns to insult the "fools" who caught it and wore it, whereupon addressing his song in the song, he tells it: "there's more enterprise/In walking naked."

In "Sailing to Byzantium," after beginning on the theme "That is no country for old men," we come upon the coat in the second stanza:

An aged man is but a paltry thing,
A tattered coat upon a stick, unless
Soul slap its hands and sing, and louder sing
For every tatter in its mortal dress,
Nor is there singing school but studying
Monuments of its own magnificence;
And therefore I have sailed the seas and come
To the holy city of Byzantium.

I take it, then, that the coat of the apparitions is to be interpreted as the representative of the poet, after he has lost the exhilaration that first came of his welcoming death in its beautifully metaphorical transfiguration. And thus it represents the quality of the self-directed realism under which Yeats so grievously suffered. In *A Vision* he had written: "Fragment delights in fragment and seeks possession, not service; whereas the Good Samaritan discovers himself in the likeness of another, covered with sores and abandoned by thieves upon the roadside, and in that other serves himself." At the last, it would seem, refusing fragmentation, still preserving his poet's "unity of being," he suffered himself however to become a kind of "Bad Samaritan" to himself, and punished himself in identification with the things about him. I recall that in the metaphorical version of the Vision's genesis, he had mentioned only three symbols, "a man torn in two by an eagle and some sort of wild beast, a man whipping his shadow, a man between a hunchback and a fool in cap and bells." The first would obviously indicate conflict of motives, the second would indicate an abuse of the self (by abuse of the shadow as *alter ego*); the man between hunchback and fool is doubtless the saint. Without this last, we are left with but the emotionally torn hunchback and the fool striking at his own shadow. They are the themes that Yeats had to contend with, in his courageous last strivings, so human, so poignantly well said.

In the Byzantium poems I am always reminded of the "Ode on a Grecian Urn"; for besides the complex quality of the exhilaration (got through subterfuges that enable the poet to welcome what he might otherwise fear), there is in Yeats an intensification of Keats's vision of immortalization, not as a *person,* but by conversion into a fabricated *thing*. It is not a religious immortality that is celebrated here, but an aesthetic one. It is "beauty," "lunar."

In the second of the Byzantium poems there is an expression, "flames begotten of flame," which is mentioned in a comment by Mr. MacNeice:

> The world of Becoming, of human beings, is a world of "mire and blood," of impermanent and unsatisfying movement. Byzantium also has its movements but they are, to use Aristotle's terminology, *energeia* instead of *kinesis;* that is, movement for its own sake, self-contained, self governing, absolute, eternal, instead of movement originated from without, a means to an end outside itself, contingent, relative, and doomed to cessation. Yeats admits that it is possible to cross from one world to the other; the "blood-begotten spirits" can join the dance of the "flames begotten of flame."

This talk of *movement*, let us remind ourselves, is talk of *motives*—and Mr. MacNeice is here distinguishing two kinds of motivation (which brings us back to the starting point of the *Vision,* quite as the book that describes the Vision had, in its closing pages, brought us to Byzantium). Here we are at the very core of the two concepts of motives. Yet have we said enough when we treat the "flames begotten of flame" as the symbol of an intrinsic motivation, in contrast with such motivation as things get by propulsion from without?

Is not this form, of a substance growing out of itself, also open to problems of narcissism, or hermaphroditism, as with his master Blake (the great problem that mystics have always faced when, beginning with a sexual analogy, they next seek to collapse the two principles into a unity)? Yeats's vision is not that of a motive in God, or in some other natural or supernatural context. At this point, it is the vision of a motive in self. In another way, after a long roundabout journey, it seems to be a return to the lake isle of Innisfree, to his own heart's core, but with white dying and gold being born out of its death.

We find the pattern repeated in the next stanza, where we read of

Those images that yet
Fresh images beget. . . .

But in "The Phases of the Moon" we read that "He has found, after the manner of his kind,/Mere images"; that "Under the frenzy of the fourteenth moon [which is just before full moon]/The soul begins to tremble into stillness,/ To die into the labyrinth of itself", and thence we are told that "those that we have loved" got their fingers "from some bloody whip in their own hands."

Or let us put it this way: There is an ecstatic *vision* of the intrinsic motive, and there is a corresponding *problem* of the intrinsic motive. In the Byzantium poem we encounter it in its ecstatic form, but elsewhere we encounter it in its problematic form.[2] Thus, in one of the last poems, we find it in a gloomy variant: "Mirror on mirror mirrored is all show." And he now complains that he is "all metaphor." And in this mood, his earlier awestruck poem, "The Mother of God,"

[2] It gets another variant in the "Meditations in Time of Civil War." In *A Vision,* distinguishing the meanings of the four terms, "sensuous," "concrete," "idealized," and "abstract," Yeats wrote of the first: "An object is sensuous if I relate it to myself, 'my fire, my chair, my sensation.' " And during the doubts of civil war, when one cannot know just what will be his identity and his properties, with relation to the identity that s taking shape among his countrymen as a whole, we find Yeats writing of "Ancestral Houses," "My House," "My Table," "My Descendants," "The Road at My Door," etc. The motif here becomes a way of reaffirming an individual integrity, with its related properties, as against the puzzles of fragmentation.

that follows "Byzantium" in his *Collected Works* and might well be read as a companion piece to the Leda sonnet, has a harsh replica in "A Nativity" of his *Last Poems*.

In these last poems one gets the feeling that the frequent refrains, in italics, represent another voice, as though the distinction between Will and Mask with which Yeats had enlivened his speculations in earlier years had become transformed into a kind of grim internal colloquy. In one instance, "The Man and the Echo," a great poignancy is got by a significant change in the pattern of voice and response. Twice, the Man has spoken long stanzas, to which the Echo answers briefly, once "Lie down and die" and next "Into the night." But the third time the Echo's answer is woven into the texture of the Man's words itself, and it is a still more cruelly directed echo—this time a symbolic one, an echo not of words, but an echoing *incident:*

O Rocky Voice,
Shall we in that great night rejoice?
What do we know but that we face
One another in this place?
But hush, for I have lost the theme,
Its joy or night seem but a dream;
Up there some hawk or owl has struck,
Dropping out of sky or rock,
A stricken rabbit is crying out,
And its cry distracts my thought.

In one of his earliest poems, "Anashuya and Vijaya," a mannered and arbitrary piece, there was a stage setting that I do greatly like the design of:

A little Indian temple in the Golden Age. Around it a garden; around that the forest. Anashuya, the young priestess, kneeling within the temple.

I like in it the widening circles: the priestess, surrounded by a temple, which in turn is surrounded by a garden, which in turn is surrounded by the forest. It is a scene promising in its expansiveness. And one might recall it when reading of the scene in the bleak play "Purgatory," published among his *Last Poems*. It is briefly: "A ruined house and a bare tree in the background." "Study that tree," the old man says to his son; "What is it like?" And the son, whom the old man is to kill, as the old man had likewise killed his father, answers: "A silly old man."

A silly old man? The poignancy, the stylistic skill, the harsh honesty, the humanness of his work, and particularly his work in this late phase even when he was thus being Bad Samaritan to himself and to the surroundings with which he identified himself, are enough to proclaim him impressively the opposite. And perhaps we should not say that he complained much in these latter years. Perhaps it would be more accurate to say that he cursed.

W. Y. Tindall

Dedicating his *Symbolist Movement in Literature* to William Butler Yeats, Arthur Symons called his Irish friend "the chief representative of that movement in our country." Symons makes it plain that Yeats belongs not to the French symbolist movement but rather to a general European movement of which the French are leaders. Later critics have been less accurate. C. M. Bowra in his *Heritage of Symbolism* (1943) takes it for granted that Yeats is heir to the French; and Edmund Wilson in *Axel's Castle* (1931), searching for connections to support his thesis, went so far as to invent a meeting between Yeats and Mallarmé. Joseph Hone, also accepting Yeats as an heir to the French, asserts in his *Life of W. B. Yeats* (1943) that Yeats was familiar with the *Herodiade* of Villiers de l'Isle Adam, an assertion which would carry more weight if Mallarmé had not written it and if Yeats had been familiar with it. These critics, whose confusions suggest only that the matter is confusing, may be forgiven for their desire to impose cause, effect, and order upon something that seems to deny these satisfactions.

Yeats was a symbolist. That much is clear. But it is also clear that his knowledge of French was so slight that he was unable to read the difficult poems to which he is supposed to be indebted. His French, which he picked up here and there without much benefit of schooling, was adequate for translating Ronsard's sonnet "When You Are Old" (1893), unless, of course, Yeats took the poem from an English version. "Ephemera" (1889) resembles Verlaine's *Colloque Sentimental.* Ronsard and Verlaine, however, are comparatively simple, and neither could have become the basis for a system of symbolism such as Yeats was to devise.

The case for *Axël* by Villiers de l'Isle Adam is stronger. Probably between 1890 and 1892 Yeats read this play slowly and laboriously, for, as he says, his French was very poor. "That play seemed all the more profound," he adds in the Preface he wrote for an English translation of *Axël* in 1925, "because I was never quite certain that I had read a page correctly." On February 26, 1894, he went to Paris to see the

"The Symbolism of W. B. Yeats," reprinted from *Accent,* V, 4 (summer, 1945), pp. 203-212; and from *Forces in Modern British Literature 1885-1946,* pp. 248-263, copyright, 1947, by William York Tindall; by permission of the publisher, Alfred A. Knopf, Inc.

production of *Axël* at the Théâtre Montparnasse in company with Maud Gonne, who assisted his memory by explaining the words of the actors. She also helped him through the almost surrealist obscurities of Jarry's *Ubu Roi* at the symbolist Théâtre de l'Oeuvre in 1896. On his return from Paris in 1894 Yeats reviewed *Axël* in the April *Bookman* as part of the spiritual reaction of his time against science, externality, and realism of Zola and Ibsen. Yeats saw no hope of a London production of this transcendental play, for the public was ready only for Pinero and Jones. The reading of *Axël* had a lasting effect upon Yeats as his short stories "Rosa Alchemica" and "Out of the Rose" demonstrate. And his symbolic play *The Shadowy Waters* (1900) is a translation of *Axël* into nautical terms.

Aside from *Axël* and a number of treatises on the occult, there is no available evidence that Yeats read anything in French. But he was acquainted with the plays of Maeterlinck in English translation. These plays were produced in English on the London stage, starting with *L'Intruse,* January, 1892, and continuing with the others through the nineties; and from 1892 on, his plays were translated and published in London almost as soon as they were published in France. Casual references from as early as 1894 in Yeats' essays and reviews show his acquaintance with Maeterlinck; and in the September, 1897, *Bookman* he reviewed Sutro's translation of *Aglavaine et Selysette*. Although he was less enthusiastic about Maeterlinck's plays and essays than he was about *Axël,* he regarded them as almost equally significant rebellions against the external, and he was fascinated with Maeterlinck's repeated symbols of mysterious intruders, lighthouses and wells in the woods.

With the other symbolists he was less familiar. In 1894 he visited Verlaine in the Rue St. Jacques and spoke with him in English—"for I had explained the poverty of my French." They talked of *Axel* and of Maeterlinck. This article in *The Savoy* (April, 1896) in which Yeats tells about this visit, is concerned with Verlaine's character and life, to the neglect of his poetry in which, except for the problematical "Ephemera," Yeats never displayed much interest When he met the English-speaking Stuart Merrill in Paris, they talked not about poetry but about politics and socialism toward which both Merrill and Yeats temporarily inclined. But at this time perhaps Merrill undertook the translation into French of three of Yeats' poems. Maud Gonne and William Sharp conducted Yeats among the French during the nineties; and in later years Iseult

Gonne, Maud's daughter, took their place. It was she who kept Yeats up to date, reading and translating for him the poems of Claudel, Péguy, and Valéry, none of whom had the slightest effect on his work, although in 1938 he remarked that only Valéry's denial of immortality prevented him from placing the "Cimetière Marine" [*sic*] among his sacred books.

These contacts with France were inconsiderable, but Yeats managed to supplement them during the late nineties through his friendship with Arthur Symons, his next door neighbor in the Temple and fellow member of the Rhymers' Club. As Symons wrote his translations from Verlaine and Mallarmé, he read them to Yeats. Yeats was particularly impressed, he tells us in his *Autobiography,* with Symons' selection from Mallarmé's *Hérodiade,* which increased his own inclination toward an art separated from "everything heterogeneous and casual," from circumstance and character, in other words, toward a poetry as unlike that of the Victorians as possible but like the self-contained, socially isolated, and integrated poetry of Mallarmé. These translations, Yeats continues, "may have given elaborate form" to the latter verses of his *Wind Among the Reeds* (1899); and he will never know, he adds, how much his theory and practice owe to these translations. It is possible, as Yeats suggests, that the verses of Symons had these effects, but it must be remembered that Symons' translation from *Hérodiade* is not a good one and that any elaborateness communicated by it is from Symons, not Mallarmé. But the case for theory is a stronger one; for it must be supposed that Symons, who understood theories of Mallarmé, talked as much as he read, and that Yeats must have acquired some knowledge at second hand of symbolic intentions. Moreover, Yeats read *The Symbolist Movement in Literature* when it appeared in 1899 and based his essay "The Symbolism of Poetry" (1900) partly upon what he had learned. "When sound, and colour, and form are in a musical relation . . . to one another," Yeats says in this essay, "they become as it were one sound, one colour, one form, and evoke an emotion that is made out of their distinct evocations and yet is one emotion." This is Mallarmé by way of Symons. That phrase about the trembling of the veil of the temple which Yeats was continually quoting comes from the *Divagations* (1897) of Mallarmé. Since this book, if not this phrase, is difficult, Yeats received it, no doubt, from Symons, who had sat on Tuesdays at the feet of the master.

A man who cannot read Mallarmé cannot be affected by Mallarmé. But it is unnecessary to look to him or to any

Frenchman for the symbolism of William Butler Yeats, who was a symbolist poet long before he had heard of the French. He based his symbolism upon the poetry of Blake, Shelley, and Rossetti and, above all these, upon the occult. In 1886, under the spell of Mme. Blavatsky, Yeats joined the Dublin Lodge of the Theosophical Society, and two years later he joined in London the Order of the Golden Dawn, a Rosicrucian and Kabalistical society, whose leader, MacGregor Mathers, maintained connections with the similar order of Stanislas de Guaita in Paris. From the works of Mme. Blavatsky, Yeats learned that Anima Mundi, a reservoir of all that has touched mankind, may be evoked by symbols. From Swedenborg, he received the doctrine of correspondences, from Eliphas Levi the doctrine of magical incantations and symbols which have power over spiritual and material reality, and from Boehme the similar doctrine of signatures. The Emerald Tablet of Hermes Trismegistus informed him that things below are as things above. And the symbolic ritual of the Rosicrucians confirmed these ideas. A rebel against the world of matter, Yeats learned that all material things correspond to concepts in the world of spirit, and that through the use of material objects as magical symbols the adept may call down disembodied powers. The essay "Magic" (1901) expresses his conviction that the great memory of nature "can be evoked by symbols." Like Baudelaire, who had read Swedenborg before him, Yeats became a poetic visionary, and like Rimbaud, who had followed Eliphas Levi, Yeats became "magus," a master of magic who through poetic symbols and trances could surprise reality in its lair. Although he had never heard of Baudelaire or Rimbaud during his reading of Levi and Swedenborg, Yeats belonged with these poets to the great transcendental movement of the nineteenth century and turned naturally to the same supernatural sources. Material reality became for him as for them a chaos of symbols through which a poet could deal directly with spiritual orders. The example of Blake, also an occultist, taught Yeats the use in poetry of magical symbols; and the poems of Shel- ey, which he carefully analyzed, confirmed his symbolic sys- em. Like Blake, Baudelaire, and Rimbaud, Yeats saw the poet s magus and priest but as poet before magus and priest. Knowing what he was about, he went to the occult in the first lace to discover, if he could, the laws of the imagination, to find ays of inducing trance and vision through which he could onfront the inner and higher realities he needed, and to find nages or symbols for his poetry.

By 1890, before he learned about the French symbolists, he had been writing symbolic poems for several years, and when Symons and others told him about the French poets. Yeats welcomed them as fellow travellers on the road he was following, as fellow transcendentalists and occultists who had, like Blake and Shelley, hit upon symbolism as the only possible way to express what they had experienced. It is notable that aside from professional occultists and Huysmans the only Frenchmen whom Yeats read were Maeterlinck, who was a kind of theosophist, and Villiers, who was also a student of Eliphas Levi and of the Rosicrucians. Occult considerations led Yeats to the laborious reading of *Axël,* and it was probably MacGregor Mathers, the Rosicrucian, who introduced him to this congenial play.

To see how congenial it was a synopsis is necessary. This play concerns the well-born Sara, a novice in a nunnery, who has read a collection of Rosicrucian works carelessly left around in the convent library. As she stands before the archdeacon in her bridal robes about to take the veil, she is overcome with longing for a more spiritual life and for a treasure she has also read about. Seizing an axe and assuming a fierce demeanor, she locks the archdeacon in a tomb, climbs out of a window, and departs. Meanwhile, Count Axel of Auersperg, living in exile from the world in his very Gothical castle in the Black Forest, pursues Rosicrucian studies, attempts the "Great Work" of alchemy, and practices magic according to the precepts of Eliphas Levi, under the supervision of Master Janus, an adept. Indifferent to the world of matter, from which he desires to detach himself for the sake of perfection, Axel refuses to hunt for the treasure buried somewhere on his premises. He speaks eloquently of Hermes Trismegistus, Paracelsus, and the Magi. During an interminable conversation with Master Janus, however, he suddenly renounces his spiritual aims and decides to use his magic to secure the treasure. Descending into the vaults beneath the very Gothical castle, he comes upon Sara, who has already discovered the treasure. She shoots him. Enchanted by her cruelty and her shape, he covers himself in her long hair and breathes the spirit of dead roses. He proposes that they take the treasure and have a good time in Paris, Kashmir, Heliopolis, London. But she shows him her cruciform dagger and the faded rose (the Rosy Cross) which are the symbol and "correspondence" of her belief, her soul, and the nature of things. He is moved. Therefore, in expiation of their passing infidelity to the spirit of the Rosy Cross, and in contempt of the world and of love, they resolve to die, and die. The spiritual allegory, filled with symbols of castle, lamp, treasure, and the like, immediately became one of Yeats' "sacred books," surpassing even *Prometheus Unbound* in his esteem. It is easier to see why it should have appealed to a member of the Order of the Golden Dawn than why it should have appealed to the most symbolical Frenchman.

The symbols of Yeats' early poems, like those of Villiers and of Levi, are occult in character. From Mme. Blavatsky he learned that the great memory of nature preserves the legends of all nations and that one may get into touch with Anima Mundi through symbols drawn from Irish legends, the symbolic characters of Oisin or Aengus, for example, or the hound with one red ear, the white deer with no horns, or the island in the sea. But equally characteristic are his arbitrary occult symbols of rose, cross, lily, bird, water, tree, moon and sun, which he could find in the Kabalistic, Theosophical, and the other profound works which constituted the greater part of his reading. The two trees in his poems of that name are the Sephirotic tree of life of the Kabala and the tree of knowledge. The "Powers" of his poem "The Poet Pleads with the Elemental Powers" are Mme. Blavatsky's elemental spirits, the "Immortal Rose" is the Rosicrucian flower, and the "Seven Lights" are the seven planets and the astral light of theosophy. The "Ineffable Name" of "To Some I Have Talked with by the Fire" is the Kabalistical *Shem Hamphorasch* or Jehovah, whose unspeakable four-lettered name in Hebrew characters admits of seventy-two combinations, as Yeats, practicing with the Kabalists in Paris, knew by experience. These symbols differ from those ordinarily employed by the French in that they are traditional, systematic, more arbitrary and definite in outline. But although they are first of all magical symbols, hence impersonal, as used by Yeats they become as personal, reverberating and mysterious as the symbols of the less systematic French.

Of these early symbols the rose is the most complex. Most of the rose poems are to be found in *The Rose* (1893), written in his first enthusiasm after reading *Axël* with its Rosicrucian roses. But as a member of the Order of the Golden Dawn Yeats had no need to pilfer *Axël*, for the symbolic ritual of his society centered about the rose and cross. Although this society was secret, the details of its ritual have been revealed; for Aleister Crowley, a member, violating dreadful vows, exposed the ritual of the Order at great length in the September, 1909, and March, 1910, numbers of *The Equinox*, a magazine which he edited. This ritual, which has escaped the attention of critics, does much to make Yeats' poetic symbolism clear.

The novices of the Golden Dawn were confronted with the Sephirotic tree of life, the seven planets, the sphinx, and with the symbols of the four elements. Candidates of the fourth grade who were called "Unicorns from the Stars" (a phrase which Yeats took as the title for one of his plays) learned the doctrine of correspondences between microcosm and macrocosm, and at one point in their spiritual development were permitted to inhale the perfume of a rose. But only the higher initiates were admitted to the secret of the Rose of Ruby and the Cross of Gold," the "fadeless Rose of Creation and the immortal Cross of Light" or life itself, ecstasy and suffering, and union with God. Light, fire, the color red symbolized, as on Zoroaster, the highest good. In the vault of initiation there was a rose on the ceiling, a rose with a cross on the floor, and the vault was lit with the ray of a luminous rose. Father Christian Rosenkreutz, about whom Yeats wrote an essay, was regarded as the founder of the society; and the symbols of dagger, cup, and rose, which appear in Yeats' diagram of the Great Wheel, were conspicuous in the ritual. Even "Hodos Camelionis," which makes its appearance in Yeats' *Autobiography* as "Hodos Chameliontos," occurs in the course of this awful ceremony.

But to return to the symbol of the rose in Yeats' poems and stories: it is even more complex than this ritual would imply, for Yeats was personal as well as occult and he used the rose to mean more than Father Christian Rosy Cross or MacGregor Mathers intended. In "The Rose of Peace" the rose means earthly love as it does in a popular song; but the rose of "The Rose of the World" is more complicated, meaning on one level transient earthly love and beauty and on another eternal love and beauty. "The Rose of Battle" is more occult, symbolizing God's side in the battle of spirit against matter or what inspires occultists and those who have failed of earthly love in their endless battle with the materialists. Here the rose is a refuge from earthly love. Wearing this militant rose of ruby and intellectual flame as the symbol of his life and hope, the Rosicrucian knight of the story "Out of the Rose" wages God's wars against outer order and fixity. The rose in "To the Rose upon the Rood of Time," as the title of the poem implies, is the Rosicrucian rose but it is also the power of the creative imagi nation and occult philosophy too, which, Yeats fears, may re move him so completely from the present world that he wil cease to be a poet. A similar fear plagues the hero of the stor

"Rosa Alchemica," an adventure in spiritual alchemy in which the rose as in Eliphas Levi means the "Great Work" of transmuting matter into spirit. Taken to the headquarters of the Order of the Alchemical Rose where adepts ceremoniously dance with spirits who wear black lilies in their hair, the hero joins the terrible dance. On the dancing floor, to increase his terror, is a great cross and on the ceiling a rose. The acting version of *The Shadowy Waters* has a passage on the rose and cross as a symbol of the union of body and soul, life and death, sleep and waking. More and more Yeats feared the isolation of spirit from matter as he had feared the isolation of matter from spirit, and with these fears the rose came to mean what he called "unity of being" or the integration and harmony of self, world, and spirit. These meanings are present in the rose or around it, but they are not all that it suggests because from each context come reverberations enriching the symbol as it in turn enriches its context. The value of a symbol, said Yeats, is this richness or indefiniteness of reference which makes it far more mysterious and potent than allegory with its single meaning. A hundred men, he continued, would advance a hundred different meanings for the same symbol; for "no symbol tells all its meaning" to any man.

These interpretations of symbolism and of the power of the imagination, which was the same thing to him, are to be found in his edition of Blake's *Prophetic Books* (1893), in his essays on Shelley, "Symbolism in Painting" and "The Autumn of the Body," and his introduction to *A Book of Images* (1898) by W. T. Horton, a fellow adept. The symbol, says Yeats in the last of these essays, gives "dumb things voices, and bodiless things bodies."

The Wind Among the Reeds (1899) does exactly this. Re-iewing this book, Arthur Symons hailed it as a triumph of ymbolist indirection. Through the swooning, luscious diction, he musical, individual rhythms, the harmonies and overtones, nd the interaction of many traditional but mysterious images ach poem becomes the symbol of an unstated idea or mood. lthough Yeats employed description and statement more lav-shly than the French were accustomed to do, the book is clos-r in feeling and method to the works of the French symbolists han any other which appeared in England in the nineties. It esembles these works not because it is indebted to them but ecause, coming from the same revolt against matter and sur-ace, it is parellel to them.

Some of the plays of William Butler Yeats resemble those of

the French symbolist stage not only because they are also transcendental reactions against the realistic stage but because he had Villiers and Maeterlinck in mind when he wrote them. The debt of *The Shadowy Waters* to Villiers is clear. *The Countess Kathleen* (1892), however, which has all the atmosphere of Maeterlinck, was written before Yeats knew of him. It is difficult to say what part of Yeats' other plays comes from the French and what from the so-called Celtic twilights or the English romantic tradition.

The poems of *The Wind Among the Reeds* and the earlier poems owe part of their richness and depth to something apart from the conscious use of occult symbols and wavering rhythms. Like Rimbaud, Yeats had discovered a way to evade the interference of his intellect and to explore his unconscious in search of symbols. Rimbaud had done this by a systematic derangement of the senses through drugs, fatigue, and depravity. Yeats, who was far too prudent for such excesses, found in the occult a way of doing the same thing. Inclined by nature to waking visions and trances in which he saw wonderful things, Yeats found that through the use of ritual and hypnotic symbols he could enjoy deeper and more effectual trances in which new images swam before his eyes. Magic, by putting his active intellect to sleep, permitted him to secure for his poems the wealth of his unconscious. Naturally he tried to give these floating images an occult value, but this did not prevent them from carrying with them to his poems, whatever his conscious intention, the richness of man's deepest reality. Like Rimbaud, then, and with the aid of Rimbaud's tutor, Eliphas Levi, Yeats discovered a poetic territory which had been neglected in England except by occasional madmen since the time of William Blake. Yeats differs from Rimbaud, however, in the formal, conscious patterns he forced upon his images.

In the second part of *The Wandering of Oisin* (1889) Yeats tells of his hero's battle on an island in the sea with an elderly demon who keeps a lady in a cave. This episode, Yeats told Katherine Tynan, came to him in a kind of vision, which plagued him night and day, and left him in a state of collapse. "Under the guise of symbolism," he told her, "I have said several things to which I only have the key." The story, he continued, was for the common reader who would remain unaware of the symbolism, yet "the whole poem is full of symbols." Aware that these unconscious symbols would bear neither an occult nor a legendary explanation, Yeats seem in this letter to Katherine Tynan, written long before

Freud commences his study of such symbols, to apprehend some part of their significance in his life with father.

From his interest in semi-conscious vision, Yeats was led by his occult interests to examine his dreams for their occult meaning and for poetic themes and images. "The Cap and Bells" (1899) is, he assures us, a dream recorded exactly as he dreamed it. Here the images of queen, garment, hair, cap and bells, door, window, and the colors of red and green would have interested Dr. Freud, who loved the literary exploitation of the unconscious.[1] Yeats says in a note that this poem meant much to him, but, as with all symbolic poems, its meaning was never twice the same. Dr. Freud could have delivered him from these ambiguities. The first two stanzas of "The Song of Wandering Aengus" (1899) are obviously another dream, which is rationalized in the third stanza. The change of fish into girl is dream material. The images of wand, stream, berry, and fire are from man's sleeping consciousness. But the sun, moon, and apple of the third stanza are conscious occult symbols meaning intellect, imagination, and the tree of good and evil. Aengus was introduced afterwards to impart an Irish significance to the mysterious and lovely poem.

After 1900 Yeats poetry became older, plainer, and more classical until in its "lofty severe quality" it came to resemble the poetry of Baudelaire. Feeling left the surface and vibrated beneath it. Far from following Baudelaire, still further from following Jean Moreas and Henri de Regnier who had turned to a kind of hardness before him, Yeats was responding bitterly to circumstance and self. The satiric and occasional poetry of the 1910 period, however, appeared symbolist to George Moore, who was unable to get Paris out of his head. In *Vale* Moore speaks of a poem Yeats wrote about a house. "What house?" Moore asks. "Mallarmé could not be darker than this," and he adds, Yeats and Mallarmé, had they ever met, would have "got on famously." But Moore, as usual, was exaggerating. The only indirection or obscurity of "Upon a House Shaken by the Land Agitation" is Yeats' failure to mention Coole Park.

After 1917 Yeats returned more or less to symbolism, retaining nobility of the tone and classical surface, and with this return came greater obscurity. Dissatisfied with the Golden Dawn, Yeats announced in *A Vision* (1925) an occult system of his own. One of the daemons who had dictated this

[1] See Morton Irving Seiden: "A Psychoanalytical Essay on William Butler Yeats," *Accent*, spring, 1946.

system to Mrs. Yeats informed her husband of its purpose: "We have come," he said, "to give you metaphors for poetry." Yeats used them in many of the poems he wrote between 1917 and 1935, but although these images belong to a private system, they are more public than those he had used in the nineties.

Some of the later poems, such as "The Double Vision of Michael Robartes," which refers to the first and fifteenth phases of the moon, are unintelligible without reference to *A Vision,* which Yeats wrote to help readers through poems like this. "Byzantium" remains an enigma even with the help of *A Vision* and of several explications; for although it has every appearance of unity and although such images as the dome are readily intelligible, other images and their connections and references are as obscure as those of Mallarme. In Yeats such privacy is uncommon. "Leda and the Swan" springs from the system, but it has an easy surface and an emotional impact which permits the unsubtle reader to enjoy it. Like those of Mallarme, this poem, however, is symbolist in the sense that the manifest level is there to suggest unstated themes: the union of matter and spirit, of god and man, of Dove and Virgin, and all the cycles of history which begin with these unnatural conjunctions. In like manner "The Saint and the Hunchback," which has a dramatic, comprehensible level, implies three attitudes toward life symbolized by the saint, the hunchback, and Alcibiades, the last of whom stands for that aristocratic wholeness toward which Yeats aspired.

"The Delphic Oracle upon Plotinus," a gay, preposterous, and very successful poem, filled with mysterious overtones, concerns the philosopher Plotinus, swimming through boisterous waves toward a shore where Plato, Minos, Pythagoras, Rhadamanthus, and the choir of love await him. This poem seems to be not only symbolist but surrealist. As the title suggests, however, the author is not Yeats but the Delphic oracle, who composed the poem in Greek a long time ago. Using Stephen MacKenna's translation (in his edition of Porphyry's *Life of Plotinus*), Yeats in turn translated MacKenna's English into poetry. I give part of the Latin version by Marcilio Ficino because it is plainer to more people than the original Greek and because, unlike MacKenna's version, it is not copyrighted:

Aurei generis magni jovis ubi agitant
Minos et Rhadamanthus fratres: ubi justus

Aeacus: ubi Plato, sacra vis: ubi pulcher
Pythagoras, et quicunque chorum statuerunt amoris . . .

By suppressing much and by selecting such beauties as the "golden race" and the "choir of love," Yeats made of this indifferent stuff the stuff of poetry. As for its meaning, the Delphic oracle, according to Porphyry, intended her symbols to imply the journey of Plotinus through the chaos of time and death to the Elysian fields. Her symbols of sea and island attracted Yeats, whose unconscious had persistently offered them to him; and also, like Milton, he was unable to resist the richness of polysyllabic names, especially those of Pythagoras and Plotinus who were among his favorite adepts. No doubt the swimming of Plotinus toward his shore had a very personal significance to Yeats, not unlike that of the voyage to Byzantium, to the island of Innisfree, or to the Land of Youth.

These symbolic poems, which seem at first so French, owe little or nothing to the French. But many of the later poems, "Among School Children," for example, and "Sailing to Byzantium," have a tight logical structure and a dependence upon statement rarely found in French symbolist verse. Until the very end where the symbols of chestnut tree and dancer represent unity of being, "Among School Children" is classical in method, not symbolist, and its difficulties are those of any compressed, coherent whole of thought and feeling. The misprint in stanza six may be responsible, or course, for some confusion, but "golden-thighed" which glimmers so strangely in the same stanza is only a classical epithet applied to Pythagoras by Plutarch in the life of Numa Pompilius.

Yeats' poems are rarely as transcendental as they seem. Whatever their occult bearing, they are also personal and worldly. In his most dramatic poems, those on Aengus or on the saint and hunchback for instance, Yeats had his own problems in mind. Whatever his romantic contempt of the world, it was never as thorough as that of Mallarmé, who saw the world merely as a store of symbols for something else. Even in his Rosicrucian days Yeats wanted to reconcile world and spirit to integrate himself with world and spirit. His symbols, like his mask, gave him a way to do this. By their triple reference to self, world, and spirit they achieve on the aesthetic plane a unity of being impossible in life.

Donald Davidson

THE LATER YEATS, writing his memories of the years between 1887 and 1891, records that the early Yeats thought "that all art should be a Centaur finding in the popular lore its back and strong legs." It is a striking utterance, and it has often been quoted to define Yeats's relation as poet to the Ireland of tradition. This intellectual poet, the quoters seem to say, had his back and strong legs in the lore of his people. The Artist Yeats, who was of the Rhymers Club, and wrote "Sailing to Byzantium," and edited William Blake, nevertheless spent his summers in Sligo, with the fox-hunting Pollexfens. The ancient Irish myths, the later popular superstitions, perhaps even the lilt of Irish folk-song somehow merge into a complex idiom that even the most advanced moderns can accept. And furthermore, the conception of unity between art and life is everywhere in Yeats's works—sometimes positively, as in "The Trembling of the Veil," where he says, "I had begun to hope, or to half hope, that we might be the first in Europe to seek unity as deliberately as it had been sought by theologian, poet, sculptor, architect, from the eleventh to the thirteenth century"; but more often negatively, as in his typical modern poems, where he bewails the lack of unity, the disintegration of arts and of society itself.

This general view of Yeat's poetry is accepted, I suppose, by all except the Marxist critics, who are determined to convict him of escapism, on one ground or another. But to talk of unity, even as well as Yeats talks, whether in poem or prose, is not to achieve it. The question of Yeats's relation, as artist, to the popular lore, remains unsettled, and indeed almost unexamined. Perhaps it cannot be settled very easily. We know a great deal about the technique of poetry; and for some time we have been very seriously engaged in discussing the relation of the poet to his tradition—meaning, especially, his literary tradition and all that goes with it. But we know almost nothing about the proper relation between the poet and popular lore. Our critics are discreetly mum on that topic. They know a great deal about *The Golden Bough;* but that is anthropology, and only obscures the question of what the poet will do with popular lore if he *has* it, as old Scotsmen and Irishmen used to *have* the Gaelic. I do not

"Yeats and the Centaur," *The Southern Review,* VII, 3 (winter, 1942), pp. 510-516.

presume to offer any conclusive answers, but it does seem possible, within brief space, to clear away a few wrong assumptions and to establish a context within which discussion might develop.

To begin with Yeats's figure of the centaur, it seems a little unfortunate. Ixion, king of the Lapithae, was the father of the race of centaurs. He begot them of a phantom sent by Zeus to represent Hera, with whom Ixion was presumptuously infatuated. Later, Ixion was punished by being bound to the famous wheel, eternally revolving. The subsequent history of the centaurs is none too encouraging. They fought the Lapithae at the marriage-feast of Pirithous, and were in general rowdy and turbulent, if not treacherous. The centaur Nessus gave Deianira the poisoned shirt, which put an end to Heracles. Among the centaurs, only Chiron seems to have a good reputation. He taught, among the Greek heroes, Jason and the Argonauts, yet evidently did not teach them enough, at that, to save them from a rather empty quest.

But aside from the Greek myth, which does not seem to put centaurs in very great honor, the figure of art as a centaur does not offer quite the proper respect either to art or to popular lore. If art grows out of popular lore and derives a certain animal strength from it, surely the union between the two deserves a less monstrous representation. Is art a hybrid, with its intelligence of one species and its solid substance of another? A tree would be a better image, if we must have an image. For its boughs and fruit make no uncouth junction with trunk and roots, but are the upward proliferation of the original germ, from which the dark, earth-seated parts are a corresponding downward proliferation. Between the upward and downward parts, the relation is organic and reciprocal: the one cannot do without the other. And yet—if one wishes to indulge in homily and pursue the image further—it is perfectly true that the stump of a tree will flourish for awhile and put out suckers when the top has been cut away, while trunk and branches perish forthwith when deprived of a root system, or survive only as sawed lumber.

I suspect that the later Yeats did not think too well of the young Yeats who could conceive art as a centaur. The context in which the famous figure is set is a little deprecatory. "I did not foresee," he adds presently, "not having the courage of my own thought: the growing murderousness of the world." And he proceeds to quote the first two stanzas of "The Second Coming." There could be no excellent unity, he perceived, between art and popular lore (let us say intelligence and vitality) in a society where

> *The best lack all conviction, while the worst*
> *Are full of passionate intensity.*

And the beast of this later vision is also a hybrid—a lion body and the head of a man—but he has become ominous and apocalyptic.

The figure of the centaur will not do to characterize the ideal relationship between art and popular lore, though, unfortunately, it may describe adequately enough the false conceptions that have long troubled and misled the poets, perhaps Yeats among others.

It is easy to say what the ideal relationship should be—as easy as it is to draw any other ideal picture. The popular lore ought to pass readily and naturally into the art; it ought not have to be sought out by specialists in special corners, collected, edited, published, and reviewed; and then, perhaps only through some accident of taste or fashion, be appropriated, at long range, by a very literary poet. The reverse of the process ought also to work naturally and not at a forbidding long range. The art ought to pass readily into the popular lore, and not remain eternally aloof and difficult. Unless both processes continue in mutual interchange, society as well as art is in a bad state of health; but the bad health of society is a cause, not a result, of this unfavorable relationship.

For further clarification, the terms need to be given a more precise content. By "art" I think Yeats would mean "high art"—the art of the greatest poems, plays, novels, paintings; by "popular lore" I conceive that he would mean not merely the beliefs, whether religious, superstitious, mythical, or historical, of the common people, but also the embodiment of these in arts and crafts. Thus, if the epic or drama is "high art," the folk-song, ballad, or folk-tale is "low art"—the term is not used, of course, in derogation.

When the "high art" and the "low art" of a nation or a society are out of a proper relationship to each other, the "high art" becomes too "arty," and the "low art" too "low." It was this condition that Yeats saw in Ireland. Along with other poets and patriots of the Celtic Renaissance, he sought to correct it while it was still not too late for correction to take hold. "We might be the *first* in Europe to seek unity," he wrote, for Ireland out of its "backwardness," if for no other reason, was not yet too deeply committed to the specializations and the dissociations prevailing in England and elsewhere. Ireland could not yet be said to have a "high art" at all, of a modern kind; and its "low art" was not yet too low, was indeed deep-seated, native, abundant, and not quite perverted in its expression. And perhaps Ireland might once more, as in former ages, lead Europe in the arts, high and low. But he did not foresee how murderous western civilization had become. I do not think Yeats meant to suggest that his labors were tragically interrupted by World War I. Long before 1914 the gaps were there, between best and worst, between high and low art. Even in peace, these gaps were murderous.

The question evidently takes us far beyond the range of any purely literary issues, but I must be content here with limiting it to more or less literary issues, as they become apparent in the works of our notable example.

The early Yeats wrote ballads, like the "Ballad of the Foxhunter" and the "Ballad of Father Gilligan," and folksongs, or quasi-folksongs, like "Down by the Salley Gardens." He also wrote "The Wanderings of Usheen," a semi-epical poem, and composed lyrics and plays that utilized the ancient Irish myths. In *The Celtic Twilight* he brought together prose tales and sketches in which he put the gleanings of popular lore that he got from Mary Battle, his uncle's servant, and from his own wanderings about the countryside in Sligo. Then, after a time, the poetry ceases to be narrative or in any way "folkish." The myths and popular lore become occasional references, or they become, in the modern sense, symbols, which are merged into the larger "frame of reference" established by the private mythology explained in *A Vision.* Yeats has become a modern poet, indistinguishable from other modern poets except in his subject-matter, which is unique, and in a superior grace of idiom, which we can never cease admiring, the more because his contemporaries fail so badly in comparison, for they rarely attain both grace of idiom and seriousness.

Does this poetry, then, have its strong back and legs in the popular lore? Probably not, so far as Yeats deliberately intended to build it upon popular lore. But probably yes, so far as he did *not* deliberately so intend.

It would not be easy to classify the poems on such a basis, but I think it is possible to discuss a principle. A popular lore is essentially a subject-matter, and its reality, to the people among whom it is communicated, is the reality of fact, not the reality of art, as we define it in our lofty discussions.

Furthermore, a popular lore is of course a subject-matter which is looking for an art—that is, a ready means of emphatic communication and preservation. The art of popular lore therefore is art in the old, and perhaps philosophic, sense of contrivance or artifice. It has much about it of the utilitarian and purely functional. And for this reason it must be a conventional art, with clearly marked patterns.

On the other hand, our literature, or art in the sophisticated sense, has become the other thing: an art looking for a subject-matter, and rather heedless of what the subject-matter is, so long as it sets the art to working.

So far as Yeats, therefore, already had, by birthright and direct, naive acquaintance, a hold on popular lore as a subject-matter, and went looking for an art to communicate it, he may be said to have built his poetry upon the popular lore, in a way which by implication is desirable. But when he began to think of himself primarily as an artist, and went looking for a subject-matter, and decided that he must have a strong back and legs in the popular lore, he did not stem from the popular lore any longer, but merely appropriated it, as he would appropriate any other subject-matter, or a metaphor, or a rhyme. The unity of the popular lore and the high art cannot be obtained in this manner. And the proof is (if my statement of the ideal condition it at all tenable) that the process does not work reciprocally. Thus Yeats might appropriate the matter or even the manner of the street ballad-singer of Dublin, but the Dublin ballad-singer could not make any use of the art of Yeats; and in fact the art of Yeats remains accessible only to a relatively small group of persons: the high art has become unquestionably very high, very distant from the low art.

In the collection of stories entitled *The Secret Rose* is a tale called "The Old Men of the Twilight," in which Yeats tells of an old smuggler who, to his surprise, saw a long line of herons flying over the sea toward the land, from an unaccustomed direction. He took his gun to hunt them, and found them standing in shallow water among the rushes.

> But when he looked along the barrel the heron was gone, and, to his wonder and terror, a man that seemed of an infinitely great age stood in its place. He lowered the gun, and once more the heron stood there with bent head and motionless feathers. He raised the gun, and no sooner did he look along the barrel than the old man was again before him, only to vanish when he lowered the gun for the second time.

It was enchantment, of course. The herons were artists of the druid time, who had been cursed by St. Patrick because the click of their knives, writing their thoughts on ogham tablets, disturbed him.

Yeats is like the old smuggler. He sees the popular lore only when his gun-barrel is leveled to bring it down. Without the weapon of the artist, he does not see it; or do we in general see it, except as hunters. Only then does it become a subject-matter that can be used.

As for the difference between popular art, as contrivance, and sophisticated art, as being almost an end in itself, another experience of Yeats's will serve as an illustration. He heard John F. Taylor, the Irish orator, speak and recite verses, and the experience gave him "a conviction of how great might be the effect of verse, spoken by a man almost rhythm-drunk, at some moment of intensity, the apex of long mounting thought. Verses that seemed when one saw them on the page flat and empty caught from that voice, whose beauty was half in its harsh strangeness, nobility and style." Rhythm and rhyme are intended, in folk poetry, to do exactly what Yeats describes them as doing. They are instruments of performance, really enacted. But on the printed page, the very fiction of performance has now gone, and we have the delicate nuances of modern art, to be enjoyed for themselves, no longer functional.

The inevitable conclusion, it would seem, is that Yeats, like other great romantic poets, has found a subject-matter for his art in the popular lore, and that it serves to develop the literary effects, but does not, except through occasional imitation, of itself produce the literary effects. There has been little more real fusion between the popular lore and the advanced art than between Keats's medieval lore and his art. Yet perhaps this is too broad a generalization. What Yeats had natively, he must have carried along, without the act of romanticizing. But it would be hard to identify the poems or passages of which this may be truly said.

Nobody would deny, of course — and least of all would I —that Yeats's use of the popular lore is in any sense illegitimate or shallow, according to our standards, or that it serves in any other way than to enrich his art. But to use popular lore is not enough in itself, if a unity such as Yeats describes is to be attained. When the subject-matter of the popular lore belongs natively to those who make the high art, as much as to the people, and does not need to be hunted or reclaimed; and when the high art is not too subtle and complex to serve as a functional instrument for the popular lore—in that time we shall approach the ideal condition. At one moment, in the eighteenth century, when the high art became conventional, we began to approach that condition, perhaps, and folk-song caught up a little of the manner of the high art of the time. But the moment quickly passed, and it has not come again, in poetry.

Elder Olson

THE CRITIC WHO seeks to discuss and the poet who seeks to construct a lyric poem are apt to discover all too quickly that in this particular province of literature, extensive and important as it is, little has been said which affords them any real guidance. At first sight, critical discussion of the lyric appears abundant, even though scarcely commensurate with the importance of the lyric itself; but closer examination readily reveals this abundance to be one of bons mots on the character of the lyric poet, of startling analogies to the psychological or physiological effects of lyric poetry, of "dull receipts how poems may be made," or oracular statement in which the tradition of ambiguous if portentous declamation is usually preserved by the oracle, and finally, in very considerable part, of mere *loci* within a general discussion of literature which is concerned with the lyric only because the lyric possesses some characteristic in common with other forms. In the last quarter of a century, to be sure, literary magazines have often been clamorous with disputations concerning the nature of the lyric; but perhaps without exception these have been declarations of purely individual predilections, or as in the case of Ezra Pound's famous ten precepts for Imagists, definitions of a doctrine or of a convention rather than of a lyric poem. One might be tempted to conclude that a subject so persistently slighted is perhaps not worth discussion, were it not for the fact that, more than frequently, the critical statements suggest abortive attempts at precisely that.

What has been so often attempted unsuccessfully must be approached with caution. To rectify all errors, to supply all deficiencies, to strike out a poetics for the lyric at a single blow would be a noble and ambitious project, but the causes that make it so also operate to make it improbable of achievement. It is only prudent to propose something at once less striking and more feasible; to propose an attempt to discover —through the analysis of a particular poem—some index as to how, eventually, a poetics of the lyric might be framed.

" 'Sailing to Byzantium' Prolegomena to a Poetics of the Lyric," from *The University Review*, VIII, 3 (spring, 1942), 209-219. Reprinted by permission of the author and the editor.

The author has asked that it be indicated that, in his opinion, the analysis of "Sailing to Byzantium" in this essay is purely grammatical in character, and very different from what he thinks a poetic analysis should be .—*Eds.*

It should go without saying that any attempt to furnish indices toward a poetics of the lyric can be significant only in a philosophy in which the arts and sciences are held distinct from each other; for, unless that is the case, the inquiry into principles peculiar to poetics would turn on a nonsense question: if, in any sense whatever, all knowledge is one, then it must must follow that the objects of knowledge must also be one in that same sense, and the question of peculiarities appears as a meaningless one. Further, it should be clear that poetics in such a system cannot deal with every question which may possibly be raised about a work of art, but only with those raised concerning it *qua* work of art; it is not merely conceivably but actually the case that questions about works of art may fall under many sciences, according to the manner of consideration. For instance, a question relevant to a poem as an existent thing falls under metaphysics, a question relevant to it as productive of, say, social consciousness, falls under politics; lacking the proper peculiarity to poetry neither of these questions would be poetic questions in the sense in which I propose to employ the term *poetic,* for *being* and *political instrumentality* are predicable of things other than poems, and whatever answers could be found to such questions would turn, not on the nature of poetry, but on a community between poetry and something else. Further, poetics in the present conception would be analytical and inductive, since the work is the object of consideration, and therefore, like any object of knowledge, must exist prior to any knowledge of it.

The scrutiny of particular poems would thus be the beginning of the critical enterprise; but the principles eventually reached, as disclosed by analysis, would not be rules governing the operations involved in the construction of any further poem, nor would the enumeration of poetic parts and poetic devices suffer extensions beyond those objects to which analysis had been turned. In other words, poetics as conceived here would not afford a series of recipes for making poems, nor a set of rules according to which they must be made, for the very character of poetics is such that it must be subsequent to the inventive utilizations of the medium by the artist. Obviously, anything which should constrain invention would be detrimental to rather than productive of art. Properly taken, poetic questions would be concerning the poetic structure of a particular work, in the sense of inquiring what form has been imposed upon the medium of words. Such an inquiry, properly prosecuted, would terminate in a discovery of the parts of a work and of the interrelations through which the parts are parts of a whole.

The philosophic criticism of literature has provided us richly with instruments for almost every other mode of consideration; but with respect to this one mode, only one treatise—the *Poetics* of Aristotle—is relevant; and while that treatise serves both to differentiate and to illustrate the manner of working of that mode, generally, its specific concern is only with such species of poetry as have for their principle a tissue of incidents, a plot. To attempt to find a plot in the lyric, however, would be a profitless if not impossible task; to attempt on the other hand to find in the lyric some analogue of plot in the drama and in epic, for the mere sake of imitating Aristotle, would be to run counter to the broader indications of his very method—a method involving the distinction of diverse departments of inquiry diversely prosecuted. In the absence of any specific formal treatment of the lyric, then, its analyst must not only fulfill his proper function, but find his own warrant for his operation as well. Complex as his task is, however, it is by no means hopeless; the procedure reduces to an attempt to discover some principle in the work which is the principle of its unity and order —a principle which, it goes without saying, will have to be a purely poetic principle, i.e., a formal principle of the poem, and not something extrinsic to it such as the differentiation either of authors, audiences, subject-matters, or orders of diction would afford. Since in a formal consideration the form is the end, and since the end renders everything else intelligible, a mark of the discovery of the formal principle would be that everything else in the poem would be found to be explicable in terms of it.

We may take as the subject of our analysis the lyric "Sailing to Byzantium" by Yeats.

That is no country for old men. The young
In one another's arms, birds in the trees,
— Those dying generations — at their song,
The salmon-falls, the mackerel-crowded seas,
Fish, flesh, or fowl, commend all summer long
Whatever is begotten, born, and dies.
Caught in that sensual music all neglect
Monuments of unageing intellect.

An aged man is but a paltry thing,
A tattered coat upon a stick, unless

Soul clap its hands and sing, and louder sing
For every tatter in its mortal dress,
Nor is there singing school but studying
Monuments of its own magnificence;
And therefore I have sailed the seas and come
To the holy city of Byzantium.

O sages standing in God's holy fire
As in the gold mosaic of a wall,
Come from the holy fire, perne in a gyre,
And be the singing-masters of my soul.
Consume my heart away; sick with desire
And fastened to a dying animal
It knows not what it is; and gather me
Into the artifice of eternity.

Once out of nature I shall never take
My bodily form from any natural thing,
But such a form as Grecian goldsmiths make
Of hammered gold and gold enamelling
To keep a drowsy Emperor awake;
Or set upon a golden bough to sing
To lords and ladies of Byzantium
Of what is past, or passing, or to come.

In "Sailing to Byzantium" an old man faces the problem of old age, of death, and of regeneration, and gives his decision. Old age, he tells us, excludes a man from the sensual joys of youth; the world appears to belong completely to the young, it is no place for the old; indeed, an old man is scarcely a man at all—he is an empty artifice, an effigy merely, of a man; he is a tattered coat upon a stick. This would be very bad, except that the young also are excluded from something; rapt in their sensuality, they are ignorant utterly of the world of the spirit. Hence if old age frees a man from sensual passion, he may rejoice in the liberation of the soul; he is admitted into the realm of the spirit; and his rejoicing will increase according as he realizes the magnificence of the soul. But the soul can best earn its own greatness from the great works of art; hence he turns to those great works, but in turning to them, he finds that these are by no means mere effigies, or monuments, but things which have souls also; these live in the noblest element of God's fire, free from all corruption; hence he prays for death, for release from his mortal body; and since the insouled monuments exhibit the possibility of the soul's existence in some other matter than flesh, he wishes reincarnation, not now in a mortal body, but in the immortal and changeless embodiment of art.

There are thus the following terms, one might say, from which the poem suspends: the condition of the young, who are spiritually passive although sensually active; the condition of the merely old, who are spiritually and physically impotent; the condition of the old, who, although physically impotent, are capable of spiritual activity; the condition of art considered as inanimate—i.e., the condition of things which are merely monuments; and finally the condition of art considered as animate—as of such things as artificial birds which have a human soul. The second term, impotent and unspiritual old age, is a privative, a repugnant state which causes the progression through the other various alternative terms, until its contrary is encountered. The first and third terms are clearly contraries of each other; taken together as animate nature they are futher contrary to the fourth term, inanimate art. None of these terms represent a wholly desirable mode of existence; but the fifth term, which represents such a mode, amalgamates the positive elements and eliminates the negative elements of both nature and art, and effects thus a resolution of the whole, for now the soul is present, as it would not be in art, nor is it passive, as it would be in the young and sensual mortal body, nor is it lodged in a "dying animal," as it would be in the body of the aged man; the soul is now free to act in its own supremacy and in full cognizance of its own excellence, and its embodiment is now incorruptible and secure from all the ills of flesh.

About these several oppositions the poem forms. The whole turns on the old man's realization, now that he is in the presence of the images of Byzantium, that these images have souls; there are consequently two major divisions which divide the poem precisely in half, the first two stanzas presenting art as inanimate, the second two, as animate; and that this is the case can be seen from such signs as that in the first half of the poem the images are stated as passive objects—they are twice called "monuments," they are merely objects of contemplation, they may be neglected or studied, visited or not visited, whereas in stanzas III or IV they are treated as gods which can be prayed to for life or death, as beings capable of motion from sphere to sphere, as instructors of the soul, as sages possessed of wisdom; and the curious shift in the manner of consideration is signalized by the subtle phrasing of the first two lines of stanza III: "O sages standing in God's holy fire/As in the gold mosaic of a wall." According to the first part, the images at Byzantium were images, and one should have expected at most some figurative apostrophe to them; "O images set in the gold mosiac of a wall, much as the sages stand in God's holy fire": but here the similitude is reversed, and lest there should be any error, the sages are besought to come from the holy fire and begin the tuition of the soul, the destruction of the flesh.

Within these two halves of the poem, further divisions may be found, coincident with the stanzaic divisions. Stanza I presents a rejection of passion, stanza II an acceptance of intellection; then, turning on the realization that art is insouled, stanza III presents a rejection of the corruptible embodiment, and stanza IV, an acceptance of the incorruptible. There is an alternation, thus, of negative and affirmative; out of passion into intellection, out of corruption into permanence, in clear balance, the proportion being 1: II: III: IV; and what orders these sections is their dialectical sequence. That is, passion must be condemned before the intellect can be esteemed; the intellect must operate before the images can be known to be insouled; the realization that the images are insouled precedes the realization that the body may be dispensed with; and the reincarnation of the soul in some changeless medium can be recognized as a possibility only through the prior recognition that the flesh is not the necessary matter of the soul. The parallel opposition of contraries constitutes a sharp demarcation: in stanza I a mortal bird of nature amid natural trees sings a brief song of sensual joy in praise of mortal things, of "whatever is begotten, born, and dies"; in stanza IV an immortal and artificial bird set in an artificial tree sings an eternal song of spiritual joy in praise of eternal things, of "what is past, or passing, or to come"; and similarly, in stanza II a living thing is found to be an inanimate artifice, "a tattered coat upon a stick," incapable of motion, speech, sense or knowledge, whereas in stanza III what had appeared to be inanimate artifice is found to possess a soul, and hence to be capable of all these. A certain artificial symmetry in the argument serves to distinguish these parts even further: stanzas I and IV begin with the conclusions, and I is dependent upon II for the substantiation of its premises, as IV is dependent upon III.

This much indication of the principal organization of the work permits the explication, in terms of this, of the more elementary proportions. The first line of stanza I presents immediately, in its most simple statement, the condition which is the genesis of the whole structure: "That is no country for old men"; old men are shut out from something, and the remainder of the first six lines indicates precisely what it is from which they are excluded. The young are given over to sensual delight, in which old men can no longer participate. But a wall, if it shuts out, also shuts in; if the old are excluded from something, so are the young; lines 7 and 8, consequently, exhibit a second sense in which "That is no country for old men," for the young neglect all intellectual things. Further, the use of "that" implies a possible "this"; that is, there is a country for the old as for the young; and, again, the use of "that" implies that the separation from the country of the young is already complete. The occupation of the young is shrewdly stated: at first sight the human lovers "in one another's arms" have, like the birds at their song, apparently a romantic and sentimental aura; but the curious interpolation of "Those dying generations" in the description of the birds foreshadows the significance they are soon to have; and the phrases immediately remove all sentimentality: "the salmon-falls, the mackrel-crowded seas" intend the ascent of salmon to the headwaters, the descent of mackerel to the deep seas in the spawning season, and the ironic intention is clear: all — the human lovers, the birds, the fish, do but spawn, but copulate, and this is their whole being; and if the parallel statement does not make this sufficiently evident, the summation of all in terms merely of animal genera—"fish, flesh, or fowl"—is unmistakable. The country of the young, then, is in its air, in its waters, and on its earth, from headwaters to ocean, wholly given over to sensuality; its inhabitants "commend all summer long" anything whatsoever, so long as it be mortal and animal—they commend "whatever is begotten, born, and dies"; and while they "commend" because they have great joy, that which they praise, they who praise, and their praise itself are ephemeral, for these mortals praise the things of mortality, and their commendation, like their joy, lasts but a summer, a mating season. The concluding lines of the stanza remove all ambiguity, and cancel all possibility of a return to such a country; even if the old man could, he would not return to a land where "Caught in that sensual music, all neglect/Monuments of unageing intellect." The young are "caught," they are really passive and incapable of free action; and they neglect those things which are unageing.

Merely to end here, however, with a condemnation of

youthful sensuality would be unsatisfactory; as the second stanza expounds, old age itself is no solution; the old man cannot justly say, like Sophocles when he was asked whether he regretted the loss of youth and love, "Peace; most gladly have I escaped the thing of which you speak; I feel as if I had escaped from a mad and furious master"; for merely to be old is merely to be in a state of privation, it is to be "a paltry thing/A tattered coat upon a stick," it is to be the merest scarecrow, the merest fiction and semblance of a man, an inanimate rag upon a dead stick. A man merely old, then, is worse off than youth; if the souls of the young are captive, the old have, in this sense at least, no souls at all. Something positive must be added; and if the soul can wax and grow strong as the body wanes, then every step in the dissolution of the body—"every tatter in its mortal dress"—is cause for a further augmentation of joy. But this can occur only if the soul can rejoice in its own power and magnificence. The soul of the aged must be strong to seek that which youth neglects. Hence the old must seek Byzantium; that is the country of the old; it is reached by sailing the seas, by breaking utterly with the country of the young; all passion must be left behind, the soul must be free to study the emblems of unchanging things.

Here the soul should be filled with joy; it should, by merely "studying," commend changeless things with song, as youth commends the changing with song; it would seem that the problem has been resolved, and the poem hence must end; but the contemplation of the monuments teaches first of all that these are no mere monuments but living things, and that the soul cannot grow into likeness with these beings of immortal embodiment unless it cast off its mortal body utterly. Nor is joy possible until the body be dissolved; the heart is still sick with the impossible desires of the flesh, it is still ignorant of its circumstances, and no song is possible to the soul while even a remnant of passion remains. Hence the old man prays to the sages who really stand in God's holy fire and have merely the semblance of images in gold mosiac; let them descend, "perning in a gyre," that is, moving in the circular motion which alone is possible to eternal things, let them consume with holy fire the heart which is the last seat of passion and ignorance, let them instruct the soul, let them gather it into the artifice of eternity and make the old man like themselves; even Byzantium, so long as the flesh be present, is no country for old men.

What it is to be like these, the soul, as yet uninstructed,

can only conjecture; at any rate, with the destruction of the flesh it will be free of its ills; and if, as in Plato's myth of Er, the soul after death is free to choose some new embodiment, it will never again elect the flesh which is so quickly corruptible and which enslaves it to passion; it will choose some such form of art as that of the artificial birds in Theophilus' garden;[1] it will be of incorruptible and passionless gold; and it will dwell among leaves and boughs which are also of incorruptible and passionless metal. And now all sources of conflict are resolved in this last: the old has become the ageless; impotency has been exchanged for a higher power; the soul is free of passion and free for its joy, and it sings as youth once sang, but now of "What is past, and passing, and to come"—of the divisions of Eternity—rather than of "Whatever is begotten, born, and dies"—of the divisions of mortal time. And it has here its country, its proper and permanent habitation.

Although the argument as we have stated it clearly underlies the poem, it would be erroneous to suppose that this in itself constitutes the poem, for in that case there would be no difference between our paraphrase and the poem itself. The poem itself comprehends the argument and and collocates with it many terms which, although they could scarcely be formulated into some order approximating the pattern of the argument, nevertheless qualify the argument and determine its course. The basic analogies of the poem—of the natural world to a country, of the aged man to a scarecrow, of the world of art to Byzantium, and of artifcial to natural generation—all these function as do the definitions of terms in actual argument; they serve to delimit the sphere of discourse and to make the argument intelligible.

This point is worth some discussion. The criticism of poetry has often turned chiefly on the so-called psychological connotations of readers with single words or phrases; but one may doubt whether the reader is at liberty to intrude such irrelevancies as the accidents of personal experience or the inevitable ambiguities of language would necessarily afford. Surely the ultimate consequence of such assumptions must be

[1] In his note to the poem (*Collected Poems*. New York, 1933, p. 450) Yeats remarks: "I have read somewhere that in the Emperor's palace at Byzantium was a tree made of gold and silver, and artificial birls that sang." Undoubtedly the Emperor was Theophilus (829-842), and the birds conform to the descriptions of certain automata constructed for him by Leo Mathematicus and John Hylilas. Cf. *Hist. Byzan. Script post Theoph.*, Anon. Cont. Theoph., 107; Constantini Manassis, *Brev. Hist.*, 107; and Michaeli Glycae, *Annales*, 292. See also Gibbon, *Decline and Fall*, Chapter LIII, and George Finlay, *History of the Byzantine Empire* (London, 1906), pp. 140, 148, where further references are given.

either that the poem becomes a mere stimulus to independent poetic activities on the part of the reader—that is, the reader becomes the true poet, his reading the true poem—or, on the other hand, that the reader becomes the matter or medium of art, in which case all the arts would have a common medium, the soul of the spectator. Neither of these consequences, it need scarcely be said, complies with the stipulations which initiated this discussion.

If the basic terms of a lyric poem do not receive their meanings from the chance associations of the reader, neither do they have their dictionary meanings; like terms in most discourse, they take their significance from their context, through juxtaposition to other terms with which they are equated, contrasted, correlated, or combined. In the present poem, for instance, the term "singing" is explicitly extended beyond its usual meaning to cover two kinds of jubilation, the rejoicing of the natural creature and that of the artificial; as a consequence, all the terms which relate to jubilation and song are affected; for example, "commend," "music," "singing-school," and "singing-masters" suffer an extension commensurate with that of singing. Similarly, the term "intellect" and all the terms associated with it suffer extension; and the monuments here are not ordinary monuments, but changeless embodiments of the changeless soul—by no means effigies, but truly living creatures, capable of will, of desire, of jubilation, of local motion, of intellection and instruction. Nor is Byzantium the historical city; the tourist is not invited to recall that here once he was overcharged, nor is the historian invited to contribute such information as that this was a city visited by Hugh of Vermandois; Byzantium is not a place upon a map, but a term in the poem; a term signifying a stage of contemplation wherein the soul studies itself and so learns both what it is and in what consists true and eternal joy.

Furthermore, if the words of a poem have meanings which the poet may arbitrarily determine, the "objects" in poetry are also given whatever "properties" the poet sees fit to assign to them. That is, whereas the physical thing has its determinate nature and is subject to physical laws such as Newton's laws, the "things" of a poem—the artificial and natural creatures here, for instance—have only such properties as statement within the poem affords them. Poetic statements must not be confused, however, with propositions; since they are not statements about things which exist outside the poem, it would be meaningless to evaluate them as true or false; they have rather the status or definitions or resolutions; and while in certain poems the coordination is dialectical, as in this poem, no criteria of dialectic could be significantly applied to them, for a dialectic is necessarily regulated by the natures of things external to the dialectic and must ultimately be evaluated, whereas the coordination of elements in a poem cannot involve reference to anything outside the poem. Even when poetic statements are incidentally true propositions, even when their coordination is also cogent argument, these coincidences would not affect their poetic status. Thus, "To His Coy Mistress" is an excellent poem, whether the lover's argument is valid or not. In a sense, every poem is a microcosmos, a discrete and independent universe with its laws provided by the poet; his decision is absolute; he can make things good or bad, great or small, powerful or weak, just as he wills; he may make men taller than mountains or smaller than atoms, he may suspend whole cities in the air, he may destroy creation or re-form it; within his universe the impossible becomes the possible, the necessary the contingent—if he but says they do.

I have said that the bare argument of "Sailing to Byzantium" is not the poem; but I should argue that the argument (considered not as a real argument, but, according to what I have said, as a certain collocation of terms) is the *principle* of this poem, in a sense analogous to that in which, for Aristitle, plot is the principle of tragedy. For if the principle is that for the sake of which all other things in the poem exist, and that, consequently, in terms of which all are intelligible, what could be the principle, other than the thing we have supposed? There is here no plot, no ordered tissue of incidents, for, first of all, the whole poem is of a moment—the moment in which the old man confronts the monuments and addresses them—whereas a tissue of incidents, a plot, must extend over a span of time. And second, there can be no plot because there are no incidents; the "events" in a lyric poem are never incidents as such, connected by necessity or probability, but devices for making poetic statements. Again, since there is no action, there is no agent, that is, *character*, in the sense in which there are differentiated agents in drama or epic, each duly discriminated for his distinct part in the action; rather, the character in the sense in which character may be said to exist here is almost completely universalized. Hence, if plot does not constitute the principle of the poem, neither does character; for not all the parts of the poem would be explicable in terms of character, nor are we presented with any precise depiction of character here, as we should be if it were the end. On the merely verbal level, again, we can account for nothing; the words must be explained in terms of something else, not the poem in terms of the words; and further, a principle must be a principle of something other than itself; hence the words cannot be a principle of their own arrangements.

Rather, it is clear as we look at the poem, that a certain problems orders the whole—the problem of finding a suitable compensation for the losses suffered in old age; the poem begins with exclusion from the pleasures of youth, develops among ordered dialectical alternatives, and ends when the problem is permanently solved. As the problem determines the limits of the poem, so it determines all else; the character is determined by it, for example, because—according to the very nature of the problem—a young man could not have conceived of the problem as it is stated, nor could a raging and sensual old man, nor could an old man who was contented with age, like Sophocles; since an ideal and permanent solution was to be given to the problem, a character conscious of loss, and capable of conceiving an ideal solution, was necessitated. Nothing beside this is indicated with respect to the speaker. Again, the words themselves are determined by the problem; while the choice of metaphors of a "country," or "song," and of modes of embodiment was initially arbitrary, once the metaphors have been stated they must be carried out according to the dictates of the problem; indeed, it is possible to trace variations in diction precisely proportional to the stages of the dialectic. For example, the stages are verbally signalized by the succession "flesh," "stick," "dying animal," "gold," in terms of expressions of embodiment, or "no country," "Byzantium," "the artifice of eternity," which is amid "holy fire," in terms of habitation; and the metaphor of the artificial bird in the fourth stanza bears such relation—in terms of setting, song, character of joy, object of joy, and "bodily form"—to the real birds—"those dying generations" —in stanza I as the solution of the problem bears to the element the negation of which generated the dialectic. In a similar manner the presence of nearly every word in the poem might be justified if space permitted.

On the basis of our examination, then, we may say that there exists a kind of poem (since we have here one instance of it) which has argument, in the sense we have stipulated, as its principle; not, let us remember, a dialectic referable to externals, but a certain formal collocation of terms which is referable to nothing outside itself and which may be called the soul of the poem in the sense in which Aristotle calls plot the soul of tragedy. This kind of poetry has the same means as tragedy, epic, and comedy, but whereas the latter are imitations of human action, so that their principle is a certain collocation of incidents organized by necessity and probability—whereas, that is, these are dynamic, for they imitate change—the kind which we have been scrutinizing is static; it abstracts from motion and change, and though it sometimes appears to recount events, these are not events as parts of a plot connected by probability or necessity, but events in the sense in which we speak of events in a philosophical dialogue—they are only dialectically separable stages in the treatment of a problem, and are reducible to statements within the problem. Whereas in the Aristotelian treatment of poems which have a plot as their principle, certain qualitative parts of the various species resulted from an analysis of the object of imitation that is, the action, a different procedure is necessary here; the principle is a tissue not of events but of ideas, and the ordering of the poem will not be by necessity and probability, by the antecedents and consequents of action, but by dialectical priority and posteriority. Lastly, while character will be necessitated here as where a plot is the principle, it will be determined, not by its share in an action, but by its role in a drama, not of action, but of thought. That is, it is determined, as the characters in a Platonic dialogue are determined, by the nature of the discourse which they are to utter.

It would be a mistake, however, to assume that all lyrics are of the order considered here. The term lyric itself has been given an extraordinary variety of applications, and the scrupulous analyst and critic will attempt to keep the variety of critical approaches almost commensurate with these, on the assumption that great art—however familiar the pattern in which it is apparently laid—is always in the last analysis *sui generis.*

A. Norman Jeffares

IT MAY NOT be generally known that Mrs. W. B. Yeats has in her possession a large collection of her husband's unpublished writings, consisting of diaries, letters and manuscripts in verse and prose. These documents are of particular importance for any student of Yeats's poetry, but are of general interest also, as they reveal the working of an unusual mind as well as different processes of poetic creation. Mrs. Yeats deserves great praise, for she has not only preserved these writings—a task which occasionally involved salving fragments which Yeats had torn up for secrecy's sake—but she has reduced them to order and established many of their dates. Her unique knowledge, which has always been made available so graciously, is very helpful in deciphering and interpreting the numerous obscurities in the poet's published and unpublished writings.

In common with most poets, Yeats had two main methods of writing verse, the one spontaneous, and the other a laborious process involving much alteration and substitution. What is meant by spontaneous is that Yeats recorded his thoughts in verse once he was aware of their existence, and did not substantially alter his first version of the particular poem in which he had recorded them. An example of his spontaneous method can be supplied by his short poem *The Wheel,* which was written on September 17th, 1921. The poet and his wife arrived at Euston *en route* for Ireland, and found themselves seats in the Irish Mail. Yeats then disappeared, but arrived a few minutes before the train started, waving a sheet of notepaper taken from the Euston Hotel on which he had written *The Wheel.* This poem was subsequently printed with a very slight alteration in the fifth line, but otherwise exactly as Yeats had written down his suddenly crystallised thought. We often find unpublished examples of this method in the poet's diaries. When Mrs. Yeats was once too busy to attend to her husband's wants, he opened an old diary and wrote these lines in it:

The Queen of Sheba's busy,
King Solomon is mute,
Because a busy woman
Is a savage brute.

"W. B. Yeats and His Methods of Writing Verse," from *The Nineteenth Century and After,* CXXXIX, 829 (March, 1946), pp. 123-128.

The second type of composition was a much more deliberate and unusual process, and justifies MacNeice's opinion that Yeats "made himself a poet and, as poet, he was essentially a maker." Very many of Yeats's poems were planned in prose drafts which were then made into poems. A typical prose draft is recorded in the entry for April 30th in his 1930 diary which reads:

> Subject for a poem. . . . Describe Byzantium as it is in the system towards the end of the first Christian millennium. A walking mummy, flames at the street corners where the soul is purified, birds of hammered gold singing in the golden trees, in the harbour, offering their backs to the wailing dead that they may carry them to paradise—These subjects have been in my head for some time, especially the last.

From this prose draft came, eventually, that fine poem *Byzantium*. These prose drafts occur not only in diaries but in the sumptuous manuscript books which Yeats often used; they are also to be found on scraps of paper or pages from loose-leaf note-books. The prose draft of a poem was usually followed by a succession of versions of the poem written in verse, which was often faulty in metre and rhyme. Yeats always chanted his verse aloud as he wrote, seeking always the right word, which would convey his meaning and yet fit into the sound effect which he desired to create. Because of his importance of sound in the composition of his poetry readers will find that the poems gain greatly in meaning and dramatic intensity if they are read aloud as the poet intended them to be.

Yeats constantly revised his verse; his letters, particularly those to Mrs. Shakespear and Lady Gerald Wellesley, show this clearly. A letter to Mrs. Shakespear, dated September 24th, 1936, quotes an alternative version of the sixth verse of *Among School Children* as follows:

> Here is a fragment of my last curse upon old age. It means that even the greatest men are old scarecrows by the time their fame has come. Aristotle, remember, was Alexander's tutor—hence the taws—(a form of birch)
>
> *Plato imagined all existence plays*
> *Among the ghostly images of things;*
> *Solider Aristotle played the taws*
> *Upon the bottom of the king of kings;*
> *World-famous golden-thighed Pythagoras*
> *Fingered upon a fiddle stick or strings*

What the star sang and careless muses heard—
Old coat, upon old sticks, to scare a bird.

Pythagoras made some measurement of the intervals between notes on a stretched string. . . .

Two other versions of this verse which exist in manuscript are interesting; they show how Yeats refined his verse to an epigrammatic terseness. This early version reveals a fumbling towards the choice of the final examples of famous men:

Caesar Augustus made all the laws
And the ordering of the century,
Plato that learned Geometry and was
The foremost man at the soul's meaning. . . .

Later Yeats developed his sketching of attributes with more detail, as in this version:

Plato has pronounced upon the weight and poise
Of the soul's heroes, and what breadth of wing
Climbs heaven quickest; Aristotle was
The first who had a place for everything
World-famous golden-thighed Pythagoras
Proved by measurement upon a fiddle string
What music the empyrean dancers heard.

Yeats often revised his published work, and Mr. G. D. P. Allt is at present compiling a variorum edition which will deal with the changes which Yeats made in his early published poems.[1]

The value of these drafts in any interpretation of Yeats's poetry is unquestionable. There seem to be three main advantages to be gained from their study. The first is that they give us an insight into the original mood and thoughts of the poet. In the majority of Yeats's poems the initial impulse was a personal emotion, often written down in the first person. As he revised the poem Yeats often removed the direct personal statement and contrived to generalise the experience slightly. While the rewriting and remodelling was proceeding new elements often crept into the lines, new illustrations were sought, new facets of the emotions stressed. Yeats once told Professor H. O. White, of Trinity College

[1] Cf. G. D. P. Allt. "Yeats and the Revision of His Early Verse," *Hermathena* LXIV (November, 1944), p. 92.

Dublin, that his poems were three-quarters emotion, one-quarter form. By form Yeats may well have meant the transformation which the initial emotions went thorugh during the laborious processes of composition. This alteration can be seen in the poem *Sailing to Byzantium,* which was first written as a record of a personal mood, as the original draft shows—

All in this land—my Maker that is play
Or else asleep upon his Mother's knees,
Others, that as the mountain people say,
Are at their hunting and their gallantries
Under the hills as in our fathers' day
The changing colours of the hills and seas
All that men know or think they know, being young
Cry that my tale is told, my story sung.

A letter to Mrs. Shakespear, dated September 5th, 1926, confirms this:

> There have been constant interruptions. The last time I wrote a poem about Byzantium to recover my spirits. . . .

If the final version of the first verse which appeared in *The Tower* of 1928 is compared to the initial draft quoted above it will be seen that Yeats left out mention of himself in the ultimate version, where he uses the first verse to set the stage for the second verse. The second verse is a dramatic introduction of the poet's personal relationship to the sensual land of the first verse, as the significant word "therefore" indicates:

And therefore I have sailed the seas and come
To the holy city of Byzantium.

The second use of the unpublished writings is that they often reveal the true Yeatsian meaning of a poem with some certainty. Take, for example, the poem *The Fisherman.* This poem's final version is dated June 4th, 1914, in the manuscript book which Maud Gonne gave to Yeats. In the poem Yeats writes:

Maybe a twelvemonth since
Suddenly I began,
In scorn of this audience,
Imagining a man. . . .

If we examine the entries in the manuscript between May 18th and 23rd, 1913, we find there this entry:

SUBJECT FOR A POEM

Who is this by the edge of the stream
That walks in a good homespun coat
And carries a fishing (rod) in his hand
We singers have nothing of our own
All our hopes, our loves, our dreams
Are for the young, for those whom
We stir into life. But (there is) one
That I can see always though he is not yet born
He walks by the edge of the stream
In a good homespun coat
And carries a fishing rod in his hand.

These lines form the substance of the last sixteen lines of *The Fisherman* and show that the poem is mainly an imagining of an idealised character. Without this knowledge of the manuscript book an eminent critic has been deceived by the ambiguity of these lines in the poem—

All day I'd looked in the face
What I had hoped 'twould be
To write for my own race
And the reality;

for he describes the lines as indicating a desire on Yeats's part for the actual world. The lines, however, refer both to the fisherman and the reality. There is a difference between the fisherman and the reality. The fisherman, as the earlier entry in the manuscript book shows, is the type of person whom Yeats had hoped to find in Ireland, a simple person, yet wise enough to appreciate great art. "The reality" is what he describes in these lines, which begin with savage directness—

The living men that I hate,
The dead man that I loved,
The craven man in his seat,
The insolent unreproved,
And no knave brought to book. . . .

In view of the earlier entry which clearly demonstrates the ideal nature of the fisherman, it would seem better to de scribe the poem as indicating not a desire for the actual world, but a dislike of it because it was so far removed from Yeats's early wishful imaginings.

We can use the unpublished writings to determine the narrower meanings of Yeats's poem; they often throw light on problems of syntax. The poem *A Coat* will serve as an example of this. In its published version the syntax of the first line—

I made my song a coat

is ambiguous. The manuscript has two extra lines—

And gave it to my song
And my song wore it

which show that the published line means

I made a coat for my song

The third benefit to be gained from the unpublished material is, perhaps, the most interesting, for the sources which Yeats used can sometimes be found from his rough work. A skilful critic might easily notice a similarity between these lines from a late Yeats's poem *The Ghost of Roger Casement:*

I poked about a village church
And found his family tomb
And copied out what I could read
In that religious gloom;
Found many a famous man there;
But fame and virtue rot. . . .

and Gray's *Elegy Written in a Country Churchyard;* but this similarity can only be suggested until the definite proof, afforded, in this case, by the early manuscripts of the poem, has been noticed. The Yeats did have the Elegy in mind and particularly these lines—

Some village Hampden that with dauntless breast
The little tyrant of his fields withstood
Some mute inglorious Milton here may rest
Some Cromwell guiltless of his country's blood.

is shown by the occurrence of the following lines in the first drafts of *The Ghost of Roger Casement:*

For all that Hampden thought
All that later Milton wrote

These became

It told of all his virtues there
His words had been his bond
Of such a man had Milton dreamed
For such had Hampden planned

and were later altered to

For all that Hampden thought
All that Milton knew
Had blazed in heart and head
Although John Hampden's dead.

When Yeats wrote

A line will take us hours maybe;
Yet if it does not seem a moment's thought,
Our stitching and unstitching has been naught.

he was concerned that his reader or hearer should feel that the verse was the spontaneous utterance of the poet. He took pains to hide his methods of poetic creation and to gain the directness and simplicity that is a sign of strength. It is now possible to discover how Yeats did gain his effects. It was ever a maxim of the ancient critics that poetic creation should be understood, and, in examining the methods of a man so gifted as to be termed a genius, there must be much of value. Through examining the poet's unpublished wrtings one comes to a closer understanding of his very unusual personality and mental processes, and, in turn, to a deeper understanding of his published works.

Delmore Schwartz

WHEN MAUD GONNE speaks of William Butler Yeats, the great poet, as Willie, does it not suggest thoughts of the veritable *ding-an-sich?* Her essay in *Scattering Branches,* a volume of English and Irish tributes to Yeats, is devoted and full of a respect for Yeats which is not destroyed by misgivings about his patriotism. But what is the English language—what is the gulf between Ireland and America—if the diminutive, Willie, does not suggest a guffaw, rather than the dignity of the great poet with "the stately head." Does it not seem even stranger when one thinks of the mask of the poet in the poems written about his love for Maud Gonne?

Perhaps this example is slight or wrong. Yet it may stand for many false notes which have been audible since the death of Yeats. At one extreme, there has been the false note that Yeats was a fop and a fool who by some miracle of a gift for language wrote great poetry. At the other extreme, a distinguished poet has permitted himself to say that, so far as he was concerned, Yeats had written more good poems than any other author in the history of English poetry.

But much more than false notes, much more than stupidities, too much praise or too much blame, or too little of each, or the wrong kind of each, have surrounded the dead poet and the deathless poetry. It is the sense of many points of view which makes one ask such endless questions as, What was in himself, beneath the deliberate mask? How shall we understand the greatness of his poetry? How shall we view his long career and many volumes, so different and various, and yet having the unity of one human being?

Some understanding can be gained merely by declaring some of the points of view from which Yeats has been looked at, and much more can be gained, perhaps, by taking some of the questions, problems, and mysteries which Yeats makes inevitable and considering them under the figure of an unwritten book, the unwritten book about Yeats which would tell the whole truth about him; or if not the whole truth, the truth we need to hear. It should be possible to state the nature of such a book, however far one is from being able to write it.

"An Unwritten Book," from *The Southern Review,* VII, 3 (winter, 1942), pp. 471-491.

The very question—what kind of author will write this unwritten book?—may shed some light. Is it not clear that this author will not be Irish? Not only have the Irish admirers and followers of Yeats seemed to miss a great deal, so that they are hardly able to distinguish Yeats from AE; but, as more than one critic has observed, Yeats's career and work must for some time be bound up with many native feelings about Ireland, both in the past which was Yeats's lifetime and in the present.

Yet, on the other hand, an American will not write this book because he will not know enough about Ireland, being an American. He may even know as little as the present writer, who must look into the 14th edition of the *Encyclopedia Britannica* in order to understand many of the names and references in Yeats's political poems—feeling then only that the inforamtion there is but a dark surface, at best; for what is said is often the kind of smugly judicious half-truth intended to make little of the long conflict between England and Ireland.

This must suggest that no Englishman will write our unwritten book, not even an unhappy Englishman who desires the death of the old gang. Might our author then be Anglo-Irish, like Yeats himself? Or perhaps Irish-American?

Conjectures such as these might go on forever. Perhaps they had better be exhausted by an extreme, that is, by suggesting that the unknown author of this unwritten book will be a poet and a critic who, although not Irish, enjoys and suffers a place in his time and country which is analogous to Yeats's: the poet of an oppressed country, during a period of nationalist activity, who has been educated in the country of the oppressor and must be read and understood and published there, although he must also give himself to the cause of national freedom and the native language and art. Perhaps—if the fancy and metaphor will be forgiven me—this author will be French-Canadian or Chinese, educated in Japan during the latter half of the twentieth century.

Consider, if it seems that too much is being made of the problem, merely the chief subjects of Yeats's poetry—romantic love, nationalist Ireland, distinguished friends and artists, the Irish aristocracy, the stories of a remote countryside, and a home-made philosophy of history and of the supernatural. In each of these subjects, how can we help but feel that there is much more worth knowing than what we know as common readers? This difficulty and need of knowledge does not exist in all poets because all poets are not, like Yeats, engaged in dramatizing their own lives; not as directly, not to the same extent, not in the same way. R. P. Blackmur has shown how, for example, one cannot understand some of Yeats's best poems if one does not apply to them Yeats's views about magic. Perhaps it is not necessary to know much about political Ireland in order to understand the political poems: but what richness of particularity such knowledge gives to the poems. It is probably not necessary to know at all about Yeats's long relationship with Maud Gonne, if we are nothing more than readers of poetry. But some readers will always look for the private life in the public poems—if in Dante and Shakespeare, then everywhere in all poets—here, at this level, the exact and particular fact would help to keep the poems free of romantic misunderstanding; they are full enough of romantic understanding.

Thus one important part of our unwritten book would consist of the valuable information which makes possible footnotes from line to line wherever proper names or special references occur, or when the rhyme depends upon the way in which Yeats pronounced some English words. That the poems of Yeats require more footnotes than most other poets might serve as a working principle with which to begin. This is made only more true by the fact that Yeats himself provided some of the material for footnotes in his prose. For the labor then becomes one of seeing and making explicit the connections in question, and also of being critical of the poet's intention, since he was not only engaged in creating an image of himself, but often he may not have known himself what the truth was, as is the case with passages in *A Vision.*

This need of the information of footnotes is more than obvious. No poet is free of particularity, nor would any poet wish to be; the need of information is a general thing and only the degree and kind required by Yeats has to be mentioned. So too with other topics which are generic traits of an adequate book. But as soon as one sets up a sharp distinction between the general subjects of a satisfactory book about a poet and the specific problems which Yeats presents, there is so much to think about that it is hard to keep one's thoughts in order. The easy order of a review of specific problems is perhaps best, beginning with the most inclusive and going forward by trying to close in on the unique and irreducible thing which is the poetry.

Yeats in Europe. What a high-sounding title! But it is impossible to avoid a recognition of how important Europe is in thinking of Yeats. Born at the height of the Victorian period, becoming a writer during the Nineties, living through the years which culminated in the first World War, arriving at his true mastery and power during the Post-War period, and dying four months after the signing of the Munich Pact, Yeats suggests, just to begin with, the kind of table of contemporary events which is often found at the beginning of a great poet's collected poems. But it is much more than a matter of interesting correspondences. Yeats died the same month that *The Criterion* was suspended, because, as the editor said, the Munich Pact seemed to make no longer possible the assumptions on which the magazine had been based. Let this stand as a sign of the international causes which have a serious effect upon the literature of our time. The Munich Pact destroyed or helped to destroy an important magazine. In Yeats himself, from the beginning of his career to the very end, what happened in the Europe of his time penetrated his whole being as a poet, despite his serious sincere belief that he was writing, for the most part, *sub specie aeternitatis*. Thus one of his last poems, "Lapis Lazuli," at once expresses this belief and reproves the fear in Europe of the coming war:

For everybody knows or else should know
That if nothing drastic is done
Aeroplane or Zeppelin will come out,
Pitch like King Billy bomb balls in
Until the town lie beaten flat. . . .

What can the London reader think of these lines at present? What anyone can think of the characteristic attitude involved in this poem is something to be considered carefully later on. The point here is not merely the number of poems which are concerned—some of them explicitly—with the long agony of Europe. Often it is the effect of Europe on the fate of Ireland which occupies the poet's mind. But it is just as often true that we cannot help but see how Yeats was a European man, intensely interested in and moved by what was happening in Paris, where the Symbolist movement reigned as he began to write, and in England, where his books were published.

To take one difficult instance which suggests the *Zeitgeist*, or perhaps, as Yeats would have said, the *Anima Mundi*, we find the obsessive symbol of the doll being used by Rilke, Stravinsky, and Yeats. Is it the same kind of feeling, the love of the artifact against the love of the natural thing, in all three? Did performances of the Russian Ballet bring Rilke and Yeats to the same symbol? Is this love of the artifact and hatred of the natural an expression of the isolation of the modern artist from the rest of society, as well as a metaphysical hatred of natural life and of change? Such are some of the questions, among many, which our unknown author might be able to answer, although we are too ignorant to do more than guess. The problem is neither general nor vague: what was happening in Europe during Yeats's career was a factor in bringing about minute details of the structure and texture of his poems. We need not take an obvious example like "Easter, 1916" or other poems in which the World War and Irish Nationalism are involved. For there is a large-scale example of great complexity and impressiveness, clear perhaps only from an angel's point of view: the shift from romantic dimness to sharp- and clear-cut harshness of texture which took place in music and painting as well as in poetry during the years that Yeats was developing his later style. Needless to say, Yeat's later style is part of this shift. From the pre-Raphaelites to Picasso, from Debussy to Stravinsky, from Swinburne, Symons and Dowson, to the Imagists, Pound, and Eliot, the transformation is such that we can hardly doubt that the source is the same, the character and changes in European civilization, whatever the diversity and individuality of all these artists. Is it not this factor which must be the source of such another resemblance amid difference of the affirmation by Yeats, Eliot, and Rilke, among others, of the landed aristocracy as the good society? We can hardly fail to see Yeats's writing of *A Vision* as being at least suggested by the movement of history in his time. We know that never before has the character of society changed as quickly as in the fifty years of Yeats's adult life. And we know that in times of rapid social change, men are moved to study the philosophy of history more frequently. Given these two generalizations, a reading of *A Vision* together with the autobiographical writings and the poems would bring forth further major problems for our unknown author.

He would undoubtedly note that "objectivity" and "subjectivity," the basic terms of Yeats's philosophy of history, are analogues or equivalents for thoughts and action. Their opposition, their mixture, and their cycle look like projections—although not merely projections—of the life Yeats lived and the lives of his friends who were also artists, so that the whole framework of this view of history from beginning to end must be suspect as a vast sublimation of a special and limited experience. This suspicion would merely be reinforced when one took into account Yeats's method in elucidating his system. To illustrate the kinds of human beings produced by each phase of the moon which was an analogue of each phase of history, Yeats chooses almost always as his examples poets, artists, or intellectuals of some kind—"Flaubert, Herbert Spencer, Swedenborg, Dostoyevsky, Darwin," "Keats, Giorgione, many beautiful women," the few exceptions being obvious: Queen Victoria, Napoleon and Parnell. Thus it would seem on the surface that when Yeats looked at Europe and at history, he could see only his own face or the faces of his friends or what was already in his mind. But we soon see that the being of all the things which concerned Yeats was bound up with what was happening in Europe, and that as Yeats follows what interests him, in his poems and in his autobiographies, he is following, in his own way, the effect of Europe upon his own life.

Another generalization inevitably suggests itself, once we have seen the poet against the background of Europe from 1890 until 1939, the generalization that the center of the work is the poet as romantic poet, just as so much other work during this period has, as its subject, art as art, because the artist is isolated from the rest of society.

Starting with a desire to write the poetic poetry of the Nineties, Yeats went through a complete experience of what it is for the poet to exist and practice his art during modern times and thus came upon a subject peculiarly fit for the romantic poet, namely, what it is to be a poet in modern times. The experience of his generation, the fate of such gifted authors as Wilde, Dowson, Lionel Johnson, and Synge, who died in misery and degradation, might by itself be taken as a sufficient cause for turning to this subject. But there is much else which makes it seem natural that the later poetry should be full of references to the artists, poets, scholars and beautiful women the poet has known, and should speak of the country house where life is ceremony, where works of art abound, where the rich are patrons of the arts. The poet intent upon Art for Art's sake so exhausted his intention and learned so much about Art from others who were of like intent that the underlying subject of his later poetry became the fate of Art and the emotion of the Artist in modern life.

Given this generalization, how much seems to be explained: the hatred of time in the later poetry is, in part, the hatred of the movement of history, which has greatly altered the bases and assumptions with which the poet began to practice his art. The ideal of a landed aristocracy is the expression of a desire for a society in which the artist can thrive, for the ruling class of industrial and finance capitalism does not need the artist and, unlike other ruling classes, when it turns to art buys Old Masters, partly because culture has become international, partly because the millionaire, like the artist, is, in his own way, removed from the rest of society. Thus too the opposition of Byzantium to nature is the opposition of a civilization in which art, artificiality and ritual dominate, to modern civilization. At the same time, it is the expression of the artist's need of fixed forms, traditions, and stability.

Another point to be emphasized is that it was the poet's experience of ceaseless social change which brought him the desire for permanence and the metaphors of permanence.

Yeats in Ireland. What has just been said of Yeats's relationship to Europe would be even more true of his relationship to Ireland. Perhaps this second instance will make it clear that when one speaks of Europe one is not summoning up an empty abstraction or convenient abbreviation for many things taken together. The most rigorous nominalist could hardly say that Ireland was some kind of abstraction endowed with illusory powers by the patriot or Platonist. And Ireland's fate was of course bound up with that of Europe and in particular with the course of the British Empire. The working principle of our gifted author here would probably be an invariable sense of his own ignorance, a knowledge that one cannot feel the full quality of the words and emotions when Yeats writes of Ireland. One must understand, knowing that one cannot feel, what names like Parnell, O'Leary, Pearse, and Connally mean to the Irish nationalists, even to such a one as Yeats, whose ambiguous and ambivalent sentiments can be heard in many poems; most directly perhaps in such a poem as "I am of Ireland," where a woman cries to a man with "a stately head," "Come dance with me in Ireland," and the man replies that the orchestra seems to be insane in Ireland, only to have her repeat her invitation, as if forever.

The question of how well the poet has generalized his experiences as an Irishman is one that can be quickly answered after explicit admission has been made of how most readers must fall short of grasping the local or national feelings. We can see how, with a knowledge of the particular references, the Irish names and events mentioned so often in the poems become signs of the common experience of human beings: the history has become poetry in that the particular event signifies a typical kind of event. Thus in "I am of Ireland," the dramatic relationship, far from being local or national or personal, is significant of any human being's effort in the disorder of our time.

But another problem which is more difficult would present itself at this point for our author, the task of making out the part that Irish Nationalism played in Yeats's career as a poet. Undoubtedly it played a great part from beginning to end, but in mixed and opposed ways. Some have said that it was Yeats's experience as a political organizer which made him a poet of the later style. Yet in his *Autobiographies,* Yeats says that the few months of his political activity were the worst months of his life, he was an utter failure at it, and he soon gave it up. Again, it is said that politics brought him in direct contact with the speech of the people; yet, in "Estrangement," written in 1909, he says that he has always been unable to speak with strangers, with any but intimate friends. If one wishes, one can rescue the worth of Yeats's political experience by means of the dialectical sleight of tongue whereby every habit, trait, or action brings forth its opposite; this was of course one of Yeats's favorite doctrines. But surely our adequate author would not rest with this kind of explanation which, since it can explain everything, really explains nothing.

The part that Yeats took in the Irish Renaissance,[1] closely connected as it is with Irish Nationalism despite such conflicts as the one over *The Playboy of the Western World,* must bring to the fore another large-scale generalization, the fact that the few great periods of the drama in Western culture have been periods of strong or triumphant nationalism; for example, Periclean Athens, Elizabethan England, and the France of Louis XIV. This should suggest a connection between nationalism and the audience which the dramatist needs more than any other kind of author. In Yeats's case, it suggests the possibility that it was here, in the Abbey Theatre, hearing again and again plays by authors who were closer to the people and their speech than Yeats could ever come directly, that Yeats acquired that knowledge of how to use speech in verse which is so important an element in

[1] It is worth remarking that Yeats's first prose work appeared in 1894 and was entitled "The Celtic Twilight."

his later style. The relationship of Yeats to Synge, who, on Yeats's advice, went among the people in order to hear and copy down their speech, the extreme admiration which Yeats felt for Synge—an admiration far in excess of what Synge's plays now seem to justify—may have been in part Yeats's intuitive anticipation of the nature of his later style.

Whatever the truth, in detail, about the effect of Irish Nationalism and the Irish theater upon Yeats, one important rule we must note, and see exemplified in Yeats as well as other authors, is the rule that authors seek the conditions which make them what they are just as much as the conditions seek out authors. Irish Nationalism must have made authors of a number of men who might otherwise have spent their lives in peace; it must have dictated their subject-matter often enough and given them an audience. But in Yeats's case one cannot avoid the notion that Yeats came to Irish Nationalism from deliberate choice, seeking out a cultural and literary *milieu* in which he might fulfill himself as an author. How this process occurred, what factors of pride, careerism, and immediate need began it, the influence of childhood attachments in Yeats's case, and the influence of Maud Gonne, how the process reached beneath such motives and became deeply-rooted—what a difficult chapter this would make in the book that is not yet written. Perhaps in Yeats, the whole process could be followed step by step, despite the evasions and gaps in the *Autobiographies*.

One fact in the back of one's mind throughout, whenever one seeks the connection between a man and the conditions of all kinds which have surrounded him and penetrated him, is the unique poet who cannot be reduced to any causes or circumstances. Yeats alone of his generation became a great poet: what cause or circumstance explains this greatness?

Yeats in Himself. The first thing that meets the reader in most volumes by Yeats is a portrait of the author next to the title page, showing the poet at a stated age. No matter how intent we are in distinguishing between a body of poetry and the poet who composed it, we cannot do so when we come to Yeats. For he is his own chief character—from the languishing and pale "I" of the early love poems to the "sixty-year-old smiling public man," Senator Yeats, of "Among School Children." The *Autobiographies* increase this connection in numerous ways because no one will read the poems without wishing also to see what is in the *Autobiographies*,

Yet this dramatized projection of himself in prose and

verse is only one view, and a most charitable one. Other views of the same human being exist and seem to contradict it. To use the most striking example, when we read *Dramatis Personae,* we cannot forget the Yeats presented by George Moore. Just as we can hardly doubt that the Yeats presented by George Moore and the George Moore of Yeats are far from being the whole truth, so too we are aware, whenever Yeats uses himself as a character in one of his poems, that this is a version made by the poet to suit his own idea of himself and of what a poet should be. What, for example, does an Irish Republican think of the Yeats who appears in "Easter, 1916?" We can be certain that he does not see Yeats as Yeats sees and presents himself.

In the *Autobiographies,* Yeats was not trying to tell the truth about himself, but to use whatever part of the truth would help him to achieve a dramatic image. When we read in the *Autobiographies* the judgment that Oscar Wilde made of *The Wanderings of Oisin,* comparing it favorably with Homer, if we have read that poem or even if we have not, we know that we are confronted with vanity and blindness; not Wilde's only, but Yeats's also.

So too when we read of Wilde himself in the *Autobiographies,* or when we come upon the many references to Maud Gonne in the prose or the verse: we know that this is not the truth about them because other people saw them so differently. And it is not only different views of the same person, but almost always a view on Yeats's part which seems the product of a will to see only what he wants to see, and a will to forget the rest. Yeats's poetry will never be separated from his *Autobiographies,* and neither work will ever be separated from the human being who was not what he wished to be and not what he saw himself as being.

How difficult it is to keep the human being and the work separate can be seen in a few more very recent instances. One reviewer of Yeats's *Last Poems and Plays* remarked that he was disgusted by the explicit sexuality displayed in these poems by a man who was, after all, over seventy. Whether or not disgust is justified in this case the present writer does not pretend to know, but it is certain that the protagonist of these poems is manifestly an old man full of sexual longings and regrets. Again, in *Scattering Branches,* L. A. G. Strong writes that several critics have attributed "the riot of copulation" in the last poems to "the gland operation Yeats underwent some five or six years before he died." Mr. Strong believes that the way to answer such an attribution is to "look to that in him which made him demand the operation: to the manner of man he was." Louis MacNiece is similarly concerned in his book on Yeats about the poet's virginity until the age of forty: how shall we tell the poet from the poem? Although we know how to make the distinction and ignore all Yeats did to dramatize himself as a human being, some will always refuse to make the distinction. Perhaps it is for this reason that Homer and Shakespeare have sometimes ceased to exist.

And, finally, our unknown author will perhaps engage in comparisons; Yeats against Arthur Symons, for the sake of what light may be shed on why one became a great poet in middle age while the other, better educated and better equipped in other ways, did not; Yeats against A. E. Housman, to show, among much else, how Yeats did perfectly what Housman did mechanically in verse; Yeats against James Joyce and against Ezra Pound; Yeats against Arnold Bennett and Andre Gide, both of them born almost at the same time as Yeats and both of them authors of journals which make a rich comparison with Yeats's *Autobiographies.*

His Lyric Poems. It is possible to read Yeats's prose for its beauties of style, although those beauties never arrive at the sustained coherence and unity which constitute a complete book. But it is clear that neither his plays nor his prose writings[2] make Yeats what he is for us. The poems which begin with the volume called *The Green Helmet* and end with *Last Poems and Plays* are for most readers the only reason why the rest of Yeats's work has anything but incidental interest. They are the center of interest, the justification of our interest, and inevitably the source of fresh instances of old problems about the nature of literature. Our gifted author, confronted with these problems, will probably be content with stating them once more as well as possible in their relationship to Yeats.

For example, there will certainly once more be the problem of what the reader who does not share Yeat's beliefs in the supernatural can take as a workable attitude while he reads. This problem is further complicated by the difficulty of knowing whether or not Yeats held those beliefs himself, and still further complicated by the grab-bag character of Yeats's view of the supernatural, arrived at through such in-

[2] Perhaps Yeats was a great lyric poet, but a poor dramatist and fragmentary prose writer because of the self-absorption, obvious throughout, which kept him from being interested in other human beings, except as they were directly related to himself.

termediaries as Irish peasants, Madame Blavatsky, and Mrs. Yeats, whatever the ultimate ontological source. But another ancient problem, which in a way contains the problem of belief and must arise even for those who believe exactly what Yeats believed, is the question of the relationship of the formal perfection of some of the poems to the kind of insight which it for the most part embodies. I mean to say that the insight is far from being the equal of the writing itself taken in abstraction.

It is true that some of Yeats's poems are full of a wisdom which must commend itself to and convince every man, Buddhist to Seventh Day Adventist. The second part of "A Dialogue of Self and Soul" is a passage the equal of Dante and Shakespeare at their best. But in general, the point of view of Yeats's verse is romantic in its assumptions and in its conclusions. Romantic love, the romantic view of death, the romantic view of the poet, the private self-made philosophy of the romantic poet—these are all basic elements of Yeats's mind as it manifests itself in his lyric poems. Even when he sees and understands much more than the romantic poet, the lurid glow of romanticism nevertheless hangs over the scene. And very often it is pure romantic perception, the consequence of all the romantic assumptions, that we find in poems which, considered as verbal expression, are faultless.

An easy instance is such a poem as "The Scholars." These academic figures, bald-headed, coughing, and respectable, would be dumbfounded, the poet suggests, if they met Catullus or the other poets whom they edit and annotate, making a learned text of the lines

That young men, tossing on their beds,
Rhymed out in love's despair
To flatter beauty's ear.

How utterly banal a view! No doubt, some scholars are worthy of contempt for the reasons advanced by the poet. It is not a question of the character of the scholar, past or present, nor is it necessary to suppose that scholars are handsome and heroic figures. What one finds essentially wrong here is the romantic triteness and stupidity of the attitude, the implied contempt for learning because it is painstaking and not spontaneous, the schoolboy's view of the absent-minded professor, and the Bohemian's notion of academicism: "All (that is, all the scholars) think what other people think," Yeats wrote, thinking what other people think. What would Catullus have thought of this poem? We are told of the *Alexandrian* sources of his poetry.

Again, to take a more striking and more characteristic example, in "An Irish Airman Foresees His Death," consider the following lines, in which the airman is supposedly revealing his reasons for participating in the first World War on the side of Great Britain:

Those that I fight I do not hate,
Those that I guard I do not love . . .
My country is Kiltartan Cross,
My countrymen Kiltartan's poor,
No likely end could bring them loss,
Or leave them happier than before.
Nor law nor duty bade me fight,
Nor public men nor cheering crowds,
A lonely impulse of delight
Drove to this tumult in the clouds . . .

The rejection of law, duty, public men, and cheering crowds, and the apotheosis of one motive, "A lonely impulse of delight," shows with exactitude how complete a romantic Yeats was.

For one more even more obvious example of the height, width and depth of Yeats's romanticism, there is the first poem of the sequence, "A Woman Young and Old" in Yeats's next to last volume of verse:

FATHER AND CHILD

She hears me strike the board and say
That she is under ban
Of all good men and women,
Being mentioned with a man
That has the worst of all bad names,
And thereupon replies
That his hair is beautiful,
Cold as the March wind his eyes.

That is of course a quasi-dramatic lyric. Hence it may be wrong to suppose that the poet is expressing an admiration without reservations for the lady's reply. Yet is it not the same lonely impulse of delight, rejecting all other appeals, which motivates not only the lady's sentiments, and not only the father, who seems to be much impressed by his daughter's reply, but the whole poem? I certainly do not mean to raise any issue of moralism or didacticism, although whatever the worst of all bad names may be, traitor, murderer, or pimp, it is hard to accept beautiful hair and cold eyes as being a counterweight from any rational point of view. Nor is it that one would wish the poem always to declare that virtue is good, evil is bad, and the wicked will surely be punished. The issue I want very much to raise is the distinction in quality between the expression, considered in abstraction, and the wisdom or rather lack of wisdom in this poem. Some instance of this issue can be found in a majority of Yeats's later poems and it is only brevity and convenience which make the weight of argument rest on this short poem. The expression here as elsewhere seems to me to have every *literary* virtue which could possibly be required for a short lyric: it has clarity, simplicity, exactness of diction, metrical exactness and sensitivity, a fine dramatic framework which finds its counterpart in the order and structure of the lines. But, by contrast, the sentiments which are given this fine expression are part of the foolish bravado of romantic adolescence: the equivalent in literary expression would be irresponsible doggerel or perhaps a quick-moving limerick.

It is here then that our unknown author would have his most difficult problem. He would have to accept and elucidate the greatness of the writing without forgetting the inferior quality of the emotions and attitudes embodied in the writing. No doubt this raises the ancient and ever-new problem of the separation of form from subject-matter. At the same time it raises the similar but more inclusive problem, stated precisely, and yet not, I think, sufficiently discussed by T. S. Eliot in an analogous context where the question was that of the religious attitude to literature: "The 'greatness' of literature cannot be determined solely by literary standards; though we must remember that whether it is literature or not can be determined only by literary standards." Our gifted unknown author will have to make that distinction again and again in writing of Yeats's poems, explicating the nature of literary standards by considering the verse as expression and at the same time making clear, in all humility, how often Yeats fell short of the wisdom which is in the Bible, Dante, and Shakespeare, and in every rational being when he thinks well enough and acts well enough to survive as a human being. There are passages and whole poems in which Yeats has that wisdom as well as any poet, but the dominant tendency of his work derives, in the direct way we have seen, from the tenets, the assumptions and the conclusions of romanticism in some of its most familiar forms.

Only if one subscribes to the theory of the identity of form and subject-matter—which can always be heard and which is never explained—is such a separate enjoyment of expression apart from doctrine, attitude, and sentiment impossible. Is it not necessary, in fact, to grasp the quality of language and expression in Yeats's later poetry without taking its romanticism with equal seriousness, or permitting a rejection of its romanticism to interfere with one's enjoyment of it as expression?

His Mastery of Expression. As expression, Yeats's later poetry suggests the possibility of endless study. The use of speed and slowness in going from word to word, the use of line lengths, of repetition, of off-rhymes, and similar devices of the versification, are matters which would be analyzed in detail in our adequate book. But it is the use of meter, above all, which would require and reward study. The metrical mastery which accomplishes so much works through variations of the iambic structure of a complexity which is such that the proper names for all the devices do not, as far as I know, exist:

> 'Old lovers *yet may have*
> All *that time denied*—
> Grave *is heaped on grave*
> *That they be satisfied*—
> Over *the blackened earth*—
> The old troops *parade,*
> Birth *is heaped on birth*—
> *That such* cannonade
> *May thunder time away,*
> Birth-hour and death-hour meet,
> Or, as great sages *say,*
> Men dance *on deathless feet.*'

I have italicized the variations of the iambic trimeter of this quotation in order to show briefly the extraordinary variety Yeats could manage with ease and without the least hint of a wrenching of accent or an imperfection of tone. I do not know the name for such a variation as is contained in "*The old troops* parade." But the expressiveness of this variation and of the wonderful last line, "*Men dance* on deathless feet," should illustrate the riches in Yeats's versification which require elucidation and analysis as well as enjoyment.[3]

Another example which illustrates more broadly the difference between formal excellence and insight which is inferior, slight, or absent is such a poem—there are many like it in this respect—as "A Thought from Propertius":

She might, so noble from head
To great shapely knees
The long flowing line,
Have walked to the altar
Through the holy images
At Pallas Athena's side,
Or been fit spoil for a centaur
Drunk with the unmixed wine.

The extraordinary effect of this short poem is largely the result of the inverted sentence structure[4] in the first three lines—"So noble from head/To great shapely knees/The long flowing lines," and the delayed rhyme of "line" and "wine," which binds the third line with the conclusion of the poem. The image of the poem simulates the visual without being visual and the classical references do not have any profound associations for the modern reader, and in any case hardly account for the beauty of the verse. This instance suggests in fact that any great translation shows how mastery of language and expression can exist in isolation from mastery of or insight into subject-matter.

Interpretation. Most important of all, I think, will be the labor of providing a system of interpretation for Yeats's poems. We have heard enough by now of the four kinds of levels of meaning in *The Divine Comedy*. A like system will have to be made and worked out for Yeats. R. P. Blackmur's emphasis on the magical kind of meaning is exemplified, in his essay on Yeats, in what he says of one of Yeats's best poems: " 'Leda and the Swan' can be read on at least three distinct levels of significance, none of which interferes with the others: the levels of dramatic fiction, of condensed insight into Greek mythology, and a third level of fiction and insight combined, as we said, to represent and hide a magical insight."

[3] There is also the question of why Yeats wrote such weak, unorganized blank verse in his plays; why, when he gave up rhyme, his metrical mastery disappeared. In the lyrics, the use of anapests and spondees is another matter worth studying.

[4] It is with thsi device of style that Yeats achieves some of the beauty of his prose: this device in the middle of artful simple declarative sentences.

Yet, since this possibility sometimes brings about a drunkenness or wanton-ness of interpretation, perhaps it is worth while citing an extreme example, an example of fruitful misunderstanding, in order to show not only how real the problem of interpretation may be, but what dangers it creates.

In another of Yeats's best poems, "Among School Children," there is a passage which becomes, I think, very much better *when it is misunderstood*. Or rather when Yeats's intended meaning is mistaken for another one. In the fifth stanza of "Among School Children," the "I" of the poem turns from the school children who have reminded him of the old age and the childhood of a woman who was once a great beauty. Her old age and her loss of beauty have made him question the worth of any natural life.

Quite naturally and appropriately, this leads to thoughts about what famous philosophers have said of Nature, and of human life as a natural process:

Plato thought nature but a spume that plays
Upon a ghostly paradigm of things;
Soldier Aristotle played the taws
Upon the bottom of a king of kings;
World-famous golden-thighed Pythagoras
Fingered upon a fiddle-stick or strings
What a star sang and careless Muses heard:
Old clothes upon old sticks to scare a bird.

Given the first two lines of the stanza, which are certainly an effort to describe Plato's view of nature, suppose one takes the next two lines as a description of Aristotle's cosmology. "A king of kings" would thus be Aristotle's Prime Mover or God; the taws or marbles [5] would be the concentric spheres which constitute the world for Aristotle and to which the Prime Mover gives impetus or movement. The reference is playful and ironic, and also exact in saying that the taws or celestial spheres were played against the bottom of the Prime Mover, since he is, in Aristotle's description of his life,

[5] In *Webster's New International,* a taw is defined as follows: "1. *Colloq. & Dial.* A line or mark from which players at marbles shoot. 2. A marble to be used as a shooter; also, a game at marbles." This is all that is given for taw as a noun.

If taws are taken as marbles, then their application to the Aristotelian-Ptolemaic cosmology might mean the sun and the stars, which are part of the celestial spheres, as well as their celestial spheres themselves. For the sun and the stars are more like marbles than the spheres, which are concentric to each other, so that the whole of nature resembles, to use a homely example, an onion, at the approximate center of which is the earth and outside of which is the Prime Mover.

turned away from all nature and wholly engaged in eternal thought about himself. And the whole sense of the passage, taken in this way, is a good extension, by example, of the contempt for nature which Yeats is trying to state. The succeeding four lines, as well as the preceding two, help this interpretation by their reference to Pythagoras on the same level of discourse, namely, different philosophies of nature expressed in concrete figures. There is nothing special to or limited to Aristotle about this interpretation of the two lines concerning him, for the Ptolemaic cosmology must be known in order to understand many other authors: the last line of the *Divine Comedy*, "The Love which moves the sun and the other stars," depends on the same cosmology and is a reference to the same Prime Mover, which should suggest that the educated reader might naturally and even spontaneously seize upon this interpretation.

Moreover, this interpretation seems to tally with what one takes to be a misprint; "Soldier Aristotle" (which appears on page 251 of the American edition of the *Collected Poems* of 1933) should then read "Solider Aristotle," a correction enforced not only by the obvious contrast between Aristotle and Plato, but also by the meter which is wrenched by "soldier."

It seems fairly certain, however, that Yeats intended nothing of the sort. "Taws" means whips, as well as marbles. The king of kings is Alexander, Aristotle's pupil, often referred to in antiquity as the king of kings. "Soldier Aristotle" may not be a misprint, but a reference to Aristotle's interest in military strategy, and the whole intention of the poet becomes a biographical-historical example, the supposition that Aristotle whipped his noble pupil.

Further evidence that Yeats had this in mind is to be seen in another of his poems, "The Saint and the Hunchback," in which it is impossible to doubt that by taws, Yeats meant whips:

I lay about me with the taws
That night and morning I may thrash
Greek Alexander from my flesh.

This historical-biographical interpretation seems to me obviously inferior, in terms of the poem itself, so far as significance goes; they seem to stick out wrongly from the rest of the stanza: what has Aristotle's whipping of his noble pupil to do with contempt for nature? It would seem rather to be contempt for monarchy.

The whole problem of the meaning or meanings of any poem is raised by this example. This particular example is extreme, as I have said, and possibly freakish, but in one form or another much of Yeats's verse raises the same questions for any reader, namely, What are the limits which define legitimate interpretation? Are there any limits? To what extent can we disregard the author's intention?

One answer fairly popular at present I suppose would be that the reader is justified in giving as many interpretations as he can to a poem: the more, the better; the more, the richer the poem. In William Empson's terms, there are any number of possible types of ambiguity, and we ought to get all we can from all of them.

This answer seems to be involved in countless difficulties. For example, some interpretations contradict one another. In "Among School Children," one cannot at the same time take the two lines in question as referring to Alexander and to the Prime Mover.

Another answer might be, An interpretation is valid only if it is consistent with the whole context of the poem taken as a literal statement. But this criterion of the whole literal context breaks down quickly. One sees that it enforces the philosophical interpretation by being consistent with the consideration of Nature which is the subject of the two preceding and the four succeeding lines. One also sees how the interpretation which makes the two lines describe Aristotle's whipping of his pupil would be also consistent, with a slight straining of one's ingenuity, with a poem which is about school children.

Whatever the answer to the whole problem of interpretation or this particular instance of it may be, this problem and all the problems I have shifted to an unknown author add up to a definition of ignorance. Yet this defined ignorance assumes, knows, and depends upon an inexhaustible substance, like Life itself. Only admiration of this substance could bring one to a concern with its problems and mysteries. It is with this admiration, with a conviction of the greatness of this poetry, that our author will began and end, All will begin and end with admiration and love of the greatness of this poetry.

V

T. S. Eliot

THE INVITATION TO address you on this occasion and in this place was at the same time irresistible and terrifying. You have instituted an annual lecture in memory of the greatest poet of our time—certainly the greatest in this language, and so far as I am able to judge, in any language. This is the first lecture, and in a theater for ever associated with his name, the center of some of his most important activity. The responsibility which I have accepted is considerable. I have thought it fit, on this the first of these annual ceremonies, to devote my words to the work of William Butler Yeats himself: that is what I should wish to do, and what I expect you would wish to hear, But even after taking this obvious decision, my subject left me a wide range of selection. The achievement of a great poet cannot be surveyed in an hour. There are many aspects of his work—cultural, political, religious—which can be better treated by a compatriot. In what way can a visitor like myself discuss Yeats's work with the greatest freshness and with the least impertinence? It seemed to me that a certain informality, and even personality, might be permitted if I was to consider a few aspects of his poetry from the point of view of his admirers and fellow practitioners outside of Ireland, and especially in England and America.

The generations of poetry in our age seem to cover a span of about twenty years. I do not mean that the best work of any poet is limited to twenty years: I mean that it is about that length of time before a new school or style of poetry appears. By the time, that is to say, that a man is fifty, he has behind him a kind of poetry written by men of seventy, and before him another kind written by men of thirty. That is my position at present, and if I live another twenty years I shall expect to see still another younger school of poetry. One's relation to Yeats, however, does not fit into this scheme. When I was a young man at the university in America, just beginning to write verse, Yeats was already a considerable figure in the world of poetry, and his early period was well defined. I cannot remember that his poetry at that stage made any deep impression upon me. A very young

"The Poetry of W. B. Yeats," The First Annual Yeats Lecture, delivered to the Friends of the Irish Academy at the Abbey Theatre, June, 1940; and *The Southern Review*, VII, 3 (winter, 1942), pp. 442-454.

man, who is himself stirred to write, is not primarily critical or even widely appreciative. He is looking for masters who will elicit his consciousness of what he wants to say himself, of the kind of poetry that is in him to write. The taste of an adolescent writer is intense, but narrow: it is determined by personal needs. The kind of poetry that I needed, to teach me the use of my own voice, did not exist in English at all; it was only to be found in French. For this reason the poetry of the young Yeats hardly existed for me until after my enthusiasm had been won by the poetry of the older Yeats; and by that time—I mean, from 1919 on—my own course of evolution was already determined. Hence, I find myself regarding him, from one point of view, as a contemporary and not a predecessor; and from another point of view, I can share the feelings of younger men, who came to know and admire him by that work from 1919 on, which was produced while they were adolescent.

Certainly, for the younger poets of England and America, I am sure that their admiration for Yeat's poetry has been wholly good. His idiom was too different for there to be any danger of imitation, his opinions too different to flatter and confirm their prejudices. It was good for them to have the spectacle of an unquestionably great living poet, whose style they were not tempted to echo and whose ideas contradicted those in vogue among them. You will not see, in their writing, more than passing evidences of the impression he made, but the work, and the man himself as poet, have been of the greatest significance to them for all that. This may seem to contradict what I have been saying about the kind of poetry that a young poet chooses to admire. But I am really talking about something different. Yeats would not have this influence had he not become a great poet; but the influence of which I speak is due to the figure of the poet himself, to the integrity of his passion for his art and his craft which provided such an impluse for his extraordinary development. When he visited London he liked to meet and talk to younger poets. People have sometimes spoken of him as arrogant and over-bearing. I never found him so; in his conversations with a younger writer I always felt that he offered terms of equality, as to a fellow worker, a practitioner of the same mystery. It was, I think, that, unlike many writers, he cared more for poetry than for his own reputaton as a poet or his picture of himself as a poet. Art was greater than the artist: and this feeling he communicated to others; which was why younger men were never ill-at-ease in his company.

This, I am sure, was part of the secret of his ability, after becoming unquestionably the master, to remain always a contemporary. Another is the continual development of which I have spoken. This has become almost a commonplace of criticism of his work. But while it is often mentioned, its causes and its nature have not been often analyzed. One reason, of course, was simply concentration and hard work. And behind that is character: I mean the special character of the artist as artist—that is, the force of character by which Dickens, having exhausted his first inspiration, was able in middle age to proceed to such a masterpiece, so different from his early work, as *Bleak House*. It is diffcult and unwise to generalize about ways of composition—so many men, so many ways—but it is my experience that towards middle age a man has three choices: to stop writing altogether, to repeat himself with perhaps an increasing skill of virtuosity, or by taking thought to adapt himself to middle age and find a different way of working. Why are the later long poems of Browning and Swinburne mostly unread? It is, I think, because one gets the essential Browning or Swinburne entire in earlier poems; and in the later, one is reminded of the early freshness which they lack, without being made aware of any compensating new qualities. When a man is engaged in work of abstract thought—if there is such a thing as wholly abstract thought outside of mathematical and the physical sciences—his mind can mature, while his emotions either remain the same or only atrophy, and it will not matter But maturing as a poet means maturing as the whole man, experiencing new emotions appropriate to one's age, and with the same intensity as the emotions of youth.

One form, a perfect form, of development is that of Shakespeare, one of the few poets whose work of maturity is just as exciting as that of their early manhood. There is, I think, a difference between the development of Shakespeare and Yeats, which makes the latter case still more curious. With Shakespeare, one sees a slow, continuous development of mastery of his craft or verse, and the poetry of middle age seems implicit in that of early maturity. After the first few verbal exercises you say of each piece of work: "This is the perfect expression of the sensibility of that stage of his development." That a poet should develop at all, that he should find something new to say, and say it equally well, in middle age, has always something miraculous about it. But in the case of Yeats the kind of development seems to me different. I do not want to give the impression that I regard his earlier and his later work almost as if they had been written by two different men. Returning to his earlier poems after making a close acquaintance with the later, one sees, to begin with, that in technique there was a slow and continuous development of what is always the same medium and idiom. And when I say development, I do not mean that many of the early poems, for what they are, are not as beautifully written as they could be. There are some, such as "Who Goes with Fergus?" which are as perfect of their kind as anything in the language. But the best, and the best known of them, have this limitation: that they are as satisfactory in isolation, as "anthology pieces" as they are in the context of his other poems of the same period.

I am obviously using the term "anthology piece" in a rather special sense. In any anthology, you find some poems which give you complete satisfaction and delight in themselves, such that you are hardly curious who wrote them, hardly want to look further into the work of that poet. There are others, not necessarily so perfect or complete, which make you irresistibly curious to know more of that poet through his other work. Naturally, this distinction applies only to short poems, those in which a man has only been able to put a part of his mind, if it is a mind of any size. With some such you feel at once that the man who wrote them must have had a great deal more to say, in different contexts, of equal interest. Now among all the poems in Yeats's earlier volumes I find only in a line here or there, that sense of a unique personality which makes one sit up in excitement and eagerness to learn more about the author's mind and feelings. The intensity of Yeat's own emotional experience hardly appears. We have sufficient evidence of the intensity of experience of his youth, but it is from the retrospections in some of his later work that we have our evidence.

I have, in early essays, extolled what I called impersonality in art, and it may seem that, in giving as a reason for the superiority of Yeats's later work the greater expression of personality in it, I am contradicting myself. It may be that I expressed myself badly, or that I had only an adolescent grasp of that idea—as I can never bear to reread my own prose writings, I am willing to leave the point unsettled—but I think now, at least, that the truth of the matter is this. There are two forms of impersonality: that which is natural to the mere skilful craftsman, and that which is more and more achieved by the maturing artist. The first is that of what I have called the "anthology piece," of a lyric by Lovelace or Suckling, or of Campion, a finer poet than either. The second impersonality is that of the poet who, out of intense and personal experience, is able to express a general truth; retaining all the particularity of his experience, to make of it a general symbol. And the strange thing is that Yeats, having been a great craftsman in the first kind, became a great poet in the second. It is not that he became a different man, for, as I have hinted, one feels sure that the intense experience of youth had been lived through—and indeed, without this early experience he could never have attained anything of the wisdom which appears in his later writing. But he had to wait for a late maturity to find expression of early experience; and this makes him, I think, a unique and especially interesting poet.

Consider the early poem which is in every anthology, "When you are old and grey and full of sleep," or "A Dream of Death" in the same volume of 1893. They are beautiful poems, but only craftsman's work, because one does not feel present in them the particularity which must provide the material for the general truth. By the time of the volume of 1904 there is a development visible in a very lovely poem, "The Folly of Being Comforted," and in "Adam's Curse"; something is coming through, and in beginning to speak as a particular man he is beginning to speak for man. This is clearer still in the poem "Peace," in the 1910 volume. But it is not fully evinced until the volume of 1914, in the violent and terrible epistle dedicatory of *Responsibilities*, with the lines

Pardon that for a barren passion's sake
Although I have come close on forty-nine. . . .

And the naming of his age in the poem is significant. More than half a lifetime to arrive at this freedom of speech. It is a triumph.

There was much also for Yeats to work out of himself, even in technique. To be a younger member of a group of poets, none of them certainly of anything like his stature, but further developed on their limited path, may arrest for a time man's development of idiom. Then again, the weight of the pre-Raphaelite prestige must have been tremendous. The Yeats of the Celtic twilight—who, begging your pardon, seems to me to have been more the Yeats of the pre-Raphaelite twilight—uses Celtic folklore almost as William Morris uses Scandinavian folklore. His longer narrative poems bear the mark of Morris. Indeed, in his pre-Raphaelite phase, Yeats is by no means the least of the pre-Raphaelites. I may be mistaken, and I may be impertinent, but the play, *The Shadowy Waters,* seems to me one of the most perfect expressions of the vague enchanted beauty of that school: yet it strikes me—and this is what may be an impertinence on my part—as the western seas descried through the back window of a house in Kensington, an Irish myth for the Kelmscott Press; and when I try to visualize the speakers in the play, they have the great dim, dreamy eyes of the knights and ladies of Burne-Jones. I think that the phase in which he treated Irish legend in the manner of Rossetti or Morris is a phase of confusion. He did not master this legend until he made it a vehicle for his own creation of character—not, really, until he began to write the Plays for Dancers. The point is, that in becoming more Irish, not in subject-matter but in expression, he became at the same time universal.

The points that I particularly wish to make about Yeats's development are two. The first, on which I have already touched, is that to have accomplished what Yeats did in the middle and later years is a great and permanent example—which poets-to-come should study with reverence—of what I have called Character of the Artist: a kind of moral, as well as intellectual, excellence. The second point, which follows naturally after what I have said in criticism of the lack of complete emotional expression in his early work, is that Yeats is pre-eminently the poet of middle age. By this I am far from meaning that he is a poet only for middle-aged readers: the attitude towards him of younger poets who write in English, the world over, is enough evidence to the contrary. Now, in theory, there is no reason why a poet's inspiration or material should fail, in middle age or at any time before senility. For a man who is capable of experience finds himself in a different world in every decade of his life; as he sees it with different eyes, the material of his art is continually renewed. But in fact, very few poets have shown this capacity of adaptation to the years. It requires, indeed, an exceptional honesty and courage to face the change. Most men either cling to the experiences of youth, so that their writing becomes an insincere mimicry of their earlier work, or they leave their passion behind, and write only from the head, with a hollow and wasted virtuosity. There is another and even worse temptation: that of becoming dignified, of becoming public figures with only a public existence—coat-racks hung with decorations and distinctions, doing, saying and even thinking and feeling only what they believe the public expects of them. Yeats was not that kind of poet: and it is, perhaps, a reason why young men should find his later poetry more acceptable than older men easily can. For the young can see him as a poet who in his work remained in the best sense always young, who even in one sense became young as he aged. But the old, unless they are stirred to something of the honesty with oneself expressed in the poetry, will be shocked by such a revelation of what a man really is and remains. They will refuse to believe that *they* are like that.

You think it horrible that lust and rage
Should dance attendance upon my old age;
They were not such a plague when I was young:
What else have I to spur me into song?

These lines are very impressive and not very pleasant, and the sentiment has recently been criticized by an English critic whom I generally respect. But I think he misread them. I do not read them as a personal confession of a man who differed from other men, but of a man who was essentially the same as most other men; the only difference is in the greater clarity, honesty and vigor. To what honest man, old enough, can these sentiments be entirely alien? They can be subdued and disciplined by religion, but who can say that they are dead? Only those to whom the maxim of La Rochefoucauld applies: *Quand les vices nous quittent, nous nous flattons de la créance que c'est nous qui les quittons.* The tragedy of Yeats's epigram is all in the last line.

Similarly, the play *Purgatory* is not very pleasant, either. There are aspects of it which I do not like myself. I wish he had not given it this title, because I cannot accept a purgatory in which there is no hint, or at least no emphasis upon Purgation. But, apart from the extraordinary theatrical skill with which he has put so much action within the compass of a very short scene of but little movement, the play gives a masterly exposition of the emotions of an old man. I think that the epigram I have just quoted seems to me just as much to be taken in a dramatic sense as the play *Purgatory*. The lyric poet—and Yeats was always lyric, even when dramatic—can speak for every man, or for men very different from himself; but to do this he must for the moment be able to identify himself with every man or other men; and it is only his imaginative power of becoming this that deceives some readers into thinking that he is speaking for and of himself alone—especially when they prefer not to be implicated.

I do not wish to emphasize this aspect only of Yeats's poetry of age. I would call attention to the beautiful poem in *The Winding Stair,* in memory of Eva Gore-Booth and Con Markiewicz, in which the picture at the beginning, of

> *Two girls in silk kimonos, both*
> *Beautiful, one a gazelle,*

gets great intensity from the shock of the later line,

> *When withered, old and skeleton gaunt,*

and also to "Coole Park," beginning

> *I meditate upon a swallow's flight,*
> *Upon an aged woman and her house.*

In such poems one feels that the most lively and desirable emotions of youth have been preserved to receive their full and due expression in retrospect. For the interesting feelings of age are not just different feelings; they are feelings into which the feelings of youth are integrated.

Yeats's development in his dramatic poetry is as interesting as that in his lyrical poetry. I have spoken of him as having been a lyric poet—in a sense in which I should not think of myself, for instance, as lyric; and by this I mean rather a certain kind of selection of emotion rather than particular metrical forms. But there is no reason why a lyric poet should not also be a dramatic poet; and to me Yeats is the type of lyrical dramatist. It took him many years to evolve the dramatic form suited to his genius. When he first began to write plays, poetic drama meant plays written in blank verse. Now, blank verse has been a dead meter for a long time.

It would be outside of my frame to go into all the reasons for that now: but it is obvious that a form which was handled so supremely well by Shakespeare has its disadvantages. If you are writing a play of the same type as Shakespeare's, the reminiscence is oppressive; if you are writing a play of a different type, it is distracting. Furthermore, as Shakespeare is so much greater than any dramatist who has followed him, blank verse can hardly be dissociated from the life of the sixteenth and seventeenth centuries: it can hardly catch the rhythms with which English is spoken nowadays. I think that if anything like regular blank verse is ever to be re-established, it can only be after a long departure from it, during the course of which it will have liberated itself from period associations. At the time of Yeats's early plays it was not possible to use anything else for a poetry play: that is not a criticism of Yeats himself, but an assertion that changes in verse forms come at one moment and not at another. His early verse-plays, including *The Green Helmet,* which is written in a kind of irregular rhymed fourteener, have a good deal of beauty in them, and, at least, they are the best verse-plays written in their time. And even in these, one notices some development of irregularity in the metric. Yeats did not quite invent a new meter, but the blank verse of his later plays shows a great advance towards one; and what is most astonishing is the virtual abandonment of blank verse meter in *Purgatory*. One device used with great success in some of the later plays is the lyrical choral interlude. But another, and important, cause of improvement is the gradual purging out of poetical ornament. This, perhaps, is the most painful part of the labor, so far as the versification goes, of the modern poet who tries to write a play in verse. The course of improvement is towards a greater and greater starkness. The beautiful line for its own sake is a luxury dangerous even for the poet who has made himself a virtuoso of the technique of the theater. What is necessary is a beauty which shall not be in the line or the isolable passage, but woven into the dramatic texture itself; so that you can hardly say whether the lines give grandeur to the drama, or whether it is the drama which turns the words into poetry. (One of the most thrilling lines in *King Lear* is the simple

Never, never, never, never, never,

but, apart from a knowledge of the context, how can you

say that it is poetry, or even competent verse?) Yeats's purification of his verse becomes much more evident in the four Plays for Dancers and in the two in the posthumous volume: those, in fact, in which he had found his right and final dramatic form.

It is in the first three of the Plays for Dancers, also, that he shows the internal, as contrasted with the external, way of handling Irish myth of which I have spoken earlier. In the earlier plays, as in the earlier poems, about legendary heroes and heroines, I feel that the characters are treated, with the respect that we pay to legend, as creatures of a different world from ours. In the later plays they are universal men and women. I should, perhaps, not include *The Dreaming of the Bones* quite in this category, because Dermot and Devorgilla are characters from modern history, not figures out of pre-history; but I would remark in support of what I have been saying that in this play these two lovers have something of the universality of Dante's Paolo and Francesca, and this the younger Yeats could not have done. So with the Cuchulain of *The Hawk's Well*, the Cuchulain, Emer and Eithne of *The Only Jealously of Emer;* the myth is not presented for its own sake, but as a vehicle for a situation of universal meeting.

I see at this point that I may have given the impression, contrary to my desire and my belief, that the poetry and the plays of Yeats's earlier period can be ignored in favor of his later work. You cannot divide the work of a great poet so sharply as that. Where there is the continuity of such a positive personality and such a single purpose, the later work cannot be understood, or properly enjoyed, without a study and appreciation of the earlier; and the later work again reflects light upon the earlier, and shows us beauty and significance not before perceived. We have also to take account of the historical conditions. As I have said above, Yeats was born into the end of a literary movement, and an English movement at that: only those who have toiled with language know the labor and constancy required to free oneself from such influences—yet, on the other hand, once we are familiar with the older voice, we can hear its individual tones even in his earliest published verse. In my own time of youth there seemed to be no immediate great powers of poetry either to help or to hinder, either to learn from or to rebel against, yet I can understand the difficulty of the other situation, and the magnitude of the task. With the verse-play, on the other hand, the situation is reversed, because Yeats had nothing, and we have had Yeats. He started writing plays at a time when the prose-play of contemporary life seemed triumphant, with an indefinite future stretching before it; when the comedy of light farce dealt only with certain privileged strata of metropolitan life; and when the serious play tended to be an ephemeral tract on some transient social problem. We can begin to see now that even the imperfect early attempts he made are probably more permanent literature than the plays of Ibsen or of Shaw; and that his dramatic work as a whole may prove a stronger defense against the successful urban Shaftesbury Avenue—vulgarity which he opposed as stoutly as they. Just as, from the beginning, he made and thought his poetry in terms of speech and not in terms of print, so in the drama he always meant to write plays to be played and not merely to be read. He cared, I think, more for the theater as an organ for the expression of the consciousness of a people, than as a means to his own fame or achievement; and I am convinced that it is only if you serve it in this spirit that you can hope to accomplish anything worth doing with it. Of course, he had some great advantages, the recital of which does not rob him of any of his glory: his colleagues, a people with a natural and unspoilt gift for speech and for acting, and this theater—it is impossible to disentangle what he did for the Irish theater from what the Irish theater did for him. From this point of advantage, the idea of the poetic drama was kept alive when everywhere else it had been driven underground. I do not know where our debt to him as a dramatist ends—and in time, it will not end until that drama itself ends. In his occasional writings on dramatic topics he has asserted certain principles to which we must hold fast: such as the primacy of the poet over the actor, and of the actor over the scene-painter; and the principle that the theater, while it need not be concerned only with "the people" in the narrow Russian sense, must be for the people; that to be permanent it must concern itself with fundamental situations. Born into a world in which the doctrine of "art for art's sake" was generally accepted, and living on into one in which art has been asked to be instrumental to social purposes, he held firmly to the right view which is between these, though not in any way a compromise between them, and showed that an artist, by serving his art with entire integrity, is at the same time rendering the greatest service he can to his own nation and to the whole world.

I have come here to do honor to the memory of a great poet. It is a pleasure to me to praise him, and to have the privilege of doing so here and before this audience; and if I had not had the conviction of praising him in all sincerity I should not have come at all. But to be able to praise, it is not necessary to feel complete agreement; and I should not think it right to dissimulate the fact that there are aspects of his thought and feeling which to myself are unsympathetic. I say this not in order to express my own beliefs, which I shall leave in silence, but rather to indicate the limits which I have set to my criticism. The questions of difference, objection and protest arise in the field of doctrine, and you have no need to be reminded how vital they are. I have been concerned only with the poet and dramatist, so far as these can be isolated. In the long run they cannot be wholly isolated. A full and elaborate examination of the total work of Yeats must some day be undertaken; perhaps it will need a longer perspective. There are some poets whose poetry can be considered more or less in isolation, for experience and delight. There are others whose poetry, though giving equally experience and delight, has a larger historical importance. Yeats was one of the latter: he was one of those few whose history is the history of their own time, who are a part of the consciousness of an age which cannot be understood without them. This is a very high position to assign to him: but I believe that it is one which is secure.

W. H. Auden

ONE DRAWBACK, AND not the least, of practising any art is that it becomes very difficult to enjoy the works of one's fellow artists, living or dead, simply for their own sakes.

When a poet, for instance, reads a poem written by another, he is apt to be less concerned with what the latter actually accomplished by his poem than with the suggestions it throws out upon how he, the reader, may solve the poetic problems which confront him now. His judgments of poetry, therefore, are rarely purely aesthetic; he will often prefer an inferior poem from which he can learn something at the moment to a better poem from which he can learn nothing. This gap between his evaluations and those of the pure critic is all the wider in the case of his immediate predecessors. All generations overlap, and the young poet naturally looks for and finds the greatest help in the work of those whose poetic problems are similar to his because they have experiences in common. He begins, therefore, with an excessive admiration for one or more of the mature poets of his time. But, as he grows older, he becomes more and more conscious of belonging to a different generation faced with problems that his heroes cannot help him solve, and his former hero-worship, as in other spheres of life, is all too apt to turn into an equally excessive hostility and contempt. Those of us who, like myself, have learned, as we think, all we can, and that is a good deal, from Yeats, are tempted to be more conscious and more critical of those elements in his poems with which we are not in sympathy than we ought to be. Our criticisms may sometimes be objectively correct, but the subjective resentment with which we make them is always unjust. Further, as long as we harbor such a resentment, it will be a dangerous hindrance to our own poetic development, for, in poetry as in life, to lead one's own life means to relive the lives of one's parents and, through them, of all one's ancestors; the duty of the present is neither to copy nor to deny the past but to resurrect it.

I shall not attempt, therefore, in this paper, to answer such questions as, "How good a poet is Yeats? Which are his best poems and why?"—that is the job of better critics

"Yeats as an Example," *The Kenyon Review,* X, 2 (spring, 1948), pp. 187-195, copyright, 1944, by Kenyon College.

than I and of posterity—but rather to consider him as a predecessor whose importance no one will or can deny, to raise, that is to say, such questions as, "What were the problems which faced Yeats as a poet as compared with ours? How far do they overlap? How far are they different? In so far as they are different, what can we learn from the way in which Yeats dealt with his world, about how to deal with our own?"

Let me begin with the element in his work which seems most foreign to us, his cosmology, his concern with the occult. Here, I think, is a curious fact. In most cases, when a major writer influences a beginner, that influence extends to his matter, to his opinions as well as his manner—think of Hardy, or Eliot, or D. H. Lawrence; yet, though there is scarcely a lyric written to-day in which the influence of his style and rhythm is not detectable, one whole side of Yeats, the side summed up in the *Vision*, has left virtually no trace.

However diverse our fundamental beliefs may be, the reaction of most of us to all that occult is, I fancy, the same: How on earth, we wonder, could a man of Yeats's gifts take such nonsense seriously? I have a further bewilderment, which may be due to my English upbringing, one of snobbery. How *could* Yeats, with his great aesthetic appreciation of aristocracy, ancestral houses, ceremonious tradition, take up something so essentially lower-middle class—or should I say Southern Californian—so ineluctably associated with suburban villas and clearly unattractive faces? A. E. Housman's pessimistic stoicism seems to be nonsense too, but at least it is a kind of nonsense that can be believed by a gentleman—but mediums, spells, the Mysterious Orient—*how* embarrassing. In fact, of course, it is to Yeats's credit, and an example to me, that he ignored such considerations, nor, granted that his Weltanschauung was false, can we claim credit for rejecting what we have no temptation to accept, nor deny that the poetry he wrote involving it is very good. What we should consider, then, is firstly, why Celtic mythology in his earlier phases, and occult symbolism in his later, should have attracted Yeats when they fail to attract us; secondly, what are the comparable kinds of beliefs to which we are drawn and why; thirdly, what is the relation between myth, belief, and poetry?

Yeats's generation grew up in a world where the great conflict was between the Religion of Reason and the Religion of Imagination, objective truth and subjective truth, the Universal and the Individual.

Further, Reason, Science, the general, seemed to be winning and Imagination, Art, and the individual on the defensive. Now in all conflicts it is the side which takes the offensive that defines the issues which their opponents have to defend, so that when scientists said, "Science is knowledge of reality, Art is a fairyland," the artists were driven to reply, "Very well, but fairies are fun, science is dull." When the former said, "Art has no relation to life," the latter retorted, "Thank God." To the assertion that "every mind can recognize the absolute truths of science, but the values of art are purely relative, an arbitrary affair of individual taste," came back the counterclaim, "Only the exceptional individual matters."

Thus, if we found Yeats adopting a cosmology apparently on purely aesthetic grounds, i.e., not because it is true but because it is interesting; or Joyce attempting to convert the whole existence into words; or even a dialectician like Shaw, after the most brilliant and devastating criticism of the pretensions of scientists, spoiling his case by being a crank and espousing Lamarckism, we must see their reactions, I think, if we are to understand them, in terms of a polemical situation in which they accepted—they probably could do nothing else—the antithesis between reason and imagination which the natural sciences of their times forced upon them, only reversing, with the excessive violence of men defending a narrow place against superior numbers, the value signs on each side.

Our situation is somewhat different. The true natural sciences like physics and chemistry no longer claim to explain the meaning of life (that presumption has passed to the so-called Social Sciences) nor—at least since the Atom Bomb—would any one believe them if they did. The division of which we are aware is not between Reason and Imagination but between the good and evil will, not between objectivity and subjectivity but between the integration of thought and feeling and their dissociation, not between the individual and the masses but between the social person and the impersonal state.

Consequently the dangers that beset us are different. We are unlikely to believe something because it would be fun to believe it; but we are very likely to do one of two things, either to say that everything is relative, that there is no absolute truth, or that those who do not hold what we believe to be absolute reject it out of malice.

When two people to-day engage in an argument, each tends to spend half of his time and energy not in producing evidence to support his point of view but in looking for the hidden motives which are causing his opponent to hold his. If they lose their tempers, instead of saying, "You are a fool," they say, "You are a wicked man."

No one now asserts that art ought to describe immoral persons or acts; but many assert that it must show those on the right side as perfectly moral and those on the wrong as completely immoral. An artist to-day is less likely than his predecessors to claim that his profession is supremely important but he is much more likely to sacrifice his artistic integrity for economic or political reward.

No private citizen to-day thinks seriously, "Here is superior me and there are all those other people"; but "Here are we, all in the same boat, and there is It, the Government." We are not likely to become snobs—the great houses have become state institutions anyway—but we can all too easily become anarchists who, by passively refusing to take part in political life, or by acting blindly in terms of our own advantage alone, promote the loss of that every individual liberty we would like to keep.

To return from life to poetry: any poet to-day, even if he deny the importance of dogma to life, can see how useful myths are to poetry—how much, for instance, they helped Yeats to make his private experiences public and his vision of public events personal. He knows, too, that in poetry all dogmas become myths; that the aesthetic value of the poem is the same whether the poet and/or the reader actively believe what it says or not. He is apt then to look around for some myth—any myth, he thinks, will do—to serve the same purpose for himself. What he overlooks is that the only kind of myth which will do for him must have one thing in common with believed dogma, namely, that the relation of the former to the poet, as of the latter to the soul, must be a personal one. The Celtic legends Yeats used were woven into his childhood—he really went to seances, he seriously studied all those absurd books. You cannot use a Weltanschauung like Psychoanalysis or Marxism or Christianity as a poetic myth unless it involves your emotions profoundly, and, if you have not inherited it, your emotions will never become involved unless you take it more seriously than as a mere myth.

Yeats, like us, was faced with the modern problem, i.e., of living in a society in which men are no longer supported by tradition without being aware of it, and in which, therefore, every individual who wishes to bring order and coherence into the stream of sensations, emotions, and ideas entering his consciousness, from without and within, is forced to do deliberately for himself what in previous ages had been done for him by family, custom, church, and state, namely the choice of the principles and presuppositions in terms of which he can make sense of his experience. There are, of course, always authorities in each field, but which expert he is to consult and which he is to believe are matters on which he is obliged to exercise his own free choice. This is very annoying for the artist as it takes up much time which he would greatly prefer to spend on his proper work, where he is a professional and not an amateur.

Because Yeats accepted the fact that we have lost the old nonchalance of the hand, being critics who but half create,

Timid, entangled, empty and abashed,
Lacking the countenance of our friends,

accepted it as a working condition and faced its consequences, he is an example to all who come after him. That is one reason why he may be called a major poet. There are others.

The difference between major and minor poetry has nothing to do with the difference between better and worse poetry. Indeed it is frequently the case that a minor poet produces more single poems which seem flawless than a major one, because it is one of the distinguishing marks of a major poet that he continues to develop, that the moment he has learnt how to write one kind of poem, he goes on to attempt something else, new subjects, new ways of treatment or both, an attempt in which he may quite possibly fail. He invariably feels, as Yeats puts it "the fascination of what's difficult"; or, in another poem,

I made my song a coat
Covered with embroideries
Out of old mythologies
From heel to throat;
But the fools caught it,
Wore it in the world's eyes
As though they'd wrought it.

Song, let them take it,
For there's more enterprise
In walking naked.

Further, the major poet not only attempts to solve new problems, but the problems he attacks are central to the tradition, and the lines along which he attacks them, while they are his own, are not idiosyncratic, but produce results which are available to his successors. Much as I admire his work, I consider Hopkins a minor poet, and one of my reasons for thinking so is that his attempt to develop a rhetoric to replace the Tennysonian rhetoric is too eccentric, the proof of which is that he cannot influence later poets in any fruitful way; they can only imitate him. Yeats on the other hand has effected changes which are of use to every poet. His contributions are not, I think, to new subject matter, nor to the ways in which poetic material can be organized—where Eliot for instance has made it possible for English poetry to deal with all the properties of modern city life, and to write poems in which the structure is musical rather than logical, Yeats sticks to the conventional romantic properties and the traditional step-by-step structure of stanzaic verse. His main legacies to us are two. First, he transformed a certain kind of poem, the occasional poem, from being either an official performance of impersonal virtuosity or a trivial *vers de societe* into a serious reflective poem of at once personal and public interest.

A poem such as *In Memory of Major Robert Gregory* is something new and important in the history of English poetry. It never loses the personal note of a man speaking about his personal friends in a particular setting—in *Adonais*, for instance, both Shelley and Keats disappear as people—and at the same time the occasion and characters acquire a symbolic public significance.

Secondly, Yeats released regular stanziac poetry, whether reflective or lyrical, from iambic monotony; the Elizabethans did this originally for dramatic verse, but not for lyric or elegiac. Thus:

What youthful mother, a shape upon her lap
Honey of generation had betrayed,
And that must sleep, shriek, struggle to escape
As recollection or the drug decide,
Would think her son, did she but see that shape

With sixty or more winters on its head,
A compensation for the pang of his birth,
Or the uncertainty of his setting forth?

Or take this:

Acquaintance; companion;
One dear brilliant woman;
The best endowed, the elect
All by their youth undone,
All, all, by that inhuman
Bitter glory wrecked.

But I have straightened out
Ruin, wreck and wrack;
I toiled long years and at length
Came to so deep a thought
I can summon back
All their wholesome strength.

What images are these
That turn dull-eyed away,
Or shift Time's filthy load,
Straighten aged knees,
Hesitate or stay?
What heads shake or nod?

In spite of all the rhythmical variations and the half-rhymes which provide freedom for the most natural and lucid speech, the formal base, i.e., the prosodic rhythms of iambic pentameter in the first, and iambic trimeter in the second, and the rhyme patterns which supply coherent dignity and music, these remain audible.

The magazine *Vogue* is preparing, I believe, to run two series of photographs, one called Contemporary Great, the other Contemporary Influences, a project which is calculated to cause considerable ill-feeling. Does a man feel prouder of what he achieves himself or of the effect he has on the achievements of posterity? Which epitaph upon a poet's grave would please him more: "I wrote some of the most beautiful poetry of my time" or "I rescued English lyric from the dead hand of Campion and Tom Moore"? I suspect that more poets would prefer the second than their readers would ever guess, particularly when, like Yeats, they are comfortably aware that the first is also true.

Morton Dauwen Zabel

THE FELICITY of the life of a man of genius can never be recognized until after the event of his achievement. His work alone justifies his acts and gifts and supports a *propter hoc* on his destiny. "The private history of any sincere work looms large with its own completeness," said Henry James: this is the retrospective logic of greatness that is most passionately envied by common men. Once the validity or strength of the artist's work is clear, every chance or mischance of his career—every risk or peril that would ordinarily deform or defeat the average existence—takes on the justice of destiny, the beatitude of his vocation. Form is imposed on the chaos or confusion of experience. Life receives the stamp of purpose and of permanence. So the dark night of Hopkins or Rilke rivals the sun's fine weather of Goethe; the agony of Baudelaire becomes more enviable than the serenity of Ronsard; Blake's madness proves as sane as Wordsworth's sobriety; Rimbaud snatches from defeat a triumph surer than Hugo's. To loom large in the dimensions of art is so great a passion in men that even those who fear or despise it are willing to submit to its price in indignity or embarrassment if they may share in its endurance. "Seven cities warr'd for Homer, being dead." The citizens of three English towns competed for the immortality of surviving as the swine of Dickens' Eatanswill. Statemen claim a share in the tragedies of Poe and Dostoevsky. Men and women of impregnable respectability sue for the honor of having been vilified by Heine or seduced by Byron. Redeem us, they plead, from our safety, our boredom, our nonentity. Proust's law touches all of us: "Life as it flows is so much time wasted, and nothing can ever be recovered or truly possessed save under the form of eternity, which is also the form of art."

An age as baffled and demoralizing as ours makes men more anxious than ever to recover themselves from its waste and stupidity by possessing an identity in the work of its image-makers and heroes of form. The impulse may be tragic: witness its results in the worship of demagogues and symbolic heroes. It may also be more happily regenerative: we live half our lives in the world that James or Proust, Eliot

"Yeats: The Book and the Image," reprinted with revisions from *The Nation*, 151, 15 (October 12, 1940), 160-161; and 156, 10 (March 6, 1943), 348-350; by permission of the author and publishers.

or Rilke, has arrested and made solid under our feet. Thus also the great appeal of the work of Yeats, with its eloquent testimony of personal success in an age of confusion and defeat. His poetry in its sixty-year evolution and triumph is already a document on its times. Now that the life out of which it issued is complete, his career becomes more than ever an object of attention and analysis. Joseph Hone's biography—the first full record of Yeats's career thus far attempted—is certainly one of the most engaging records of the poetic life our century is likely to yield.[1]

Of the two difficulties that alternately harass the biographers of poets—the embarrassment of poverty that comes of finding little or nothing in the life to account for the poetry; the rarer embarrassment of riches that comes of finding too much —the historian of Yeats obviously works under the second. His problem is further complicated by the fact that Yeats anticipated him, in verse, prose, and autobiography, at every point of his task. Yeats took his life, almost from the beginning, as "an experiment that needs analysis and record" ("at least my generation so valued personality that it thought so"). He sought "an image not a book"—the continuous vitality of symbolic experience and action, not the tact and decorum of a purposive career. ("Self-interest and self-preservation," said his greatest teacher, his father, "are the death of poetry.") His energies were held in tension between purpose and instinct: between seeking spiritual victory in "an intellectual daily recreation of all that exterior fate snatches away" and making an art that should be "a fountain jetting from the entire hopes, memories, and sensations of the body." ("I must," he wrote in his diary in 1909, "keep one note from leading to another that I may not surrender myself to literature. . . . Neither Christ nor Buddha nor Socrates wrote a book, for to do that is to exchange life for a logical process.") He took it as his supreme task to "understand why there is a deep enmity between a man and his destiny, and why a man lives nothing but his destiny." The life he lived exists for us in two realities: historic and imaginative, actual and symbolic, book and image. It is with both those realities—with their mutual necessity, their complementary existence—that every biographer or critic of Yeats is taxed and every reader faced if Yeats's value for the men of his time is to be realized.

It was the book of Yeats's life rather than its image that

[1] Joseph Hone, *W. B. Yeats, 1855-1939* (New York, 1943).

Mr. Hone set himself to write, as it was the symbolic image, in its fullest derivation and reference, that concerned Louis MacNeice in his recent study of the poetry.[2] The work of biography could hardly, at this early stage of Yeats's posthumous history, have fallen into abler hands than Mr. Hone's. His skill and tact—already seen in his excellent *Life of George Moore* of 1936, a better book than this one by virtue of its simpler subject and freer conditions—here work under official privileges which, though they have imposed inhibitions that make the poet's later career obscure at a good many points, will be enjoyed by none of his successors. What Keats said of Shakespeare is far more explicitly true of Yeats: he led a life of allegory upon which his work is the comment. So we examine the full record: childhood in Dublin and Sligo among those "old fathers" and "half legendary men" of the West — Butlers, Pollexfens, Corbets, Middletons; schooldays in Dublin and London with Yeats's father a mentor in wisdom and sympathy apparently unrivalled among the fathers of poets; the Eighties and Nineties in London and Paris where Yeats was divided between the "tragic generation"—Dowson, Wilde, Johnson—and those men of "militant action"—Morris, Henley, O'Leary, Shaw, Maud Gonne, the Parnellites —who were preparing the future; the return to Ireland, a dramatic moment in modern literature, to join with Lady Gregory, Martyn, Moore, and Synge in the battles of the Abbey Theatre; the return to the larger world and to a poetry of responsibilities; the drama of 1916, of civil war, and of the new Free State; marriage at fifty-two; the final creative phase announced by *The Tower;* and the apotheosis of old age. We learn the importance to Yeats's thought or verse of mystics like W. T. Horton, Mohini Chatterji, and MacGregor Mathers the cabbalist, of T. W. Rolleston, Ian Hamilton, Thomas Davis, Olivia Shakespear, and Mabel Beardsley; of the women who so decisively influenced Yeats's character (though here the facts are still shrouded); of the conflicting politics of Maud Gonne, the Parnellites, the Unionists, the Treaty party, and the O'Duffy Blueshirts with whom he temporized in his last decade. Yeats saw his friends and enemies in a hierarchy of values, and the pageant of these people—"Ireland's history in their lineaments"—not only furnishes a drama of causes unrivalled in modern poetic experience but an annotation of the materials whereby Yeats substanced and tested the conceptions his imagination and philosophical ex-

[2] Louis MacNeice, *The Poetry of W. B. Yeats* (London and New York, 1941).

periments were yielding him.[3]

His life has a greater import that that of its rich opportunities and contacts. It is an emblem of modern experience, a parable of intellectual and moral conflict in an age of unstable thought, "skeptical faith," moral irresponsibility and evasion. The shape his career assumes is the shape imposed on it not only by his experiments in art, thought, and action, but by the conflict of personal will at grips with the typically modern passivity to fate and historical necessity which he saw as an evil of his times. His art is so urgent and compelling that it tends to make his readers impose an excessive justice, a kind of *ex post facto* idealism, on his experience and ideas. But this tendency, which may often go to extremes, is countered by another: the critical repudiation of Yeats's way of art and thought—the acceptance of his poetry without admitting the truth of the forces and conditions that brought it into being. One critic has already stressed Yeats as "ignorant of philosophy" and presented as literal the poet's own statement in *A Vision* that his symbolic system may be regarded as "stylistic arrangements of experience" that "have helped me to hold in a single thought reality and justice." Another has announced that Yeats "never thought well" and that, while their "transmutation into poetry" is convincing, "his excursions into Berkeley and Plotinus, his attempts to rebut Bertrand Russell, his gleeful infatuation with viscous Oriental mysticism, are pathetic." All this comes from the contemporary habit of looking on beliefs and spiritual processes as mainly if not wholly instrumental, justified only after the fact of their utility or stimulus is demonstrated in a result. It tends to be the stress made by Mr. MacNeice in his highly resourceful and suggestive study, which interprets Yeats from the vantage-point of a "reality" of which he was largely innocent but which a later generation has at its command; and it reappears in W. H. Auden's review of the Hone book when he says that

> Yeats's temptation—he never succumbed to it completely—to regard art as a religious ritual damages the art for it prevents the artist from taking serious risks of failure. Magnificent as is their diction, I cannot but feel that his poems lack a certain inner resonance. Each exists solidly enough in its frame of reference, but rarely transcends it. Comparing his poetry with that, for instance, of T. S. Eliot and Robert Graves, I find it, beautiful as it is, lacking in seriousness, which,

[3] Cf. "The Thinking of the Body: Yeats in the Autobiographies," by the present writer in *The Southern Review*, VII, No. 3 (winter, 1941), pp. 562-591.

of course, has nothing to do with solemnity.

This point is serious and it is legitimately raised, but its implication must be clarified. Yeats's work undoubtedly lacks a fully convincing "architectonic" (to revive Arnold's word for it), a consistent and applicable structure of belief and reference. The structure it has often appears personal, provisional, eclectic, and unstable except in terms of a personal need and imperative. I mean to join in no aspersion on Yeats's verse—to me it is inferior to nothing in modern literature—when I admit that its recurring provisionality keeps it from having the integrated seriousness, superior to both personal and historical emotion, that is the strength of Eliot's. Of this lack—but also of the compensating zeal, energy, and sincerity of his interests—Yeats's life supplies an explanation. He *was* aesthetic in his origins and temperament. He did accept Lionel Johnson's idea of life as ritual well past the age when such consciousness of function and attitude can remain safely overt in a poet. He did risk the laming of his faculties and the enervation of his motives by constant manipulation and curiosity, and his achievement is in a serious degree a victory over willful indulgences of temperament and sensation. Yet it is a sign of Yeats's real capacities that he knew he had to grow from sensation to emotion, from reverie to thought, from passivity to action, from aestheticism to art; and the growth is as much marked by intention as by natural or instinctive process. The growth was personal, sensible, moral, before it was anything else—historical, philosophical, critical. To deprive it of reality or seriousness is to set up a paradox between Yeats's character and his poetry that admits no solution. If the poetry is real, sound, and true, the experience and "thinking" out of which it issued must—*for him*—be so likewise; and if they are not, it is not.

Yeats would never admit thinking to be an exclusive prerogative of the intellect. It must be a process and occupation of the whole man and of the objects to which his thought is applied—his actions, his friends and enemies, the cones and gyres of *A Vision* that describe the processes of history; of experience in good and evil alike. His father once praised a man because he "loved humanity too much to hate any man, and knew too much of history to hate any opinion." Yeats "studied hatred" and cultivated "rage," but however valuable he felt them in his creative life, he knew there is a love that transcends them and without which knowledge, sympathy, forgiveness, and wisdom are impossible. This is perhaps not the moment to hope that such a counsel will be adopted by civilized men. An uncivilized work must first be finished. But to those who tend to regard squeamishly Yeats's ideas of history, of the aristocratic principle, and of what many are now emphasizing as his "proto-Fascist sympathies," it may be a good moment to suggest that unless Yeats's doctrine is recurred to after present disasters are put by, we may entertain little hope of emerging from "the growing murderousness of the world" or the anarchy of righteousness that has brought it about. Yeats's realities are the realities of our human capacity for vitality and sincerity. His resonance is that of the poetic integrity, whose imagination includes philosophy. If the framework of his thought and images deprives him, through its specialized symbolism, of taking a place among the very greatest poets, it nevertheless establishes him as a poet preeminent in modern times for his sense of the moral wholeness of humanity and history.

Yeats's life had the superb advantages of its drama and its heroism. But before we claim the drama and heroism as our own, with the ready vicariousness which his poetry encourages, it would do us well to remember that they were the achievements of a man who had the power to shape and control them; who wrought them and the poetry that expresses them out of ordeal, division, and a full share of bitterness. It is also necessary to remember that the success of art is never easy. Yeats's life may appear felicitous now that his work is done, but its felicity will prove misleading and his poetry deluding if we imagine that we can enjoy them by assuming our own superiority, as thinkers, realists, and exponents of justice, to the man upon whom it fell to *prove* that his life was fortunate and his talent genuine. There was nothing unreal or facile about that task. And it would be the last irony if Yeats, who hated abstraction, should end by having an abstraction made of his art through its divorce from the truth of his experience or from the realism of thought and imagination which made that truth possible.

II

The tragedy of the poet who dies young is an accepted tradition of martyrdom and heroism in the mythology of literature. It thrives with all the benefits of rarity, moral indignation, and potentialities that remain safely undecided in the pathos of speculation. The tragedy of the poet who dies old is another story—commonplace, human, seldom inspiring. It too is a matter of common acceptance, but chiefly as evidence on the ways of human compromise, or as a source of grim satisfaction to the laity who look to the frustrations of genius for consolation in their own defeats. Even in cases of popularly successful talent, reaction can make the old age of art a bitter experience in isolation and lonely endurance. If a poet placates or defeats the enemies that contrive the martyrdom of a young genius—social hostility, moral conventions, practical necessity—his success carries the odium of a truce. A Goethe, Hardy, or Yeats is permitted to rely on none of the arguments that make the silencing of a Keats, Pushkin, or Rimbaud heroic. Every deviation he shows from consistency or organic maturity is held suspect as a mark of eccentricity or imposture. *"Peu de gens savent être vieux."* A poet is usually dishonored not only when he fails to learn but when he tries.

Yeats's long life and achievement have not lacked recognition during the past twenty years, but it seems to be the thing once more to hold his career in renewed skepticism, to discount his struggle with modern life, and to diminish his spiritual ordeal to "the quarrel he made with himself." He is written down as an exotic by-product of the major European tradition. His peak was reached in *The Tower* and *The Winding Stair*, and Mr. F. R. Leavis was right in noting in the *Last Poems* an inferiority of organization, a weakening of the positives of "sensual music" and "monuments of unaging intellect" that created the subtle and majestic tension of "Sailing to Byzantium." But even he underestimated the fact that Yeats wrote for over a decade after that poem's appearance and was constitutionally unwilling to make it an end-stop of his art or to accept the common definition of the moment in life at which organization should be permanently established. What is more confusing is that this skepticism has shifted from Yeats's artistry and thought to his character. Mr. Auden, reducing Yeats's gift to one of diction and word-magic ("always more concerned with whether or not a phrase sounded effective than with the truth of its idea or the honesty of its emotion") and impugning his sincerity for an "utter lack of effort to relate his aesthetic *Weltanschauung* with that of science," has denied him the refuge of selfhood itself, that "foul rag-and-bone shop of the heart" to which the desertion of his masks and legends finally abandoned him. Mr. MacNeice, reviving the notion that the public considered Yeats "safe because he was an exotic" and that "his ingredients become odder and odder," has also emphasized the idea that Yeats's temperament was dominantly histrionic, veering between aristocratic sympathies and a "praise of war" falsely inferred from his envy of "lust and rage," and failing in its reaction against the aesthetic isolation of his youth because of a "constitutional inhumanity." Yeats provoked and survived many such shifts of respect and skepticism in his lifetime. But when the complex integrity of his whole career, his passionate sense of the conflict between art and life, and his hard-won insights are thus reduced by moral analysis—when, indeed, we hear of a young English poet's verdict that he was "a bad old man"—we begin to feel that his critics are not a thousand miles removed from the musician who once wrote him: "You should have heard my setting of your 'Innisfree' as it was sung in the open here by two thousand Boy Scouts."

Yeats made his life and art vulnerable to accusations of vanity and instability because he combined the exorbitant self-consciousness of his post-romantic generation with continuous efforts to resist the confines of his age and its hostile abstractions of science and society, which to him spelled the blight not only of poetry but of the personal life. He is, superficially viewed, the major escapist of modern literature. His first flight was from the moral and scientific determinism of the Eighties (Ibsen, Tyndall, Huxley) to the mysteries of legend and poetic symbolism as the Irish myths, Pater, and Paris taught them. His induction into these rites ("traditional sanctity and loveliness") was barely achieved when the disgust and reaction of an intense personal crisis drove him, in the middle Nineties, to nationalism and Irish political culture. This extraversion enriched his art and energies at the cost of convincing him of the enmity of popular emotions to art and idealism, and of the sacrifice of human worth that even the noblest heroism entails. ("Did that play of mine send out/ Certain men the English shot?") He turned again: to abstractions of "pure mind" in the quietism of India; from this to Balzac's aggressive principle or the compulsions of human personality as shown by the Blakean symbolism of the Great Wheel; from the Wheel, intractably altering its phases in the successive editions of his essays and of *A Vision*, back to the simplest elements of folk nature as they exist in ballad and martial chant. The last phase of all, final in its unflattering austerity, was his inescapable retreat to the secret courage of the heart where, bereft of his "circus animals" and no longer transfigured as "character isolated by a deed," he faced his fundamental identity as a man. In that confrontation he found, like Baudelaire before him, his highest realism and his severest passion as a lyric poet.

To demand that a career as bred in conflict as this, exposing itself with this courage and refusing the protective mandates of moral or political orthodoxy, should emerge without an exaggeration of personality or with its passionate sense of hostilities "organized" into a perfectly lucid balance, is to go beyond the scale of human merit. Yeats's whole animus derives from his hatred of such mandates, of the tyranny of abstraction. The travail of his people's soul meant less to him, when it hardened into ignorant persecution, than the suffering and death of John Synge. The rough justice of modern warfare collapsed into ignominious baseness when the punishing of treason meant that Roger Casement's character must be officially slandered and an unpopular man be denied "his last refuge—Martyrdom." It is true that Yeats's insistence, in his last poems, on his isolation, his scorn of complacency, and his prolonged virility suggests the failure of another balance, that of personal certitude. The pride and contempt in Yeats's later manner are continuously harassed by a persecuting sense of guilt. "Lust and Rage" were his goads to the end of his life. He was never able to rise to the serenity of a grand old age. But it is a question if the true poet ever should—if a restlessness of vision and the continuous distress of human sympathies are not more important to him. "I got sleep & tired & spent my day in bed and thought of my soul," he wrote Dorothy Wellesley in 1936. "Then I noticed that every time I thought of my soul I used some second-hand phrase & knew by that that I was thinking of my soul from ambition & vanity. I said to myself 'Your job is to avoid deep places & die blaspheming' & I got well at once."

The *Last Poems* revive the the full range of Yeats's personae and symbols. Their oppositions are fixed in peasant character or political action and in the timeless and indifferent superiority of aesthetic and ideal absolutes: on the one hand in love, gallantry, wickedness, faith, sensual delight and misery, and self-reckless courage as embodied in "High Talk" and "Hound Voices," the martyrs of 1916, the tragedies of Parnell and Casement, in O'Rahilly, Colonel Martin, John Kinsella, the lady and the chambermaid; on the other hand in "Beautiful Lofty Things," the arrested image of perfection in the bronze head of a museum ("As though a sterner eye looked through her eye. On this foul world in its decline and fall"), in a memory of Maud Gonne ("Pallas Athene in that straight back and arrogant head"), in the eternal figure of a young girl. It has been said that in later life Yeats turned only to the simplest or most complex things, scorning all middle grounds. But the truth is that simple and complex things existed for him only in a state of constant attraction and repulsion, of continuous interdependence. This oscillation of qualities made all reality a complex middle ground of polarities, refusing simplification and dreading the purity of abstract synthesis. His humanism is that of Hopkins:

Nor angel insight can
Learn how the heart is hence:
Since all the make of man
Is law's indifference.

It is right to ascribe to Yeats an obsession by dialectic. His oppositions play restlessly and imperatively against one another. The antithesis is never resolved. It was his special role as man and poet to represent that inexhaustible tension and irresolution in all its meanings.

The letters he wrote to Dorothy Wellesley in the last five years of his life[4] show that it kept him alive and writing to the end, the source of his energy and delight. As a poet's letters they are without pompous authority or didactic benevolence, even though they also lack the intense critical and moral perception that appears in the letters of Keats, Hopkins, or Rilke. They form an annotation of his last years and his last poems. They show no easy tranquillity, no flattering satisfaction of mind or achievement, if also little power of piercing with a phrase or an insight. Their wisdom is agitated. In this they reflect the last poems. Of these only a small number are in Yeats's richest manner ("A Bronze Head," "To D.W.," "The Statues," "John Kinsella's Lament," "Politics," "Under Ben Bulben." "The Circus Animals' Desertion," and the two Casement ballads). The others are often marginal, or echo his earlier work. Yeats lacked the anguish of extreme penetration as Hopkins knew it. His rhetorical habit and symbolist derivations deprived him of that "terrible pathos." He lacked on the other hand a mastery of critical

[4] *Letters on Poetry from W. B. Yeats to Dorothy Wellesley* (London and New York, 1940).

organization, of condensing allegory and controlled vision as they appear in Rilke and Eliot. The "antinomies" were always too close to him. His last two plays show an exaggeration of disgust that makes them dramatically flaccid through their excess of anti-human revulsion. Lyrics like "Sweet Dancer" and "The Wild Wicked Old Man" revive the simple pathos of his earliest years. The grand manner and the naive, the terror and the pathos of beauty, were never harmonized in his thought. What Goethe achieved in old age in the *West-Oestlicher Divan* is never fully arrived at. But Yeats shows us anew—he is perhaps the only modern British poet to do so—what Thomas Mann has reminded us of in Goethe: how the ideal of aesthetic autonomy must be constantly forced out of superiority or abstraction by the "Antaean compensation" of the earth, of human fact and necessity. Yeats lacked Goethe's intellectual and moral capacities but he is Goethe's superior as a lyric poet by the fact that art and earth were never separated in his life or verse. They exist only by their mutual inadequacy. It is in their complementary necessity that they enter his poetry, bringing the full realism of the lyric experience and giving his work both its emotional validity and its unflagging beauty as song.

If this realism, and its power to illuminate human struggle and aspiration, is to stand convicted of "constitutional inhumanity," the question is: What kind of humanity do we want? Yeats lived in an age that gave him opportunities to see all types of human energy and ambition at work. He found reasons to be edified or enlightened by few of them. He had no taste for prophetic or moral arrogance. He knew that no one can be blinder than a self-sufficient artist. He saw that no one can be crueler than the common man. He summoned men into a society, an order, where aristocrats of spirit might give the ignorant a standard to live by, but where the passionate and the miserable also give the proud a reason to be humble. This was his conception of the artist's mediation, and he not only used the historic opportunities that came his way to make that mediation active, but gave his own nature and character over to the learning of the lesson. He provides an occasion for learning the meaning of the present moment in history, not from frenzied oracles and spokesmen of righteousness, but from the ordeal and truth of self-knowledge which every man must face before he may claim a knowledge of humanity. This was for Yeats the one genuine source of energy and fortitude, and it saved him from despair when he saw Europe standing, at the moment of his death, at the edge of a new disaster:

All things fall and are built again,
And those that build them again are gay.

Yeats took forty years to learn what Lady Gregory meant when she taught him Aristotle's maxim: "To think like a wise man but to express oneself like the common people." It took the long endurance of his troubled and distracted career to justify his epitaph: "Cast a cold eye/On life, on death." When, at the age of sixty, he received from the Swedish Academy the medal of the Nobel Award, he wrote, after the ceremony: "All is over, and I am able to examine my medal . . . It shows a young man listening to a Muse, who stands young and beautiful with a great lyre in her hand, and I think as I examine it, 'I was good-looking once like that young man, but my unpractised verse was full of infirmity, my Muse old as it were; and now I am old and rheumatic, and nothing to look at, but my Muse is young. I am even persuaded that she is like those Angels in Swedenborg's vision, and moves perpetually toward the day-spring of her youth.' " In 1937 he wrote: "I have recovered a power of moving the common man I had in my youth. The poems I can write now will go into the general memory." A month before his death he wrote: "I do nothing but write verse."

Walter E. Houghton

WRITING IN 1906, Yeats spoke of two ways before literature —upward into ever growing subtlety until poetry was written for only a small and learned audience or downward until all was "simplified and solidified again."

"That is the choice of choices—the way of the bird until common eyes have lost us, or to the market carts." By and large, Yeats had gone the first road, both in substance and in style. After the poetry addressed to Maud Gonne and his friends at Coole Park and the satire of Dublin Philistines, the range and density increased, until such complex poems as "The Second Coming" and "Nineteen Hundred and Nineteen" not only expressed a whole vision of modern society plunging toward anarchy but "placed" that vision in a larger perspective of historical cycles. At the same time, this terrifying picture of "the growing murderousness of the world" forced him again, though not so completely as in the eighties and nineties, to escape inward to a happier world of the imagination:

I need some mind that, if the cannon sound
From every quarter of the world, can stay
Wound in mind's pondering
As mummies in the mummy-cloth are wound.

By 1916 this necessity led him upward in the further sense of mystical elevation, renewed the early desire for trance, and brought the deeper study of occult literature that resulted in *Per Amica Silentia Lunae* (1917) and the philosophical poetry of Michael Robartes and Owen Aherne. When *A Vision* appeared in 1925, he seemed lost again "upon *Hodos Chameliontos*"; and two years later he was rejecting the sensual music of "whatever is begotton, born, and dies" for the music of the soul, singing the "monuments of unaging intellect," and was longing to sail from Ireland to the holy city of Byzantium, out of nature into the artifice of eternity. In the meanwhile, as his thought had grown more subtle and esoteric, his medium had become increasingly packed and allusive, the symbols often drawn from occult sources;

"Yeats and Crazy Jane: The Hero in Old Age," from *Modern Philology*, XL, 4 (May, 1943), 316-329.

and the complex orchestration of the ode supplanted the lyric as the principal form. In 1928, the year of *The Tower* and Yeats's sixty-third year, it seemed impossible that he would ever go downward to the market carts. And then suddenly, with his amazing flexibility, he wheeled away from the intellectual and exotic to the simple and elemental, from the mystical to the sensual, from the lords and ladies of Byzantium to Crazy Jane and Jack the Journeyman, and wrote, as I think, his finest single volume, *Words for Music Perhaps* (1932).[1]

The new departure was not a reversal of direction but a radical shift in emphasis. Yeats never abandoned his metaphysic; it appears even in the Crazy Jane poems. On the other hand, a strain of natural passion cuts through the visionary mood of the preceding work. As Cleanth Brooks has pointed out, "Sailing to Byzantium" is a poem of conflict: the desire to pass out of nature is unfulfilled, the sensual music still beats in the veins. And the same tension is often present in *The Tower*. Indeed, the preface to *A Vision* had prophesied that a new poetry, simple and passionate, would take the place of "philosophy":

> I am longing to put it [*A Vision*] out of reach that I may write the poetry it seems to have made possible. I can now, if I have the energy, find the simplicity I have sought in vain. . . .
>
> I would forget the wisdom of the East and remember its grossness and its romance.

Yet the poetry that immediately followed, with the exception of "A woman young and old," was neither simple nor gross; and the wisdom of the East remained dominant. When the proof sheets of *A Vision* were corrected, Yeats plunged even more deeply into metaphysics, read Berkeley and all of Plotinus, went from Plotinus "to his predecessors and successors." And he might have gone on in this direction but for the long and severe illness, or illnesses, from October, 1927, to the spring of 1929, when he lived under almost constant physical and nervous depression, and twice, from pneumonia in the fall of 1927 and from Malta fever a

[1] The only criticism I know is "Crazy Jane," by Louis MacNeice, in *The Poetry of W. B. Yeats* (1941), chap. viii; and the review by Theodore Spencer in *Hound and Horn,* VII (1933), 164-74. MacNeice fails to recognize the fundamental pattern of heroic tragedy or the close relation of the volume to Yeats's early criticism; but his remarks on lyric form and its connection with Blake are excellent. Spencer does not attempt much more than an analysis of Yeats's use of refrain. My chief obligation is to my friend C. L. Barber for his stimulating suggestions made in conversation.

year later, nearly died. The crucial connection between these facts and the new poetry is partly revealed by Yeats' important note:

> "A Dialogue of Self and Soul" was written in the spring of 1928 during a long illness, indeed finished the day before a Cannes doctor told me to stop writing. Then in the spring of 1929 life returned as an impression of the uncontrollable energy and daring of the great creators; it seemed that but for journalism and criticism, all that evasion and explanation, the world would be torn in pieces. I wrote "Mad as the Mist and Snow," a mechanical little song, and after that almost all that group of poems called in memory of those exultant weeks "Words for Music Perhaps." . . . Since then I have added a few poems to "Words for Music Perhaps," but always keeping the mood and plan of the first poems.

In the implied relationship between the illness, the "Dialogue," and the group of lyrics, the second term provides an invaluable clue to the effect of the first and the interpretation of the third. For the "Dialogue" is the autobiographical record of the same experience which a year later, in the greater detachment of convalescence, Yeats projected into the dramatic characters of Crazy Jane and Tom the Lunatic.

In Part I of the "Dialogue" the Soul reiterates the escapist appeal of *A Vision.* "Fix every wandering thought," it tells the Self, "upon that quarter where all thought is done" and continues with the promise that, if imagination scorn the earth, ancestral night can "deliver from the crime of death and birth." In answer the Self holds up Sato's blade, "emblematical of love and war," and claims "as by a soldier's right a charter to commit the crime once more." In Part II the pretense of impersonal debate is dropped, as Yeats speaks out himself. The sickening review of his life as one of clumsiness and calumny, failure and frustration, is countered by triumphant acceptance and self-assertion:

My Self. I am content to follow to its source,
Every event in action or in thought;
Measure the lot, forgive myself the lot!
When such as I cast out remorse
So great a sweetness flows into the breast
We must laugh and we must sing,
We are blest by everything,
Everything we look upon is blest.

In the crisis of his illness Yeats discovered what alone could sustain him—not escape from the body but return to the body, to the personality as a whole; not Platonic ecstasy but what he called "heroic ecstasy." And this discovery is the basic theme of *Words for Music Perhaps.* He was thinking of himself when he wrote to Dorothy Wellesley, after a similar illness of hers in 1938: "It brings the soul back to itself: we sink down into our own soil and take root again."

This is true in a further sense, for the roots of *Words for Music Perhaps,* in form as well as in thought, lie far in the past. Many years earlier Yeats had formulated his conception of the hero and heroic tragedy.[2] After a first embodiment in the Pre-Raphaelite plays on legendary kings and queens, the whole program was abandoned, as Yeats moved upward to his intellectual and philosophical poetry. Then when his illness turned his mind back to the past and called up the heroic attitude, he rededicated his art to the early ideal, but in a new and more profound form. He stripped it of romantic distortions, gave it deeper contact with the common lot of men—and so at last sang "the heroic song I have longed for." Only by returning through the "Dialogue" to the critical definition of the hero and heroic poetry can we recognize, not merely the crucial place of *Words for Music Perhaps* in Yeats's whole development, but its full meaning and instrinsic weight.

II. THE CONCEPT OF THE HERO

Almost every influence of his early life drew Yeats to the heroic idea. The conscious sense of a family tradition of soldiers and sailors, "swift indifferent men"; the aristocratic tradition of "the proud, the heroic mind," which he found still existing in Ireland, "where a woman was remembered for her beauty, a man admired for his authority, his physical strength, his birth or his wildness"; and the third tradition, Irish legend, first revived in the eighties when "Standish O'Grady, his mind full of Homer, retold the story of Cuchulain that he might bring back an heroic ideal." These influences from the past were deepened by Yeats's reaction to the Victorian present. We may discount his early scheme for a "Castle of Heroes," built on an island in Loch Gill, as the escapist tendency from which he presently re-

[2] In the first essay on Blake (1897), in *The Irish Dramatic Movement* (1907), and in the essays called "Discoveries" (1906), "Poetry and Tradition" (1907), and "The Tragic Theatre" (1910).

covered. But the conscious need for religious faith and a tougher character was permanent. When Huxley and Darwin robbed him of Christian belief and he made a new religion out of myth and legend, its central dogma was the truth of whatever "those imaginary people" had spoken: the revelation of Odysseus was the revelation of heaven. This identification of god and the hero was reaffirmed just after the publication of the Crazy Jane poems, in *The Resurrection,* where the Greek says of the gods: "The man who lives heroically gives them the only earthly body that they covet. He, as it were, copies their gestures and their acts." This is Yeats's doctrine of discipline by conscious imitation. Early in life the Mask he set up, at the opposite pole from the gentle and dreamy Willie, was the heroic image as seen in Hamlet:

> I wished to become self-possessed, to be able to play with hostile minds as Hamlet played, to look in the lion's face, as it were, with unquivering eyelash. . . . Discovering that I was only self-possessed with people I knew intimately, I would often go to a strange house where I knew I would spend a wretched hour for schooling sake. I did not discover that Hamlet had his self-possession from no schooling but from indifference and passion-conquering sweetness, and that less heroic minds can but hope it from old age.[8]

This was a prophecy at once true of Crazy Jane and of Yeats himself. In the last analysis, however, it was "the romantic movement with its turbulent heroism, its self-assertion," that provoked the worship of dynamic personality and led him to define "an exciting person, whether the hero of a play or the maker of poems," as one who "will display the greatest volume of personal energy."

If energy is good in itself, if the highest praise is to say of a man " 'What a nature,' 'How much abundant life' " the hero must enjoy a special code of morals, an inner sense of "purity," and a gigantic pride. In the essays on Blake (1897) Yeats often cites the assertion of impulse against the repressive code of rational morality:

> Passions, because most living, are most holy . . . and man shall enter eternity borne upon their wings.
>
> Those who are cast out are all those who, having no passions of their own, because no intellect, have spent their lives in curbing and governing other people's lives by the various arts of poverty and cru-

[8] Cf. *The Autobiography of William Butler Yeats* (1938 ed.), pp. 43-44: "For many years Hamlet was an image of heroic self-possession for the poses of youth and childhood to copy, a combatant of the battle within myself."

elty of all kinds. The modern Church crucifies Christ with the head downwards.

These were the weapons that Yeats sharpened for his defense of amoral art against bigoted Catholics and Dublin Philistines. And, in doing so, he drew for support on the heroes of Shakespeare. Their violation of the Ten Commandments he found justified by the higher court of our instinctive sympathy:

> This character who delights us may commit murder like Macbeth, or fly the battle for his sweetheart as did Antony or betray his country like Coriolanus, and yet we will rejoice in every happiness that comes to him and sorrow at his death as if it were our own. It is no use telling us that the murderer and the betrayer do not deserve our sympathy. . . . We are caught up into another code, we are in the presence of a higher court.

And yet, he added, "there is some law, some code, some judgment." Anthony must not rail at Cleopatra or Coriolanus abate "that high pride of his in the presence of death." It is the positive virtues of courage, love, physical strength, decisive action, and above all, abounding energy that win our sympathy and form the higher law of heroic morality.

It follows that the hero is freed from every form of hesitation, both moral and physical. Acting from impulse that is good, he feels, as Yeats says, an "instinctive harmony" a sense of joyous confidence and inner purity. Cuchulain "seemed to me a heroic figure because he was creative joy separated from fear." The statues of Mausolus and Artemisia became "images of an unpremediated joyous energy, that neither I nor any other man, racked by doubt and inquiry, can achieve." Nor is the hero troubled by regret or remorse: Kevin O'Higgins was

A soul incapable of remorse or rest;
A revolutionary soldier kneeling to be blessed.

It was with O'Higgins' assassination in mind that Yeats wrote, in the lyric called "Death":

A great man in his pride
Confronting murderous men
Casts derision upon
Supersession of breath.

We remember the "high pride" of Coriolanus in the presence of death. It is, of course, at the moment of tragedy that the hero reaches his full stature, since "only the greatest obstacle that can be contemplated without despair, rouses the will to full intensity." He must at once accept his destiny, not only without rage or fear but with all the strength of heroic fortitude. It is the paradox of self-surrender and self-assertion.

As I implied in the description of the Mask, this whole conception was a discipline Yeats set himself as a man. Timid and fearful, painfully self-conscious and critical, beset by his Protestant ancestry with a Puritan conscience, he tried for repose, for self-possession, through the deliberate assumption of the heroic image. A passage from "Anima Hominis" (1917) illuminates for a moment the psychological pattern. He speaks of coming home from public meetings full of "gloom and disappointment," having

> overstated everything from a desire to vex or startle, from hostility that is but fear. . . . But when I shut my door and light the candle, . . . I begin to dream of eyelids that do not quiver before the bayonet: all my thoughts have ease and joy, I am all virtue and confidence.

Part II of the "Dialogue of Self and Soul" develops on the same basic pattern, but in a deeper groove; for then it was no question of social clumsiness capable of dispersion by aesthetic revery but a tragic crisis to be sustained only by full realization of the heroic attitude. In the final stanza the acceptance of life as tragedy, the self absolution and purification followed by exultant joy, culminate in the sense of sanctity, also ascribed to O'Higgins but extended, by a natural transference, to the whole universe. A year later he achieved again the same high mood and also projected his own tragic heroism into Crazy Jane and Tom the Lunatic.

III. FORM

When the heroic theme was reborn in Yeats's old age, its image and its medium were new. Both innovations had the same source—a fresh sympathy with the common man. In the early period the hero still meant for Yeats the hero of Aristotelian tradition, not peasant but warrior-king. He was more concerned, he admitted in 1905, "with the heroic legend than with the folk"; and it is significant that he divided Irish drama into two kinds—"plays of peasant life and plays of a romantic and heroic life," that is to say, those of Synge, with their "ugly, deformed or sinful people," and those of Yeats, in which the "masterful spirits" are kings and queens. Outside of legend, his heroes were his own aristocratic circle in idealized form—Lady Gregory and her son ("our Sidney and our perfect man"), Maud Gonne in the role of Helen of Troy, Synge himself, "a sick man picturing energy, a doomed man picturing gaiety." But when the suffering of 1927-1929 brought him acutely back to elemental life, he came to feel, however vicariously, much of that sympathy with the folk he had lacked before. Or, to put it differently, Yeats the poet and Yeats the aristocrat were submerged beneath the powerful sense of Yeats the man. And if we add to this the uprush of physical strength in convalescence, stimulating the pronounced sexual vitality of his old age, we need not look further to account for the new heroic image—a crack-pated, bawdy, old woman and a lunatic beggar.

Under pressure of the same forces, earlier theories of verse were similarly transmuted into a new medium. When he first rejected the temporal and the psychological for a poetry of "simple emotions" common to all men in all ages, Yeats naturally thought of the ballad, and for a time he had even denied merit to all Irish poetry but a few ballads "written out of a personal and generally tragic experience." In the Crazy Jane poems, however, the ballad has become what Yeats called a broadside. Taking her cue from his practice, Dorothy Wellesley wrote in 1936: "Broadsides should be vigorous, tragic, bawdy, wild, any of those things. Am I right? But not contemplative." And, with the same contrast in mind, Yeats remarked in 1937: "I have several ballads, poignant things. . . . They have now come to an end I think, and I must go back to the poems of civilization"—that is to say, to the sophisticated and intellectual poetry at the opposite pole from the downward road to the market carts, where all is "simplified and solidified." In 1935 and 1937 the Cuala Press published a monthly *Broadside*, containing two ballads (Yeats himself first printed in this way many of the poems later published as *Last Poems*). A distinctive feature was the accompanying music often arranged from an old folk tune by Arthur Duff. The early ideal of verse set to musical notation, like the rest of his early theory, returned with fresh conviction when Yeats sank down to his roots again. The Wellesley letters are filled with its importance and its close association with the elemental and the permanent:

'Music, the natural words in the natural order.' Through that formula we go back to the people. Music will keep out temporary ideas, for music is the nation's clothing of what is ancient & deathless.

His last projective thought seems to me to have been this wish for 'words for melody.' Melody, not music conventionally spoken of: folk, ballad, &c.

All these poems are words for music perhaps, but they are not all broadside-ballads. Though not worked out rigidly, the "plan" Yeats had in mind was an antiphonal pattern in which the dramatic lyrics of Jane and Tom were to be played off against the more traditional lyrics of the poet speaking in his own voice. This too, is the development of an old idea, for in 1901 Yeats had set up, in opposition to the bad poetry of the middle class, a "good poetry" which embraced both these categories:

> There is only one kind of good poetry, for the poetry of the coteries, which presupposes the written tradition, does not differ in kind from the true poetry of the people, which presupposes the unwritten tradition.

With a subtle modulation the theme of sleep in "Three Things," with its imagery of bones and its earthly idiom, is rehandled in the next poem through images of Paris and Helen, Tristram and Leda; and the rhythm lifted from the unevenness of speech to sensuous grace. Jane's anxiety, expressed dramatically in poem iv, is recast in poem x into general statement and lyrical form. The "madness" of genius (poem xviii) is the counterpart, in contrasting mode, of the lunacy of Jane, and Tom the dancer at Cruachan (poem xxi) proclaims what Tom, in the next poem, discovers from his 'ghostly' experience; and Jane herself exemplifies the supreme theme of art and song (poem xvii):

> *Bodily decrepitude is wisdom; young*
> *We loved each other and were ignorant.*

The broad effect is that "balance or reconciliation of . . . the general with the concrete, the idea with the image, the individual with the representative" which Coleridge ascribed to the imagination of its highest level.

The application of Coleridge's remark to a whole group of poems is not loosely made. *Words for Music Perhaps,* written out of a single, if complex, experience is itself a work of art; it has, as Yeats said, a unity of "mood and plan."

Taken individually, these poems cannot be measured against "The Second Coming," "Among School Children," and a dozen more; and they can be matched, in substance and form, by a number of the lyrics in *Last Poems*. But, when read together, in close association, their apparent slightness disappears, and we come to realize that the volume as a whole embodies a broad and profound vision of life that makes it one of Yeats's highest achievements.

IV. MEANING

Crazy Jane and Tom the Lunatic stand in violent opposition to every form of asceticism—intellectual, mystical, or moral; to every dichotomy of the unified being, whether body and soul or thought and feeling. Their "insanity" is the wisdom of the natural man. In contrast to "my recent work," Yeats said at the time of their composition, "these 'Poems for Music' are all praise of joyous life." But at once he added a clause that implies their broader and deeper theme of heroic tragedy, "though in the best of them it is a dry bone upon the shore that sings the praise." As in the "Dialogue," we have, on the one hand, the same recognition of suffering seen from the perspective of old age: the inhumanity of man to man, the brevity of love and its essential loneliness—even the choice of a lover "not kindred" to the soul; the corruption of the ideal in the "Frog-spawn of a blind man's ditch." And, on the other side, we have the triumphant assertion of the same heroic will, claiming the validity of love against moral repression, accepting, with quiet or defiant courage, the destruction of "what life cannot rebuild."

In the opening poem Crazy Jane faces the Bishop. When Yeats spoke in 1904 of the opposition of heroic passion "with the law that is the expression of the whole, whether of Church or Nation," he thought of pulpit and press as the "enemies of life"; and every bishop as the Bishop of Connaught who "told his people a while since that they 'should never read stories about the degrading passion of love.'" That is the "source" of the poem and part of its meaning; but a deeper insight, gained in the intervening years, has given the original opposition a closer fidelity to life. The Bishop is not the symbol of law but of the letter of the law, the letter that killeth. He is not misguided, like his predecessor at Connaught, but cruel, and cruel because, as Yeats realized, without charity "our moral sense can be but cruelty." The poem is therefore not, or not merely, an attack on clericism but on man's inhumanity to man. This is skilfully pointed when Jane picks up the Bishop's charge that the lovers "lived like beast and beast" and turns *him* into beast—and a "heron's hunch upon his back," beneath the hypocritical robes of the priest. Jane herself is the tragic hero, defeated by the Bishop, "when his ban banished Jack the Journeyman," and by the conditions of life (Jack is dead)—but proud, defiant, without remorse. And the refrains, as often through these poems, are a kind of tragic chorus, offering consolation in *"All find safety in the tomb"* and ironic sympathy in *"The solid man and the coxcomb."*

In their second meeting (poem vi) the Bishop asserts the dichotomy of soul and body: the spirit is good, the flesh evil; the virtuous life is ascetic, in a heavenly mansion, evil life is natural life, in a bodily mansion. It is the voice of Blake's enemies, and his reply is Yeats's and Jane's, "But that which is Sin in the sight of cruel man is not sin in the sight of our kind God":

'Fair and foul are near of kin,
And fair needs foul,' I cried.
'My friends are gone, but that's a truth
Nor grave nor bed denied,
Learned in bodily lowliness
And in the heart's pride.

'A woman can be proud and stiff
When on love intent;
But Love has pitched his mansion in
The place of excrement;
For nothing can be sole or whole
That has not been rent.'

Fair needs foul ("What you call foul"), and soul and body are two halves of a single whole, a truth "learned in bodily lowliness." This last image, which is to be read literally, is then extended in the closing lines into one of Yeats' boldest figures, for the reference is neither to suffering nor to the "necessity of descretion," as MacNeice would have it, but to the physical union through which alone love is made "sole or whole."

The same conviction is given a different setting in poem iii, which is also related to the first encounter with the

Bishop. The title, "Crazy Jane on the Day of Judgment," is purposely ambiguous. It is *this* day when Jane sits in self-judgment. The Bishop is wrong—and yet, what is true love? Doesn't the soul need the body? All will be known when time is gone, on the Judgment Day.

'Love is all
Unsatisfied
That cannot take the whole
Body and soul';
And that is what Jane said.

'Take the sour
If you take me,
I can scoff and lour
And scold for an hour.'
'That's certainly the case,' said she.

'Naked I lay,
The grass my bed;
Naked and hidden away,
That black day';
And that is what Jane said.

'What can be shown?
What true love be?
All could be known or shown
If Time were gone.'
'That's certainly the case,' said he.

As with most of these poems, the apparent simplicity is deceptive, for natural love in its fulness is only part of the meaning. There is the important contrast, here and elsewhere, between Jane and Jack. Her character, fierce and defiant by moments (even her love is "like the lion's tooth"), is also sensitive, perceptive, capable of devotion. Jack is simply Jack the Journeyman, ready enough to desert one woman for another, since for him body alone is the meaning of love. Hence the juxtaposition of the hero and the common man. One must be aware of Jack's tone of voice—rapid, a bit shrill, offhand and casual (he is bored with the whole discussion). Jane speaks slowly, seriously, the pitch low. One must read the last line in key with stanza two, and with a marked difference of tone from Jane's previous use of the same words. Not to do so is to miss the underlying pathos.

The contrast of Jane and Jack reappears, in clearer outline and deeper implication, in "'I am of Ireland.'" This poem is perhaps the finest of the group—to Horace Gregory the finest lyric in contemporary literature; but this is not evident without close analysis, for a powerful rhythm tends to conceal the full and elusive meaning:

'I AM of Ireland,
And the Holy Land of Ireland,
And time runs on,' cried she
'Come out of charity,
Come dance with me in Ireland.'

One man, one man alone
In that outlandish gear,
One solitary man
Of all that rambled there
Had turned his stately head.
'That is a long way off,
And time runs on,' he said,
'And the night grows rough.'

'I am of Ireland,
And the Holy Land of Ireland,
And time runs on,' cried she.
'Come out of charity
And dance with me in Ireland.'

The fiddlers are all thumbs,
Or the fiddle-string accursed,
The drums and the kettledrums
And the trumpets all are burst,
And the trombone,' cried he,
'The trumpet and trombone,
And cocked a malicious eye,
'But time runs on, runs on.'

'I am of Ireland,
And the Holy Land of Ireland,
And time runs on,' cried she.
'Come out of charity
And dance with me in Ireland.'

Granting that any explanation of a poem so delicate must be too literal and crude, let us say that a woman very like Crazy Jane is in a pub somewhere outside of Ireland. As she looks at the rowdy scene (even the orchestra is drunk—the fiddlers are all thumbs), suddenly she thinks of Ireland, of everything romantic the name can suggest, its heroic past, its holy miracles, its national aspiration, its beauty—everything which Yeats has captured in her song.[4] No one pays any attention, except one man, another Jack the Journeyman ("stately" in line 10 means "showing a sense of superiority; repellently dignified; not affable or approachable"—N.E.D., 2.b), who first pretends to take her literally ("that's a long way off and it's getting late"), and then, when she repeats her appeal, he "cocks a malicious eye"—gives her the wink, and agrees that there's no time to lose: they better get going. On which the woman sings her romantic vision all the more fiercely in the face of this coarse and common reduction of the ideal. Technically, the reduction is brilliantly made by having the man pick up the phrase about time running on and twist it to his own meaning; so that we feel at once, intuitively, the contrast between two very different dances, holy and unholy, between charity and lust. In short, the greatness of the poem lies in its simple statement of tragic contrast. What Yeats wrote in 1909 of Synge's characters is true of this Crazy Jane heroine:

> Person after person in these laughing sorrowful, heroic plays is, 'the like of the little children do be listening to the stories of an old woman, and do be dreaming after in the dark night it's in grand houses of gold they are, with speckled horses to ride, and do be waking again in a short while and they destroyed with the cold, and the thatch dripping, maybe, and the starved ass braying in the yard.'

In the poem, however, this general pattern is given a specific form—the image of the hero as reflected in the malicious eye of the world. It is therefore the dramatic answer to the question in the "Dialogue":

[4] Cf. a remark in "J. M. Synge and Ireland" (1910), *Essays by W. B. Yeats* (1924), p. 401, where Yeats sums up the "lineaments" of Ireland in a phrase of Borrow's: " 'Oh, Ireland, mother of the bravest soldiers and of the most beautiful women!' " The refrain is a brilliant adaptation of a medieval lyric called "The Irish Dancer," printed in *A Treasury of Middle English Verse*, ed. Margot R. Adamson (1930), p. 56:

> *"I come from Ireland*
> *From the Holy Land*
> *Of Ireland.*
> *Good sir, I pray to thee,*
> *For of Saint Charity,*
> *Come out and dance with me*
> *In Ireland!"*

The finished man among his enemies?—
How in the name of Heaven can he escape
That defiling and disfigured shape
The mirror of malicious eyes
Casts upon his eyes?

There is no escape; there is only the counteraffirmation of heroic song. A few years later Yeats was to say that "the east has its solutions always and therefore knows nothing of tragedy; it is we, not the east, that must raise the heroic cry."

That remark sums up the interpretation so far advanced of Yeats's development from *A Vision* to *Words for Music Perhaps*. But the later work contains other poems, not yet mentioned, which do involve the solutions of the east. Does this introduce the earlier mood of mystical search? Or is the tragic and heroic note sustained and the unity of the volume preserved?

The philosophical theme is the permanence or survival of individual life, and even of specific events. Its immediate source at the moment was Plotinus, especially the section of the *Enneads* which is entitled, "It there an Ideal Archetype of Particular Beings?" It was Plotinus's affirmative answer to that question which led Yeats to prefer him to Plato:

> So far the Ideas had been everything, the individual nothing; beauty and truth alone had mattered to Plato and Socrates, but Plotinus thought that every individual had his Idea, his eternal counterpart.
>
> We may fail to express an archetype or alter it by reason, but all done from nature is its unfolding in time. Some other existence may take the place of Socrates. Yet Socrates can never cease to exist.

In the second of these quotations, taken from the important comment on Plotinus in the Preface to *The Words upon the Window-pane* (1931), Yeats is thinking of the passage in the fifth *Ennead* which he refers to specifically a moment later:

> We have to examine the question whether there exists an ideal archetype of individuals, in other words whether I and every other human being go back to the Intellectual, every (living) thing having origin and principle There.
>
> If Socrates, Socrates' soul, is eternal then the Authentic Socrates—to adapt the term—must be There; that is to say, the individual soul has an existence in the Supreme as well as in this world.

And thus, he goes on to say, everything has "permanent endurance," and the individual soul returns back, at death, to his "archetype existence there" Yeats recognized that Plotinus gave no sanction for a second descent into time; and yet it seemed to him—naturally enough when we remember *Anima Mundi*—"that it [the soul] can at will re-enter number and part and thereby make itself apparent to our minds." From that assumption he drew his final deduction:

> If we accept this idea many strange and beautiful things become credible. The Indian pilgrim has not deceived us; he did hear the bed where the sage of his devotion slept a thousand years ago creak as though someone turned over in it; . . . *the Irish country-woman did see the ruined castle lit up* [cf. poem v] . . . those two Oxford ladies did find themselves in the garden of the Petit Trianon with Marie Antoinette and her courtiers, see that garden as those saw it . . .

And he might have added—as he certainly remembered in poem v—his statement years earlier in *Anima Mundi* that "Spiritualism . . . will have it that we may see at certain roads and in certain houses old murders acted over again and in certain fields dead huntsmen riding with horse and hound, or *ancient armies fighting above bones or ashes*." [cf. poem v]. In short, as the Preface concludes,

> All about us there seems to start up a precise inexplicable teeming life, and the earth becomes once more, not in rhetorical metaphor, but in reality, sacred.

This, then, is the philosophy Yeats offers for support against the tragedy of existence: that "all things remain in God" (poem v) or stand in His "unchanging eye" (poem xxii); that nothing can "fail," cease to exist, because "things out of perfection sail" (poem xxiv), and return at death to the "light lost" at birth (poem iv); that old age is merely the mask of the young beauty that was "before the world was made" and will be always (poem ix); and that the experience of ghosts and ghostly re-enactment is the proof of this "saving" metaphysic (poems v and xxii).

Curiously enough, however, when we examine its embodiment in the dramatic poems, we discover that its whole spirit and emotion are transformed or submerged by the predominant passion of heroic assertion. What I mean appears, for example, when Tom the lunatic sees the ghosts of his old companions:

Sang old Tom the lunatic
That sleeps under the canopy;
'What change has put my thoughts astray
And eyes that had so keen a sight?
What has turned to smoking wick
Nature's pure unchanging light?

"Huddon and Duddon and Daniel O'Leary,
Holy Joe, the beggar-man,
Wenching, drinking, still remain
Or sing a penance on the road;
Something made these eyeballs weary
That blinked and saw them in a shroud.

'Whatever stands in field or flood
Bird, beast, fish or man,
Mare or stallion, cock or hen,
Stands in God's unchanging eye
In all the vigour of its blood;
In that faith I live or die.'

Tom's faith in what MacNeice has aptly called "the spirituality of blood" is, in effect, a faith in the indestructibility of energy. That is why, in spite of the religious orientation, the experience in the last stanza is scarcely different in quality from that which closes the "Dialogue." Here, as there, the feeling of sanctity, which is extended in both cases from he individual to "everything we look upon," does not rise from any Neo-Platonic faith, but from an inner and wholly natural sense of supreme strength. The accent of heroic joy s therefore precisely the same. As soon as the metaphysic passes from statement to dramatic expression, its emotional ontext is sensual and heroic.

The implication that Yeats was not sustained, at bottom, y the solutions of the east is acutely revealed by "Crazy ane on God," for there the supernatural metaphors are learly rhetorical, and the earth is not in reality sacred at ll, but entirely 'profane'—and heroic.

CRAZY JANE ON GOD

That lover of a night
Came when he would
Went in the dawning light
Whether I would or no;

Men come, men go;
All things remain in God.

Banners choke the sky;
Men-at-arms tread;
Armoured horses neigh
Where the great battle was
In the narrow pass:
All things remain in God.

Before their eyes a house
That from childhood stood
uninhabited, ruinous,
Suddenly lit up
From door to top:
All things remain in God.

I had wild Jack for a lover;
Though like a road
That men pass over
My body makes no moan
But sings on:
All things remain in God.

It might seem that Yeats has projected his metaphysic into a dramatic situation, but closer inspection proves, I think, that the doctrines are not *in the poem* at all. Their function ended, so to speak, when they had given the imagination its angle of vision and its images. Yeats said himself that his system "helped me to hold in a single thought reality and justice" and that the voices who dictated *A Vision* had come to give him "metaphors for poetry." The final stanza makes it clear that Crazy Jane is not sustained by any philosophy of ghostly permanence or by any atom of faith that she will find her lover again when time is gone. Her fortitude rests on an act of acceptance and the permanent possession *in time* of a love once realized. That is why the refrain does not carry its literal and Plotinian meaning and why the images of stanzas two and three, however "true" in Jane' mind—or in Yeats's—are metaphorical analogies to illustrate a permanence wholly natural. In short, as Yeats once said of a dramatic poem which starts from a bundle of ideas "gradually philosophy is eliminated until at last the onl philosophy audible . . . is the mere expression of one char acter"—and *that* philosophy is not Plotinian. Nor is it Christian. Though the refrain is reminiscent of Dante's "nella sua volonta e la nostra pace," the act of acceptance is not one of Christian humility. Jane is not filled with the love of God but the love of Jack; and, however she may describe her destiny as the providence of God, she accepts it with the same heroic fortitude that stands alone, without religious reference, at the close of the "Dialogue." Unless this were so, we should miss the poignant sense of tragedy.

V. EVALUATION

If *Words for Music Perhaps* is the final crystallization of Yeats's art, its evaluation is an index to this achievement. Some remarks of Spender's in 1934 state the derogatory position:

> Yeats' poetry is devoid of any unifying moral subject.
> Although he has much wisdom, he offers no philosophy of life, but, as a substitute, a magical system . . . not socially constructive.
> In his later poems, although there is great show of intellectualism, he rests really always on certain qualities, rather than ideas, such as breeding and courtesy. For the thought is hopelessly inadequate to his situation.

The force of this attack is vitiated by overstatement. A magical system is not what Yeats *substituted* for a philosophy of life; nor are breeding and courtesy the qualities affirmed in the later heroic poems (they are hardly conspicuous in Crazy Jane). But, if Spender's criticism is distorted, it is the distortion of a truth, for *Words for Music Perhaps* is indeed devoid of any unifying moral subject, and for that reason is not socially constructive.

For all his citation of Sophocles and Shakespeare, Yeats produces a very different tragic effect. Because the hero is not at war with evil, within or without, we cannot feel that profound sense of pity and terror which comes from witnessing a world of moral disorder. On the contrary we "*rejoice* in every happiness that comes to him, and *sorrow* at his death as if it were our own." This is hardly the mood of tragic catharsis. It is the mood which Yeats, in 1938, rightly defined as the aim of his plays, "tragic ecstasy;" the mood described in the essay of "Poetry and Tradition" and in terms which show its close connection with the heroic psychology of self-surrender and self-assertion (he had just mentioned the death scenes of Timon and Cleopatra):

> The nobleness of the Arts is in the mingling of contraries, the extremity of sorrow, the extremity of joy, perfection of personality, the perfection of its surrender, overflowing turbulent energy, and marmorean stillness.[5]

Throughout all his criticism, Yeats spoke only once, that I recall, of "the purification that comes with pity and terror to the imagination and intellect," precisely the effect mos lacking in *Words for Music Perhaps.*

Those emotions, however, were dominant in one perio of his work, and dominant because Yeats was then writing for the first and last time, from a full awareness of evil brought home to him by the First World War and the Irish Revolution. "The Second Coming," "Meditations in Time o Civil War," and "Nineteen Hundred and Nineteen" ar great tragic odes, but their pity and terror is not "purified because there is no counteraffirmation. "The growing mur derousness of the world" stands unchallenged; no hero face "the Savage God." In "The Second Coming" the failure c aristocracy and the association of energy with evil mark fo the moment the complete eclipse of heroic faith:

> *The blood-dimmed tide is loosed, and everywhere*
> *The ceremony of innocence is drowned;*
> *The best lack all conviction, while the worst*
> *Are full of passionate intensity.*

Overwhelmed by this nightmare vision, Yeats could onl revolt with a "rage to end all things." Had he come throug this period of despair and, with renewed faith in the herois latent in man, still held fast to the moral problem, he wou have created a tragic art in the same kind as Shakespeare' but after the recoil toward mysticism he returned to th earlier mode of heroic art, however deepened and widene

John F. Taylor was right when he said that Yeats's imag nation was "aesthetic rather than ethical." But for that v must hold the time largely responsible. His little-known ess on Lady Gregory's *Cuchulain of Muirthemne,* written 1902, reveals the permanent effect of the age upon Yea developing imagination:

> The Church when it was most powerful created an imaginative u ty, for it taught learned and unlearned to climb, as it were, to t

[5] Cf. the description of Synge's work (*Essays,* p. 383) as "these laughing, s rowful, heroic plays."

> great moral realities. . . . The storytellers of Ireland, perhaps of every primitive country, created a like unity, only it was to the greatest aesthetic realities that they taught the people to climb. They created for learned and unlearned alike, a communion of heroes, a cloud of stalwart witnesses.

Yeats's thought was inadequate to his situation, not because he hated democracy, and Karl Marx, but because when Huxley and Darwin destroyed his Christianity, they divorced his poetry from a moral basis and therefore from society. How serious that was for his tragic art is sharply exposed by an autobiographical passage of 1925, put into the mouth of Owen Aherne: although "Mr. Yeats has intellectual belief, . . . he is entirely without moral faith, without that sense, which should come to a man with terror and joy, of a Divine Presence." And he added that, "though he may seek, and may have always sought it, I am certain he will not find it in this life." What he did find was an amoral faith in the heroic man.

That is the case against *Words for Music Perhaps,* but we must not be tempted—and the temptation is strong at the moment—into letting it determine a final estimate. It limits, but it does not invalidate, the claim of high achievement. A poetry of personality built on however defective a philosophy is a greater *poetry* than one which has sacrificed vitality of life to any abstraction of belief no matter how adequate. This is the validity behind Yeats's insistence, throughout the criticism of the 1930's, upon the superiority of Irish heroic art to the new movements in England. In England, he said, the recovery of legend "checked by the realism of Eliot, the social passion of the war poets, gave way to an impersonal philosophical poetry"; while in Ireland, "a still living folk tradition," deepened by the civil war, made her poets harden their personalities and restore "the emotion of heroism to lyric poetry." Beside his own fulfillment of that ideal, it seems true, as he claimed, that "most of the 'moderns'—Auden, Spender, etc., seem thin." Even Eliot, though his poetry is never thin and its later values have become Christian, has not yet welded together his intense but fugitive sense of life into a rich and sensuous whole. When in *Murder in the Cathedral* he presented a hero facing his destiny, the result was a little dry and abstract, a trifle archeological, beside the immediacy of Crazy Jane.

For Yeats's imagination, however aesthetic and nonmoral,

has attained in *Words for Music Perhaps* the power of condensing a wide vision of life into symbols that keep that vision fully alive. Without ceasing to be flesh and blood and brain, "the persons upon the stage," as he wrote in "The tragic theatre," "greaten till they are humanity itself." Jack and Jane and Tom the Lunatic recreate the elemental experiences of man. What "seems to the hasty reader a mere story is completely life"—though not the complete moral life of Shakespeare. The greatness and also the limitation of these poems cannot be stated better than by Yeats himself:

Art . . . shrinks . . . from every abstract thing, from all that is of the brain only, from all that is not a fountain jetting from the entire hopes, memories, and sensations of the body. Its mortality is personal, knows little of any general laws.

Artists and poets . . . come at last to forget good and evil in an absorbing vision of the happy and the unhappy.

A Select Bibliography

OF ARTICLES AND BOOKS, IN WHOLE OR IN PART, ON YEATS

As its title indicates, this bibliography—though it lists most of the best, and most of the recent, work on Yeats—is not exhaustive. It is, however, representative of the various people—with various points of view, at various dates, and in various places—who have interested themselves in the man and his work.

The following notes concern form and method of the bibliography. (1) Asterisks before entries indicate that the works listed are reprinted in this volume. (2) Names of authors are those under which they wrote; and, where these names are pseudonyms, maiden names, etc., cross references are provided, as they are in other instances where helpful. (3) In general, entries for periodical articles follow this form: author, title of article, periodical, volume and number, date, and page; entries for books, this form: author, chapter or section title (if any), book title, editor(s) (if any), place of publication, publisher, date of publication, and pages. (4) In a few instances periodical articles and books which the editors were unable to examine are listed, and in some of these instances one or more of the items included in (3) are missing. (5) *A, an, the, die, la,* etc. are omitted where they are first words in titles of periodicals. (6) Names of publishers are shortened. (7) Where entries represent articles or books which deal with the particular works of Yeats, and the titles of these articles or books do not indicate the works, the titles of the works are in parentheses after the entries. (8) Where entries for reviews of important books on Yeats are included, the titles of the books are in parentheses after the entries. (9) Where periodical articles are reprinted in books, entries are given only for the books. (10) In general, entries are given only for first editions of books.

Aas, L., "William Butler Yeats og hans Verker Dramatikeren. Yeats og det irske teater," *Ord och Bild,* XXXVI (1927), 461-468.

——, "William Butler Yeats og hans Verker Lyrik, prosodiktning og kritik," *Ord och Bild,* XXXVI (1927), 145-152.

Abbott, Claude Colleer, ed., *Further Letters of Gerard Manley Hopkins,* London: Oxford University Press, 1938, *passim.*

Academy, LXIII, n. s. 1597 (December 13, 1902), 661-662 (*Where There is Nothing*).

——, LXIV, n. s. 1619 (May 16, 1903), 475 (*Ideas of Good and Evil*).

A.E. *See also* "Some Passages . . ."

—— [Russell, George William], *The Living Torch,* New York: Macmillan, 1938, *passim.*

——, "Poet of Shadows," *Imaginations and Reveries,* Dublin:

Maunsel, 1915, 24-28 (see also, *ibid., passim*).

———, *Some Irish Essays,* Dublin: Maunsel, 1906.

———, "Yeats's Early Poems," *Living Age,* CCCXXVII, 4247 (November 28, 1925), 464-466 (*Early Poems and Stories*).

Alexander, Ian W., "Valery and Yeats: The Rehabilitation of Time," *Scottish Periodical,* I, 1 (summer, 1947), 77-106.

Allt, G. D. P., "W. B. Yeats," *Theology,* XLII (1941).

———, "Yeats and the Revision of His Early Verse," *Hermathena,* LXIV (November, 1944).

Alspach, Russell K., "Some Sources of Yeats's *The Wanderings of Oisin,*" *Publications of the Modern Language Association,* LVIII, 3 (September, 1943), 849-866.

———, "Two Songs of Yeats," *Modern Language Notes,* LXI, 6 (June, 1946), 395-400 ("Red Hanrahan's Song about Ireland," "The Song of Wandering Aengus").

———, "The Use by Yeats and Other Irish Writers of the Folklore of Patrick Kennedy," *Journal of American Folk-Lore* LIX, 234 (October-December, 1946), 404-412.

———, "Yeats's First Two Published Poems," *Modern Language Notes,* LVIII, 7 (November, 1943), 555-557 ("Song of the Faeries," "Voices").

Andreus, Irene D., "A Glimpse of Yeats," *Reading and Collecting,* II, 3 (February-March, 1938), 8-9.

Archer, William, "William Butler Yeats," *Poets of the Younger Generation,* London: Lane, 1902, 531-557.

Arns, Karl, "Der Träger des Nobelpreises," *Literatur,* XXVI, 5 (February, 1924), 261-265.

———, "William Butler Yeats," *Schone Literatur,* XXX, 6 (June, 1929), 248-256.

Auden, W. H., "In Memory of W. B. Yeats" (a poem), *New Republic,* XCVIII, 1266 (March 8, 1939), 123; and *London Mercury,* XXXIX, 234 (April, 1939), 578-580.

———, "The Public v. the Late Mr. W. B. Yeats," *The Partisan Reader—1934-44,* ed. William Phillips and Philip Rahv, New York: Dial Press, 1946.

* ———, "Yeats as an Example," *Kenyon Review,* X, 2 (spring, 1948), 187-195.

———, "Yeats: Master of Diction," *Saturday Review of Literature,* XXII, 7 (June 8, 1940), 14 (*Last Poems and Plays*).

Aynard, Joseph, "W. B. Yeats, lauréat du prix Nobel," *Revue de Paris,* yr. 31, vol. I (January 1, 1924), 176-189.

Bailey, Ruth, *A Dialogue on Modern Poetry,* London: Oxford University Press, 1939, *passim.*

Baker, Howard, "Domes of Byzantium," *Southern Review,* VII, 3 (winter, 1942), 639-652 ("Sailing to Byzantium," "Byzantium").

Baring, M., "Mr. Yeats's Poems," *Punch and Judy and Other Essays,*

London: Heinemann, 1924, 228-232.

Barnes, T. R., "Yeats, Synge, Ibsen and Strindberg," *Scrutiny*, V, 3 (December, 1936), 257-262.

Bax, Sir Arnold, *Farewell My Youth*, London: Longmans, Green, [1943].

Bax, Clifford, ed., *Florence Farr, Bernard Shaw and W. B. Yeats*, Dublin: Cuala Press, 1941.

* Beach, Joseph Warren, "Without Benefit of Clergy," *A History of English Literature* by Craig, Anderson, Bredvold, and Beach, New York; Oxford University Press (in press).

———, "Yeats and AE," *The Concept of Nature in Nineteenth-Century Poetry*, New York: Macmillan, 1936, 535-538.

Beerbohm, Max, "Some Irish Plays and Players," *Saturday Review*, XCVII, 2528 (April 9, 1904), 455-457 (*The King's Threshold*).

[Beerbohm], Max, "In Dublin," *Saturday Review*, LXXXVII, 2272 (May 13, 1899), 586-588 (*The Countess Cathleen*).

B[enet], W[illiam] R[ose], "William Butler Yeats, 1865-1939," *Saturday Review of Literature*, XIX, 15 (February 4, 1939), 8.

* Bentley, Eric, "Yeats as a Playwright," *Kenyon Review*, X, 2 (spring, 1948), 196-208.

Bickley, Francis, "The Development of William Butler Yeats," *Living Age*, CCLXIV, 3429 (March 26, 1910), 802-805.

———, "Yeats and the Movement," *J. M. Synge and the Irish Dramatic Movement*, London: Constable, 1912, 49-66.

Binyon, Laurence, "William Butler Yeats," *Bookman* [London], LXIII, 376 (January, 1923), 196-199 (*Later Poems* [1922], *Plays in Prose and Verse, The Trembling of the Veil*).

Blackmur, R. P., "Between Myth and Philosophy: Fragments, of W. B. Yeats," *Southern Review*, VII, 3 (winter, 1942), 407-425.

* ———, "The Later Poetry of W. B. Yeats," *The Expense of Greatness*, New York: Arrow Editions, 1940, 74-106.

———, "Under a Major Poet," *American Mercury*, XXXI, 122 (February, 1934), 244-246 (*The Collected Poems . . .* [1933]).

Bogan, Louise, "The Cutting of an Agate," *Nation*, CXLVIII, 9 (February 25, 1939), 234-235.

———, "William Butler Yeats," *Atlantic Monthly*, CLXI, 5 (June, 1938), 637-644.

Bönninger, K., "W. B. Yeats neue gedichte," *Neue Zürcher Zeitung*, No. 663 (1934).

Bose, Abinash Chandra, "William Butler Yeats," *Three Mystic Poets*, Kolhapur (India): School & College Book Stall, 1945, 1-46.

Bottomley, Gordon, "His Legacy to the Theatre," *Arrow*, summer, 1939, 11-14.

Bowra, C. M., "William Butler Yeats," *The Heritage of Symbolism*, London: Macmillan, 1943, 180-218.

Boyd, E. A., "William Butler Yeats," *Contemporary Drama of Ireland*, Boston: Little, Brown, 1917, 47-87.

———, "William Butler Yeats," *Portraits: Real and Imaginary,* New York: Doran, 1924, 236-245.

———, "William Butler Yeats: The Poems," ". . . The Plays," and ". . . Prose Writings," *Ireland's Literary Renaissance,* New York: Lane, 1916, 122-144, 145-165, 166-187.

Bradbrook, M. C., "Songs of Experience," *Scrutiny,* II, 1 (June, 1933), 77-78 (*Words for Music Perhaps . . .*).

Braun, H., "William Butler Yeats. Irische Schaubühne," *Deutsche Zeitschrift,* XLVII, 11-12 (August-September, 1934), 576-578.

Brenner, Rica, "William Butler Yeats," *Poets of Our Time,* New York: Harcourt, Brace, 1941, 355-411.

Brock, A. Clutton. *See* Clutton-Brock.

Bronowski, J., "William Butler Yeats," *The Poet's Defense,* Cambridge: Cambridge University Press, 1939, 229-252.

Brooks, Cleanth, Jr., "Yeats's Great Rooted Blossomer," *The Well Wrought Urn,* New York: Reynal & Hitchcock, 1947, 163-175 ("Among School Children").

* ———, "Yeats: The Poet as a Myth-Maker," *Modern Poetry and the Tradition,* Chapel Hill: University of North Carolina Press, 1939, 173-202 (*A Vision*).

Brooks, Cleanth, Jr., and Warren, Robert Penn, *Understanding Poetry,* New York: Holt, 1938, 224-230 ("After Long Silence"), 273-277 ("A Deep-Sworn Vow"), 615-621 ("Two Songs from a Play").

Brooks, Van Wyck, *Opinions of Oliver Allston,* New York: Dutton, 1941, *passim.*

Brown, Forman G., "Mr. Yeats and the Supernatural," *Sewanee Review,* XXXIII, 3 (July, 1925), 323-330.

Brunius, August, "Yeats och Moore," *Var Tid Arsbok Utgiven av Samfundet De Nio 1923,* Stockholm: Wahlstrom & Widstrand, 1923, 75-95.

Bullough, Geoffrey, "W. B. Yeats and Walter De la Mare," *The Trend of Modern Poetry,* Edinburgh: Oliver & Boyd, 1934, 27-43.

* Burke, Kenneth, "On Motivation in Yeats," *Southern Review,* VII, 3 (winter, 1942), 547-561.

———, "The Problem of the Intrinsic," *A Grammar of Motives,* New York: Prentice-Hall, 1945, 465-484 (in part, reply to Elder Olson, *op. cit. infra*).

Bush, Douglas, *Mythology and the Romantic Tradition,* Cambridge: Harvard University Press, 1937, *passim.*

Byrne, Dawson, *The Story of Ireland's National Theatre,* Dublin: Talbot Press, 1929, *passim.*

C., R. J., "Yeats' 'The Wild Swans at Coole,'" *Explicator,* II, 4 (January, 1944), query 20.

Carswell, Catherine. *See* Fay.

Cary, Elisabeth Luther, "Apostles of the New Drama," *Lamp,*

XXVII, 6 (January, 1904), 593-598.

Cazamian, Madeleine L., "W. B. Yeats, poète de l'Irlande," *La Vie des Peuples,* January, 1924.

———, "William Butler Yeats, 1865-1939," *Études Anglaises,* III, 2 (April-June, 1939), 127-131.

Chesterton, G. K., "Efficiency in Elfland," *Living Age,* CCLXXIV, 3552 (August 3, 1912), 317-319 (*The Land of Heart's Desire*).

Chew, Samuel C., *A Literary History of England,* ed. Albert C. Baugh, New York & London: Appleton-Century-Crofts, 1948, 1508-1512.

Chislett, W., "On the Influence of Lady Gregory on William Butler Yeats," *Moderns and Near-Moderns,* New York: Grafton Press, 1928, 165-167.

Church, Richard, "The Later Yeats," *Eight for Immortality,* London: Dent, 1941, 41-54.

———, "A Poet's Design for Living," *Fortnightly Review,* CLIII [o. s. CLIX], 916 [o. s. 951] (April, 1943), 258-262 (Hone's *W. B. Yeats, 1865-1939*).

Clarke, Austin, "Poet and Artist," *Arrow,* summer, 1939, 8-9.

———, "W. B. Yeats," *Dublin Magazine,* April-June, 1939.

Clarke, Egerton, "William Butler Yeats," *Dublin Review,* CCIV, 409 (April-May-June, 1939), 305-321.

Clemens, Cyril, "The Passing of W. B. Yeats," *Canadian Bookman,* XXII, 2 (June-July, 1939), 21-25.

Clemens, Katharine, "Some Recollections of William Butler Yeats," *Mark Twain Quarterly,* VI, 1 (summer-fall, 1943), 17-18.

Clutton-Brock, A., *Academy,* LXIV, n. s. 1624 (June 20, 1903), 617-619 (reply to "The State Called Reverie," *infra*).

Colum, Mary M., "Memories of Yeats," *Saturday Review of Literature,* XIX, 18 (February 25, 1939), 3-4, 14.

———, "The Yeats I Knew," *Life and the Dream,* Garden City: Doubleday, 1947, 127-141 (see also *ibid., passim*).

Colm, Padraic, "A Dublin Letter," *Saturday Review of Literature,* XIII, 16 (February 15, 1936), 24.

———, "The Greatness of W. B. Yeats," New York *Times Book Review,* February 12, 1939, 1, 17.

———, "Mr. Yeats's Plays and Later Poems," *Yale Review,* XIV, 2 (January, 1925), 381-385 (*Plays in Prose and Verse* and *Later Poems* [1924]).

———, "On Yeats," *Commonweal,* XX, 3 (May 18, 1934), 70-71.

Cowley, Malcolm, "The Hosting of the Shee," *New Republic,* CVIII, 6 [w. n. 1471] (February 8, 1943), 185-186 (Hone's *W. B. Yeats, 1865-1939*).

———, "Poet in Politics," *New Republic,* XCVI, 1242 (September 21, 1938), 191-192 (*The Autobiography . . .*).

———, "Yeats and O'Faolain [*sic*]," *New Republic,* XCVIII, 1263 (February 15, 1939), 49-50.

[Cowley, Malcolm?], "Yeats," *New Republic,* XCVIII, 1262 (February 8, 1939), 4.

Cunliffe, John W., "The Irish Movement," *English Literature During the Last Half Century,* New York: Macmillan, 1919, 223-243.

———, "William Butler Yeats," *English Literature in the Twentieth Century,* New York: Macmillan, 1933, 101-105.

———, "William Butler Yeats," *Leaders of the Victorian Revolution,* New York: Appleton-Century, 1934, 305-311.

* Daiches, David, "W. B. Yeats—I" and "W. B. Yeats—II," *Poetry and the Modern World,* Chicago: University of Chicago Press, 1940, 128-155, 156-189.

Daly, J. J., "The Paganism of Mr. Yeats," *Cheerful Ascetic, and Other Essays,* New York: Bruce, 1931, 87-102.

David, Paul, "Structure in Some Modern Poets," *New English Weekly,* XXVII, 4 (July 26, 1945), 131-132.

* Davidson, Donald, "Yeats and the Centaur," *Southern Review,* VII, 3 (winter, 1942), 510-516.

Davison, Edward L., "Three Irish Poets," *Some Modern Poets,* New York: Harper, 1928, 173-196.

Day, Lewis C., "A Note on W. B. Yeats and the Aristocratic Tradition," *Scattering Branches,* ed. Stephen Gwynn, New York: Macmillan, 1940, 157-182.

Desmond, Shaw, "Dunsany, Yeats, and Shaw: Trinity of Magic," *Bookman* [New York] LVIII, [3] (November, 1923), 260-266.

Deutsch, Babette, *This Modern Poetry,* New York: Norton, 1935, *passim.*

Dodds, E. R., ed., *Journal and Letters of Stephen MacKenna,* New York: Morrow, [1936], *passim.*

Doorn, Willem van, "William Butler Yeats," *English Studies,* II, 9 (June, 1920), 65-77.

Dottin, Paul, "La Littérature anglaise en 1938 (II)," *Revue de France,* XIX, 14 (July 15, 1939), 236-249 (*The Herne's Egg* . . .).

D[owden?], E[dward?] M., "The Writings of Mr. W. B. Yeats," *Fortnightly Review,* LXXXV [o. s. XCI], 506 [o. s. 541] (February, 1909), 253-270 (*The Collected Works in Verse and Prose* . . . [1908]).

Draws-Tychsen, H., "Die Dramen von William Butler Yeats," *Berliner Tageblatt,* No. 71 (1934).

Drew, Elizabeth, and Sweeney, John L., "W. B. Yeats," *Directions in Modern Poetry,* New York: Norton, 1940, 148-171 (see also *ibid., passim*).

Dubois, Louis Paul, *See* Paul-Dubois.

Duffy, Sir Charles Gavan, "Books for the Irish People," *The Revival of Irish Literature,* London: Unwin, 1894, 35-60.

Dulac, Edmund, "Without the Twilight," *Scattering Branches,* ed. Stephen Gwynn, New York: Macmillan, 1940, 135-144.

Edgar, Pelham, "The Enigma of Yeats," *Queen's Quarterly*, XLVI, 4 (November, 1939), 411-422.

Edwards, Oliver, "W. B. Yeats and Ulster: and a Thought on the Future of the Anglo-Irish Tradition," *Northman*, XIII, 2 (winter, 1945).

———, "Yeats's 'The Fisherman,'" *Wales*, VII, 25 (spring, 1947), 222-223.

Eglinton, John [Magee, W. K.], *A Memoir of A E, George William Russell*, London: Macmillan, 1937, *passim*.

———, "Mr. Yeats's Autobiographies," *Dial*, LXXXIII, [2] (August, 1927), 94-97.

———, "Yeats and His Story," *Irish Literary Portraits*, London: Macmillan, 1935, 17-38.

———, "Yeats at the High School," *Erasmian*, June, 1939, 11-12.

Eichler, Albert, "'Erzahlungen u. Essans' von William Butler Yeats," *Beiblatt zur Anglia*, XXVIII, 10 (October, 1917), 298-302.

Eliot, T. S., *After Strange Gods*, London: Faber & Faber, 1934, 43-47.

———, *The Music of Poetry*, Glasgow: Jackson, 1942, 17.

* ———, "The Poetry of W. B. Yeats," *Southern Review*, VII, 3 (winter, 1942), 442-454.

———, *The Use of Poetry and the Use of Criticism*, London: Faber & Faber, 1933, 140.

E[liot], T. S., "A Commentary," *Criterion*, XIV, 57 (July, 1935), 610-613.

Ellis, Stewart M., "W. B. Yeats," *Mainly Victorian*, London: Hutchinson, n. d., 280-286 (*The Trembling of the Veil*).

Ellis-Fermor, Una, "W. B. Yeats," *The Irish Dramatic Movement*, London: Methuen, 1939, 91-116 (see also *ibid., passim*).

Ellmann, Richard, *Yeats: The Man and the Masks*, New York: Macmillan, 1948.

Elton, Oliver, *Modern Studies*, London: Arnold, 1907, 299-307.

Emery, Florence Farr. *See* Bax.

Empson, William, *Seven Types of Ambiguity*, rev. ed., London: Chatto & Windus, 1947, 187-190 ("Who Goes with Fergus?").

Ervine, St. John R., "W. B. Yeats," *Some Impressions of My Elders*, New York: Macmillan, 1922, 264-305.

Evans, B. Ifor, "W. B. Yeats and the Continuance of Tradition," *Tradition and Romanticism*, London: Methuen, 1940, 201-208.

Farmer, Albert J., *Le Mouvement esthétique et "décadent" en Angleterre (1873-1900)*, Paris: Librairie Ancienne Honore Champion, 1931, *passim*.

Farr, Florence. *See* Bax.

Farren, Robert [O'Farachàin, Roibeárd], *The Course of Irish Verse in English*, New York: Sheed & Ward, 1947, 64-78.

Fay, W. G., "The Poet and the Actor," *Scattering Branches*, ed. Stephen Gwynn, New York: Macmillan, 1940, 115-134.

Fay, W. G., and Carswell, Catherine, *The Fays of the Abbey Theatre,* New York: Harcourt, Brace, 1935, *passim.*

Fehr, Bernhard, *Die englische Literatur des 19. u. 20. Jahrhunderts,* Potsdam: Akademie Verlagsges. Athenaion, 1923, 454-456, 500-503.

———, "W. B. Yeats, der Träger des Nobelpreises," *Neue Zürcher Zeitung,* XXI (November, 1923).

Fermor, Ellis, Una. *See* Ellis-Fermor.

Figgis, Darrell, "Mr. W. B. Yeats' Poetry," *Studies and Appreciations,* London: 1912, 119-138.

Firkins, O. W., "Cathleen Ni Houlihan at the Bramhall Playhouse," *Weekly Review,* III, 63 (July 21, 1920), 76.

———, "Mr. Yeats and Others," *Review,* I, 7 (June 28, 1919), 151-153 (*The Wild Swans at Coole*).

Flaccus, Kimball, "Yeatsiana," *Saturday Review of Literature,* XII, 20 (September 14, 1935), 9.

Freyer, Grattan, "The Politics of W. B. Yeats," *Politics and Letters,* I, 1 (summer, 1947), 13-20.

Frothingham, Eugenia Brooks, "An Irish Poet and his Work," *Critic,* XLIV, 1 (January, 1904), 26-31.

Frye, Northrop, "Yeats and the Language of Symbolism," *University of Toronto Quarterly,* XVII, 1 (October, 1947), 1-17.

"The Gaelic Revival in Literature," *Quarterly Review,* XCCV, 390 (April, 1902), 423-449 (*Samhain* [October, 1901], *Poems*).

Garnett, David, "W. B. Yeats," *New Statesman and Nation,* XVII, n. s. 415 (February 4, 1939), 174 (replied to by Sean O'Faoláin, "W. B. Yeats," *New Statesman . . . , infra*).

Garnett, Edward, "The Work of W. B. Yeats," *English Review,* II, [1] (April, 1909), 148-152 (*The Collected Works in Verse and Prose . . .* [1908]).

Gassner, J. W., "John Millington Synge and the Irish Muse," *Masters of the Drama,* New York: Random House, 1940, 524-574.

Gibson, Wilfrid, "W. B. Yeats," *Bookman* [London], LXXVII, 460 (January, 1930), 227-228 (*Selected Poems . . .* [1929]).

Gillet, Louis, "W. B. Yeats," *Revue des Deux Mondes,* yr. 109, per. 8, vol. L, [no. 2] (March 1, 1939), 219-223.

Gilomen, Walther, "George Moore and His Friendship with W. B. Yeats," *English Studies,* XIX, 3 (June, 1937), 116-120.

Gogarty, Oliver St. John. *See also* Rothenstein.

———, *As I Was Going Down Sackville Street,* New York: Reynal & Hitchcock, 1937, *passim.*

Goldring, Douglas, *Smith Lodge,* London: Constable, 1943, *passim.*

Gonne, Maud. *See also* MacBride.

Gonne, Maud, "Yeats and Ireland," *Scattering Branches,* ed. Stephen Gwynn, New York: Macmillan, 1940, 15-34.

Gorman, Herbert. *See also* Joyce.

———, "The Later Mr. Yeats," *Outlook,* CXXX, [15] (April 19,

1922), 655-656 (*Selected Poems*).

Gregory, Horace, "On William Butler Yeats and the Mask of Jonathan Swift," *The Shield of Achilles,* New York: Harcourt, Brace, 1944, 136-155.

———, "Personae and Masks," *Nation,* CXLVIII, 6 (February 4, 1939), 153-154 (*The Autobiography . . .*).

———, "Yeats: Envoy of Two Worlds," *New Republic,* LXXVII, 993 (December 13, 1933), 134-135 (*The Collected Poems . . .* [1933], *The Winding Stair . . .*).

———, "Yeats: Last Spokesman," *New Republic,* LXXXIV, 1085 (September 18, 1935), 164-165 (*The Collected Plays . . .* [1935], *Wheels and Butterflies, The King of the Great Clock Tower . . .*).

Gregory, Lady. *See also* Robinson.

———, "The Coming of the Irish Players," *Collier's,* XLVIII, 5 (October 21, 1911), 15, 24.

Grierson, Herbert J. C., "Fairies—from Shakespeare to Mr. Yeats," *Dublin Review,* CXLVIII, 297 (April, 1911), 271-284; and *Living Age,* CCLXIX, 3492 (June 10, 1911), 651-658.

Grierson, Herbert J. C., and Smith J. C., *A Critical History of English Poetry,* rev. ed., London: Chatto & Windus, 1947, 476-479.

Griffin, Gerald, "William Butler Yeats," *The Wild Geese,* London: Jarrolds, n. d., 151-163.

Grubb, H. T. Hunt, "William Butler Yeats: His Plays, Poems and Sources of Inspiration," *Poetry Review,* XXVI, [5, 6] (September-October, 1935; November-December, 1935), 351-365, 455-465.

Gurd, Patty, *The Early Poetry of William Butler Yeats,* Lancaster (U.S.A.), 1916.

Guthrie, William Norman, "W. B. Yeats," *Sewanee Review,* IX, 3 (July, 1901), 328-331 (*The Shadowy Waters*).

Gwynn, Denis, "The Irish Literary Theatre," *Edward Martyn and the Irish Revival,* London: Cape, 1930, 109-170.

Gwynn, Stephen L., "Ageing of a Poet," *Garden Wisdom,* Dublin: Talbot Press, 1-19.

———, "The Irish Literary Theatre and its Affinities," *Fortnightly Review,* LXX [o. s. LXXVI], 420 [o. s. 455] (December, 1901), 1050-1062.

———, *Irish Literature and Drama in the English Language,* London: Nelson, 1936, *passim.*

———, "The Passing of W. B. Yeats," *Fortnightly Review,* CXLV [o. s. CLI], 867 [o. s. 902] (March, 1939), 347-349.

———, "Poetry and the Stage," *Fortnightly Review,* LXXXV [o. s. XCI], 506 [o. s. 541] (February, 1909), 337-351.

———, "Scattering Branches," *Scattering Branches,* ed. Stephen Gwynn, New York: Macmillan, 1940, 1-14.

———, "An Uncommercial Theatre," *Fortnightly Review,* LXXII [o. s. LXXVIII], 432 [o. s. 467] (December, 1902), 1044-1054.

———, "Yeats's Poetry and Work," *Fortnightly Review*, CXXXVIII [o. s. CXLIV], 824 [o. s. 859] (August, 1935), 234-238.

Hackett, F., "William Butler Yeats," *The Invisible Censor*, New York: Huebsch, 1921, 114-118.

Haüsermann, H. W., "W. B. Yeats's Criticism of Ezra Pound," *English Studies*, XXIX, 4 (August, 1948), 97-109.

———, "W. B. Yeats's Idea of Shelley," *The Mint*, ed. Geoffrey Grigson, London: Routledge, 1946, 179-194.

Haydn, Hiram, "The Last of the Romantics: An Introduction to the Symbolism of William Butler Yeats," *Sewanee Review*, LV, 2 (April-June, 1947), 297-323.

Hayes, Richard, "His Nationalism," *Arrow*, summer, 1939, 10-11.

Headlam, Maurice, *Irish Reminiscences*, London: Hale, [1947].

Healy, J. V., " 'Ancient Lineaments,' " *Poetry*, LXII, 4 (July, 1943), 223-228 (Hone's *W. B. Yeats, 1865-1939*).

———, "Yeats and His Imagination," *Sewanee Review*, LIV, 4 (autumn, 1946), 650-659.

Heiseler, Bernt von, "Erzählungen und Lyrik," *Deutsche Zeitschrift*, XLVII, 11-12 (August-September, 1934), 579-580.

———, "William B. Yeats," *Neue Rundschau*, yr, 50, vol. II, no. 8 (August, 1939), 142-149.

Henderson, Philip, "Politics and W. B. Yeats," *The Poet and Society*, London: Secker & Warburg, 1939, 132-153.

Henry, Marjorie Louise, *Stuart Merrill*, Paris: Librairie Ancienne Honore Champion, 1927, *passim*.

Herts, B. Russell, "The Shadowy Mr. Yeats," *Depreciations*, New York: Boni, 1914, 33-39.

Hesse, I., "William Butler Yeats," *Kolnische Volkzeitung*, no. 192 (1935).

Hicks, Granville, *Figures of Transition*, New York: Macmillan, 1939, *passim*.

Higgins, F. R., "Yeats as Irish Poet," *Scattering Branches*, ed. Stephen Gwynn, New York: Macmillan, 1940, 145-156.

Higgins, F. R., "Yeats and Poetic Drama in Ireland," *The Irish Theatre*, ed. Lennox Robinson, London: Macmillan, 1939, 65-88.

Hillyer, Robert, "A Poet Young and Old," *New Adelphi*, III, 1 (September-November, 1929), 78-80 (*The Tower*).

Hind, C. L., "W. B. Yeats," *Authors and I*, New York: Lane, 1921, 318-324.

Hinkson, Katharine Tynan. *See* Tynan.

Hinkson, Pamela, "Letters from W. B. Yeats," *Yale Review*, n. s. XXIX, (December, 1939 [winter, 1940], 307-320.

Hoare, A. D. M., *The Works of Morris and Yeats in Relation to Early Saga Literature*, Cambridge: University Press, 1937.

Hodgins, James Cobourg, "William Butler Yeats," *The World's Best Literature*, ed. John W. Cunliffe and Ashley H. Thorndike, New York: Warner Library, 1917, XXVI, 16260a-16260h.

Hone, Joseph, ed., *J. B. Yeats' Letters to His Son, W. B. Yeats, and Others,* London: Faber & Faber, [1944].

———, *The Life of George Moore,* New York: Macmillan, 1936, *passim.*

———, "A Scattered Fair," *Wind and the Rain,* III, 3 (1946).

———, *W. B. Yeats, 1865-1939,* New York: Macmillan, 1943.

———, *William Butler Yeats: The Poet in Contemporary Ireland,* London: Maunsel & Roberts, 1915.

———, "Yeats as Political Philosopher," *London Mercury,* XXXIX, 233 (March, 1939), 492-496.

Hopkins, Gerard Manley. *See* Abbott.

* Houghton, Walter E., "Yeats and Crazy Jane: the Hero in Old Age," *Modern Philology,* XL, 4 (May, 1943), 316-329 (*Words for Music Perhaps . . .*).

Hughes, Glenn, *Imagism and the Imagists,* Stanford University: Stanford University Press, 1931, *passim.*

Huttemann, G., *Wesen der Dichtung und Aufgabe des Dichters bei William Butler Yeats,* Bonn, 1929.

Jackson, Holbrook, "The Discovery of the Celt," *The Eighteen Nineties,* New York: Knopf, 1922, 147-156.

Jackson, Schuyler, "William Butler Yeats," *London Mercury,* XI, 64 (February, 1925), 396-410.

James, R. A. Scott. *See* Scott-James.

Jameson, Grace E., "Mysticism in A E and in Yeats in Relation to Oriental and American Thought," *Ohio State University Abstracts of Doctors' Dissertations,* No. 9 (1932), 144-151.

Jarrell, Randall, "The Development of Yeats's Sense of Reality," *Southern Review,* VII, 3 (winter, 1942), 653-666.

Jeffares, A. Norman, "An Account of Recent Yeatsiana," *Hermathena,* LXXII (1948), 21-43.

———, "The Byzantine Poems of W. B. Yeats," *Review of English Studies,* XXII, 85 (January, 1946), 44-52.

———, " 'Gyres' in the Poetry of W. B. Yeats," *English Studies,* XXVII, 3 (June, 1946), 65-74.

———, " 'The New Faces': A New Explanation," *Review of English Studies,* XXIII, 92 (October, 1947), 349-353.

———, *A Poet and a Theatre,* Groningen: Wolters, 1946.

———, "The Source of Yeats's 'A Meditation in Time of War,' " *Notes and Queries,* CXCIII, 24 (November 27, 1948), 522.

———, "Thoor Ballylee," *English Studies,* XXVIII, 6 (December, 1947), 161-168.

———, " 'Two Songs of a Fool' and Their Explanation," *English Studies,* XXVI, 6 (December, 1945), 169-171.

*———, "W. B. Yeats and His Methods of Writing Verse," *Nineteenth Century and After,* CXXXIX, 829 (March, 1946), 123-128.

Johnson, Lionel, *Academy,* XLII, n. s. 1065 (October 1, 1892), 278-

279 (*The Countess Cathleen . . .*).

Johnson, W. R., "Crazy Jane and Henry More," *Furioso*, III, 2 (winter, 1947), 50-53 ("Crazy Jane Talks with the Bishop").

Johnston, Charles, "Personal Impressions of W. B. Yeats," *Harper's Weekly*, XLVIII, 2461 (February 20, 1904), 291.

Jones, Llewellyn, "The Later Poetry of Mr. W. B. Yeats," *First Impressions*, New York: Knopf, 1925, 137-148.

Joyce, James, "The Day of the Rabblement," *Two Essays*, Dublin, 1901; quoted at length in Herbert Gorman's *James Joyce*, New York: Farrar & Rinehart, 1939, 71-73.

———, *A Portrait of the Artist as a Young Man*, New York: Modern Library, 1928, Ch. V, 265-266 (*The Countess Cathleen*).

Kellner, Leon, *Die englische Literatur der neuesten Zeit*, Leipzig: Tauchnitz, 1921, 368-380.

Killew, A. M., "Some French Influence in the Works of W. B. Yeats at the End of the Nineteenth Century," *Comparative Literature Studies*, VIII (1942), 1-8.

King, Richard Ashe, "Mr. W. B. Yeats," *Bookman* [London], XII, 72 (September, 1897), 142-143.

Knights, L. C., "Poetry and Social Criticism: The Work of W. B. Yeats," *Explorations*, London: Chatto & Windus, 1946, 170-185.

Krans, H. S., *William Butler Yeats and the Irish Literary Revival*, New York: McClure, Philips, 1904.

Lawrence, C. E., "Poetry and Verse and Worse," *Quarterly Review*, CCLXII, 520 (April, 1934), 299-314 (*The Collected Poems . . .* [1933]).

Leacock, Stephen B., "Thinking of Tomorrow," *Too Much College*, New York: Dodd, Mead, 1939, 200.

Leavis, F. R., "The Great Yeats, and the Latest," *Scrutiny*, VIII, 4 (March, 1940), 437-440 (*Last Poems and Plays*).

———, "The Latest Yeats," *Scrutiny*, II, 3 (December, 1933), 293-295 (*The Winding Stair . . .*).

*———, *New Bearings in English Poetry*, London: Chatto & Windus, 1932, 27-50.

Lewis, C. Day. *See* Day Lewis.

Lichnerowicz, Jeanne, "Le dernier prix Nobel de litterature W.-B. Yeats," *Revue Politique et Littéraire* (*Revue Bleue*), LXI, 23 (December 1, 1923), 793-794.

———, "William Butler Yeats," *Europe*, V, 18 (June 15, 1924), 162-174.

Lienhardt, R. G., "Hopkins and Yeats," *Scrutiny*, XI, 3 (spring, 1943), 220-224 (Menon's *The Development of William Butler Yeats*).

Lucas, F. L., "Sense and Sensibility," *Authors Dead and Living*, New York: Macmillan, 1926, 241-246 (*Plays and Controversies*).

Luce, A. A., *Berkeley's Immaterialism*, London: Nelson, [1945].

Lynd, Robert, "Mr. W. B. Yeats," *Old and New Masters,* New York: Scribner's, n. d., 156-170.

Mabbott, T. O., "Yeats' 'The Wild Swans at Coole,' " *Explicator,* III, 1 (October, 1944), item 5.

MacBride, Maud Gonne, *A Servant of the Queen,* London: Gollancz, 1938, *passim.*

MacCarthy, Desmond, "The Irish National Theatre," *Saturday Review,* CIX, 2851 (June 18, 1910), 782-783.

———, "W. B. Yeats," London *Sunday Times,* No. 6043 (February 5, 1939), 6.

———, "Yeats," *Criticism,* London: Putnam, 1932, 81-88.

McGill, Anna Blanche, "Concerning a Few Anglo-Celtic Poets," *Catholic World,* LXXV, 450 (September, 1902), 775-785.

McGrath, John, "W. B. Yeats and Ireland," *Westminster Review,* CLXXVI, 1 (July, 1911), 1-11.

McGreevy, Thomas, "Mr. W. B. Yeats as a dramatist," *Revue Anglo-Americaine,* VII, 1 (October, 1929), 19-36.

MacKenna, Stephen. *See* Dodds.

Mackey, William F., "Yeats's Debt to Ronsard on a *Carpe Diem* Theme," *Comparative Literature Studies,* XIX (1946), 4-7 ("When You Are Old").

MacLeish, Archibald, "Public Speech and Private Speech in Poetry," *Time to Speak,* Boston: Houghton Mifflin, 1940, 59-70.

Macleod, Fiona [Sharp, William], "The Later Work of Mr. W. B. Yeats," *North American Review,* CLXXV, 551 (October, 1902), 473-485.

MacNeice, Louis, *Modern Poetry: A Personal Essay,* London: Oxford University Press, 1938, *passim.*

———, *The Poetry of W. B. Yeats,* London: Oxford University Press, 1941.

———, "Yeats's Epitaph," *New Republic,* CII, 26 [w. n. 1334] (June 24, 1940), 862-863 (*Last Poems and Plays*).

Magee, W. K. *See* Eglinton.

Malvil, Andre, "William Butler Yeats," *Le Monde Nouveau,* October, 1928.

Marble, A. R., "W. B. Yeats and His Part in the Celtic Revival," *Nobel Prize Winners in Literature,* New York: Appleton, 1925, 253-263.

Masefield, John, "On Mr. W. B. Yeats," *Recent Prose,* New York: Macmillan, 1933, 193-199.

———, *Some Memories of W. B. Yeats,* New York: Macmillan, 1940

———, "William Butler Yeats," *Arrow,* summer, 1939, 5-6.

Mason, H. A., "Yeats and the English Tradition," *Scrutiny,* V, 4 (March, 1937), 449-451 (*Oxford Book of Modern Verse*).

———, "Yeats and the Irish Movement," *Scrutiny,* V, 3 (December, 1936), 330-332 (*Dramatis Personæ*).

Masterman, C. F. G., "After the Reaction," *Living Age,* CCXLIV, 3160 (January 28, 1905), 193-208.

Matthiessen, F. O., "The Crooked Road," *Southern Review,* VII, 3 (winter, 1942), 455-470 (" 'I am of Ireland,' " "After Long Silence").

———, "Yeats and Four American Poets," *Yale Review,* XXIII, 3 (March, 1934), 611-617 (*The Collected Poems . . .* [1933]).

[Mayhew, Joyce], *Ad Multos Annos: William Butler Yeats in his seventieth year,* Mills College, California: Eucalyptus Press, 1935.

Maynard, Theodore, "W. B. Yeats: Fairies and Fog," *Our Best Poets,* New York: Holt, 1922, 67-83.

Megroz, R. L., *Modern English Poetry 1882-1932,* London: Nicholson & Watson, 1933, *passim.*

Mellers, W. H., "A Book on Yeats," *Scrutiny,* IX, 4 (March, 1941), 381-383 (MacNeice's *The Poetry of W. B. Yeats*).

Menon, V. K. Narayana, *The Development of William Butler Yeats,* Edinburgh: Oliver & Boyd, 1942.

Mercier, Vivian, " 'Speech after long silence,' " *Irish Writing,* No. 6 (1948).

Millett, Fred B., *The Rebirth of Liberal Education,* New York: Harcourt, Brace, 1945, 166-168 ("After Long Silence").

Minton, Arthur, "Yeats' 'When You Are Old,' " *Explicator,* V, 7 (May, 1947), item 49.

"Mr. Yeats's Poems," *Academy,* LVI, n. s. 1409 (May 6, 1899), 501-502 (*The Wind Among the Reeds* and *Poems* [new edition]).

* Mizener, Arthur, "The Romanticism of W. B. Yeats," *Southern Review,* VII, 3 (winter, 1942), 601-623.

Monahan, Michael, "Yeats and Synge," *Nova Hibernia,* New York: Kennerley, 1914, 13-37.

Monroe, Harriet, "Mr. Yeats and the Poetic Drama," *Poetry,* XVI, 1 (April, 1920), 32-39.

Moore, George, *Hail and Farew*[illegible]ew York: Appleton, 19[illegible] 1920, I (*Ave*), *passim;* III ([illegible]), 170-212.

Moore, Isabel, "William [illegible]utler Yeats," *Bookman* [New Yo[illegible] XVIII, [4] (D[illegible]cember, 1903), 360-363.

Moore, T. St[illegible]ge, "Yeats," *English,* II, 11 (1939), 273-278.

More, [illegible] Elmer, "Two Poets of the Irish Movement," *Shelburn[illegible] Essays* (First Series), New York: Putnam's, 1906, 177-193.

Morgan, A. E., "The Irish Pioneers: 1. Yeats," *Tendencies of Modern English Drama,* New York: Scribner's, 1924, 139-147.

Morris, Lloyd R., *The Celtic Dawn,* New York: Macmillan, 1917, *passim.*

Muddiman, Bernard, *The Men of the Nineties,* London: Danielson, 1920, *passim.*

Muir, Edwin, *The Present Age from 1914,* New York: McBride, 1940, *passim.*

———, "W.-B. Yeats," *Aspects de la Littérature Anglaise 1918-1945* eds. Kathleen Raine and Max-Pol Fouchet, Paris: Fontaine

[1947], 94-105.

Murphy, Gwendolen, *The Modern Poet,* London: Sidgwick & Jackson, [1938].

* Murry, J. Middleton, "Mr. Yeats's Swan Song," *Aspects of Literature,* rev. ed., London: Jonathan Cape, 1934, 53-59 (*The Wild Swans at Coole*).

Nevinson, Henry W., "The Poet of the Sidhe," and "The Latter Oisin," *Books and Personalities,* London: Lane, 1905, 218-225, 226-232.

———, "W. B. Yeats, The Poet of Vision," *London Mercury,* XXXIX, 233 (March, 1939), 485-491.

Noguchi, Yone, "A Japanese Poet on W. B. Yeats," *Bookman* [New York], XLIII, [4] (June, 1916), 431-433.

Notopoulos, James A., " 'Sailing to Byzantium,' " *Classical Journal,* XLI, 2 (November, 1945), 78-79.

O'Connell, J. P., *Sailing to Byzantium* (*Harvard Honors Theses in English,* No. 11), Cambridge: Harvard University Press, 1939.

O'Connor, Frank, "A Classic One-Act Play," *Radio Times,* XCIV, 1214 (January 3, 1947), 4.

———, "The Old Age of a Poet," *Bell,* February, 1941.

———, "The Plays and Poetry of W. B. Yeats," *Listener,* XXV, 643 (May 8, 1941), 675-676.

———, "Two Friends: Yeats and A. E.," *Yale Review,* n. s. XXIX, 1 (September, 1939 [autumn, 1939]), 60-88.

O'Connor, William Van, *Sense and Sensibility in Modern Poetry,* Chicago: University of Chicago Press, 1948, *passim.*

O'Conor, Norreys Jephson, "Yeats and His Vision," *Changing Ireland,* Cambridge: Harvard University Press, 1924, 72-82.

———, "A Note on Yeats," *Essays in Memory of Barrett Wendell,* ed. His Assistants, Cambridge: Harvard University Press, 1926, 285-289.

O'Faoláin, Sean, "Æ and W. B.," *Virginia Quarterly Review,* XV, 1 (winter, 1939), 41-57.

———, *Criterion,* IX, 36 (April, 1930), 523-528 (*Selected Poems . . .* [1929]).

———, "W. B. Yeats," *English Review,* LX, [6] (June, 1935), 680-688.

———, "W. B. Yeats," *New Statesman and Nation,* XVII, n. s. 416 (February 11, 1939), 209 (reply to David Garnett, *op. cit. supra*).

———, "Yeats and the Younger Generation," *Horizon,* V, 25 (January, 1942), 43-54.

O'Faracháin, Roibeárd. *See* Farren.

O'Hegarty, P. S., "Yeats and the Revolutionary Ireland of His Time," *Dublin Magazine,* July-September, 1939.

* Olson, Elder, " 'Sailing to Byzantium': Prolegomena to a Poetics

of the Lyric," *University Review,* VIII, 3 (spring, 1912), 209-219.

O'Neill, George, "Irish Drama and Irish Views," *American Catholic Quarterly Review,* XXXVII, 146 (April, 1912), 322-332.

Orage, A. R., "Ireland: Diagnoses," *Selected Essays and Critical Writings,* London: Nott, 1935, 54-56 (*Reveries Over Childhood and Youth*).

Orwell, George, "W. B. Yeats," *Dickens, Dali and Others,* New York: Reynal & Hitchcock, 1946, 161-169.

O'Sullivan, Donal, *The Irish Free State and Its Senate,* London: Faber & Faber, 1940, *passim.*

Paul-Dubois, Louis, "M. Yeats et la mouvement poétique en Irlande —I: le poète du rêve," *Revue des Deux Mondes,* yr. 99, per. 7, vol. LIII, [no. 3] (October 1, 1929), 558-583.

———, "M. Yeats et le mouvement poétique en Irlande—II: le philosophe et l'influence," *Revue des Deux Mondes,* yr. 99, per. 7, vol. LIII, [no. 4] (October 15, 1929), 824-846.

Pauly, M.-H. "W. B. Yeats et les symbolistes français," *Revue de Littérature Comparée,* XX, 1 (January-March, 1940), 13-33.

Peacock, Ronald, "Yeats," *The Poet in the Theatre,* New York: Harcourt, Brace, 1946, 117-128.

Pearson, Hesketh, *G. B. S.: A Full Length Portrait,* New York: Harper, 1942, *passim.*

Pellizzi, Camillo, *Il Teatro Inglese,* Milan: Fratelli Treves, 1934, 234-242 (translation: *English Drama: The Last Great Phase,* tr. Rowan Williams, London: Macmillan, 1935, 176-183).

Pfister, Kurt, "Der irische Dichter William Yeats," *Frankfurter Zeitung,* No. 80-81 (February 14, 1934), 9.

Phelps, William Lyon, "The Irish Poets," *The Advance of English Poetry in the Twentieth Century,* New York: Dodd, Mead, 1918, 157-193.

Pollock, J. H., *William Butler Yeats,* Dublin: Duckworth, 1935.

Porteus, Hugh Gordon, *Criterion,* XIII, 51 (January, 1934), 31[illegible] (*The Winding Stair . . .*).

Pound, Ezra, ed., *Passages from the Letters of John Butler Yeats,* Churchtown, Dundrum: Cuala Press, 1917.

Pourrat, Henri, "W. B. Yeats," *Nouvelle Revue Francaise,* XXII (1924), 124-128.

Prokosch, Frederic, "Yeats's Testament," *Poetry,* LIV, 6 (September, 1939), 338-342 (*Last Poems and Two Plays*).

Quinn, John, "Lady Gregory and the Abbey Theatre," *Outlook,* XCIX, [16] (December 16, 1911), 916-919.

Quinn, Kerker, "Blake and the New Age," *Virginia Quarterly Review,* XIII, 2 (spring, 1937), 271-285.

R., "Synge a Yeats," *Jeviste,* II (1921-1922), 638.

Ransom, John Crowe, "The Irish, the Gaelic, the Byzantine," *Southern Review*, VII, 3 (winter, 1942), 517-546.

———, "Old Age of a Poet," *Kenyon Review*, II, 3 (summer, 1940), 345-347 (*Last Poems and Plays*).

———, "The Severity of Mr. Savage," *Kenyon Review*, VII, 1 (winter, 1945), 114-117 (reply to D. S. Savage, "The Aestheticism of W. B. Yeats," *infra*).

* ———, "Yeats and His Symbols," *Kenyon Review*, I, 3 (summer, 1939), 309-322.

Read, Herbert, "The Later Yeats," *A Coat of Many Colours*, London: Routledge, 1945, 208-212 (*The Collected Poems . . .* [1933], esp. "The Sorrow of Love").

———, "Révolte et réaction dans la poésie anglaise moderne," *Presence*, April, 1946, 56.

Reid, Forrest, *W. B. Yeats: A Critical Study*, London: Secker, 1915.

Reynolds, Horace, Introduction to W. B. Yeats, *Letters to the New Island*, Cambridge: Harvard University Press, 1934, 3-66.

Rhys, Ernest, *Academy*, XLIX, n. s. 1242 (February 22, 1896), 151-152 (*Poems* [1895]).

———, "W. B. Yeats: Early Recollections," *Fortnightly Review*, CXXXVIII [o. s. CXLIV], 823 (July, 1935), 52-57.

Richards, I. A., *Coleridge on the Imagination*, New York: Harcourt, Brace, 1935, *passim*.

———, *Science and Poetry*, 2nd ed., London: Kegan Paul, Trench, Trubner, 1935, 79-82.

Richardson, Dorothy M., "Yeats of Bloomsbury," *Life and Letters To-Day*, XXI, 20 (April, 1939), 60-66.

Ricketts, Charles, *Self-Portrait*, eds. T. Sturge Moore and Cecil Lewis, London: Davies, 1939, *passim*.

Robinson, Lennox, "As Man of the Theatre," *Arrow*, summer, 1939, 20-21.

———, ed., *Further Letters of John Butler Yeats*, Churchtown, Dundrum: Cuala Press, 1920.

———, "The Man and the Dramatist," *Scattering Branches*, ed. Stephen Gwynn, New York: Macmillan, 1940, 55-114.

———, ed., *Lady Gregory's Journals, 1916-1930*, New York: Macmillan, 1947, 259-266.

R[obinson?], L[ennox?], "Foreward," *Arrow*, summer, 1939, 5.

Rolleston, C. H., *Portrait of an Irishman*, London: Methuen, [1939].

Rosenberger, Coleman, "Consuming Its Rag and Bone," *Accent*, I, 1 (autumn, 1940), 56-57 (*Last Poems and Plays*).

Rothenstein, Sir William, *Men and Memories*, New York: Coward-McCann, 1931, 1935, I, *passim*; II, *passim*.

———, *Since Fifty*, London: Faber & Faber, 1939, *passim*.

Rothenstein, Sir William, "Yeats as a Painter Saw Him," *Scattering Branches*, ed. Stephen Gwynn, New York: Macmillan, 1940, 35-54.

Rothenstein, Sir William, Turner, W. J., and Gogarty, Oliver St.

John, "Three Impressions: I," "II," and "III," *Arrow,* summer, 1939, 16-17, 17-19, 19-20.

Russell, George. *See* A.E.

Saul, George Brandon, "Literary Parallels: Yeats and Coppard," *Notes and Queries,* CLXVIII, 18 (May 4, 1935), 314.

———, "Yeats's Hare," *Times Literary Supplement,* [XLVI], 2345 (January 11, 1949), 23 ("The Collar-Bone of a Hare" and "Two Songs of a Fool").

* Savage, D. S., "The Aestheticism of W. B. Yeats," *The Personal Principle,* London: Routledge, 1944, 67-91 (replied to by John Crowe Ransom, "The Severity of Mr. Savage," *supra*).

———, "Two Prophetic Poems," *Adelphi,* XXII, 1 (October-December, 1945), 25-32 ("The Second Coming").

Schneider, Elisabeth, "Yeats' 'When You Are Old,'" *Explicator,* VI, 7 (May, 1948), item 50.

"A School of Irish Poetry," *Edinburgh Review,* CCIX, 427 (January, 1909), 94-118 (*Poems, 1899-1905* [1906], *Poems* [1908]).

* Schwartz, Delmore, "An Unwritten Book," *Southern Review,* VII, 3 (winter, 1942), 471-491.

Schweisgut, Elsbeth, *Yeats' Feendichtung,* Darmstadt: Bender, 1927.

Scott, Winfield Townley, "The Foolish, Passionate Man," *Accent,* I, 4 (summer, 1941), 247-250 (Masefield's *Some Memories of W. B. Yeats,* Gwynn's *Scattering Branches,* MacNeice's *The Poetry of W. B. Yeats, Letters on Poetry from W. B. Yeats to Dorothy Wellesley*).

———, "Yeats at 73," *Poetry,* LIII, 11 (November, 1938), 84-88 (*New Poems* [1938]).

Scott-James, R. A., "The Farewell to Yeats," *London Mercury,* XXXIX, 233 (March, 1939), 477-480.

Seiden, Morton Irving, "A Psychoanalytic Essay on William Butler Yeats," *Accent,* VI, 3 (spring, 1946), 178-190 (*The Wanderings of Oisin*).

Shanks, E. B., "The Later Poetry of Mr. W. B. Yeats," *First Essays on Literature,* London: Collins', 1923, 238-244.

Shapiro, Karl, *Essay on Rime,* New York: Reynal & Hitchcock, 1945, 19.

Sharp, Elizabeth A., *William Sharp,* New York: Duffield, 1910, *passim*.

Sharp, William. *See* Macleod.

Shaw, Bernard. *See* Bax.

Shaw, Francis, "The Celtic Twilight," *Studies,* XXIII, 89 (March, 1934), 25-41.

———, "The Celtic Twilight: Part II.—The Celtic Element in the Poetry of W. B. Yeats," *Studies,* XXIII, 90 (June, 1934), 260-278.

Sinclair, F., "A Poet's World in Woburn Walk," *St. Pancras Journal,* December, 1948.

Sitwell, Edith, "William Butler Yeats," *Aspects of Modern Poetry,* London: Duckworth, 1934, 73-89.

Smith, A. J. M., "A Poet Young and Old—W. B. Yeats," *University of Toronto Quarterly,* VIII, 3 (April, 1939), 309-322.

Smith, J. C. *See* Grierson.

Some Passages from the Letters of Æ to W. B. Yeats, Dublin: Cuala Press, 1936.

Southworth, James G., "Age and William Butler Yeats," *Sowing the Spring,* Oxford: Blackwell, 1940, 33-45.

Sparrow, John, "Extracts from a Lecture on Tradition and Revolt in English Poetry," *Bulletin of the British Institute in Paris,* April-May, 1939.

———, *Sense and Poetry.* New Haven: Yale University Press, 1934, *passim.*

Speaight, Robert, "William Butler Yeats," *Commonweal,* XXIX, 23 (March 31, 1939), 623-624.

Spencer, Theodore, "The Later Poetry of W. B. Yeats," *Literary Opinion in America,* ed. Morton Dauwen Zabel, New York: Harper, 1938, 263-277 (*Words for Music Perhaps . . .*) (reply to Yvor Winters, *op. cit. infra*).

———, "The Tower," *New Republic,* LVI, 723 (October 10, 1928), 219-220.

[Spencer, Theodore], "Mr. Yeats," *Nation and Athenæum,* XLIII, 3 (April 21, 1928), 81 (*The Tower*).

Spender, Stephen, "La crise des symboles," *France Libre,* VII, 39 (January 15, 1944), 206-210 ("The Second Coming").

———, "The 'Egotistical Sublime' in W. B. Yeats," *Listener,* XXI, 527 (February 16, 1939), 377-378.

* ———, "Yeats as a Realist," *The Destructive Element,* London: Jonathan Cape, 1935, 115-132.

Squire, J. C., "Mr. W. B. Yeats's Later Verse," *Essays on Poetry,* London: Hodder & Stoughton [1924], 160-170 (*Later Poems* [1922]).

Stace, W. T., "The Faery Poetry of Mr. W. B. Yeats," *British Review,* I, 1 (January, 1913), 117-130.

Stageberg, Norman C., "Yeats' 'Sailing to Byzantium,'" *Explicator,* VI, 2 (November, 1947), item 14.

Stamm, Rudolf, "'The Sorrow of Love,'" *English Studies,* XXIX, 3 (June, 1948), 79-87.

———, "Three Anglo-Irish Plays," *Bibliographia Anglicana,* V (1943).

———, "Von Theaterkrisen und ihrer Uberwindung," *Jahrbuch der Gesellschaft für Schweizerische Theaterkultur,* 1943.

Starkie, W., "W. B. Yeats," *Nuova Antologia,* ser. 6, vol. CCXXXIV, of the coll. CCCXIII (April 1, 1924), 238-245.

"The State Called Reverie," *Academy,* LXIV, n. s. 1623 (June 13, 1903), 589-590 (*Ideas of Good and Evil*) (replied to by A. Clutton-Brock, *loc. cit. supra*).

Stauffer, Donald A., "Artist Shining through His Vehicles," *Kenyon Review*, XI, 2 (spring, 1949), 330, 332-334, 336 (Ellmann's *Yeats: The Man and the Masks*).

———, "Yeats and the Medium of Poetry," *English Literary History*, XV, 3 (September, 1948), 227-246.

Strong, L. A. G., *A Letter to W. B. Yeats*, London: Hogarth Press, 1932. (July, 1937), 14-29.

———, "W. B. Yeats: An Appreciation," *Cornhill Magazine*, CLVI, 931 4468 (January, 1939), 438-440.

———, "William Butler Yeats," *Scattering Branches*, ed. Stephen Gwynn, New York: Macmillan, 1940, 183-229.

"The Success of Yeats," *Times Literary Supplement*, [XXXVIII], 1931 (February 4, 1939), 73.

Sweeney, John L. *See* Drew.

Swinnerton, Frank, *The Georgian Scene*, New York: Farrar & Rinehart, 1934, *passim*.

Symons, Arthur, "Mr. W. B. Yeats," *Studies in Prose and Verse*, London: Dent; New York: Dutton, [1904?], 230-241.

Tallqvist, C. E., "William Butler Yeats. En studie," *Finsk Tidskrift*, CII, [2, 4] (1927), 119-141, 281-307.

Tate, Allen, *Reactionary Essays on Poetry and Ideas*, New York: Scribner's, 1936, *passim*.

———, "Winter Mask: to the Memory of W. B. Yeats" (a poem), *Chimera*, I, 4 (spring, 1943), 2-3.

* ———, "Yeats's Romanticism: Notes and Suggestions," *On the Limits of Poetry*, New York: Swallow Press & Morrow, 1948, 214-224.

Taylor, Joseph R., "William Butler Yeats and the Revival of Gaelic Literature," *Methodist Review*, LXXXVII, [2] (March, 1905), 189-202.

Tennyson, Charles, "Irish Plays and Playwrights," *Quarterly Review*, CCXV, 428 (July, 1911), 219-243 (*The Collected Works . . .* [1908]).

———, "The Rise of the Irish Theatre," *Contemporary Review*, C, [2] (August, 1911), 240-247.

Tery, Simone, "W. B. Yeats, poete irlandais," *Grande Revue*, CXIII, [2] (December, 1923), 259-272.

Thompson, Francis, "A Schism in the Celtic Movement," "William Butler Yeats," and "Fiona Macleod on Mr. W. B. Yeats," *Literary Criticisms*, ed. Terence L. Connolly, New York: Dutton, 1948, 326-332 (*Literary Ideals in Ireland*), 370-373 (*The Secret Rose*), 373-376 (reply to Fiona Macleod, *op. cit. supra*).

Tietjens, Eunice, *The World at My Shoulder*, New York: Macmillan, 1938, 59-61.

Tillyard, E. M. W., *Poetry Direct and Oblique*, rev ed., London: Chatto & Windus, 1945, *passim*.

* Tindall, W. Y., *Forces in Modern British Literature 1885-1946*,

New York: Knopf, 1947, 248-263 (See also *ibid., passim*).

———, "The Symbolism of W. B. Yeats," *Accent*, V, 4 (summer, 1945), 203-212.

———, "Transcendentalism in Contemporary Literature," *The Asian Legacy and American Life*, ed. Arthur E. Christy, New York: Day, 1945, 175-192.

Todhunter, J., *Academy*, XXXV, n. s. 882 (March 30, 1889), 216-217 (*The Wanderings of Oisin . . .*).

Turner, W. J. *See also* Rothenstein.

———, "Ode (In memory of W. B. Yeats)," *New Statesman and Nation*, XVII, n. s. 417 (February 18, 1939), 243.

———, "Words and Tones," *New Statesman and Nation*, XVIII, n. s. 439 (July 22, 1939), 141-142.

———, "Yeats and Song-Writing," *New Statesman and Nation*, XVII, n. s. 426 (April 22, 1939), 606-607.

Tuve, Rosemond, *Elizabethan and Metaphysical Imagery*, Chicago: University of Chicago Press, 1947, *passim*.

Tychsen, H. Draws. *See* Draws-Tychsen.

Tynan, Katharine [Hinkson, Katharine Tynan], *The Middle Years*, London: Constable, 1916, *passim*.

———, *Twenty-five Years: Reminiscences*, New York: Devin-Adair, 1913, *passim*.

———, "William Butler Yeats," *Sketch*, IV, 44 (November 20, 1893), 256.

Untermeyer, Louis, *From Another World*, New York: Harcourt, Brace, 1939, *passim*.

Ure, Peter, *Towards a Mythology: Studies in the Poetry of W. B. Yeats*, Liverpool: University Press of Liverpool; London: Hodder & Stoughton, 1946.

W[alkley?], A. B., "Mr. W. B. Yeats and 'The Wind Among the Reeds,'" *Academy*, LVIII, n. s. 1446 (January 20, 1900), 63.

W[alsh], E. R., "Some Reminiscences of W. B. Y.," *Irish Times*, February 10, 1940.

* Warren, Austin, "William Butler Yeats: The Religion of a Poet," *Rage for Order*, Chicago: University of Chicago Press, 1948, 66-84.

Warren, C. Henry, "William Butler Yeats," *Bookman* [London], LXXXII, 492 (September, 1932), 284-286.

Warren, Robert Penn. *See* Brooks.

Watkins, Vernon, "The Last Poems of Yeats" (a poem), *Life and Letters To-Day*, XXIII, 28 (November, 1939), 312-313.

———, "Yeats in Dublin" (a poem), *The Lamp and the Veil*, London: Faber & Faber, 1945, 7-19.

———, "Yeats' Tower" (a poem), *Selected Poems*, Norfolk: New Directions, 1948, 24.

Weeks, Donald, "Image and Idea in Yeats's *The Second Coming*,"

Publications of the Modern Language Association, LXIII, 1 [Part 1] (March, 1948), 281-292.

Welek, René, and Warren, Austin, *Theory of Literature,* New York: Harcourt, Brace, 1949, *passim.*

Wells, Henry W., *New Poets from Old,* New York: Columbia University Press, 1940, *passim.*

Weygandt, Cornelius, "Mr. William Butler Yeats," *Irish Plays and Playwrights,* Boston: Houghton Mifflin, 1913, 37-71.

———, "William Butler Yeats and the Irish Literary Renaissance," *Time of Yeats,* New York: Appleton-Century, 1937, 167-251.

———, "With Yeats in the Woods at Coole," *Tuesdays at Ten,* Philadelphia: University of Pennsylvania Press, 1928, 176-185.

White, Terence de Vere, *The Road of Excess,* Dublin: Browne & Nolan [1946].

Whitridge, Arnold, "William Butler Yeats 1865-1939," *Dalhousie Review,* XIX, 1 (April, 1939), 1-8.

Wild, Friedrich, *Die englische Literatur der Gegenwart seit 1870,* Wiesbaden: Dioskuren-Verlag, 1928, 83-88.

Wilder, Amos N., "W. B. Yeats and the Christian Option," *The Spiritual Aspects of the New Poetry,* New York: Harper, 1940, 196-204.

Williams, Charles, "W. B. Yeats," *Poetry at Present,* Oxford: Clarendon Press, 1930, 56-69.

"Willie Yeats and John O'Leary," *Irish Book Lover,* XXVII (November, 1940).

Wilson, Edmund, "Proust and Yeats," *New Republic,* LII, 670 (October 5, 1927), 176-177a.

* ———, "W. B. Yeats," *Axel's Castle,* New York: Scribner's 1931, 26-64.

———, "W. B. Yeats," *New Republic,* XLII, [Part II] (April 15, 1925), 8-10.

———, "Yeats's Memoirs," *New Republic,* L, 638 (February 23, 1927), 22-23 (*Autobiographies*).

Winters, Yvor, *Hound and Horn,* VI, 3 (April-June, 1933), 534-545 (replied to by Theodore Spencer, "The Later Poetry of W. B. Yeats," *supra*).

Witt, Marion W., "William Butler Yeats," *English Institute Essays, 1946,* New York: Columbia University Press, 1947, 74-101.

——— ,"Yeats' 'The Collar-Bone of a Hare,'" *Explicator,* VII, 3 (December, 1948), item 21.

———, "Yeats' 'A Dialogue of Self and Soul,'" *Explicator,* V, 7 (May, 1947), item 48.

———, "Yeats's Hare," *Times Literary Supplement,* [XLVI], 2385 (October 18, 1949), 535 ("The Collar-Bone of a Hare" and "Two Songs of a Fool").

———, "Yeats' 'Mohini Chatterjee,'" *Explicator,* IV, 8 (June, 1946), item 60.

———, "Yeats' 'The Moods,'" *Explicator,* VI, 3 (December, 1947), item 15.

———, "Yeats' 'When You Are Old,'" *Explicator,* VI, 1 (October, 1947), item 6.

———, "Yeats' 'The Wild Swans at Coole,'" *Explicator,* III, 2 (November, 1944), item 17.

Wrenn, C. L., *W. B. Yeats: A Literary Study,* London: Murby, 1920.

"Yeats and the Abbey Theatre," *Theatre Arts Monthly,* XXIII, 3 (March, 1939), 160-161.

"Yeats's Inner Drama," *Times Literary Supplement,* [XXXVIII], 1931 (February 4, 1939), 72, 74.

Yeats, John Butler. *See also* Hone, Pound, and Robinson.

———, *Early Memories,* Churchtown, Dundrum: Cuala Press, 1923.

Yeats, John Butler, *Letters to His Son W. B. Yeats and Others, 1869-1922,* ed. Joseph Hone, New York: Dutton, 1946.

Zabel, Morton Dauwen, "The Last of Yeats," *Nation,* CLI, 15 (October 12, 1940), 333-335 (*Last Poems and Plays, Letters on Poetry from W. B. Yeats to Dorothy Wellesley*).

———, "The Summers of Hesperides," *Poetry,* XLIII, 5 (February, 1934), 279-287 (*The Collected Works* [1933] and *The Winding Stair . . .*).

———, "The Thinking of the Body: Yeats in the Autobiographies," *Southern Review,* VII, 3 (winter, 1942), 562-590.

———, "Yeats: The Image and the Book," *Nation,* CLVI, 10 (March 6, 1943), 348-350 (Hone's *W. B. Yeats, 1865-1939,* MacNeice's *The Poetry of W. B. Yeats*).

Z[abel], M[orton] D[auwen], "Yeats at Thirty and Seventy," *Poetry,* XLVII, 5 (February, 1936), 268-277.